Diversification through Acquisition

Diversification through Acquisition

Strategies for Creating Economic Value

Malcolm S. Salter
Wolf A. Weinhold

THE FREE PRESS
A Division of Macmillan Publishing Co., Inc.
NEW YORK

Collier Macmillan Publishers
LONDON

The Free Press
A Division of Macmillan Publishing Co., Inc.
866 Third Avenue, New York, N. Y. 10022

Collier Macmillan Canada, Ltd.

Library of Congress Catalog Card Number: 79–7370

Printed in the United States of America

printing number
1 2 3 4 5 6 7 8 9 10

Library of Congress Cataloging in Publication Data

Salter, Malcolm S
   Diversification through acquisition.

   Includes bibliographical references and index.
   1. Diversification in industry. 2. Consolidation
and merger of corporations. I. Weinhold, Wolf A.,
joint author. II. Title.
HD38.S31374   1979   658.1'6   79-7370
ISBN 0-02-928020-6

Passages from the following works have been quoted here by permission of the author(s) and/or publishers:

Abernathy, W. J. and K. Wayne, "The Limits of the Learning Curve," *Harvard Business Review*, September–October 1974.

Christenson, C. R., N. A. Berg, and M. S. Salter, *Policy Formulation and Administration: A Casebook of Top-Management Problems in Business*, seventh ed. (Homewood, Illinois: Richard D. Irwin, 1976).

Donaldson, G. M., "Financial Goals: Management vs. Stockholders," *Harvard Business Review* 41, June 1963.

Genstar, Ltd., "A Submission to the Royal Commission on Corporate Concentration," Montreal, November 1975.

Ibbotson, R. G. and R. A. Sinquefield, *Stocks, Bonds, Bills, and Inflation: The Past (1926–1976) and the Future (1977–2000)* (Charlottesville, Virginia: The Financial Analysts Research Foundation, 1977).

Mason, E. S., *The Corporation in Modern Society* (Cambridge, Massachusetts: Harvard University Press, 1964).

Myers, S. C. and S. M. Turnbull, "Capital Budgeting and the Capital Asset Pricing Model: Good News and Bad News," *Journal of Finance* 32, May 1977.

Rumelt, R., *Strategy, Structure, and Economic Performance* (Boston, Massachusetts: Harvard University, Division of Research, 1974).

Rumelt, R., "Diversity and Profitability," UCLA Working Paper MGL-51, 1977.

Salter, M. S. and W. A. Weinhold, "Diversification via Acquisition: Creating Value," *Harvard Business Review* 56, July–August 1978.

Scherer, F. M., *Industrial Market Structure and Economic Performance* (Skokie, Illinois: Rand McNally College Publishing Co., 1970).

Schoeffler, S., Buzzell, R. D., and D. F. Heany, "Impact of Strategic Planning on Profit Performance," *Harvard Business Review* 52, March–April 1974.

Contents

List of Figures

List of Tables

Preface

The objective of this book is to help managers develop strategies of diversification through acquisition that offer the potential for creating real economic value. The book addresses five basic issues: (1) Diversification objectives: How related or unrelated should diversifying acquisitions be, and how can economic value be created by various kinds of diversifying acquisitions? (2) Acquisition guidelines: How can meaningful acquisition guidelines be developed? (3) Screening systems: How can high-potential acquisition candidates be effectively identified? (4) Analysis of diversifying acquisitions: What kind of in-depth strategic and economic analyses should be made to determine the worth of high-potential candidates to the diversifying company? and (5) Antitrust: What is the evolving antitrust environment for companies pursuing diversification through acquisition?

The impetus for preparing this book is the concern of an increasing number of managers, investors, academic researchers, and public officials that many diversification programs have failed to provide the shareholder benefits once expected. During the past twenty-five years an increasing proportion of U.S. companies have seen wisdom in pursuing strategies of diversification. In recent years the productivity of capital of many (but not all!) multibusiness companies has lagged behind the economy. Nevertheless, diversification through acquisition remains popular. In light of this continuing interest and the apparent risks in following such a strategy, we think a review and synthesis of the current state of thought about diversifying acquisitions is both useful and timely.

The book is divided into four sections. In Part I we introduce the subject of diversification through acquisition and summarize the principal conclusions of our study. Throughout our summary we indicate where the reader can turn in the later chapters for a more detailed discussion of various points of interest.

In Part II we present an analytical framework based on recent extensions of capital market theory, market planning models developed during the past decade, and more established strategic-planning practices. While this section does not present a comprehensive, empirically validated theory of corporate diversification, it does show how concepts drawn from three analytic traditions complement each other and how this set of complementary concepts can help companies create value for their investors through well-planned, diversifying acquisitions. Part II is the conceptual part of the book, forming the underpinnings of subsequent chapters, which deal with the recurring challenges facing acquisitive diversifiers. Despite the rigor that we have tried to sustain through this discussion, it is presented with a certain modesty. The diversification decision, like most policy decisions, does not lend itself to totally convincing theoretical modeling. This characteristic of the diversification decision explains why the tasks of the policymaker in multibusiness companies are so painfully difficult and why so many men of wisdom differ over what constitutes appropriate policy.

Part III of the book demonstrates the power of the concepts presented in Part II by showing how they can help managers resolve the managerial issues outlined above. Each of the issues is discussed in light of the histories of several well-known diversifiers. These include such companies as Heublein, Genstar, Continental Group, General Cinema, Ciba-Geigy, Rockwell International, and INCO (International Nickel).

Part IV treats the relevant antitrust issues. After summarizing the principal barriers to diversification through acquisition posed by current antitrust policy, we examine two initiatives to raise new barriers. The first argues for more aggressive enforcement (and interpretation) of existing antitrust legislation; the second calls for the enactment of new legislation.

In each section of the book we emphasize diversification through acquisition rather than diversification through internal development. We do this for several reasons. First, the exchange of assets presumed in our analytic approach allows us to highlight an economic logic that is applicable to *both* forms of corporate diversification. Where a market exchange takes place, this economic logic can be most crisply demonstrated. Second, the increased number and size of diversifying acquisitions taking place in the late 1970s suggest that a focus on diversifying acquisitions corresponds to contemporary business policy interests. Finally, and perhaps most important from a research point of view, diversification through internal development—whether managed by an R&D group, a new-venture division, or a more mature operating entity—deserves its own contemporary study. While such a study would have to stress a host of organizational issues, it could usefully build upon the economic and strategic concepts presented here.

Early versions of the chapters of this book were prepared in connection with the development of a new elective course at the Harvard Business School entitled "Managing Diversification." The pedagogical goals of this course are (1) to identify general management problems associated with creating and managing different kinds of diversified companies, (2) to develop skills in evaluating alternative ways of dealing with these problems, and (3) to develop an awareness of the major public policy issues affecting the future of diversified companies. This book clearly reflects the goals of the Managing Diversification course; it does not treat, however, the full range of ideas presented there. Our present emphasis is on the creation of diversified companies, not their subsequent management. Materials similar to those included in this book have been discussed over the past five years at Harvard by MBA candidates as well as more experienced managers in Harvard's Advanced Management Program located in Boston and its sister program, the International Senior Managers Program, located in Vevey, Switzerland. Chapter 2 has appeared in slightly different form in the *Harvard Business Review*.

Several faculty colleagues at the Harvard Business School, including Professors Norman Berg, Joseph L. Bower, Robert H. Hayes, Daniel M. Kasper, Thomas R. Piper, Michael E. Porter, and Irwin Tepper, reviewed early versions of several chapters and provided valuable counsel. Special thanks must be paid to Professors Hayes and Piper, who as colleagues in Switzerland during 1977–1978 withstood with grace and great intelligence our constant probings and invariably provided creative comments on numerous drafts. Professor Berg's continued support in an effort that piggybacked on his earlier work in the Managing Diversification course is also greatly appreciated. In addition, we are grateful for the financial support provided by Professor Richard S. Rosenbloom, Associate Dean for Research and Course Development, and the Associates of the Harvard Business School.

Two former students have also made important contributions to our study. W. Curtis Francis prepared an early analysis of the Rockwell-Admiral merger. Steven E. Hengen prepared an antitrust working paper from which we have borrowed freely in Chapter 11.

Two professional colleagues, David Notestein and Douglas Smith, deserve special mention: Mr. Notestein for both his help in locating data important to this study and the inestimable value of his time spent questioning our premises, assumptions, and analyses; Mr. Smith for his constant exhortations about not forgetting the "real world" of mergers and acquisitions.

We wish to thank Helen Kosakowski for her typing of many pages of the manuscript while organizing our lives and the office during our work on this book. We are also indebted to Mary V. Day and Muriel Drysdale, whose typing of numerous drafts of the manuscript enabled it to become both legible and comprehensible. Carole Sihver, our secretary in Vevey, provided considerable help while we were in Switzerland. The members of the Word Processing Group also provided considerable support.

An especially sympathetic wife also deserves a special acknowledgment. Barbara Salter helped sustain this project in many important ways. Her good cheer, while she bore with our preoccupations during the past several years and took the heavier load in raising a family, has been extraordinary. Finally, we want to thank our parents for their continued interest and commitment to our academic work. The encouragement and moral support of Wolf K. and Marjorie Weinhold was a particularly important contribution to this completed project.

With these expressions of gratitude go our personal affirmations of responsibility for the conclusions of this book and their presentation.

Diversification through Acquisition

PART I

The Diversification Decision: An Overview

CHAPTER 1

Introduction to Corporate Diversification

THERE ARE MANY REASONS AND pressures leading companies to consider diversification. One reason to diversify is to mitigate the effects of a slowdown in sales and earnings accompanying the mature phase of a business's life cycle. Another pressure is a fruitful R&D effort, like Du Pont's or Hewlett-Packard's, which leads to a rich collection of new product ideas and prototypes waiting to be exploited. The desire to build on an existing franchise, like the Gillette Company's desire to develop new products that can be moved through its distribution system, is another realistic pressure. Competitive pressure can also force companies to diversify. How else can one explain the interest of Xerox in electric typewriters and IBM's in copiers? The desire to smooth the swings of cyclical income streams provides another reason to diversify, one that is consistent with the desire to build a balanced portfolio of businesses where the cash generators can help finance high-potential cash takers.

Some companies diversify to avoid takeovers; others diversify to use more fully the general management skills of their top operating executives. Still other companies diversify so that they can attract and retain first-rate managers. These companies believe that the ability to recruit new managers at all levels depends to a great extent on the ability to provide a wide range of new responsibilities and opportunities for self-development. Finally, and possibly most important, U.S. antitrust laws often press growth oriented companies into a search for bold diversification opportunities. As reported by Gilbert Burck several years ago, aggressive antitrust action during the 1960s "has made companies reluctant to enter fields closely related to their own. . . . So expansion-minded companies with money or access to money have been unwilling or unable to use it in horizontal or vertical expansion and naturally have been drawn to new fields." [1]

3

Companies can diversify through acquisition or through internal development. Diversification through internal development is implemented by relying on existing internal resources as the basis for establishing a business new to the company. Typically, this approach to diversification is supported by an explicit planning process that focuses on reviewing both a company's technological competences and its opportunities for new business development on a continuing basis. Such a strategy of diversification requires special technological and organizational capacities and can take as long as a decade to implement.[2] A recent study by Ralph Biggadike of forty large U.S. companies that diversified through internal development showed that eight years was typically required before their new ventures generated a positive return on investment.[3]

In contrast, diversification through acquisition can take weeks rather than years to execute. While such a strategy can be the result of detailed planning, it often is not. Acquisition candidates tend to become available without advance notice. Favorable environmental conditions—such as the state of the equity market—can develop and disappear without a clear warning signal. Unexpected competitive bids for previously identified acquisition candidates can often raise both the "ante" and the pressure for corporate strategists. Swift, decisive action—not sustained planning—is thus a hallmark of many diversifying acquisitions.

Diversification through acquisition is often an attractive option for diversifying companies not only because it can save a company time but also because the *cost of entry* into a new industry or business through acquisition may be less than the cost of diversification through internal development. Diversification through acquisition is especially attractive when the key success variables of a business consist of such intangibles as patents, trademarks, copyrights, product image, exclusive distribution, specialized management knowhow, and research-and-development skills. These intangibles are often impossible to duplicate within reasonable limits of cost and time. Indeed, the risk of failing to develop intangible resources critical to the success of an enterprise is often a more important deterrent to new entrants in industries earning above-average, long-run rates of return than such structural barriers as production scale economics and absolute size. Where such intangible barriers exist, the *risk of entry* is often high. This risk naturally serves to discourage entry by companies outside the industry pursuing diversification through internal development. Only companies willing to "buy into" the industry through acquisition are in a position to participate in its above-average profitability without running overwhelming entry risks.[4]

Recognizing the special conditions surrounding the execution of diversification through acquisition, we aim in this book to develop a practical framework for analyzing diversifying acquisitions and developing an intelligent diversification program. In pursuing this goal, we will limit our discussion to primarily domestic acquisitions. Furthermore, we will not concentrate on the financial packaging of acquisitions or the legal details of corporate reorganizations that often accompany major acquisitions. Neither will we address the administrative challenges of managing different kinds of diversified companies. While these topics represent important aspects of the process of diversification through acquisition, our interest here is primarily strategic in nature. Our principal concern is helping managers design a program of diversification through acquisition that can serve the long-run goals held by a company and its shareholders.

The time is right for a fresh look at diversification through acquisition. During the past two decades an increasing proportion of large American companies have seen wisdom in pursuing strategies of diversification. Many of these companies have diversified through acquisition. In recent years the return on capital of widely diversified companies as a group has been below the "all industry" averages. As we shall see, there is sufficient evidence now to suggest that businessmen should approach the analysis and execution of corporate diversification with extreme caution. However, before we examine this evidence and the questions it raises, it is essential that we define what "diversification" will come to mean in the context of our discussion.

Definitions

The terms "diversified" and "diversification" can suggest innumerable meanings. In a historical review of the role of chief executive at the General Electric Company, James P. Baughman has noted that Ralph Cordiner used the terms in at least six different senses during his tenure as CEO: "developmental (R&D) diversification," "functional diversification," "product diversification," "customer diversification," "geographic (international) diversification," and "diversification of the means of financing." Thus, diversification, according to Cordiner, was a change in any of the above-mentioned elements of General Electric's corporate strategy.[5]

A more traditional meaning of diversification is limited to product market diversification. This is the meaning we will adopt. The key to this definition is an understanding of what constitutes different markets, since trying to define diversification on the basis of products alone is not very precise. The problem is one of agreeing on a definition of a product. Is a product defined by the raw materials in it? If so, a transistor and a vacuum tube are two different products although they serve similar functions. Is a product defined by the type of customer to which it is sold? If so, dresses for women and dresses for "misses" are two different products. Is a product defined by the manufacturing process? If so, a handcrafted pot and a machine-made pot are two different products, or are they?

The only way out of this ambiguous situation is to accent the heterogeneity of markets as well as products in the definition. Market heterogeneity can be defined according to two criteria. The first stems from the concept of substitutability, or cross-elasticity of demand. If the cross-elasticity of demand for two products is high, it means that the two products are close substitutes and therefore belong to the same market. High cross-elasticity exists where the demand for one product increases more or less proportionally with a rise in price for the other—assuming, of course, that the price of the first product remains constant. Low elasticity of demand, or low substitutability, would define separate markets. The second criterion stems from the notion of immobility of productive resources. When resources can be shifted rapidly from the manufacturing of one product to the manufacturing of others, then the products are most likely very similar. Thus, in Michael Gort's words,

> Diversification may be defined in terms of the heterogeneity of output from the point of view of the number of markets served by that output. Two products may be specified as belonging to separate markets if their cross-elasticities of demand are low and if, in the short run, the necessary resources employed in the production and distribution of one cannot be shifted to the other.[6]

According to this definition, a company's degree of diversification increases as the heterogeneity of the markets served by that company increases. In addition, this definition implies that heterogeneity of product is distinct from diversification if it involves only minor differences of essentially the same product.[7]

Corporate diversification, as defined above, is a broad enough concept to encompass a variety of forms. Perhaps the most sophisticated classification of diversified companies and diversification strategies has been developed by Richard P. Rumelt, who identified nine differentiable types.[8] These diversification strategies differ in terms of the strengths, skills, or purposes that underlie the "cumulative total of a firm's diversification moves" and the way new activities are related to old activities.

For our purposes Rumelt's simplified scheme of three basic categories of diversified companies—dominant-business companies, related-business companies, and unrelated-business companies—provides the most useful framework for thinking about diversification options. Dominant-business companies, according to Rumelt's framework, derive 70 to 95 percent of sales from a single business or vertically integrated chain of businesses. Representative companies include General Motors, IBM, Texaco, Scott Paper, and U.S. Steel. Related-business companies have diversified by adding activities that are tangibly related to the collective skills and strengths possessed by the company. No single business accounts for more than 70 percent of such a company's sales. Du Pont, Eastman Kodak, General Electric, and General Foods are some companies that fall into this category. Unrelated-business companies, commonly called conglomerates, have diversified without necessarily relating new businesses to old. In this class of company no single business accounts for as much as 70 percent of sales. Such companies as Litton, LTV, Rockwell International, Olin, and Textron are representatives of this particular class.

Rumelt has defined his categories of diversified companies in terms of a "specialization ratio," showing the proportion of a company's revenues derived from its largest business, and a "related ratio," showing the proportion of a company's revenues derived from its largest single group of related businesses. Businesses are considered related if they (1) serve similar markets and use similar distribution systems, (2) employ similar production technologies, or (3) exploit similar science-based research.

Rumelt's concept of relatedness is consistent with the distinctions that Gort makes in defining diversification. Both researchers' focus is on the technological properties and market characteristics associated with a particular product or business. The more similar the technology of two businesses or the more similar the market and the marketing system required to reach the market of two businesses, the more related the two businesses are.

In practice, relatedness has as much to do with required management skills as it does with product market characteristics. If one believes that business experience and management skills are the critical elements of success, then it makes sense to classify diversification strategies by these criteria. Business experience can best be defined in terms of the company's product market profile. Management skills can be divided into two broad categories—general management skills and functional activities. Functional activities can be further divided into research and development, production and manufacturing, and marketing and distribution.

Using these criteria it becomes relatively easy to identify diversification strategies. An unrelated diversifier is a company pursuing growth in product markets where the key success factors are unrelated to each other. Such a company, whether an actively managed conglomerate or a more passively managed holding company, expects little or no transfer of functional skills between its various businesses (divisions). In contrast, a related diversifier is a company that uses its skills in a specific functional activity or product market as a basis for diversification.

Related diversifiers can be usefully divided into two basic types. If a related diversifier expands its business by entering product markets requiring functional skills identical to those already possessed by the company, we can call this strategy "related-supplementary diversification." The purest form of this strategy would be horizontal integration where the expansion involves minimal departure from key functional activities. An example of related-supplementary diversification is one specialty chemical company acquiring another. Horizontal integration would take place where one blast furnace acquires another in a different locality.

If a related diversifier expands its business base by adding key functional activities and skills to its existing set (but not substantially changing its final product market), then we can call this strategy "related-complementary diversification." Here, the purest form of related-complementary diversification would be vertical integration where the expansion involves adding key functional skills with minimal changes in product market orientation. An example of related-complementary diversification is a food processor acquiring a food wholesaler.

Figure 1-1 depicts the variety of related diversification strategies that companies can pursue. The horizontal axis measures the change in product market(s) of the company, while the vertical axis measures the change in key functional activities. A diversifying acquisition will involve a change in one or both of these criteria. Acquisitions that involve a greater change in product market than in key functional activities are related-

FIGURE 1-1. Related Diversification Strategies

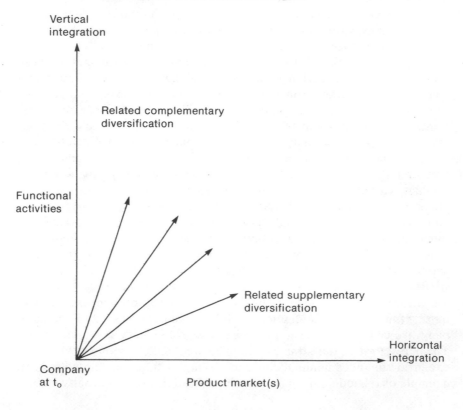

supplementary diversification moves. Conversely, acquisitions that involve a greater change in key functional activities than in product markets are related-complementary diversification moves. It is important to emphasize that the scales of these axes are not absolute—they merely reflect the relative direction of a diversification alternative.

Similarly, it is important not to overdraw distinctions between related and unrelated diversification. If two businesses have similar product market characteristics, it would be natural to expect that many common skills are required to manage the two businesses. It is conceivable, however, that businesses normally classified as different from each other in a product market sense could require similar strategic, organizational, and operating skills. A diversifying acquisition linking these two businesses together into one company may therefore be viewed by its managements as being related, although the details of technology and marketing may be quite different. Thus, the distinction we wish to make between related and unrelated diversification cannot always be a perfectly clear one.

Related diversification often leads to synergy, a topic that has received a good deal of publicity in recent years.[9] Synergy is said to exist when the combined return on a company's resources is greater than the sum of its parts. This can occur (1) when the products of two or more businesses use common distribution channels, common sales administration, and common warehousing, (2) where there is an opportunity for tie-in sales that can increase the productivity of the sales force, (3) where opportunities for common advertising and sales promotion exist, (4) where common facilities can be utilized and overhead spread over larger volume, (5) when there is research-and-development carryover from one product to another, and so on. In theory, one would expect that the greater the potential for synergy between two businesses, the more closely related they are in terms of key functional skills or product markets. In practice, managers of diversified companies realize how difficult it is to take advantage of potential synergies. When this potential cannot be exploited for organizational or other reasons, the administration of a group of so-called related businesses will have many similarities with conglomerate management. Here, again, we see that such distinctions as "related" and "unrelated" diversification have to be made with great care. Given the importance and the subtleties of this distinction, we will return to the subject later, in our discussion of diversification objectives.

History of Corporate Diversification through Acquisition

Although mergers and acquisitions constitute only one route to corporate diversification, their visibility has facilitated extensive economic research.[10] This research shows that acquisition activity in the United States runs in cycles and that the peaks of these cycles typically accompany peaks in either economic activity or stock prices. Figure 1-2 shows the three major cycles between 1895 and 1978.

The first peak in merger and acquisition activity just prior to 1900 was reached in a period of economic expansion following a decade of economic stagnation. The wave of mergers between 1895 and 1905 involved an estimated 15 percent of all manufacturing assets and employees, and accompanied major changes in the nation's social and technological infrastructure.[11] An important characteristic of this merger wave was the simultaneous consolidation of producers within numerous industries. These mergers, mostly horizontal integrations, were typically made in search of market dominance. George Stigler has characterized this merger wave as "merging for monopoly." Many of today's industrial giants,

FIGURE 1-2. Number of Manufacturing and Mining Firms Acquired, 1895-1978

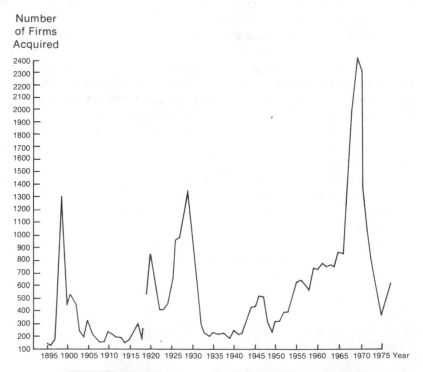

Sources: F. M. Scherer, *Industrial Market Structure and Economic Performance* (Chicago: Rand McNally, 1970), p. 104; Bureau of Economics, FTC, *Current Trends in Merger Activity, 1971,* May 1972; and Bureau of Economics, FTC, *Statistical Report on Mergers and Acquisitions,* December 1978.

including the several descendants of the Standard Oil Trust, U.S. Steel, General Electric, United Fruit, Eastman Kodak, American Can, American Tobacco, U.S. Rubber, Du Pont, P.P.G., International Harvester, and U.S. Gypsum, among others, have their origins in this period. The tail end of this merger wave in 1903–1904 coincided with a severe economic recession and the *Northern Securities* decision, which established that mergers could be successfully attacked under the then existing antitrust law.[12]

The second wave of merger and acquisition activity occurred during the 1920s. This wave was marked by the formation of numerous electric, gas, and water utility holding companies. In the manufacturing sector, most mergers involved either small market share additions or vertical integration. Worthy of special note was the formation of strong "number two companies" in numerous industries previously dominated by one giant firm. The consolidations of Bethlehem Steel, Allied Chemical, Continental Can, and Kraft all date from this era. George Stigler has characterized this period of merger activity as "merging for oligopoly." The end of this wave of activity came with the stock market crash in 1929 and the worldwide depression from 1930 to 1933. During the 1930s many of the recently created utility holding companies collapsed into bankruptcy, and major segments of American industry underwent severe contractions.

The third cycle of merger activity started after World War II and peaked in the late 1960s. In contrast to mergers of previous periods, the typical merger did not involve the nation's largest companies or result in a substantial degree of intra-industry concentration. Most of the acquirers were small to medium-sized companies whose acquisitions were small to medium-sized companies operating outside the acquiring company's narrowly defined industry. What developed during this period was a new class of firms, generally known as conglomerates, with activities in several unrelated product markets. The growing importance of conglomerates in American industry during this period can be seen in Figure 1-3, where the terms "conglomerate" and "unrelated business" are roughly equivalent. An emerging trend toward diversification by the country's largest companies, indicated by the increasing number of the businesses in the related-business category, can also be seen in Figure 1-3.

The most important characteristic of the third merger and acquisition wave was diversification. While a continuing concentration of the nation's industrial assets occurred, it did not result in significantly increased concentration within industries. (Despite the Celler–Kefauver Amendments to the Clayton Act in 1950, the country's antitrust laws had little effect on limiting both related and unrelated mergers.) Since this wave of activity brought corporate growth but not concentrated market power, as defined in classical economic terms, we can refer to this third wave as "merging

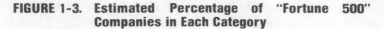

FIGURE 1-3. Estimated Percentage of "Fortune 500" Companies in Each Category

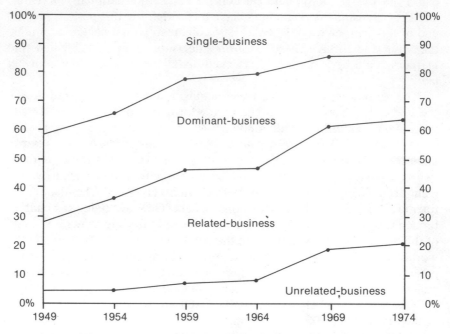

Source: Richard Rumelt, "Diversity and Profitability" (Los Angeles: University of California at Los Angeles Working Paper, 1977), p. 21. Reprinted by permission of the author.

for growth.'' For conglomerates, the wave subsided in 1969–1970 with the collapse of the stock market; for other acquirers, it subsided in 1973 with the advent of the nation's severest economic recession since the 1930s.

The most recent merger and acquisition cycle stretched from a peak in the bull market of the late 1960s, through the economic slowdown of the mid-1970s, and into an upsurge in economic activity during the latter half of the 1970s. Tables 1-1 to 1-4 provide a comparative profile of merger and acquisition activity during this most recent cycle. Table 1-1 shows recent trends in the number and size of acquisitions. Note the surge in small to medium-sized acquisitions in the 1967–1973 period. During 1967–1969, conglomerates were responsible for most of the acquisition activity, whereas during 1970–1973 second tier, industrial firms expanding their product market commitments tended to be the most acquisitive. In 1976–1978 the number of large and very large acquisitions increased dramatically, although the total number of recorded acquisitions remained relatively level.

TABLE 1-1. Trend in Recorded Acquisitions[a]

	All Acquisitions			Mining and Manufacturing Acquisitions		
	Number of Acquisitions[b]	Number over $10 million	Number over $100 million	Number of Acquisitions	Number over $10 million	Number over $100 million
1951–55[c]	NA	NA	NA	378/yr.	30/yr.	2/yr.
1956–60[c]	NA	NA	NA	705/yr.	48/yr.	1/yr.
1961–66[c]	1514/yr.	NA	NA	920/yr.	63/yr.	5/yr.
1967–69[c,d]	3403/yr.	NA	NA	2070/yr.	150/yr.	27/yr.
1970	2854	NA	NA	1351	91	12
1971	2303	NA	NA	1011	59	5
1972	2758[e]	NA	NA	NA	60	6
1973	1919[e]	137	28	697	64	7
1974	1276[e]	129	26	505	62	11
1975	889[e]	112	16	355	59	11
1976	1081[e]	159	23	461	81	14
1977[f]	1182[e]	195	38	619	99	19
1978[f]	1350	260	45	NA	NA	31

a The FTC's Bureau of Economics changed its method of reporting acquisitions in 1972. Therefore, the data reported before and after this year are not exactly comparable.

b Does not include partial acquisitions.

c Numbers shown for these periods are yearly averages.

d In the three-year period 1967–1969, $32.5 billion in large mining and manufacturing assets changed hands.

e As originally reported. The December 1978 *Statistical Report on Mergers and Acquisitions* reports revised totals of 2839, 2359, 1474, 1047, 1171, and 1182 for the years 1972–1977 respectively.

f 1977 figures are subject to revision; 1978 figures are preliminary.

Sources: Bureau of Economics, FTC, *Current Trends in Merger Activity,* May 1972; Bureau of Economics, FTC, *Statistical Report on Mergers and Acquisitions,* July 1974, October 1975, November 1976, November 1977, and December 1978; and various editions of *Mergers and Acquisitions.*

TABLE 1-2. Percentage of Total Large Acquisitions by 200 Largest Industrial Companies[a]

Year	Number	Assets
1950–1959[b]	60.9	57.8
1960–1969[b]	40.4	59.4
1970	34.1	55.9
1971	28.8	40.1
1972	38.3	51.6
1973	40.6	57.1
1974	40.3	48.1
1975	32.2	52.4
1976	25.9	44.7
1977[c]	32.3	60.4
1978[d]	35.0	50.0

[a] Large acquisitions are those involving acquired assets exceeding $10 million.

[b] Averages for the period.

[c] 1977 figures are subject to revision.

[d] 1978 figures are preliminary.

Source: Bureau of Economics, FTC, *Statistical Report on Mergers and Acquisitions,* December 1978.

Table 1-2 shows the percentage of large acquisitions made by the nation's two hundred largest industrial companies. In terms of the relative numbers of acquisitions made, this group's activity has fallen continuously from 1950 on; however, in terms of the relative assets acquired, it has remained relatively constant. These statistics confirm the notion that while the two hundred largest industrial companies were making fewer acquisitions in the late 1970s, they were making significantly larger acquisitions than before.

Table 1-3 shows what percentage of large acquisitions were recorded by the FTC as diversifying acquisitions. Sketchy as the evidence is, it indicates how important diversifying acquisitions have become in the context of overall acquisition activity. From 1961 to 1978, over 70 percent of the total assets acquired by the industrial companies have resulted from acquisitions falling into the FTC's "broad definition" of diversifying acquisitions. This category includes all acquisitions extending operations beyond present product or geographic markets. The FTC's "narrow definition" of diversifying acquisitions is more meaningful for our purposes, since it closely corresponds to unrelated or pure conglomerate diversifications. It is clear from these data that at the height of acquisition activity in the late 1960s a special interest in "pure conglomerate" or unrelated mergers developed. After a decline in interest during 1972–1974, a dramatic resurgence of investment in unrelated diversifying ac-

TABLE 1-3. Large Diversifying Acquisitions by Industrial Companies: Percentage of Total Assets Acquired[a]

Year	FTC Broad Definition[b]	FTC Narrow Definition[c]
1952–1955[d]	52.0	3.6
1956–1959[d]	N.A.	14.0
1961–1970[d]	78.5	30.4
1971	79.2	45.3
1972	59.2	16.8
1973	65.3	36.7
1974	68.2	38.0
1975	94.6	68.3
1976	83.6	54.8
1977[e]	77.7	44.6
1978[f]	76.0	46.7

[a] Large acquisitions are those involving acquired assets exceeding $10 million.

[b] All acquisitions extending operations beyond present product or geographical markets.

[c] Acquisitions where the two companies are functionally unrelated in marketing or production.

[d] Averages for the period.

[e] 1977 figures are subject to revision.

[f] 1978 figures are preliminary

Sources: Bureau of Economics, FTC, *Statistical Report on Mergers and Acquisitions,* July 1974, October 1975, November 1977, and December 1978; and Jesse W. Markham, *Conglomerate Enterprise and Public Policy,* Division of Research, Harvard Business School, 1973.

quisitions took place, starting in 1975. These data, along with those of Tables 1-1 and 1-2, suggest that many of the recent large and very large acquisitions have been unrelated diversification moves by the country's largest firms.

Table 1-4 helps place the most recent upsurge in merger and acquisition activity in much broader perspective. From a historical perspective, we can see that the acquisition activity during 1975–1978 was comparatively mild. While total acquired assets in 1975–1978 were reaching the 1967–1969 peak, the amount of acquired assets relative to existing assets was just approaching the average acquisition rate for the 1960–1966 period and still far below that for the 1967–1969 period. In fact, the background data show the years 1955–1956 and 1963–1971 having as high or higher merger and acquisition activity, relative to either new investment or total existing assets, than that during the active 1977–1978 period. Table 1-4 also reveals that acquisition activity in recent years has had little or no effect on the level of new investment in plant and equipment despite numerous claims to the contrary.

TABLE 1-4.   Comparison of Large Acquired Assets to New and Existing Investments for Manufacturing and Mining Companies

Year	New Investment[a] ($ billions)	Acquired Assets[b] ($ billions)	Acquired Assets as Percentage of New Investment	Acquired Assets as Percentage of Existing Assets
1948–1953[c]	$10.6/yr.	$ 0.3/yr.	2.8%	0.18%
1954–1959[c]	14.8/yr.	1.7/yr.	11.4	0.80
1960–1966[c]	20.2/yr.	2.9/yr.	14.5	0.92
1967–1969[c]	31.2/yr.	11.6/yr.	37.2	2.47
1970	33.8	6.6	19.5	1.14
1971	32.2	3.1	9.8	0.51
1972	33.8	2.7	7.9	0.41
1973	40.8	3.6	8.7	0.50
1974	49.2	5.1	10.4	0.69
1975	51.7	5.5	10.7	0.68
1976	56.5	6.9	12.2	0.79
1977[d]	65.5	9.6	14.7	1.02
1978[e]	73.2	12.3	16.8	1.19

[a] Total expenditures for new plant and equipment by manufacturing and mining firms.

[b] Acquired firms with assets of $10 million or more.

[c] Numbers shown for these years are averages for the period.

[d] 1977 figures are subject to revision.

[e] 1978 figures are preliminary.

Source: Bureau of Economics, FTC, *Statistical Report on Mergers and Acquisitions,* December 1978, and Standard & Poor's Statistical Service, *Current Statistics*, January 1979.

The upswing in merger and acquisition activity beginning in 1975 appears to indicate a fourth wave of corporate marriages. While all the important characteristics of this wave cannot be confidently predicted until time has passed, several distinct features are observable. Table 1-5 presents a partial profile of the major transactions that took place from 1975 to 1978.

Most of the mergers and acquisitions during this period involved payments of cash or a package of cash and cash equivalents. This is in marked contrast to the 1960s, when common stock or convertibles were the principal medium of exchange. In addition, hostile tender offers were much more common than during earlier periods. In 1975 and 1976 almost twice as many hostile offers were initiated than in 1968, although there were only half as many mergers. A further increase in the number of hostile offers as well as the "degree of hostility" occurred in 1977 and

1978. Open bidding wars between two, three, or even four corporate suitors developed for particularly desirable properties. As a result tender premiums over going market prices were driven up from an average of 10 to 20 percent in the 1960s to almost 50 percent, with premiums of 100 percent over market value not uncommon.

The nature and size of the assets involved in mergers and acquisitions during 1975–1978 also give this period a distinctive profile. An acquisition by one company more frequently than before was a division being divested by another company. In 1976 divestitures involved over half of all acquisitions versus approximately 10 percent in the 1960s. These divestitures, as well as outright corporate acquisitions, also tended to be much larger than before. Acquisitions over $10 million grew threefold between 1970 and 1977–1978, while very large acquisitions (those over $100 million) grew ninefold. Table 1-5 shows that since 1976 over twenty transactions have fallen into the $300 million class.

Finally, in contrast to earlier periods many of the acquisition-oriented companies in the late 1970s were well-established, conservative, old-line giants with a substantial bulk of their activities concentrated in a few closely related business. U.S. companies such as Mobil, General Electric, Atlantic-Richfield, United Technologies, Johns Manville, Phillip Morris, R. J. Reynolds, Pepsico, and Continental Group fall into this class. None of these companies was considered to be an acquisitive diversifier in the 1960s. Not to be outdone were the foreign acquirers of U.S. companies, such as Bayer, Nestlé, British Oxygen, Imetal, Sandoz, Société Générale, Ciba-Geigy, and INCO. Where foreign companies could not obtain total ownership, substantial minority interests were bought, as in the case of Robert Bosch's 9.9 percent interest in Borg-Warner and the Flick Group's 30 percent interest in W. R. Grace.

A basic difference between U.S. and foreign acquirers was the type of diversification pursued. Acquisitions by foreign acquirers were mostly related to their existing businesses, while their American counterparts tended to pursue unrelated diversifying acquisitions. If history shows that the redeployment of assets by U.S. companies into unrelated businesses reflects attempts to reduce their risk exposure in an increasingly volatile economic and political environment at home, then this most recent wave of activity may be characterized as "merging for economic stability." Ironically, this epithet may also characterize the objectives of many foreign acquirers, who were attempting to transfer assets out of their home countries to the United States, which appeared to have a more stable economy. The natural first step for these acquirers, having relatively few activities in the United States, was to extend their traditional businesses through related diversification.

TABLE 1-5. Acquisitions Exceeding $100 Million, 1975–1978

Acquiring Company	Acquired/Merged Company	Market Value ($ Millions)	Type[a]
1975			
International Paper Co.	General Crude Oil Co.	486.	unrelated
Standard Oil of California	Amax Inc. (20%)	333.	unrelated
United Technologies Corp.	Otis Elevator Co.	280.	unrelated
Standard Oil of Indiana	Pasco Oil & Gas (Wyoming Properties)	225.	vertical integration
Esmark, Inc. International	Playtex Co. (sub. Rapid American)	210.	unrelated
Signal Companies, Inc.	UOP, Inc.	120.	unrelated
Baker Oil Tools, Inc.	Reed Tool Co.	120.	related-complementary
Int'l Minerals & Chemicals Co.	Commercial Solvents Co.	118.	related-complementary
1976			
General Electric Co.	Utah International Inc.	2,170.	unrelated
Mobil Oil Corp.	Marcor Inc. (46%)	900.	unrelated
Peabody Holdings Inc.	Peabody Coal (sub. Kennecott Copper)	900.	unrelated
R. J. Reynolds Industries, Inc.	Burmah Oil & Gas Co.	520.	unrelated
Marathon Oil Co.	ECOL Ltd.	402.	vertical integration
Marathon Oil Co.	Pan-Ocean Oil Corp.	265.	vertical-integration
Herald Co.	Booth Newspapers Inc.	260.	horizontal integration
Sandoz Ltd.[b]	Northrup King & Co.	190.	related
Colgate Palmolive Co.	Riviana Foods, Inc.	170.	related
Southland Royalty Corp.	Aztec Oil & Gas Co.	170.	horizontal integration
Gould, Inc.	ITE Imperial Co.	164.	related
Atlantic Richfield Co.	Anaconda Co. (27%)	162.	unrelated
Federated Dept. Stores Inc.	Rich's Inc.	160.	horizontal integration
Natomas Company	Apexco Inc.	127.	horizontal integration
Foremost-McKesson Inc.	C. F. Mueller Co.	115.	related-complementary
Warner-Lambert Company	Deseret Pharmaceutical, Inc.	110.	related-complementary
Flick Group[b]	W. R. Grace & Co. (11%)	105.	related

18

Company		
DuPont Co.	Christiana Securities Co.	1,567.	consolidation
McDermott (J. Ray) Co. Inc.	Babcock & Wilcox Co.	687.	related
Kennecott Copper Corp.	Carborundum Co.	567.	unrelated
Atlantic Richfield Co.	Anaconda Co. (73%)	622.	unrelated
Gulf Oil Co.	Kewanee Industries	455.	vertical integration
Continental Group Inc.	Richmond Corp.	366.	unrelated
Getty Oil Co.	Mission Corp./Skelly Oil Co.	357.	consolidation
Taubman-Allen-Irvine Inc.	Irvine Corp.	337.	related
Pepsico Inc.	Pizza Hut Inc.	326.	unrelated
Champion International Corp.	Hoerner Waldorf Corp.	317.	related
Nestle SA[b]	Alcon Laboratories Inc.	276.	related
Int'l Tel. & Tel. Corp.	Carbon Industries Inc.	256.	unrelated
Bayer AG[b]	Miles Laboratories Inc.	254.	related
Carrier Corp.	Inmont Corp.	244.	unrelated
Union Oil of California	Molycorp Inc.	240.	unrelated
Allegheny Ludlum Industries Inc.	Chemetron Corp.	231.	unrelated
St. Regis Paper Co.	Southland Paper Mills Inc.	222.	horizontal integration
Fluor Corp.	Daniel International Corp.	221.	related-complementary
Northwest Industries Inc.	Coca-Cola Co. of Los Angeles	205.	unrelated
Norton Simon Inc.	Avis Inc.	174.	unrelated
Gannett Co. Inc.	Speidel Newspapers Inc.	173.	horizontal integration
Tenneco Inc.	Monroe Auto Equip. Co.	167.	related-supplementary
NL Industries Inc.	The Rucker Co.	165.	unrelated
Farmers Group Inc.	Farmers New World Life Insurance Co.	159.	related-complementary
Combustion Engineering Inc.	Vetco Inc.	158.	unrelated
Houston Natural Gas Corp.	Pott Industries Inc.	147.	unrelated
Union Carbide Corp.	Amchem Products Inc.	140.	related-supplementary
Beneficial Corp.	Interstate Securities Co.	137.	related
Int'l Tel. & Tel. Corp.	Eason Oil Co.	133.	unrelated
Textron Inc.	Allied Chem. (9.6%)	127.	unrelated
Dresser Industries Inc.	Marion Power Shovel Co.	126.	related
Borg-Warner Corp.	Baker Industries Inc.	119.	unrelated
B.C. Forest Products Ltd.[b]	Blandin Paper Co.	115.	related
General Signal Corp.	Sola Basic Industries	113.	related-supplementary

(Table 1-5 continues on next page.)

19

TABLE 1-5. Acquisitions Exceeding $100 Million, 1975–1978 (Continued)

Acquiring Company	Acquired/Merged Company	Market Value ($ Millions)	Type[a]
Jack Eckerd Corp.	Eckerd Drugs Inc.	110.	horizontal integration
Beatrice Foods Co.	Harman Int'l Industries	103.	unrelated
American Can Co.	Pickwick International	101.	unrelated
Norton Co.	Christenson Inc.	100.	unrelated
1978			
Johns-Manville Corp.	Olinkraft Corp.	$585.	unrelated
Phillip Morris Inc.	Seven-Up Co.	515.	related complementary
Beatrice Foods Co.	Tropicana Products Inc.	490.	related complementary
Unilever N.V.[b]	Nat'l Starch & Chemical Co.	480.	related
United Technologies Corp.	Carrier Corp. (49%)	476.	related
IC Industries	Pet Inc.	410.	unrelated
BOC International Ltd.[b]	Airco Inc. (65%)	405.	related
Eaton Corp.	Cutler-Hammer Inc.	378.	unrelated
Standard Chartered Bank Ltd.[b]	Union Bancorp.	372.	related
Humana Inc.	American Medicorp	300.	horizontal integration
Sun Co. Inc.	Becton, Dickinson & Co. (34%)	293.	unrelated
Dayton-Hudson Corp.	Mervyn's	287.	related complementary
Time Inc.	Inland Container Corp.	280.	related supplementary
Thyssen A.G.[b]	Budd Co.	272.	related
Flick Group[b]	W.R. Grace & Co. (24%)	255.	related
Johnson Controls Inc.	Globe-Union Inc.	251.	related supplementary
Consolidated Foods Inc.	Hanes Corp.	249.	unrelated
Dart Industries Inc.	P.R. Mallory & Co. Inc.	245.	related complementary
Warner-Lambert Co.	Entenmann's Inc.	233.	related complementary
United Technologies Corp.	AMBAC Industries	210.	related supplementary
Barclays Bank Int'l Ltd.[b]	American Credit Corp.	191.	related

GDV	Servomation Corp.	189.	unrelated
LTV Corp.	Lykes Corp.	188.	related supplementary
Nat'l Distillers & Chem Co.	Emery Industries, Inc.	185.	related supplementary
Tenneco Inc.	Philadelphia Life Ins. Co. (76%)	170.	unrelated
Superior Oil Co.	Austral Oil Co.	170.	horizontal integration
General Signal Corp.	Leeds & Northrup Co.	167.	related
Time Inc.	American T.V. & Communications	151.	related complementary
Allis Chalmers Corp.	American Air Filter	148.	unrelated
Pepsico Inc.	Taco Bell	148.	related supplementary
Int'l Tel. & Tel. Corp.	Qume Corp.	147.	unrelated
Gulf United Corp.	Equitable General Corp.	140.	horizontal integration
Cavenham Ltd.[b]	Colonial Stores Inc.	133.	horizontal integration
Pillsbury Co.	Green Giant Co.	130.	related
Bow Valley Industries Ltd.[b]	Flying Diamond Oil Co.	128.	horizontal integration
American Can Co.	Fingerhut Corp.	127.	unrelated
Schering Plough Corp.	Scholl Inc.	127.	related-complementary
Signal Cos.	UOP Inc. (49.5%)	120.	unrelated
Esmark Inc.	STP Corp.	117.	unrelated
General Cable Corp.	Automation Industries Inc.	114.	related
Davy International	McKee Corp.	106.	related
Eli Lilly & Co.	Cardiac Pacemakers Inc.	103.	related complementary
Kaneb Services Inc.	Diamond M Co.	102.	unrelated
Greyhound Corp.	Verex Corp.	102.	unrelated
Flick Group[b]	U.S. Filter Corp. (34.5%)	100.	unrelated

[a] This column identifies the kind of diversification involved in each acquisition. If the acquisition is related and sufficient information is available, it is then categorized as related-complementary or related-supplementary. If a nondiversifying acquisition is involved, it is characterized as either horizontal or vertical integration.

[b] Non-U.S. purchaser.

Source: *Mergers and Acquisitions: The Journal of Corporate Venture*, 1975–1979.

21

The Performance of Diversified Firms

As we have seen, U.S. industry has experienced several waves of merger and acquisition activity. In contrast to earlier ones, the merger waves of the 1960s and the late 1970s have seen corporations emphasizing strategies of diversification rather than those leading to intra-industry concentration. While increasingly volatile economic and political environment may help explain the recent interest in diversifying acquisitions, there exists no economically based theory to justify wide-ranging corporate diversification. In fact, a strict reading of classical microeconomic theory (especially the concept of specialization) implies that by spreading resources among several businesses, corporate diversification can lead to lower profitability and reduced competitive strength. This divergence between theory and recent corporate practice suggests that it may be useful to look at the performance record of diversifying companies.

The performance of diversified companies can be analyzed in many ways. Many contemporary economists have studied the question of whether or not corporate diversification, particularly unrelated or conglomerate diversification, has led to superior means of reducing investment risk or improving capital returns.[13] More recently, several students of business policy and corporate strategy have attempted to analyze the performance of diversified companies relative to that of other classes of companies. Finally, the business press has tracked the performance of various samples of companies for years.

Let us turn to the work of economists first. Several economists, including Reid; Weston and Mansingkha; Conn; Holzman, Copeland, and Hayya; and Melicher and Rush, among others, have looked at whether or not diversification has led to increased corporate returns.[14] The general conclusion of these studies is that unrelated diversification does not lead to higher corporate returns. Weston and Mansingkha's work, which has been supported by other studies, did note, however, that defensive diversification (diversification out of industries with low profitability) often enabled firms to increase their profitability from inferior to average levels. Smith and Scheiner; Westerfield; Weston, Smith, and Shieves; and Lev and Mandelker in particular have looked at whether corporate diversification offered superior risk-reduction capabilities.[15] These studies conclude that while conglomerates may have achieved some risk reduction relative to individual firms, it typically came by reducing company specific risk while increasing the more relevant market-related risks of the company. In virtually every comparison, mutual funds provided more efficient diversification than unrelated corporate diversifiers as well as better risk/return tradeoffs. One of the more persuasive economic studies of conglomerate performance was done by Mason and Gondzwaard.[16] They found that even during the heyday of conglomerates mergers (1962–1967) investors could have earned higher rates of return by randomly selecting portfolios of securities from the industries where conglomerates participated than through ownership of conglomerates themselves. These higher returns on the randomly selected portfolios came in spite of the conglomerates' greater use of financial leverage and the assessment of transaction costs and taxes on the randomly selected portfolios.

Turning now to students of business policy and corporate strategy, we find that Rumelt's research provides better insight about the relative performance of diversifying companies than most of the previous studies relying on traditional, economic definitions of diversity.[17] Table 1-6, based on his categories of companies referred to earlier, shows the performance of companies following various diversification strategies. Most noteworthy is the fact that dominant-business companies underperformed, on average, all other classes of companies according to the five performance measures. Single-business companies outperformed the average in terms of capital productivity but underperformed it in terms of corporate growth. The statistics on unrelated-business companies, the group that grew the most in number during two decades under study, do not suggest that unrelated diversification was necessarily the answer. While this class of companies showed significantly higher corporate growth rates, it also showed the lowest rates of capital productivity. The statistics on related-business companies are more consistent than those of unrelated-business companies in that this class of companies outperformed the averages on

TABLE 1-6. Annualized Performance of Listed NYSE Companies, 1950–1970

	Sales Growth	Earnings Growth	EPS Growth	ROI	ROE
Single-business companies	7.17%	4.81%	3.92%	10.81%	13.20%
Dominant-business companies	8.03	7.95	5.99	9.64	11.64
Related-business companies	9.14	9.39	7.64	11.49	13.55
Unrelated-business companies	14.24	13.86	7.92	9.49	11.92
Average for all companies	9.01	8.72	6.57	10.52	12.64

Source: Richard P. Rumelt, *Strategy, Structure and Economic Performance,* Division of Research, Harvard Business School, 1974.

all five measures. This group had the second highest set of growth rates while achieving the highest returns on capital.

Recognizing that industry effects could have a significant effect on relative corporate performance, Rumelt reevaluated his work by attempting to neutralize any industry effects on corporate profitability.[18] His preliminary results are shown in Table 1-7. Column 3 shows the difference between what companies actually earned and what they should have earned as average members of the industry. The constantly declining residual from +1.51 for single businesses to −1.66 for unrelated portfolio businesses (or conglomerates), while statistically untestable, suggests that increasing diversification leads to decreasing relative profitability. According to Rumelt, "*given an industry,* those specializing in it will tend to be more profitable than those for which it is a sideline." Rumelt's two studies neatly summarize the dilemma many companies face. Sticking close to traditional businesses can condemn a company to mediocre performance. However, wide-ranging diversification places the produc-

TABLE 1-7. Performance Differences among Rumelt's Strategic Categories [Weighed for Industry Affiliation (1962–1971)]

Category	Actual ROC	Expected ROC[a]	Residual
Single Business	11.45%	9.94%	1.51*
Dominant–constrained[b]	12.09	11.01	1.08
Related–constrained[b]	12.28	11.67	.61
Related Linked[b]	10.53	10.83	− .30
Multibusiness[c]	8.30	10.13	−1.83*
Unrelated portfolio[c]	8.80	10.46	−1.66*
Average for all companies	11.00	10.89	0.11

[a] Average return on capital over the period for all the companies in each strategic category if they were average performers in the industries in which they participated.

[b] Rumelt's "constrained" categories closely correspond to related-complementary diversification while his "linked" categories closely correspond to related-supplementary diversification.

[c] Rumelt expanded his original unrelated category into a multibusiness segment, or companies with 2–4 relatively balanced though unrelated businesses, and an unrelated portfolio segment, or companies with numerous unrelated businesses.

* Significant at the 5% level.

Source: Richard Rumelt, "Diversity and Profitability," University of California at Los Angeles Working Paper MGL-51, 1977. Reprinted by permission of the author.

tivity of capital at significant risk. And the chances for successful related diversification will highly depend on the characteristics of the industry a company is in.

Table 1-8 provides a glimpse at the performance of diversified companies relative to overall measures of the economy and stock prices. While stock prices, in general, have not kept pace with inflation or the economy's growth since 1967, conglomerate stock-price performance has been way below that of the two Standard & Poor indices. While the choice of the base year does influence the relative performance of the conglomerate index (1967–1968 was the peak in conglomerate stock prices), it was also the peak in real terms for the stock market.

Tables 1-9 and 1-10 show the recent peformance of unrelated diversifiers as presented by two business publications, *Forbes* and *Business Week*. The 1973–1978 period is a useful one, since it starts at the top of a business cycle and goes through the 1975 recession into the 1976–1978 economic upswing. It also includes the most recent upsurge in merger and acquisition activity. Both tables indicate that conglomerates were poor performers relative to industry averages during this period. This is particularly true concerning their productivity of capital. The extensive use

TABLE 1-8. Relative Economic and Stock Price Performance, 1965–1978

Year	Consumer Price Index	Fed. Res. Index of Ind. Prod.	S&P 400 Index of Ind. Co's.	S&P 500 Index of Major Co's.	S&P Index of 10 Congl.[a]
1965	94.5	89.8	93.6	95.4	36.7
1966	97.2	97.7	91.3	92.7	55.5
1967	100.0	100.0	100.0[b]	100.0[b]	100.0[b]
1968	104.2	106.3	108.4	107.4	122.1
1969	109.8	111.1	108.1	106.4	88.5
1970	116.3	107.8	92.0	90.5	51.4
1971	121.3	109.6	109.3	106.9	65.7
1972	125.3	119.7	122.8	118.8	67.2
1973	133.1	129.8	121.5	116.8	45.1
1974	147.7	129.3	93.7	90.1	32.7
1975	161.2	117.8	97.4	93.7	40.0
1976	170.5	129.8	115.5	110.9	58.0
1977	181.5	137.1	109.3	106.8	58.1
1978	195.8	145.0	107.1	104.5	57.6

[a] Companies included in the index are City Investing, Gulf+Western Industries, Walter Kidde, Litton Industries, Teledyne, Tenneco, Textron, U. S. Industries, and United Brands.

[b] Actual 1967 Standard & Poor's Indexes for the S&P 400, 500, and 10 conglomerates were 99.18, 91.93, and 26.85 respectively. Index base for the S&P 400 and 500 are 1941–1943 = 10. Index base of the 10 conglomerates is 1965 = 10.

TABLE 1-9. Forbes Industry Comparisons[a]

Year	Multicompanies-Multi-Industry[b]			Multicompanies-Conglomerates[b]			All Industries		
	Median Return on Equity[c]	Median Return on Capital[c]	Median 5 yr. Sales Growth[c]	Median Return on Equity[c]	Median Return on Capital[c]	Median 5 yr. Sales Growth[c]	Median Return on Equity[c]	Median Return on Capital[c]	Median 5 yr. Sales Growth[c]
1969–73[d]	9.5%	7.9%	6.5%	11.2%	7.7%	14.2%	11.4%	8.2%	10.7%
1973	11.5	9.2	6.5	13.1	7.8	14.2	12.8	9.0	10.7
1974	12.8	10.2	7.2	14.4	7.4	11.7	13.3	9.6	11.0
1975	10.9	8.4	8.5	11.7	7.7	10.9	11.7	8.2	10.9
1976	13.0	9.1	9.3	12.5	8.4	10.2	12.9	9.8	11.8
1977	12.8	10.2	9.8	13.1	8.8	10.1	13.9	10.2	12.4
1978	13.0	10.0	9.7	16.6	9.3	10.3	15.4	10.5	12.9

[a] Based upon Forbes' Annual Report on American Industry.

[b] These categories differ on the basis of Forbes perception of how acquisitive a diversifying company is. The composition of these categories is shown in the Appendix to this chapter (p. 261).

[c] Median figures are not averages, but the point which divides a sample into two equal parts. A skewed sample may have an average significantly different from the median.

[d] Average.

TABLE 1-10. *Business Week* **Survey of Business Profits**[a]

	Conglomerates[b]		All Industry Composite	
Year	Average Return on Equity	Average Price–Earnings Ratio[c]	Average Return on Equity	Average Price–Earnings Ratio[c]
1973	11.3%	6	14.0%	11
1974	11.8	5	14.0	9
1975	11.3	8	11.8	12
1976	13.2	8	14.0	10
1977	12.9	7	14.1	9
1978	13.5	6	15.1	8

[a] Based on *Business Week*'s Quarterly Survey of Business Profits.
[b] The composition of *Business Week*'s conglomerate category is shown in the Appendix to this chapter (p. 261).
[c] Based on price–earnings ratios in effect on evaluation date.

of financial leverage by conglomerates is seen in their volatile return-on-equity figures. We can also see that the average price/earnings ratio for conglomerates (which reflects investors' future outlooks for these companies) has continually been at a severe discount from the average price/earnings ratio for the market as a whole.

Data presented in Table 1-11 show in greater detail the economic risks of corporate diversification. This table tracks the performance of a sample of firms originally selected by the Federal Trade Commission in the late 1960s as representative of companies pursuing strategies of diversification and not classifiable in the standard industrial categories. Once again, the relatively low capital productivity of widely diversified companies is quite apparent. While the average return on equity (ROE) of the sample was 20 percent higher than the average of the Fortune 500 (because of accounting conventions) in 1967, it has remained below the Fortune 500 average since then. Even the surge in corporate profits during the 1976–1978 period and the impact of nonoperating profits at several corporations failed to bring the sample average up the Fortune 500 average. Even more telling than the return on equity figures is the sample's return on total assets; this has been approximately 20 percent below the Fortune 500 average throughout the ten-year period. One other useful observation is the highly skewed nature of this sample's returns. While 10 companies had an ROE greater than 10 percent above the Fortune 500 average in 1978, fifteen companies had an ROE greater than 10 percent *below* the Fortune 500 average.

The evidence presented in Tables 1-8 to 1-11 suggests that unrelated diversification is not a panacea for lagging corporate performance. When

TABLE 1-11. Performance Data on 36 Diversified Manufacturers (1967, 1973, 1975, 1978)

Company[a]	1967			1973		
	Year-end total assets (in millions of dollars)	Return on assets	Return on equity	Year-end total assets (in millions of dollars)	Return on assets	Return on equity
Avco	$1,618.5	3.4%	14.7%	$1,412.2	(1.3)%	(3.6)%
Bangor Punta	144.4	4.0	13.6	328.1	0.5	1.3
Bendix	833.4	5.5	11.3	1,427.0	4.1	11.1
Boise Cascade	865.2	3.3	11.3	1,585.4	9.0[b]	21.1[b]
City Investing	338.9	4.0	18.5	3,622.8	2.0	10.3
Colt Industries	197.1	6.1	16.7	266.0	4.0	10.0
FMC	931.8	6.6	13.6	680.5	5.7	11.6
GAF	473.5	4.1	6.9	627.0	4.6	8.7
General Tire	741.7	4.1	8.4	1,233.9	6.2	12.9
W. R. Grace	1,578.4	3.4	8.6	2,003.8	4.2	11.3
Gulf+Western	749.4	6.4	26.8	2,364.1	3.8	13.4
IC Industries	865.5	2.3	4.0	1,736.0	3.0	6.0
ITT	2,961.2	4.0	11.4	10,133.0	5.2	14.1
Kidde	253.1	7.0	14.7	739.5	5.1	12.5
Koppers	326.5	4.3	7.7	520.3	5.7	11.2
LTV	845.1	4.8	18.3	1,829.1	2.7[b]	23.7[b]
Litton	945.0	7.4	19.0	2,116.2	2.0	5.2
Martin Marietta	527.2	7.0	11.9	1,074.0	5.3	11.4

3M	1,034.7	14.2	19.9	2,280.9	13.0	20.6
N L Industries	576.4	8.9	13.4	987.8	4.8	10.9
Northwest Industries	1,286.3	3.0	6.0	964.8	5.9[b]	13.4[b]
Norton Simon	463.8	3.3	6.7	1,120.0	7.0	15.5
Ogden	381.7	5.3	14.1	713.6	3.7	12.9
Rapid-American	337.8	4.8	14.9	1,755.5	1.7	13.7
SCM	451.4	5.6	19.7	552.7	3.3	7.8
Signal	1,090.3	4.5	9.1	1,378.1	4.2	8.7
Singer	1,049.2	4.8	11.1	1,897.0	5.0	11.9
Sperry Rand	1,095.2	5.9	11.9	1,840.6	4.9	10.6
Studebaker-Worthington	561.0	5.9	12.1	995.1	3.3	10.5
TRW	710.9	7.6	17.3	1,446.1	6.6	15.1
Teledyne	337.7	6.4	15.8	1,229.6	5.3	12.6
Tenneco	3,589.3	4.1	11.8	5,127.3	4.5	12.3
Textron	669.7	9.2	20.4	1,310.4	7.7	16.1
U.S. Industries	162.3	7.4	20.5	1,033.5	6.5	12.7
White Consolidated	277.3	3.8	14.7	597.4	5.9	15.1
Whittaker	118.0	7.4	29.3	589.4	(1.0)[b]	(3.3)[b]
Sample Average		5.3	13.9		4.0	12.2
Fortune "500"		7.8	11.7		5.0	12.4

(Table 1-11 continues on the next page.)

TABLE 1-11. *(Continued)*

	1975			1978			EPS growth rate 1968–1978
	Year-end total assets (in millions of dollars)	Return on assets	Return on equity	Year-end total assets (in millions of dollars)	Return on assets	Return on equity	
Avco	$1,250.4	4.9%[b]	12.1%[b]	$4,634.2	2.7%[b]	20.4%[b]	6.1
Bangor Punta	234.9	3.6	8.7	441.6	5.4	15.4	6.5
Bendix	1,567.6	5.1	11.1	2,037.4	6.4	13.9	8.8
Boise Cascade	1,569.5	4.1	7.5	1,981.9	6.7	12.5	8.2
City Investing	3,938.0	0.8	5.0	5,783.4	1.9	18.7	6.6
Colt Industries	866.3	6.0	14.8	1,263.8	6.9	15.4	10.3
FMC	1,843.9	5.9	13.7	2,248.8	6.3	13.4	6.2
GAF	705.4	4.4	8.4	785.3	4.4	9.7	5.7
General Tire	1,427.3	4.4	9.1	1,701.7	6.8	12.1	9.6
W. R. Grace	2,523.8	6.6	18.8	3,268.4	5.2	12.2	10.1
Gulf+Western	3,305.7	4.2	17.5	4,507.8	4.0	13.1	12.0
IC Industries	2,241.7	2.2	5.3	3,223.8	3.0	8.2	6.6
ITT	10,408.0	3.8	9.6	14,034.9	4.7	12.0	5.3
Kidde (Walter)	854.9	5.1	12.3	1,299.8	5.3	12.1	7.8
Koppers	679.7	8.9	17.6	1,034.2	7.4	12.7	6.6
LTV	1,962.8	0.7	3.9	3,720.3	1.1	7.2	(9.6)
Litton	2,185.7	1.6	4.4	2,278.9	(4.0)	(12.0)	—
Martin Marietta	1,139.0	4.9	9.4	1,565.2	8.7	15.7	10.3

MMM	3,016.8	8.7	15.0	4,088.4	13.8	21.7	12.5
NL Industries	1,059.5	4.3	9.1	1,715.3	5.0	11.5	1.9
Northwest Industries	1,184.1	8.6	18.6	1,933.7	7.8	18.6	7.5
Norton Simon	1,355.7	6.1	11.9	2,004.4	5.8	14.5	12.6
Ogden	926.0	5.1	14.8	1,165.1	4.7	15.5	11.5
Rapid-American	1,481.0	(0.6)	(4.9)	1,485.3	3.1[b]	22.1[b]	13.0
SCM	704.1	4.0	10.1	844.6	4.5	10.1	9.7
Signal	1,866.8	2.2	5.3	2,423.5	6.6	16.1	8.1
Singer	1,797.1	(25.2)	(96.0)	1,435.4	4.4	12.5	8.1
Sperry Rand	2,533.1	5.2	12.9	3,286.6	5.4	12.3	10.1
Studebaker-Worthington	883.6	3.4	9.1	1,087.9	11.0	24.2	17.1
TRW	1,686.5	6.2	14.1	2,327.0	7.5	16.9	9.7
Teledyne	1,141.9	8.9	20.5	1,557.0	16.0	28.7	32.5
Tenneco	6,584.2	5.2	15.0	10,134.0	4.6	13.2	6.6
Textron	1,433.3	6.7	13.1	1,988.0	8.5	16.5	7.9
U.S. Industries	941.7	1.1	2.1	863.2	5.8	9.6	(2.6)
White Consolidated	858.2	5.5	16.0	995.1	5.5	14.4	7.4
Whittaker	508.9	0.6	1.6	550.2	5.7	16.4	3.9
Sample Average		3.6	9.5		5.3	13.9	5.3
Fortune "500"		5.7	11.6		6.9	14.2	6.9

[a] Criteria for the selection of companies in this sample:
   Each company in 1969 had total assets of $250 million or more.
   Each company had 50% or more of its total sales derived from manufactured products.
   Each company had less than 50% of its total sales in any one industry and was engaged in three or more product lines.
[b] Extraordinary items included.

Sources: The Fortune Directory of the 500 Largest U. S. Industrial Corporations, 1967, 1973, 1975, 1978; company annual report; and 10-K reports.

this evidence is combined with that developed by contemporary economists and students of business policy, it should become clear that corporate diversification, in general, and unrelated diversification, in particular, need to be planned and executed with utmost care. The evidence also indicates, however, that both related and unrelated diversification can be rewarding for both investors and managers alike. This possibility, along with the economic and political risks facing many industries, will inevitably lead more companies to try their hand at diversification. The mixed track record of their predecessors should warn these companies that their task will not be an easy one.

Questions Raised by the Performance Data

The performance data relating to various categories of diversified companies should be considered suggestive rather than definitive. Averages are often misleading, and categorization schemes often lead to oversimplification and inappropriate classifications. Yet, despite these inevitable weaknesses, the data raise a cluster of related questions that capture the essence of the conceptual and practical problems facing businessmen who are either considering or pursuing strategies of corporate diversification:

1. Why have related-business companies consistently outperformed unrelated-business companies over the past two decades?

2. Why is the productivity of capital in widely diversified companies significantly lower than for other businesses? More specifically, why does the FTC sample of thirty-seven diversified manufacturing companies underperform the Fortune 500 on both a return-on-equity and a return-on-capital basis?

3. How can the large degree of variance of performance within the unrelated diversified categories be explained?

There are several possible explanations that serve as useful starting points in grappling with these questions. Perhaps the most acquisitive diversifiers—typically the unrelated-business companies—paid too much for their acquisitions in the late 1960s and early 1970s. Perhaps the managers of acquisitive diversifiers simply did a careless job of analyzing the prospects and potential of businesses targeted for acquisition. Or perhaps related-business diversifiers were more successful in maintaining their productivity of capital than unrelated-business diversifiers because of their willingness and ability to diversify in only certain types of businesses.

Perhaps as product-market diversity increases, so too does the risk of losing control of the various operating units and divisions. Perhaps the cost of controlling and coordinating the diversified corporation can rise faster than the benefits the corporation gains from that control. Perhaps very few companies have discovered how to design an operating format and to promote a set of administrative practices that provide safeguards against "control loss." Perhaps the notion that new management techniques can help an emerging breed of general managers to handle several businesses at once more effectively than the old-time specialists could manage a single business is simply unrealistic. Perhaps this new breed of generalists—characterized by one observer of the current business scene as adaptable and versatile, with minds spacious enough to see beyond the company and yet disciplined and informed enough to solve its special problems—never developed. Perhaps Du Pont's former president, Lammot du Pont Copeland, was correct when he quipped that "running a conglomerate is a job for management geniuses, not for mortals like us at Du Pont."

Hypotheses abound; definitive answers are few. However, these hypotheses cluster around three major issues, which remain unresolved for many companies:

1.   What logic can serve as a sound basis for corporate diversification? What does this logic have to say about each type of diversification strategy, and what are its prescriptions for successful corporate diversification?

2.   What constitutes an appropriate analysis of diversifying acquisitions and, more fundamentally, what constitutes a carefully designed program of diversification through acquisition?

3.   How can diversified companies be most effectively managed during their post-acquisition phase?

While the performance data suggest that each issue must be addressed by managers of diversifying companies, our present concern lies with the first two issues. Part II of the book, therefore, introduces a framework for strategic and economic analysis. Building on this framework, Part III demonstrates how carefully prepared diversification objectives and acquisition guidelines, along with a conceptually sound acquisition-screening process, can increase the probability of selecting a merger partner that will create real economic value for the diversifying company's shareholders. It also shows how the framework developed in Part II can help decision makers enrich their analysis of diversification opportunities. Part IV concludes the book with a discussion of the antitrust challenge facing diversifying companies.

Notes and References

1. Gilbert Burck, "The Perils of the Multi-Market Corporation," *Fortune,* February 1967.

2. For an in-depth discussion of diversification through internal development see Ilan Kusiatin, "The Process and Capacity for Diversification through Internal Development" (doctoral dissertation, Harvard Business School, 1976).

3. Ralph Biggadike, "Entry, Strategy and Performance" (doctoral dissertation, Harvard Business School, 1976).

4. For a further discussion of market entry through acquisition, see Robert J. Stonebaker, "Corporate Profits and the Risks of Entry," *Review of Economics and Statistics 58,* February 1976, pp. 33–40.

5. James P. Baughman, "Problems and Performance of the Role of Chief Executive in the General Electric Company, 1892–1974," Mimeo, July 5, 1974.

6. Michael Gort, *Diversification and Integration in American Industry* (Princeton: Princeton University Press, 1962).

7. Antitrust lawyers and economists sometimes use a different product market nomenclature. Their language system is reviewed in Chapter 11, pp. 235–237.

8. Richard P. Rumelt, *Strategy, Structure and Economic Performances,* Division of Research, Harvard Business School, 1974.

9. See, for example, Igor H. Ansoff, *Corporate Strategy* (New York: McGraw-Hill, 1965).

10. See, for instance, George Stigler, "Monopoly and Oligopoly by Merger," *American Economic Review, Papers and Proceedings,* 40, May 1950; Jesse W. Markham, "Survey of Evidence and Findings on Mergers," *Business Concentration and Price Policy* (Princeton, 1955); and Ralph L. Nelson, *Movements in American Industry 1895–1956* (Princeton, 1959).

11. Markham, "Survey of Evidence," p. 157.

12. *U.S. v. Northern Securities Co.,* 120 Fed. 721 (April 1903), 193 U.S. 197 (March 1904).

13. Other economists have been interested in empirically testing capital market theory and determining whether certain financial and investment strategies of businesses are indeed efficient. Many of these studies are relevant to the diversification decision and are referenced in Chapters 3–10.

14. Samuel Reid, *Mergers Managers and Economy* (New York: McGraw-Hill, 1968); J. Fred Weston and Surrenda Mansingkha, "Test of the Efficiency Performance of Conglomerate Firms," *Journal of Finance* 26 (September 1971): 919–36; Ronald W. Melicher and David F. Rush, "The Performance of Conglomerate Firms: Recent Risk and Return Experience," *Journal of Finance* 28 (May 1973): 381–88; Robert G. Conn, "Performance of Conglomerate Firms: Comment,"*Journal of Finance* 28 (May 1973): 381–88; and

Oscar J. Holzman, Ronald M. Copeland, and Jack Hayya, "Income Measures of Conglomerate Performance," *Quarterly Review of Economics and Business* 15 (Summer 1975): 67–78.

15. K. J. Smith and J. C. Scheiner, "A Portfolio Analysis of Conglomerate Diversification, *Journal of Finance* 24 (June 1969); Randolph Westerfield, "A Note on the Measurement of Conglomerate Diversification," *Journal of Finance* 25 (September 1970): 909–14; J. Fred Weston, Keith V. Smith, and Ronald V. Shieves, "Conglomerate Performance Using the Capital Asset Pricing Model," *Review of Economics and Statistics* 54 (November 1972): 357–63; and Baruch Lev and Gershon Mandelker, "The Micro-Economic Consequences of Corporate Mergers," *Journal of Business* 45 (January 1972).

16. R. Hal Mason and Maurice B. Gondzwaard, "Performance of Conglomerate Firms: A Portfolio Approach," *Journal of Finance* 31 (March 1976): 39–48.

17. Richard P. Rumelt, *Strategy, Structure and Economic Performance*.

18. Richard P. Rumelt, "Diversity and Profitability," University of California at Los Angeles Working Paper, 1977.

CHAPTER 2

Some General Propositions

BEFORE WE TURN to a detailed discussion of our framework for strategic and economic analysis, it is useful to summarize what it suggests as appropriate strategies for creating real economic value through diversification. This summary will help orient the reader toward our basic conclusions and also allow us to indicate where the reader can turn for a more detailed explanation of particular points of interest. We will proceed in this summary by first highlighting seven common misconceptions about diversification through acquisition and then presenting several general propositions, which are developed more fully in succeeding chapters.[1]

Common Misconceptions

1. Acquisitive diversifiers create larger returns (through increased earnings and capital appreciation) for their shareholders than nondiversifiers.

The misconception that acquisitive diversifiers outperform nondiversifiers gained a certain currency during the 1960s. In part, this was due to the enormous emphasis placed on earnings-per-share growth by both security analysts and corporate executives. Acquisitive diversifiers that didn't collapse from ingesting too many acquisitions often showed sustained levels of EPS growth. However, once it became apparent that a large proportion of this EPS growth was an accounting mirage and that capital productivity was a more accurate indicator of management's ability and a company's economic strength, the market value of many acquisitive diversifiers declined radically. Since many widely diversified companies have had low rates of capital productivity in recent years, as shown in Chapter 1, it is not surprising that acquisitive diversifiers have relatively low price/earnings ratios. Throughout 1977 and 1978, the P/E ratio for the FTC sample, which includes many acquisitive diversifiers, has averaged

36

30 percent below that of the New York Stock Exchange as a whole. This discount has not changed much since then, even for such high ROE performers as Northwest Industries, Teledyne, and Textron.

As discussed in Chapter 6, such low market values relative to current earnings imply high uncertainty concerning the size and variability of future cash flows. Where high uncertainty exists, investors typically discount future earnings quite heavily since they are less valuable than more certain earnings streams. The high discount rates associated with acquisitive diversifiers mean that their growth will result in relatively less capital appreciation than that available to nondiversifiers, whose earnings streams may be more certain or predictable and whose discounts on future earnings are therefore lower.

2. Unrelated diversification offers shareholders a superior means of reducing their investment risk.

This argument has often been offered as a justification or defense of conglomerate mergers. However, as we will argue in Chapters 5 and 6, while unrelated diversification may be attractive from a corporate point of view, it is certainly not a unique or superior means of reducing investment risk. (By investment risk we mean the variability of returns over time, returns being defined as capital appreciation plus dividends paid to investors.)

According to contemporary financial theory, summarized in Chapter 5, a security's risk and return can be decomposed into two elements: (1) what is specific to each company and called "unsystematic" because it can be diversified away and (2) what is "systematic" because it is common to all securities (the securities market) and hence nondiversifiable. Since the unsystematic risk of any security can be eliminated through simple portfolio diversification, the investor does not need widely diversified companies like Litton Industries or Textron to eliminate the risk for him.

A risk/return analysis of Gulf + Western Industries, presented in Chapter 7, elaborates this point. Based on the assumption of a reasonably efficient U.S. capital market (where large numbers of rational buyers and sellers, making choices based on all economically available information, cause market prices to reflect what is knowable about the prospects for the companies whose securities are being traded), this analysis suggests that Gulf + Western has little to offer investors with respect to risk reduction over a diversified portfolio of comparable securities. It also suggests that if highly profitable companies like Gulf + Western cannot create returns in excess of those of comparable portfolios, they can at best only offer the investor value comparable to that of a mutual fund. In many cases, widely diversified companies with returns equivalent to those of a mutual fund may actually be less attractive investment vehicles because they cannot move into and out of assets as quickly and cheaply as mutual funds do.

3. Adding countercyclical businesses to a company's portfolio leads to a stabilized earnings stream and a heightened valuation by the marketplace.

This misconception is an extension of the previous one. While misconception No. 2 focuses on risk reduction, this one focuses on market valuation, a subject also covered in Chapter 6.

For decades, proponents of unrelated or conglomerate diversification have argued that when a company diversifies into an industry with a business cycle or set of economic risks different from its own, the safety of that company's income stream is enhanced. In essence, this is a very simple form of the risk-pooling concept underlying insurance. Supposedly, when one industry is "down," another will be "up"; and the average will remain much more stable than its parts.

In the light of the recent performance of many diversified companies, it should be obvious that this stability is very difficult to achieve. First, with the complex interactions of the U.S. and world economies, it is very hard to find exactly countercyclical businesses. At best, what one observes are industry cycles that either lead or lag the general economy (housing and capital goods, respectively) or that are not as cyclical as the economy in general (such as consumer goods and tobacco). Second, even if countercyclical businesses can be identified, it is difficult for diversifying companies to construct a balanced portfolio of businesses where the variable returns of individual businesses are balanced out. This stems from the problem of finding "countercyclical" companies of the appropriate size. Finally, since businesses grow at different rates, widely diversified companies face the continuing challenge of rebalancing their business portfolios through very selective acquisitions.

Quite apart from this argument, the relatively low market values associated with widely diversified companies during the past eight years indicate that the future cash returns to investors in companies comprising purportedly countercyclical businesses have been heavily discounted in the marketplace. While there are undoubtedly many reasons for this, it suggests that the market may be more interested in growth and the productivity of invested capital than earnings stability per se. In addition, investors have little incentive to bid up the price of diversified companies, since the benefits of stabilizing an income stream can be obtained by an investor through simple portfolio diversification, as explained in Chapter 5.

4. Related diversification is always safer than unrelated diversification.

This misconception rests on the notion that operating risks are reduced when diversifying companies stick to businesses that they think they understand.

It is commonly thought that management judgment can be most effectively exercised when companies limit their diversification to businesses with similar marketing and distribution characteristics, or similar production technologies, or similar science-based research operations. While this presumption often has merit, making "related" acquisitions does not guarantee results superior to those stemming from unrelated diversification. For example, Xerox's entry into data processing via its acquisition of Scientific Data Systems, justified on the grounds of technological, marketing, and manufacturing compatibility, led to a significant drain on corporate earnings. The management of Singer decided to take advantage of the company's competence in electromechanical manufacturing as the basis for its diversification program. The result was dramatic failure, leading to a $500 million writeoff of assets.

A close reading of the Xerox and Singer cases suggests that successful related diversification depends on both the quality of the companies acquired and the organizational integration required to achieve the benefits of synergy. Even more important, the perceived relatedness must be real and the merger must provide an improved competitive advantage to the partners. Unless these conditions are met, there can be no way of justifying related diversification as superior or even comparable to unrelated diversification as a means of reducing operating risks or increasing earnings. Chapters 3, 4, and 5, which present the basic concepts used throughout the book, and Chapters 7 and 8, which discuss diversification objectives and acquisition guidelines, discuss these conditions and suggest how diversifying companies can satisfy them.

5. A strong management team at the acquired company ensures realization of the potential benefits of diversification.

Many diversifying companies try to limit their pool of acquisition candidates to well-managed companies. This policy is rarely the necessary condition for realizing the potential benefits of diversification.

As we stress in Chapter 7, the potential benefits of related diversification stem from opportunities to increase the profitability of the incoming or the acquiring company by more effectively utilizing the company's core skills and resources. Usually such improvement requires an exchange of core skills and resources among the partners. In order for such an exchange to take place without an increase in overall costs, the top management of the acquiring company must be able to direct the transfer efficiently and effectively. This involves the extremely difficult task of creating structures that both encourage interdivisional cooperation and focus attention of divisional management on the performance of their semiautonomous operating units.

Apart from the acquiring of undervalued and underutilized assets that can be profitably revitalized by the acquiring company, the benefits of unrelated diversification, also discussed in Chapter 7, are rooted in two conditions: (1) increased efficiency in cash management and in the allocation of investment capital and (2) the capability of calling on profitable low-growth businesses to provide cash flow for high-growth businesses that require significant infusions of cash. Our discussion of Genstar, Ltd., a widely diversified Canadian company, will show the reader that achieving these benefits requires the corporate office of the acquiring company to possess not only the requisite financial talent but also managers capable of performing comprehensive strategic analysis of a wide range of industries and individual businesses.

The Genstar case will also demonstrate that achieving the benefits of unrelated diversification requires general managers at the corporate and group levels who can build and administer a flexible organization that is responsive to the multitude of demands created by differing operating characteristics, problems, and opportunities.

Whether pursuing related or unrelated diversification, it is often the acquiring company's management skills and resources—not those of the acquired company—that are critical to achieving the potential benefits of diversification. Indeed, where the acquired company is recognized as a well-managed company and priced accordingly by the capital market, the acquirer must exploit the potential synergies with the acquiree in order for the transaction to be economically justifiable.

6.   The diversified company is uniquely qualified to improve the management performance of acquired businesses.

During the height of the merger and acquisition activity of the 1960s, it was not uncommon for acquisitive conglomerates to argue that they could improve the profitability of acquired companies by "modernizing" administrative practices and introducing a greater degree of operating discipline than that demanded by the external marketplace. For example, in Chapter 7 we will refer to the testimony of Harold S. Geneen, Chairman and President of ITT, before the House Antitrust Subcommittee on November 20, 1969, which strongly echoes this argument. The claims invoked by Mr. Geneen and many other successful diversifiers are not benefits of diversification per se but rather simply the benefits of "good management." Single-business companies pursuing vertical integration or horizontal expansion through acquisition can achieve the identical benefits. To achieve the benefits claimed by Mr. Geneen, a company needs only to allow those managers with the requisite skills to implement their desired improvements in the organization.

It can be argued that it is a rare organization that willingly embarks on changes that could drastically affect its traditional administrative and managerial practices. Under these circumstances change will occur only when forced from the outside, and diversifying companies often represent such a force. Nevertheless, the benefits achieved are not, strictly speaking, benefits of diversification.

7.   Great deals are typically made by professional "deal makers."

Potentially the most dangerous misconception on our list is that many diversifying acquisitions owe their success to the imaginative work of experienced investment bankers and other kinds of business brokers. Every experienced corporate diversifier has learned, however, that he must live with an acquisition long after it has ceased being "a great deal."

The role of investment bankers is to provide attractive ideas, but it is the company's role to select those ideas that have the greatest economic and strategic value. As discussed in Chapters 7–10 (Part III), this role involves developing diversification objectives and acquisition guidelines that fit a carefully prepared concept of the corporation. It also involves the ability to recognize and exploit the potential for creating value through diversifying acquisitions. The following section reviews the various ways in which companies can create value for their shareholders through diversifying acquisitions.

Creating Value through Diversifying Acquisitions

Our brief discussion of common misconceptions reflects several basic notions about how economic value can be created through diversifying acquisitions. Put most succinctly, value can be created for the shareholders of a company pursuing diversifying acquisitions only when the combination of the two companies' skills and resources satisfies at least one of the following conditions:

1.   Increased returns—that is, an income stream for the combined company greater than that which could be realized from a portfolio investment in the two companies, or

2. Reduced risk—that is, a reduction in the variability of the income stream for the combined company greater than that which could be realized from a portfolio investment in the two companies.

Included in both conditions is an explicit comparison between corporate diversification on behalf of the shareholder and independent portfolio diversification by the investor. This comparison, discussed in Chapter 5, deserves special emphasis.

Recalling the distinction between systematic (market-related) risk and unsystematic (company-specific) risk, it is important to emphasize once again that most benefits of reducing unsystematic risk through diversification are as available to individual investors as they are to corporate investors. While diversified companies have the potential of creating a superior tradeoff between total risk and return relative to single-business companies, they will not create value for their shareholders by merely diversifying away unsystematic risk. In efficient capital markets, unsystematic risk is irrelevant in the equity valuation process since investors can diversify away unsystematic risk for themselves. Value can only be created for shareholders when the company's risk/return trade-offs include benefits not available through simple portfolio diversification.

Increasing Returns

There are six principal ways in which acquisition-minded companies can obtain returns in excess of those available from simple portfolio diversification. The first three are particularly relevant to related diversification. The last three are more relevant to unrelated diversification, although related diversifiers can also benefit from similar diversification effects. Each of these strategies and clues to their successful pursuit are discussed in Chapters 7–10 (Part III).

1. A diversifying acquisition can raise the productivity of capital when the special skills and industry knowledge of one merger partner can be applied to the competitive problems and opportunities facing the other partner.

Where the reinforcement of skills and resources critical to success of one of the combined company's businesses leads to increased profitability, value will be created for the shareholders of an acquisition-minded company. This transfer of skills and/or resources between businesses has been characterized by the term "synergy." The creation of value is the realization of potential synergy. Our discussion of Heublein's acquisition of United Vintners in Chapter 7 provides a good case in point.

2. Investments in markets closely related to current fields of
   operation can lead to a reduction in long-run average costs.

A reduction in average costs can accrue from scale effects, rationalization
of production and other important managerial tasks, and new opportunities for technological innovation. For example, a marketing department's budget as a percentage of sales will decline if existing resources
can be used to market new or related products. Similarly, a company like
Proctor & Gamble can expect to see its per-unit distribution costs decline
if the existing distribution system can be used to move more products to
the marketplace. This notion has been the basis of many acquisitions by
so-called "consumer-product companies."

3. Business expansion in an area of competence can lead to
   the development of a "critical mass" of resources
   necessary to outperform the competition.

Business expansion in an area of competence can lead to the generation of
additional resources, which can be used to develop competences equal to
or even superior to those of the competition. In many industries, managers claim that companies have to achieve a certain size or critical mass
before they can compete effectively with their competition. In the laboratory instrumentation field, for example, the only way many small companies can hope to offer sustained competition against such entrenched
companies as Hewlett-Packard, Tektronix, Beckman Instruments, and
Technicon is to attain a size where they have sufficient cash flow to fund
competitive research and development programs. One of the ways of
attaining this required size is by making closely related, diversifying
acquisitions.

4. The diversified company can route cash from units
   operating with a surplus to units operating with a deficit
   and can thereby reduce the need of individual businesses to
   purchase working-capital funds from outside sources.

Through centralizing cash balances, the corporate office of a diversified
enterprise can act as the banker for its operating subsidiaries. More
specifically, the widely diversified company has the opportunity to balance the working capital needs and surpluses of its divisions as the
economy progresses through a business cycle or as its divisions experience seasonal fluctuations. It must be emphasized that this type of
working-capital management is an operating benefit and completely separate from the recycling of cash on an investment basis.

5. Managers of a diversified company can direct its currently high net cash flow business to provide investment funds to businesses in which net cash flow is presently zero or negative but in which management expects positive cash flow to develop. This can improve the long-run profitability of the corporation as a whole.

In Chapter 7, we show how a well-managed, widely diversified company can call on its low-growth businesses to maximize net cash flow and profits so that funds can be reallocated to those high-growth businesses needing investment. We also point out that by so doing, such a company can reap economic benefits beyond those available from a comparable portfolio of securities, and the public, as a whole, can benefit from lower costs and, presumably, prices.

The cross-subsidization argument, as stated above, has an important extension. Since diversified companies have operating subsidiaries in several business, they have access to information that is often unavailable to the investment community. This information is the internally generated market data on each industry in which it operates—data that include "intelligence" on the competitive position and potential of each company in the industry. With this "insider" information, diversified companies are often in a significantly better position than individual investors to assess the investment merits of both specific projects and entire industries. In short, the exposure of diversified companies to a greater number of investment opportunities than single-business companies and their access to internally generated market data enables them to choose the most attractive investment projects and thereby allocate capital among industries more efficiently than the capital markets. Using the language of the financial economist, we can say that the capital budgeting process (or the internal capital market) of the diversified company can be more "efficient" than that of the external capital market.

6. Through the impact of risk pooling, the diversified company can lower its cost of debt and leverage itself to a greater extent than its nondiversified equivalent. The company's total cost of capital thereby goes down and provides shareholders with returns in excess of those available from a comparable portfolio of securities.

As the number of businesses in the portfolio of an unrelated diversifier increases and the overall variability of its operating income or cash flow decreases, the diversified company's risks of illiquidity or bankruptcy as perceived by its creditors will decrease. This altered risk perception leads to two benefits. First, the lower perceived risk should result in a smaller risk premium on the funds borrowed by the diversified company than by its nondiversified, more volatile components. More important, since the overall variability of the diversified company's cash flow is reduced, it is in a position to borrow funds to a greater extent than otherwise possible. This ability to incur a greater amount of financial leverage enables a company's shareholders to shift some risk to the government (since interest, in contrast to dividends, is deductible for tax purposes, the government shoulders a portion of the cost of capitalizing a business venture) and thereby reduce the company's total cost of capital. These potential benefits—reduced risk premiums on borrowed funds and increased borrowing ability—only become significant factors, however, when the diversifying company aggressively manages its financial risks by employing a high debt/equity ratio or having several highly risky, unrelated projects within its portfolio of business.

While the total cost of capital of a widely diversified company can conceivably be lower than that of less diversified companies of comparable size, it is important to note that its cost of *equity* capital can conceivably be higher. This stems from the probability that investors' perceptions of risk are not solely conditioned by the degree of diversification of a company's assets. The risks and opportunities perceived by professional investors also depend on the amount and the clarity of information that investors can effectively process. As companies become more diversified and the nature of their business becomes less clearly defined, investor uncertainty with respect to a company's risks and opportunities will increase. The greater this uncertainty, the greater the return or risk premium demanded by the equity investor and the higher the company's cost of equity capital. In addition, one should not forget that as debt is added to a company's capital structure, its cost of equity capital will increase because of the increased financial risk.

Decreasing Risk

Many of the possibilities for reducing risk through diversifying acquisitions are implied by the benefits of risk pooling discussed above. This is natural, since risk and return are directly related. This relationship is most obvious in the case of capital efficiencies stemming from unrelated diversification, stressed in propositions 4 through 6 above. In addition, related diversification can also benefit the diversifying company's shareholders where an acquisition results in a reduction in the variability of the acquiring company's income stream to a greater extent than that which its shareholders could obtain from simple portfolio diversification.

Although there is no evidence that General Motors' strategy was developed with this notion in mind, an important result of GM's diversification within the motor vehicle industry has been its ability to absorb easily changes in demand for any one automotive product. GM's extensive related-product line reduces the company's marketing risk and enables GM's managers to concentrate on production efficiencies. As a result, GM's income stream tends to be less volatile than those of its competitors and of portfolios of discrete investments in unassociated, though automotive-related, companies.

A Concluding Observation

A point worth stressing in this summary concerns two major reasons why programs of diversification through acquisition fail. Both reasons arise directly out of the lack of comprehensive diversification plans at many companies employing diversification as part of their overall corporate strategy. The first reason for failure is that companies often tend to acquire what is available, not what meets sound strategic and economic criteria. This type of acquisition typically comes disguised as a great opportunity, but unless the acquiring company understands the opportunity and has the resources to develop it and the management commitment to exploit it, chances for failure are high. The second reason is closely related to the first: No matter how attractive an opportunity is or how well it fits with a company's needs, there exists a price over which it ceases to be an attractive venture. The danger of overpaying particularly arises when "glamour" businesses are considered, or when pressures for corporate growth become paramount.

An important element to long-run corporate success is the ability to avoid big mistakes. A company need only be slightly better than average on a consistent basis to enable compound growth and time to work their magic. To the extent that the concepts and analytical techniques stressed in Parts II and III aid the diversifying company in avoiding the wrong acquisition or paying too much for the right one, the company's skills and resources will not be squandered. If, in addition, our strategic and economic logic can help the diversifying company to utilize its distinctive competences and/or unique resources better, its competitive position will be improved and significant value can be created for its shareholders.

Notes and References

1. Adapted from Malcolm S. Salter and Wolf A. Weinhold, "Diversification via Acquisition: Creating Value," *Harvard Business Review* 56, July–August 1978. Copyright © 1978 by the President and Fellows of Harvard College; used by permission.

Framework for Strategic and Economic Analysis

Introduction to Part II

As in most planning contexts, companies interested in diversification through acquisition face the difficult task of formulating precise objectives. This task typically forces managers to ask how related or unrelated their several businesses should be and how economic value can be created by various kinds of diversifying acquisitions.

Once diversification objectives have been formulated, three additional issues still need to be resolved by companies intent on making diversifying acquisitions: How can meaningful acquisition guidelines be developed? How can high-potential acquisition candidates be efficiently identified? And what kind of in-depth strategic and economic analysis should be made to determine the worth of high-potential acquisition candidates to the diversifying company?

Each company will naturally approach these issues in a somewhat idiosyncratic way. However, an analytical framework based on recent extensions of capital market theory, planning models developed during the past decade, and more established strategic-planning practices can help many kinds of companies create value for their investors through well-planned, diversifying acquisitions. Presenting this framework and related analytical tools is the purpose of Parts II and III of this book. We will develop in Part II the conceptual foundation for our discussion in Part III of diversification objectives, acquisition guidelines, screening systems, and the analysis of diversifying acquisitions.

There are several clusters of concepts and theories that we can draw upon, extend, or modify for our purposes. The most general and, perhaps, most established set of relevant concepts stems from notions of corporate strategy and strategic planning developed in the works of Andrews, Ansoff, Drucker, and others. A second set of relevant concepts is concerned with the composition and management of a company's product/ market portfolio. While not incompatible with the general notion of corporate strategy, this cluster of concepts focuses more narrowly on product/market commitments. The best known and most widely applied product/market-portfolio concepts have been developed by the Boston Consulting Group and the Marketing Science Institute. A third set of relevant concepts has its roots in the financial theory developed and tested by such economists as Markowitz, Tobin, Sharpe, Lintner, and Fama. These concepts, which stress notions of market efficiency in the pricing of capital assets and hypothesized relationships between risk and return, have been gaining in use as a tool for financial decision making by both the investment community and corporate financial staffs.

In the following discussion we will refer to each set of concepts— and the analytical approaches they imply—as the strategy model, the product/market-portfolio model, and the risk/return model. In Chapters 3 to 5 we will summarize each of these models and their implications for the diversification decision. In Chapter 6 we will show how each of the models relates to the others conceptually and how they complement one another in use.

The analytical framework suggested in Part II and applied in Part III concentrates on the strategic and economic aspects of diversification through acquisition rather than on the administrative and organizational aspects. To be sure, experienced diversifiers could be the first to acknowledge that such issues as the compatibility between the bureaucratic traditions and administrative practices of the target company, on the one hand, and those of the acquiring company, on the other, should be key concerns of managers responsible for managing diversification through acquisition. While such issues may often turn out to be the critical ones in managing a successful diversification program, they will not be highlighted in this book. Lest readers suspect, however, that we have irresponsibly ignored the core issues, we hasten to add that issues of administrative and organizational compatibility are irrelevant if the proposed diversifying acquisition does not make sense in the first instance from both a strategic and economic point of view.

CHAPTER 3

The Strategy Model

THE STRATEGY MODEL is based on the work of several practitioner-oriented researchers and thinkers writing in the period between the mid-1950s and the early 1970s.[1] The model focuses on the process of defining how an enterprise should compete in its economic environment and how its performance can be measured. The model places heavy emphasis on the concept of strategy, which has been defined by Alfred Chandler as "the determination of basic long-term goals and objectives of an enterprise and the adoption of courses of action and the allocation of resources necessary for carrying out these goals.[2]

There are two important characteristics of the strategy model. First, it does not pretend to describe common policymaking behavior; rather it presents a normative approach to policy formulation that has been designed to fit the well-documented needs of general managers. Second, in its basic form the strategy model is most applicable to single-business enterprises, whether they be independent companies or divisions of diversified companies. While the model addresses issues relevant to all classes of companies, including the diversification decision, it does not treat the strategic problems of multibusiness companies in great detail. Thus, the logic of the model is most relevant to companies or divisions pursuing diversification from a single, core business.

The key relationship stressed in the strategy model is the relationship between a business enterprise and its environment. The model asserts that this relationship can best be fashioned by matching market opportunities with the available corporate resources, the special competences of the company, the personal values and aspirations of managers, and the obligations to both stockholders and other segments of society. Similarly, the model assumes that strategic decisions are concerned with defining the long-term relationship between the company and its environment (objectives) and planning for the realization of this relationship through the establishment of a timed sequence of moves (plan of action).

According to the strategy model, a company's special competences are defined in terms of a set of core skills—that is, what the company is good at. In one case, this might mean the manufacture of high-volume, low-value-added metal assemblies; in another, the mass distribution of frequently purchased consumer products. This set of core skills is not just what the company does well, but what it does particularly well. The model's test of consistency asks strategists and policymakers to look at the fit of these skills and resources with the profit and service opportunities in the company's environment.

The goal of the strategy model is to facilitate a rational choice among the strategic options facing the company. By identifying the company's capabilities and limitations and the risks and opportunities facing it, the model leads management to seek alternate ways of exploiting these opportunities or accommodating those risks. The overall purpose of the model is to help general managers provide the enterprise with direction and cohesion. This is the reason for its emphasis on consistency among the company's business activities.

Propositions of the Strategy Model

Being basically normative in content, the model is explicit in prescribing specific steps for the decision-making process to follow. The model says that managers should try to match internal capabilities with external opportunities when formulating corporate strategy. This same process is recommended for selecting the best strategic option from among several. As the model helps identify adequate and inadequate strategic options in general, so too does it help identify right and wrong diversification tracks. The right diversification track is based on consistency, the wrong track on a mismatch of skills and opportunities.

The strategy model stresses the need for consistency. Put more strongly, it maintains that consistency between a company's internal resources and its external opportunities is the primary determinant of success or failure.

Assumptions of the Strategy Model

Although the model emphasizes the process of formulating a business strategy, it is based on a set of assumptions about what should constitute the objectives of a business. The most important assumption is that managing a business requires judgment in balancing a variety of needs and objectives and that searching for a single objective is essentially an irrational quest for a magic formula that will make judgment unnecessary.

Thus, to emphasize only profit maximization, for instance, is irrational and may misdirect managers to the point where they endanger the survival of a business.

Assuming that the very nature of business enterprise requires multiple objectives, what should these objectives be? Peter Drucker answers this question very succinctly: "Objectives are needed in every area where performance and results directly and vitally affect the survival and prosperity of the business."[3] These areas include market standing, innovation, productivity, physical and financial resources, profitability, manager performance and development, worker performance and attitude, and public responsibility.

While profitability is only one of several objectives of an enterprise, the strategy model assumes that it is the ultimate test of business performance. Not only does profitability measure the net effectiveness and soundness of a business's efforts and constitute the "risk premium" that covers the costs of staying in business, but profits ensure the supply of future capital for innovation and expansion. Paraphrasing Drucker, profits enable businesses to finance their future development not only through retained earnings but also through providing sufficient inducement for new outside capital in the form in which it is best suited to the enterprise's objectives.

Significantly, the strategy model's approach to profit objectives has nothing to do with the economist's concept of profit maximization. Indeed, according to the model, profits measure not the maximum profit the business can produce but the minimum it must produce to satisfy the capital market for the risks it bears in supplying capital to the business.[4] This assumption does not nullify the importance of other economic objectives such as sales growth, market share growth, cash generation, or increased market or liquidation value; nor does it reduce the role of noneconomic objectives in defining the broad purpose of a business enterprise. Rather, it suggests a minimum condition that must be met in order for managers to retain control over policy governing the use and allocation of corporate resources.

The Decision-Making Process Implied by the Strategy Model[5]

Decision making is a choice among options. The choices defined by the model concern which opportunities to exploit, which strengths to build on, which risks to defend against, and what policies to pursue toward these ends. The consequences of choosing a particular option are viewed in terms of the "fit" they provide. A mismatch would carry the company into areas where it could not exploit its strengths or where it would have to compete on the basis of skills it may not possess or skills that are not unique relative to those of the competition. Thus, options are judged in terms of whether they permit exploitation of existing strengths or provide defense against perceived risks, or whether they would require new skills or present unbearable risks.

The first step in the decision-making process as implied by the model is the preparation of strategic intelligence. The inputs to this preparation include: (1) a detailed description of what the company does and how it defines its business, (2) a prediction of future environmental opportunities and risks and their likely impact on the company's competitive position, and (3) an identification of the company's strengths and weaknesses and resources required to cope with the perceived opportunities and risks. Strategic questions that policymakers are led to ask by the corporate strategy model are:

1. What business are we in?
2. Where, in our perceived industry, are future opportunities for profit and service? Where are the risks?
3. How will these new opportunities and risks affect us? What resources will we need to cope with them?
4. What are our strengths? How have we succeeded in our business?
5. What are our weaknesses, or competitive liabilities? What skills could we not successfully use as a basis of competition? What skills would enable us to compete more successfully?

Analysis of the answers to these general questions leads to a ratification or reformulation of an appropriate concept of the corporation. This notion of how the business is to compete and how performance is to be measured leads to the setting of strategic goals and objectives for the company.

Preparation and analysis of this strategic intelligence requires the ordering of a great deal of data. The systematic inquiry and logical argument needed for this effort must be complemented by the feelings, sentiment, and judgment of the policymaker. Analytical tools must be used side by side with gut feel and rational intuition.

Alternate policies for attaining these goals and objectives need to be defined. Consequences of the alternatives are then evaluated in terms of how they satisfy corporate objectives and how likely these consequences are to occur. Top management must select from these alternatives the policy or set of policies that best matches corporate resources with perceived opportunities and best serves the corporate purpose. This shows one key feature of the model: corporate goals and purposes are established before strategic choice is made. The concept of the business provides a framework within which the decision making process takes place.

Two other steps follow management's commitment to a set of operating policies. Conditional moves must be plotted in response to potential competitive reactions, and a time sequence for these moves must be formulated. Finally, it is necessary to review periodically the inherent assumptions of the corporate strategy and the performance of the corporation under that strategy. Such a review often leads to a reformulation of corporate strategy as internal and external conditions change. Table 3-1 summarizes in idealized form the decision-making process implied by the strategy model.

There are several distinguishing features of the planning and decision-making process suggested by the strategy model. First, as noted above, there is the attempt to define objectives before the final analysis of policy alternatives is considered. This provides an important set of criteria for evaluating alternate ways of exploiting environmental opportunities and reducing risks.

Second, while such criteria help to structure the analytic process, the consideration of policy alternatives remains comprehensive in nature. More specifically, evaluating policy alternatives involves assessing the strengths and weaknesses of a wide range of alternatives that could be followed under a large number of environmental conditions.

Another characteristic of this approach to planning and decision making is the presumption on the part of the policymaker that major changes in strategy can and will be made if the comprehensive, analytical process indicates that major change is required. Great confidence is placed in the ability of the organization to change course when the imperative to do so is logically laid out and supported by detailed analysis and a sequenced plan of action. Change is thus considered a necessity rather than an insurmountable organizational problem by practitioners of the strategic mode of planning.

While major change is considered a feasible alternative by the "strategist," comprehensive strategic planning often tends to limit the frequency of major policy changes in large organizations. Strategic planning in the modern corporation requires that top-level policymakers devise and administer a complex process for capturing the detailed knowledge of opportunities and risks that exists at lower levels in the organization.[6] Once this elaborate and time-consuming process leads to a major strategic decision and steps are taken toward implementing that decision, the need and the incentive to modify key goals is often minimal over the short run.[7] Thus, another hallmark of the process suggested by the strategy model is that it tends to result in "discontinuous policymaking" rather than in continued modifications of policy.

The characteristics of what we can call the strategic mode of planning

TABLE 3-1. Decision-Making Process Implied by the Strategy Model

I	II	III	IV	V	VI
Strategic Intelligence[a]	Definition of Purpose	Policy Analysis	Strategic Choice[b]	Time Sequencing	Strategy Review
– Description of current strategy	– Concept of the business	– Generation of a comprehensive list of policy alternatives	– Selection of an internally consistent set of policies which best fits corporate resources and best serves corporate purpose	– Designation of a timed sequence of conditional moves	
– Environmental analysis	– Objectives	– Assessment of the probabilities of the consequences of each alternative		– Action step 1	
– Strategic forecasts				– Etc.	
– Audit of corporate resources, strengths and weaknesses		– Evaluate each set of consequences for corporate objectives			

[a] Information—questions, insights, hypotheses, evidence—relevant to policy.

[b] The establishment of specific policy represents the most visible evidence of a strategic commitment.

Source: C. Roland Christensen, Norman A. Berg, and Malcolm S. Salter, *Policy Formulation and Administration: A Casebook of Top-Management Problems in Business* (Homewood, Ill.: Richard D. Irwin, 1976), p. 9. © 1976 by Richard D. Irwin, Inc. Used by permission of the publisher.

and decision making differ radically from those of the incremental mode.[8] Incrementalists believe that nonincremental alternatives usually do not lie within the range of choice possible in complex organizations. They claim that complex structures can only avoid intolerable dislocation by meeting certain preconditions, among them that major changes of a political nature are admissible only if they occur slowly.[9] Since most decisions leading to a departure from current strategy affect internal coalitions of interests and power, incrementalists believe in proceeding through a sequence of approximations. Rather than undertake both a comprehensive review of the external environment and internal resources and an assessment of major strategic alternatives when faced with a specific problem, attention is focused by the incrementalists on that problem (or opportunity). The first satisfactory policy alternative is tried, altered, tried in its altered form, altered again, and so forth.[10]

Thus, the critical feature of the incremental approach to planning is that the analysis accompanying decisions proceeds through comparative analysis of marginal or incremental differences in states of being rather than through attempts at more comprehensive analysis of broadly contrived alternatives.[11] A related feature of this planning mode is that while the policymaker contemplates means, he continues to contemplate objectives as well, unlike the strategic planner who ideally must stabilize his objectives at some point and then select the proper strategic alternative.[12]

It would be foolish, of course, to overdraw this dichotomy in planning behavior. Seldom do organizations practice one mode to the total exclusion of the other. The real issue is therefore which planning mode dominates the behavior of managers and whether or not this planning behavior is effective.

The strategy model stresses the more comprehensive approach to planning and action because the risks of incrementalism are extremely high. The principal risk is the misallocation of corporate resources. Without systematic strategic planning, financial and management resources will most probably be allocated in an ad hoc manner. Without a broad assessment of corporate resources and opportunities, and a precise statement of objectives and priorities, the vast expenditures of time and money typically devoted to new programs and activities cannot be judged in terms of the benefits and costs involved. The strategic mode of planning and decision making serves to reduce this risk. While the strategy model and the mode of planning and decision making derived from it cannot guarantee future success, proponents of this model emphasize that strategic planning can increase the probability that timely revisions of goals, standards, and administrative mechanisms will take place. Proponents of the strategic mode also argue that this approach to planning will ensure that an organization will develop to meet emerging needs.

Implications for the Diversification Decision

The strategy model provides specific guidelines within which managers are to approach the diversifying acquisition. The key issue to be considered in the evaluation of an acquisition candidate is the fit it provides with the company's resources and the extent to which it furthers the attainment of corporate goals and objectives.

The notion of "fit" is worth some additional emphasis. Kenneth Andrews, who has played a major role in developing the strategy model, argues that diversification imposes the most severe requirements when it calls for knowledge of present situations and future possibilities in industries where a company has no prior experience to guide it.[13] He also stresses the point that for many companies opportunity abounds but not the ability to capture it.[14] His telling case in point is the old Underwood Company, once the leading manufacturer of typewriters in the world, which thought in the years before its acquisition by Olivetti that it should (and could) diversify into computers.

The strategy model reflects Andrews's strong bias against pursuing new business opportunities in areas where a company possesses little experience and competence. It encourages managers to face the fact that "diversification is often an illusory diversion from the opportunities a company is best able to capitalize."[15]

Put in different terms, users of the strategy model favor closely related diversification. The underlying theory is both simple and intuitively appealing: Really successful results in business require the development of a distinctive competence or competitive advantage and the ability to anticipate trends in markets and technology. The ability to maintain a distinctive competence and to anticipate is greatly enhanced by a knowledge of the industry and its environment. Thus, where diversification is related to a company's current industrial environment, the advantages of special competence and industry knowledge can create more opportunity for above-average results than unrelated diversification can.

It is not surprising that, seen in this light, questions relevant to the diversification decision posed by the model stress the notions of strategic fit and operating compatibility. These questions can be summarized as follows:

1. What opportunities and risks does the potential acquisition present?
2. What is the basis of competition in the acquisition candidate's industrial environment? What must he do well to succeed there?

3. Can we assist the acquisition candidate in any way? Do our resources and skills fit the needs of the acquisition candidate? Which of our resources are transferable?

4. Quite apart from assisting the acquisition candidate, do we understand the strategic logic, or key success factors, of this new business sufficiently well to make intelligent resource allocation decisions?

5. Does the potential acquisition fit our concept of the corporation?

The questions raised by the strategy model about the decision to diversify through acquisition are, of course, similar to those raised in the context of general business planning. The implications should be clear. Decisions regarding acquisitions should be made through essentially the same process as that by which general strategic options are evaluated and selected.

Using the Strategy Model

Given the model's emphasis on strategic fit, any analysis of diversification options involving acquisitions must include a careful assessment of whether or not the resource requirements of the two companies are sufficiently similar to warrant a combined or linked strategy of some sort. Where the resource requirements are similar for each company and where the diversifying company's strengths can be reinforced or extended and/or its weaknesses minimized or eliminated, the elements of strategic fit will be present and a diversifying acquisition will represent an attractive strategic option.

Such an analysis presumes, of course, the capacity of an enterprise to identify and evaluate its own strengths and weaknesses. Research has shown, however, that this is often a difficult task to complete in a useful fashion. In many instances managers from the same company find it difficult to reach a consensus about the strengths and weaknesses of their own company.[16] Positional and other biases, it appears, tend to affect their analyses.

How, then, can an assessment of corporate resources be systematically pursued so that a company's conclusions about its strengths and weaknesses are sufficiently detailed and objective to serve as the basis for serious diversification planning? Such an assessment requires, first, that a company develop a profile of its principal resources and skills. These tend to cluster around three dimensions:

1. *financial dimension,* including such resources as cash flow, debt capacity, and the ability to attract new capital;

2. *operating dimension,* including tangible assets, such as office buildings, manufacturing plant and equipment, warehouses, inventories, and service and distribution facilities, and more intangible resources, such as high-quality products, low-cost production methods, and high brand loyalty; and

3. *management and organization dimension,* including such resources as scientists, engineers, sales personnel, financial analysts, general managers, and bureaucratic traditions embodied in quality assurance systems, cash-management systems, and management-control systems.

Once such a profile has been developed, a company then should compare the strength of its resources with those factors critical to the company's success in its relevant product markets to see what characteristics make the company uniquely qualified to carry out its key tasks or inhibit the company's ability to fulfill its purpose. This step in the analysis yields what is called a capability or competence profile. The final step in the process is to compare this capability profile with that of major competitors in order to identify those areas where the company may be able to build a competitive advantage in the marketplace.

The most difficult characteristics to categorize as strengths and weaknesses are nonfinancial in nature. An effective way of coping with this difficulty is to sketch a capability profile along the nonfinancial dimensions by functional area (R&D/engineering, manufacturing, marketing, control, and so on). This can proceed as outlined below for the marketing function of McCord Corporation.[17]

McCord Corporation was one of the first companies to start supplying the automotive industry. As the automotive market grew to maturity, McCord became a major supplier of gaskets, radiators, and other automotive equipment. By 1963 the company was a well-established manufacturer selling most of its production in the original equipment (O/E) market. The consolidated 1963 sales of $45 million and profits of $1.8 million had some fluctuations but little real change over the previous five years.

In 1963 management attention was focused on growth and diversification through acquisition and internal development. The company was dependent on three major auto makers in the O/E market for over half its total corporate sales. Previous efforts of internally generated diversification and recent attempts at acquisition had borne no fruits. The question facing McCord was how could the company build on its strengths and compensate for or eliminate its weaknesses? This question needed to be answered in the context of the company's four principal objectives:

- to minimize the pressure of the cyclical O/E market
- to find more productive uses for the company's financial resources
- to grow at a more rapid pace
- to generate a greater level of public interest and confidence in the company.

An examination of McCord's strengths and weaknesses as of 1963 reveals a long list of characteristics that, taken together, help define the company's strategic needs. Table 3-2 summarizes a few of the principal strengths and weaknesses in the marketing area.

With this overview of the marketing area, McCord was then in a good position to make similar assessments for other functional areas. Further analysis of strengths and weaknesses revealed a very strong financial base and a reasonably active R&D group. These strengths were somewhat mitigated, however, by the relatively poor state of the company's manufacturing complex.

What happened to McCord? A merger in 1964 with the Davidson Rubber Corporation, a manufacturer of padded trim products for the automotive industry, provided a certain degree of fit from a marketing, financial, and manufacturing point of view even though the company was not able to build a strong hedge against the market power of the "Big Three" automakers. As it turned out, many of each company's resource requirements were similar, and Davidson offered McCord a broader product line, a position in the emerging safety market, more modern plants, and a younger middle-level management experienced in the auto supply market. But in the final analysis, the extent to which Davidson fit McCord's strategic needs can only be judged in light of McCord's strengths and weaknesses in the automotive supply market and the overall attractiveness of that market or industry. As depicted in Figure 3-1, both business position (defined in terms of relative market share, relative product quality, price, marketing strength, new product activity, manufacturing scale, and overall experience) and industry or market attractiveness (defined in terms of market size and growth, number and size of competitors, position in the product of life cycle, rate of technological change, and industry profitability) can help define appropriate related diversification strategies for companies like McCord. Without going into all the details of McCord's situation in 1963–1964, we can show that while Davidson offered McCord some benefits of related-supplementary diversification, the company's real needs, based on an analysis of its strengths and weaknesses and industry attractiveness, lay more in the direction of related-complementary diversification. Let's look first at this argument in conceptual terms and then return to the McCord case.

TABLE 3-2. Abstract of a Functional (Marketing) Capability Profile: McCord Corporation, 1963

	Strengths	Weaknesses
Operating Dimension	1. Despite competing in difficult O/E market, McCord has remained reasonably profitable. Simply staying above water in this type of market is a marketing plus.	1. Most products are vulnerable to backward integration and/or intensive integration because of maturity of competitors fighting for the same O/E business.
	2. Gasket lines protected from backward integration by high entry costs.	2. "Divide and conquer" methods used by the automakers keep suppliers' margins low.
	3. Some product lines sold in "aftermarket." This affords some protection against cyclical demands of O/E market.	3. Risks of being dependent on a few buyers who may go out of business (Studebaker) or have bad models (Edsel) are not compensated by high margins.
		4. Insufficient depth in replacement market is indicated by need to find new lines for replacement product sales force.
		5. Efforts to develop and market new products have been unsuccessful.
Management and Organization Dimension	4. Because of their length of service, most McCord executives have considerable experience in the auto industry.	6. Management has not recruited younger replacements with new ideas.
	5. Despite little formal planning, McCord's information system shows profitability by product line on a monthly basis.	7. Management has been unable to find a successful strategy for market growth.

60

FIGURE 3-1.   Framework for Selecting Appropriate Related Diversification Strategy

Business Position

		High	Medium _vert_	Low
Industry Attractiveness	High	No Diversification	Related-Complementary Diversification	Related-Complementary Diversification
	Medium	Related-Supplementary Diversification	No Diversification	Related-Complementary Diversification
	Low	Related-Supplementary Diversification	Related-Supplementary Diversification	No Diversification

Horizontal

The Related Diversification Grid

Recall from Chapter 1 that related-complementary diversification involves expanding a business by adding new functional activities and skills to its existing set without substantially changing its product-market orientation. Related-supplementary diversification involves expanding a business by entering new product markets requiring functional skills similar to those already possessed by the company. Figure 3-1 suggests the following guidelines regarding related-complementary and related-supplementary diversification:

1. *No diversification*   First, where a company has a strong position in an attractive industry, diversification is usually unnecessary from an economic perspective. Second, where a company possesses few unique strengths but operates in an industry of average or medium attractiveness, it may make sense to work at developing existing skills and improving its business position before considering any diversification. Finally, a weak company in an unattractive industry is clearly in a desperate situation, unlikely to be able to afford diversification or to present itself as an attractive merger partner.

2. *Related-Complementary Diversification*   Where a company participates in a highly attractive industry but possesses only average or even below-average skills, related-complementary diversification can help that company add functional skills critical

to improving its overall business position. Even where a company finds itself as a weak competitor in an industry of average or medium attractiveness, some benefits can accrue from improving its competitive position through related-complementary diversification.

3. *Related-Supplementary diversification*   Where a company has a strong business position but participates in a market of only average attractiveness or low attractiveness, there is the obvious potential to increase rates of growth and profitability by committing existing functional skills and resources to new, more attractive markets. Where a company qualifies as only an average competitor in a specific industry or market, but where that market has become relatively unattractive, there are potential benefits of using existing skills and resources to enter more attractive, related product markets.

Using the related diversification grid requires a healthy dose of judgment since there is no simple, useful system for assessing relative business position or relative industry attractiveness. Nevertheless, the grid does suggest some crude propositions that can channel thinking along the lines of the strategy model. More specifically, the grid can help companies study their related diversification options in the light of corporate strengths and weaknesses as well as industry or market characteristics.

Returning to the case of the McCord Corporation, the company can be characterized as having "low to medium" business position in an industry of "medium" attractiveness. The automotive equipment industry has two major segments, the O/E market and the replacement market, commonly referred to as the aftermarket. McCord participated in both segments. As indicated above, the O/E market experienced severe cyclical swings, while overall growth was more or less on a par with that of the economy as a whole. This market was also dominated by a powerful oligopoly who posed a continuous threat of backward integration into McCord's lines.[18] Any failure of McCord to meet preestablished product specifications, delivery schedules, or price expectations would cause a punitive shift of purchases away from McCord. The aftermarket, supplied by chains such as Sears and independent wholesale distributors who sold to service stations and the public, was more fragmented, less price-sensitive, and less cyclical. On balance, however, the automotive equipment industry was not a "growth" industry, nor was it characterized by above-average returns to automotive-equipment suppliers. In addition, while McCord was a competitive participant in the industry, the company was not a leader either in terms of market-share position, product quality, new-product activity, or manufacturing efficiency.

Viewed from the perspective of the related-diversification grid, McCord appeared to be in a position to benefit either from reinforcing its current strategic posture or, possibly, from pursuing related-complementary diversification. With respect to diversification, one can argue that the company could have improved its business position and performance by acquiring companies with the ability to place McCord in a stronger market-share position in the aftermarket or a stronger technological position in the O/E market. Had McCord been able to broaden its participation and increase its power in the automotive aftermarket or to develop a more proprietary position in the O/E market through more fruitful product development activities, the traditional core of McCord's business might have been strengthened. While the Davidson acquisition clearly offered McCord the opportunity to exploit a new technology and a new market segment, it is less clear that the attendant economic advantages were superior to those offered by a complementary diversifying acquisition. Indeed, a quick assessment of McCord's strengths and weaknesses and the attractiveness of the automotive-equipment industry suggests that significant opportunity costs may have been incurred.

Interestingly enough, the history of McCord through the mid-1970s shows a concerted effort to increase emphasis on marketing programs in the automotive aftermarket. On the other hand, no new level of commitment to product development in McCord's traditional business has been apparent. By 1975 it was the Davidson Division that was showing the most active product development activity, mainly in the rubber-parts side of the business.

A Summary Comment

The message of the strategy model is that only after a company's strengths and weaknesses in each functional area have been identified is its management in a position to begin thinking about the company's future needs and the potential of pursuing diversification through acquisition. In addition, the strategy model suggests that the best approach to developing a diversification program is not to begin by constructing measures of product-market attractiveness but rather by identifying those organization strengths that may be transferable to other product markets and the weaknesses that need to be corrected. Where a company's distinctive capabilities can be reaffirmed or extended into new areas through acquisition or, as we have seen in the McCord case, where a company's capability profile can be strengthened through a diversifying acquisition, the criterion of strategic fit will be satisfied.

Notes and References

1. See Peter F. Drucker, *The Practice of Management* (New York: Harper & Row, 1954); H. Igor Ansoff, *Corporate Strategy* (New York: McGraw-Hill, 1965); Kenneth R. Andrews, *The Concept of Corporate Strategy* (Homewood, Ill.: Dow Jones–Irwin, 1971), and Hugo E. R. Uyterhoeven et al., *Strategy and Organization,* (Homewood, Ill.: Richard D. Irwin, 1973).

2. Alfred D. Chandler, *Strategy and Structure: Chapters in the History of Industrial Enterprise* (Cambridge, Mass.: MIT Press, 1962), p. 12.

3. Drucker, *Practice of Management,* p. 65.

4. Ibid., pp. 65–67. Drucker's discussion of this point, written over twenty-five years ago, foreshadows our attempts in Chapter 5 to unite capital-market theory with notions of corporate strategy.

5. This section draws heavily from C. Roland Christensen, Norman A. Berg, and Malcolm S. Salter, *Policy Formulation and Administration* (Homewood, Ill.: Richard D. Irwin, 1976), pp. 9–11.

6. For a full treatment of this idea see Norman A. Berg, "Allocation of Strategic Funds," Division of Research, Harvard Business School, 1972, and Joseph L. Bower, *Managing the Resource Allocation Process,* Division of Research, Harvard Business School, 1970.

7. The corporate histories presented by Chandler, *Strategy and Structure,* provide evidence on this point.

8. David Braybrooke and Charles E. Lindblom, *A Strategy of Decision* (New York: The Free Press, 1963), pp. 48–57.

9. Ibid, p. 73.

10. Ibid, p. 73.

11. Ibid, p. 86.

12. Ibid, p. 93.

13. Andrews, *Concept of Corporate Strategy,* p. 82.

14. Ibid., p. 89.

15. Ibid, p. 40.

16. Howard H. Stevenson, "Defining Corporate Strengths and Weaknesses," *Sloan Management Review* 17 (Spring 1976).

17. Harvard Business School case #9-373-171.

18. Indeed, in 1975 Ford Motor Company did decide to start manufacturing auto air conditioner condensers, thereby forcing McCord to close its Washington, Indiana, plant.

CHAPTER 4

The Product/Market-Portfolio Model

WHILE THE STRATEGY MODEL was developed to deal with overall corporate environment, the several variants of the product/market-portfolio model focus on the overall economic characteristics of a company's business or portfolio of businesses. One of the early expressions of the product/market-portfolio model was developed by the Boston Consulting Group (BCG) and emphasizes a matrix of relative market share and market growth. This framework has been used widely during the past decade as a way of analyzing the competitive position of a business and the business portfolios of multiproduct, multimarket companies.

The PIMS (Profit Impact of Market Strategy) model, developed into its present form by the Marketing Science Institute, has also become widely used in recent years. This model, based on empirically tested relationships among approximately thirty-five measures of business characteristics, can be used to estimate the appropriate return on investment of a single business. One should note that the BCG framework focuses on a company's portfolio of businesses, while PIMS focuses on individual businesses within the portfolio. A third product/market-portfolio model, developed by General Electric Company with McKinsey and Company, is based on a matrix employing qualitative measures of "industry attractiveness" and "company position" within the industry. These two measures encompass considerably more company and market variables than BCG's notions of relative market share and market growth.

The following discussion will emphasize the BCG variant of the product/market-portfolio model, since it is the most widely known and easily used of the three. Furthermore, important aspects of the G.E.–

McKinsey and PIMS variants are developed in the strategy and risk/ return models. The Appendix to this chapter (p. 263) describes in more detail the PIMS and G.E.–McKinsey variants, their relationship to the BCG approach, and some common difficulties in using product/market-portfolio models.

Product/market-portfolio models focus on the strengths of a company's portfolio of products or businesses, such strengths being defined in terms of market position and market attractiveness. The key relationship stressed by the BCG variant is the relationship between the cash flow of a business and its market-share/market-growth characteristics. These characteristics are used as key indicators of a company's market position and the attractiveness of its market commitments. The model tells managers to look at the competitive situation and market growth within their business units and then construct a cluster of businesses through which high cash flow can be achieved.

The goal of the product/market-portfolio model is to maximize the total strength of the company. This goal can be best achieved, according to the model, by balancing the generation and use of cash within the company. While the model focuses primarily on the internal generation and use of cash, it does not exclude the possibility of external financing. In fact, it suggests that in certain business environments debt financing can be highly desirable. The advantage of internally generated cash is that it has greater reliability than external funding. By identifying corporate patterns of cash flow, the model leads decision makers to make strategic portfolio decisions in such a way as to optimize the financial strength of the total company and to judge unit performance as it relates to this end.

Propositions of the Product/Market-Portfolio Model

The BCG variant of the product/market-portfolio model holds that in most competitive environments relative market share and market growth determine the cash-generation or cash-usage characteristics of businesses. The logic of this proposition can be explained as follows.

When companies pursue marketing and pricing strategies geared to increasing production volume faster than their competitors, cost advantages relative to competitors will normally follow. This relationship between the accumulated experience associated with increased production volume and declining costs is referred to by BCG as the "experience-curve" effect. The experience curve relationship, as described by BCG, states that unit costs decline by approximately 20 to 30 percent (in constant dollars) with each doubling of accumulated production. While similar to the well-known and documented learning-curve phenomenon,[1] BCG has found this effect to extend to most elements of value added, including capital, labor, and overhead. The reasons for this empirically observed relationship are not known with certainty, but the underlying forces are believed to include (1) labor efficiency, (2) new processes and improved methods, (3) product redesign that conserves material, allows greater efficiency in manufacture, and takes advantage of less costly resources, (4) product standardization, and (5) scale effects. Each of these forces is related to growth in accumulated production experience and provides

FIGURE 4-1. The Experience Curve at Ford—the Model T

Price of Model T, 1909-1923 (average list price in 1958 dollars)

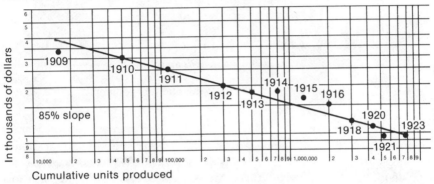

Cumulative units produced

Source: W. J. Abernathy and K. Wayne, "The Limits of the Learning Curve," *Harvard Business Review 52*, September-October 1974, p. 112. Reprinted by permission of the *Harvard Business Review.*

The Experience Curve for Integrated Circuits

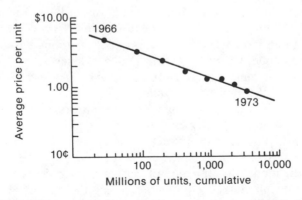

Source: Texas Instruments, Inc., First Quarter and Stockholders' Meeting Report, April 18, 1973.

FIGURE 4-2. Value of Market Share

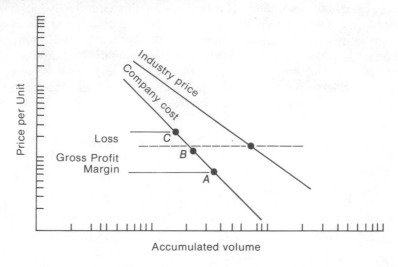

Source: Texas Instruments, Inc., First Quarter and Stockholders' Meeting Report, April 18, 1973.

opportunities that alert managements can exploit. The experience-curve relationship is often shown in a log-log graph of unit costs (or prices if a constant profit margin is assumed) versus total production, such as those shown for both the Model T and Integrated Circuits in Figure 4-1.

As is the case with accumulated experience, market share can have enormous value. Indeed, according to the model, a company's accumulated experience can best be measured by relative market share. When competitors follow similar experience curves, the dominant producer in an industry will have the greatest accumulated experience and the lowest unit costs. Assuming a single industrywide price, he will therefore have the highest profit margins. This is seen in Figure 4-2, where three different companies in an industry have different cost positions based upon their cumulative volume. Company C, the smallest, loses money, while Company B is at best marginal. The value of market share to Company A is clearly seen. As the industry's dominant producer, it is able to generate a significantly larger cash flow than its competitors because of both its greater volume and a greater contribution per unit sold.

While cash generation is a function of accumulated experience, best summarized through relative market share, cash use or investment, according to the model, is a function of market growth. To maintain market share in a growing market requires the infusion of cash for both working capital and capacity expansion. Attempting to gain additional market share further increases the business unit's growth rate and thus com-

FIGURE 4-3. Market-Share/Market-Growth Portfolio Chart

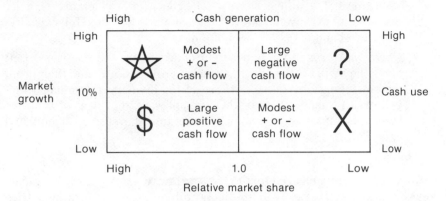

In a diversified company this chart would apply to the smallest units for which *strategic decisions* can be made. There is no necessary relationship between these business units and existing profit centers.

pounds the need for cash. Where the investment is financially attractive and capital funds are not internally available, the use of external financing, preferably debt, is called for.

Based on the general proposition outlined above, the product market-portfolio model isolates businesses into four categories reflecting their cash-use and cash-generation characteristics. Market growth is separated into high or low by an arbitrary dividing line, usually 10 percent, and cash use is depicted as high or low accordingly. Market share is viewed in terms of relative share—that is, company sales in that business divided by the sales of the company's leading competitor.[2] Since only one competitor can have a relative market share greater than 1.0, this figure is used to identify companies within an industry with high or low relative market shares and, therefore, high or low levels of relative cash generation. These four business categories are portrayed by BCG in a portfolio chart depicted in Figure 4-3.

Each quadrant in Figure 4-3 has its own pattern of cash generation and use, and BCG has given each its own name to reflect these characteristics.

- *Stars* in the upper left quadrant are the investment opportunities. With high cash use and cash generation (due to a favorable cost position in its industry), they are relatively self-sufficient.
- *Cash Cows* in the lower-left quadrant generate high cash flows yet use little in their low-growth market. These are net providers of cash.
- *Dogs* in the lower-right quadrant are cash traps in that additional

cash investments cannot be recovered. Increasing market share in a stable market is futile because no one can afford to increase capacity any more than they can afford to run at much less than full capacity. Dogs are candidates for liquidation.

– *Question Marks* in the upper-right quadrant are the real risks. Left alone they will become dogs as market growth slows, and their profit margins contract relative to those of the industry's dominant competitors. To make stars of them requires a great deal of cash for investment in increased market share and, therefore, accumulated experience.

It should be emphasized that the relationships among cash flow, market share, and market growth are likely to be most evident in industries where (1) there is a substantial experience phenomenon and (2) lower costs can be translated into competitive advantage either through lower prices, higher marketing and technical expenses, or some other means. Where lower costs are not critical to success, such as in highly differentiated markets or where experience-curve effects are limited in time because of a high rate of technological change or when product obsolescence occurs, these relationships may be tenuous.

So far we have only described the static situation as viewed by the product/market-portfolio model. The dynamics of the product life cycle yield the model's prescriptions for developing a balanced portfolio of businesses. As market growth slows, stars become cash cows. The throwoff from the cash cows must be either distributed to investors or reinvested in new assets. According to this model, the most rewarding investment is in market share to turn question marks into stars before their market growth slows. The underlying logic for this investment sequence is that the highest cash returns (and profits) occur when a dominant market share position can be obtained. Since this dominant position can be most easily achieved during the early phases of rapid market growth, when competitive positions and purchasing patterns have not yet been firmly established, it can be worthwhile for aggressive investment in question marks (high-market-growth/low-market-share businesses). Such a successful sequence is depicted in Figure 4-4.

The technological leader, or the company with a strong new venture organization, has another option available to it. In this case cash throw-off can be invested in new product activity rather than in market-share gains. Figure 4-5 portrays such a sequence.

Policymakers who employ the product/market-portfolio model for planning purposes typically try to place each of their company's businesses in one of the quadrants of the market-share/market-growth matrix. They also prepare similar historical charts (three to five years in the past)

FIGURE 4-4. Successful Portfolio Dynamics [a]

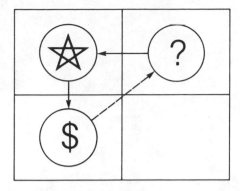

[a] The solid line connotes product movement over time. The dotted line connotes the optimal cash-flow pattern.

for both themselves and their competitors in order to understand the competitive interaction taking place and to ascertain where competitive commitment is heaviest. An ideal product/market-portfolio would be similar to the one shown in Figure 4-6. The size of the company's commitment to each business is indicated by the size of the circle used for it. The reason this portfolio is close to an ideal one is the cash flow balance of the company's assets concentrated in the cash-cow–star–question-mark half of the matrix. Cash flow from the cows can be invested in the question marks to turn them into stars.

FIGURE 4-5. Portfolio Dynamics for the New-Product Leader [a]

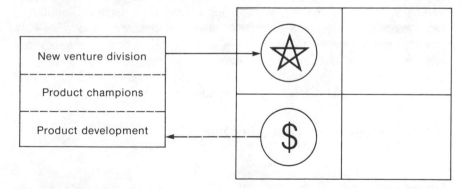

[a] The solid line connotes product movement over time. The dotted line connotes the optimal cash-flow pattern.

FIGURE 4-6. Idealized Product/Market Portfolio[a]

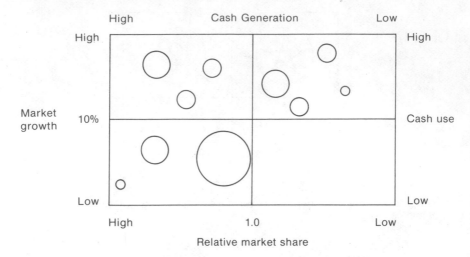

[a] The size of each circle is usually representative of the company's commitment to that business. The size of the circles relative to each other, therefore, reflects their importance in the company's total portfolio of businesses.

In addition to product/market-portfolio charts, users of this model typically look at the trend of their company's strategic investments over time. This is done by plotting, for each business in a company's portfolio, market growth rate versus the growth rate in the company's production capacity. This allows managers to see where they are planning to change their competitive commitments and by how much. Figure 4-7 depicts a trend chart for an ideal portfolio. Along the left side of the chart are two groups for which no capacity expansion is planned. These are the dogs and those question marks that are being managed for cash or liquidated. Cash cows are kept growing with the market, and stars are receiving only slightly more support. Along the right side are those question marks that are receiving investment for market-share growth in order to become stars. The model suggests that managers study similar charts for competitors to show the nature of their commitments over time.

Assumptions of the Product/Market-Portfolio Model

Underlying the basic propositions of this planning model are several explicit assumptions about the behavior of costs, prices, and profit margins in competitive markets. Since the prescriptive power of the model

FIGURE 4-7. Trend Chart for an Ideal Product/Market Portfolio

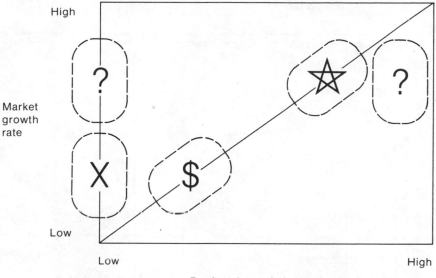

depends on the strength of these assumed economic rules, they are worth highlighting.

The first economic rule assumed by the model is that in a stable competitive marketplace, *prices will decrease as costs decrease,* because of the experience-curve effect. Where profit margins remain constant, average industry costs and prices should decline in parallel with the difference between the two equal to the profit-margin percentage.

In unstable markets where (1) new product prices are less than average costs for.the industry because of pricing policies based on anticipated costs or (2) supply is generally small relative to demand, thereby causing prices to remain firm as production increases, the parallel relationship between costs and prices in the short run may be absent. However, at some point prices on new products will begin to fall faster than costs because of either increased competition from new entrants in the market or decreased relative demand for the product. Eventually a parallel relationship between costs and prices will be reestablished. This typical cost-price relationship for unstable markets is seen in Figure 4-8, where the periods *A, B, C,* and *D* depict the evolution in relationships described above.

Another economic rule assumed by the model is that the average cost for an industry is greatly influenced by the costs of the dominant producer. If its costs are declining 25 percent per year, then so must the costs

FIGURE 4-8. Typical Cost-Price Relationship for Unstable Markets (Total Accumulated Industry Production in Units)

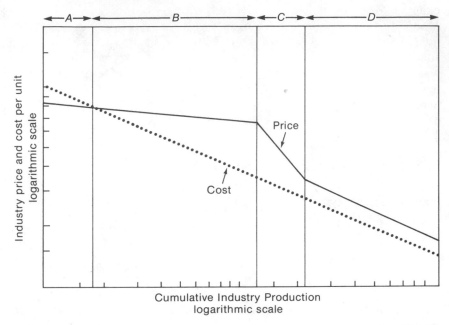

Source: "Note on the Use of Experience Curves in Competitive Decision Making," Harvard Business School, ICH 9-175-174.

of every other producer if they are to survive. If their costs decrease at a lower rate, either because they are not pursuing cost reductions as aggressively as the leader or because they are growing at a slower rate than the leader, then profits will eventually disappear, thereby eliminating those producers from the market.[3]

This leads to a third economic rule assumed by the model: profit margins are a function of sustained market share. For most companies the products that make the greatest profit contribution are those in which their share in the relevant market is the greatest. The logic is consistent with the previous assumptions and a good deal of evidence as well. If all competitors keep the same relative market share (and relative experience), then cost differentials should remain roughly constant. However, any competitor who gains market share should be able to convert this into a relative cost advantage and increased margins.[4]

Underlying each of these assumptions is the notion that experience-curve effects do drive business decision making. Providing strong support for their use is a good deal of microeconomic theory, although an ever-descending cost curve is never indicated. On the other hand, managers should not forget that numerous variables not specific to the firm, such as product obsolescence, technological innovation, government intervention, or inaccessibility to critical resources, may mean that the perceived benefits of accumulated experience are unobtainable. Perhaps the best example of the limits of using the experience curve is provided by Ford's Model T. Following a cost-minimization strategy with extensive capital investment in vertical integration, Ford achieved spectacular short-term success. In the mid-1920s, however, consumer demand shifted, and Ford was faced with both product obsolescence and a new production technology. By the time Ford designed a new car and renovated its production process, General Motors, following a more flexible strategy, had achieved permanent market leadership in the auto industry.[5]

Managers should not forget that the experience curve does not cause cost reductions, it merely provides the opportunity for an alert aggressive management to exert downward pressure on costs. The source and magnitude of these opportunities will vary over time. At one stage, they may arise out of labor efficiencies while at another from product redesign. Wherever they come from, they are observed only when management has been able to successfully exploit them.

Implications for the Diversification Decision

The focus of the product/market-portfolio model is on the cash-flow characteristics of a business. A high-potential business is one with the opportunity to stake out a leadership position in a growing industry. If this business can maintain or expand its market share position before industry growth slows, it will subsequently be in the best position to "harvest" the investments it made during the market's period of growth. The product/market-portfolio model argues and empirical evidence supports the notion that higher market share leads to higher cash flow and return on investment. Evidence, presented in Figure 4-9, indicates that, on the average, a 5 percent increase in ROI typically accompanies every 10 percent increase in market share. Experience also shows that the market-share investments with the highest incremental returns are those made during a business' growth phase. Since stars are relatively self-sufficient and already have dominant market share positions, such investments are best made for businesses that are question marks.

These observations on market-share investments and cash-flow returns reveal the benefits of constructing a portfolio of businesses through unrelated diversifying acquisitions. A company with a balanced portfolio of cash cows feeding question marks and stars is in a position both to reap the current benefits of its high market share and advantageous cost position and to develop sources of future cash flow. Sustained growth is thus

FIGURE 4-9. Relationship between Market Share and Profitability

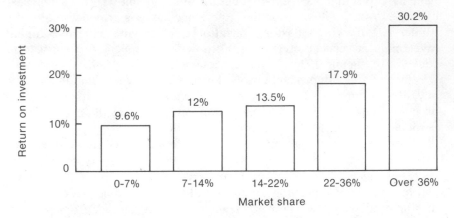

Source: Sidney Shoeffler, Robert D. Buzzell, and Donald F. Heany, "Impact of Strategic Planning on Profit Performance," *Harvard Business Review 52,* March-April 1974, p. 141. Reprinted by permission of the *Harvard Business Review.*

ensured by investing surplus cash from mature businesses in less mature, high-potential businesses.

The benefits of a balanced product/market-portfolio suggest a set of criteria by which to evaluate a potential diversifying acquisition. The key criterion is the fit of the target company's cashflow characteristics with those of the existing portfolio. The degree of fit will be governed by the target company's competitive position, the expected growth of its market, the cost of retaining or improving its competitive position, and the cashflow characteristics of the acquiring company's existing portfolio of businesses. Thus, managers would ask of the acquisition candidate:

1. What are its cash-flow characteristics?
2. How will these characteristics evolve over time in view of the competitive situation?
3. What investment on our part would be required over time to make a success of this business? And finally,
4. How does this cash-flow pattern fit with our existing portfolio of products and businesses?

According to the logic of the model, changes in the business portfolio are intended to fill in financial weak spots or build upon financial strengths. For example, a company in a high-growth industry may feel that access to a secure (and inexpensive) cash-flow source would enable it to maintain its present growth and possibly improve its market share position. This situation is similar to that faced by Tyco Labs, a manufacturer of high-technology products, in the mid-1970s. To fund both its rapid growth and its research-and-development programs, Tyco acquired (at a price equivalent to only four times cash flow) the Grinnel Co. from ITT. Grinnel was a major competitor in the low-growth, low-capital-intensity business of fire protection. The cash flow from Grinnel was able to fuel Tyco's internal growth as well as its active acquisition program. Alternatively, a mature company generating substantial cash flows may see an opportunity to nourish emerging growth companies or to convert a so-called question mark into a star. This was the situation in which Philip Morris found itself in the late 1960s with its tobacco business. The question mark Philip Morris acquired was Miller High Life, at the time number five in the brewing industry. With an infusion of over $500 million in production facilities and Philip Morris's marketing talent, Miller's growth exploded. By 1978 Miller was second in the industry with strong prospects of becoming number one. Armed with two cash cows, in mid-1978 Philip Morris acquired Seven-Up, a distant number three in the soft-drink industry that nevertheless led the growing noncola segment. Philip Morris apparently hoped to repeat its successful strategy with Miller High Life at Seven-Up.

Philip Morris's acquisition of Miller High Life provides an interesting insight into the product/market-portfolio model and its implications for the diversification decision. Philip Morris brought to Miller not only a large, surplus cash flow but also a formidable marketing talent that had established Philip Morris as the strongest competitor in the cigarette market. Prior to Philip Morris's entry, the brewing business was production oriented; brewmasters brewed beer and let the beer sell itself. Philip Morris's enormous cash flow enabled Miller to compete on this basis by building large, low-cost breweries; but Philip Morris's marketing skills also introduced a new competitive tactic into the industry. Miller High Life was both brewed and marketed. Caught between Miller's low-cost production and high marketing expenditures, the brewing industry underwent a major strategic and competitive transition in the mid-1970s.

While the notion of a balanced portfolio of cash flows appears to argue for broadly based or unrelated diversification, further reflection on the concepts underlying the model reveals even stronger arguments for related diversification. The logic behind related diversification rests on a company's ability to develop "overlapping experience curves" or the ability to transfer accumulated experience from one business to another. This, in fact, is a part of what happened at Miller as Philip Morris brought its marketing talent to bear. When distinct product markets have overlapping experience curves, exposure to each alters the markets' cost curves. Relevant cumulative volume no longer depends on the industry's narrowly defined experience curve, since a business's costs in one product market can reflect the experience gained in the other and vice versa. Thus, diversifying acquisitions that offer overlapping experience curves can be highly desirable.

Managers following this line of analysis would review three basic questions in examining a potential, related acquisition:

1. Where is experience accumulated in this business and how similar is it to our existing businesses?
2. What are the opportunities for overlapping experience curves?
3. What is the cash flow impact of the reduced relative costs arising from this related diversifying acquisition?

In summary, the product/market-portfolio model can help managers travel both the related and unrelated diversification routes. Related diversification is suggested when overlapping experience curves exist. In this environment, analytic attention should be focused on how the relative cost positions of the related business will be affected by the acquisition. Alternatively, an interest in balancing the cash flow characteristics of a portfolio of businesses will lead to unrelated diversification. This choice calls for understanding the product life cycle and investment requirements of the potential acquisition, as well as its relative cost position, so that the fit of its cash flow with the acquiring company's existing portfolio can be determined.

Using the Product/Market-Portfolio Model

Conducting a product/market-portfolio analysis as part of the diversification process is difficult for many reasons. Foremost is the difficulty that managers, consultants, and economists face in accurately defining relevant businesses or markets. Within a company, resources may be widely shared or the organizational structure may cut across what are economically independent businesses. In the marketplace, distinctly different products may compete for the same customer group, or the same product may be bought by distinctly different customers. Then again, the relevant market for a particular business might be only a small segment of a traditionally defined market. Thus, the key to successful use of the product/market-portfolio model is careful attention to how the business can be most meaningfully defined and where the boundaries of markets served by the business are assumed to be.

Once these definitional problems are overcome and the necessary data collected, a company can proceed to plot its current portfolio of businesses on a market-share/market-growth matrix. Often the impetus for this analysis is a shortfall in corporate cash needs. Alternatively, the impetus may arise out of a change in the competitive environment a business is facing or the proddings of a new CEO. The resulting portfolio chart may well be like the one shown in Figure 4-10.

This chart reflects the portfolio of a $1 billion corporation in 1974 as the economy entered the severest recession in the post–World War II period. The company had grown up in two closely related, presently mature businesses, represented by *A* and *B* in the figure. These two markets were large, fragmented ones, though oligopolistic in nature because of their high capital requirements and common resource requirements. In the mid-1960s, the company had adopted a growth strategy under the prodding of a new CEO and over the next decade made over forty acquisitions, mostly in the $5 to $25 million asset size. Growth was the company's prime objective, despite the fact that it barely survived the 1970–1971 recession. However, as the economy turned down in 1974, the company found that it did not have the cash it needed for its existing operations, let alone the funds required for several new capital-investment projects. Facing a cash flow constraint that promised to develop into a major strategic crisis, the company brought in new management.

This management undertook a product/market-portfolio analysis and concluded that the company's previous diversification efforts had seriously undermined the company's viability. Most of the acquisitions were either small companies or companies in low-growth industries, a consequence of prior efforts to spread business risks. These businesses,

FIGURE 4-10. 1974 Product/Market Portfolio Chart for a Major Industrial Company

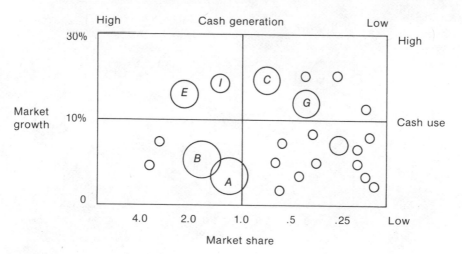

as seen in Figure 4-10, were concentrated in the dog and question mark quadrants. Nevertheless several acquisitions, namely businesses *C*, *E*, and *I*, were stars or potential stars.

Facing a major turning point, management decided to restructure its business portfolio utilizing the concepts of the product/market-portfolio model. In-depth analysis of each business was undertaken. Assessments of present and potential competitive strengths were stressed. (Similar studies were also done for its major competitors to assess their long-run commitments.) This information was then combined to prepare an estimate of the company's cash flow balance over the next ten years. The conclusion from this exercise was that the existing shortfall of funds would continue despite a growing contribution of funds from business E in addition to the funds provided by businesses *A* and *B*. Facing this scenario, senior management decided to concentrate its efforts on approximately ten businesses where it felt it had the best chance to become a significant competitor. The remaining businesses were to be either sold or managed for cash to provide the investment funds necessary to pursue aggressive market share strategies for the remaining businesses.

The portfolio resulting from this strategy is shown in Figure 4-11. Comparison of this portfolio with the idealized portfolio shown in Figure 4-6 shows a high degree of congruence between the two. Businesses A and B remain as the cash cows with business E showing signs of becoming one in the near future. Of particular interest was the decision to further invest in I, already a star, so as to further increase its market share. This undoubtedly reflected management's highly optimistic outlook for this

**FIGURE 4-11. 1978 Product/Market Chart for a
Major Industrial Company**

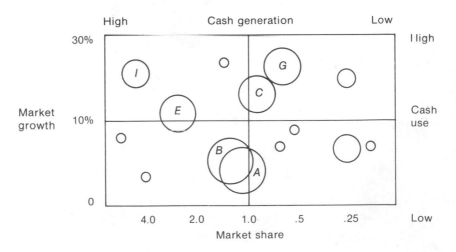

industry. The several dogs that remained in the portfolio were businesses more or less related to the company's activities in *A* and *B*.

The value of utilizing product/market-portfolio models has been well demonstrated by other companies in the last few years. Probably the first major strategic decision made using this framework was General Electric's exit from the computer mainframe business in the late 1960s. Analyzing its portfolio of businesses, G.E. decided that it could not fund businesses in three capital intensive, high-growth industries (computers, turbines, and nuclear power plants) at the same time. Its analysis led it to abandon computers by selling out to Honeywell and recouping as much of its investment as possible. RCA, making a similar decision to leave the mainframe computer business several years later, had to write off over $400 million from a smaller investment base. Another company showing the impact of successful product/market-portfolio management is Mead Corporation. Before adopting this analytic model, Mead was among the lowest performers on an ROI and ROE basis in the forest products industry. Following the divestiture of numerous marginal businesses and a renewed emphasis on obtaining strong market share positions, Mead in 1977 was among the three highest performers and had the highest five-year e.p.s. growth rate in the industry. So successful was Mead's turnaround that it became the target of an unsuccessful acquisition attempt by Occidental Petroleum in 1978.

These examples of the product/market-portfolio model in use suggest two basic guidelines for managers involved in diversification decisions and strategic planning. The first reflects the model's focus on the cash-use cash-generation properties of an individual business and is most relevant to related diversification:

- *Successful related diversification* will improve a business' competitive position by either increasing its relevant market share position or by reducing its relative costs through overlapping experience curves. Reduced relative costs or increased market share positions typically result in higher cash flow and return on investment for that business than would otherwise be the case.

The second guideline reflects the model's implications for the management of a group of businesses within a company's portfolio and is most relevant to unrelated diversification:

- *Successful unrelated diversification* will improve a company's short-run and long-run cash flow balance and therefore lead to an improved financial and strategic position. This arises because the successfully diversified company with a balanced product/market portfolio generates both its investment funds as well as its investment opportunities. Surplus cash flow from mature, dominant businesses will be available for aggressive investment in increasing the market shares of businesses in growing industries. After attaining high relative market shares, these growing businesses subsequently become the portfolio's high net cash flow generators as industry growth slows and investment needs diminish.

A Summary Comment

As we have seen, the product/market-portfolio model suggests guidelines for both related and unrelated diversification. As one would expect, the related diversification guidelines are very similar in scope and content to those offered by the strategy model. Of perhaps more interest are the product/market-portfolio model's guidelines for unrelated diversification, since they greatly expand the scope of possible analysis. These guidelines emphasize the long-run economic strength of a portfolio of businesses in cash flow balance. In both cases, it is important to note that the product/market-portfolio model provides no specific guidelines about how excess cash flow can be most effectively invested in a business's operation (or, conversely, how a business can be most effectively managed for cash). Developing these business policies is the goal of the strategy model. Thus, the detailed analysis suggested by the strategy model can and does play an important complementary role in the decision-making process once the product/market-portfolio model has helped management identify those businesses where cash flow could properly be generated or invested.

It is also important to stress that the product/market-portfolio model does not provide a fully satisfactory basis for relative comparisons. Consider, for example, the problem of comparing the relative attractiveness of two businesses with similar product/market or cash-use/cash-generation characteristics; or the difficulty in knowing when the costs of further investment in a business outweigh the potential cash flow benefits. Neither the strategy nor the product/market-portfolio models were designed to handle these issues. However, the risk/return model can. We shall turn our attention to this model in the next chapter.

Notes and References

1. The impact of the learning curve on an industry's production costs was already well established in the early 1950s. See, for instance, F. J. Andress, "The Learning Curve as a Production Tool," *Harvard Business Review* 32, January–February 1954, and M. A. Requero, *An Economic Study of the Military Airframe Industry*, Department of the Air Force, October 1957.

2. Business growth and market share are typically measured in dollar terms. Ideally, these measures should be stated in unit terms, so that ''real'' growth and market share can be determined.

3. ''Note on the Use of Experience Curves in Competitive Decision Making,'' Harvard Business School, ICH 9-175-174, p. 9.

4. Boston Consulting Group, *Perspectives on Experience*, 1968, p. 26.

5. Interesting accounts of the Ford experience appear in W. J. Abernathy and K. Wayne, ''The Limits of the Learning Curve,'' *Harvard Business Review* 52, September–October 1974, and Alfred P. Sloan, Jr., *My Years with General Motors* (New York: Doubleday, 1972).

CHAPTER 5

The Risk/Return Model

THE RISK/RETURN MODEL is an amalgam of related concepts drawn from contemporary financial economics.[1] In contrast to the strategy and product/market-portfolio models, it reflects the interests and concerns of investors rather than operating managers. The key concepts stressed in the model include (1) the tradeoff between expected risk and return of a particular security or capital asset, (2) the means by which an investor's risks and returns can be altered through portfolio diversification, and (3) the mechanism by which the capital market apparently prices or values both individual securities and investment portfolios.

Since securities are financial claims on a company and, in turn, a company can be viewed as a portfolio of investments in capital assets, several important aspects of the risk/return model can be applied in an analysis of corporate strategy, particularly in diversification. The model can help managers view their company as a set of investment opportunities and construct an investment portfolio that creates real economic value for investors. The model can also help assess the potential effect of a diversifying acquisition on the market value of a company.

Propositions of the Risk/Return Model

The risk/return model is based on several basic propositions. They are summarized here and discussed in varying degrees of detail below.

1. The return of a particular security is the compensation to investors of bearing its risk; the greater the risk, the greater the required return.

2. An investor can alter his level of risk and return through portfolio diversification.

84

3. Portfolio diversification cannot eliminate that component of a security's total risk related to the performance of the capital market. Only that component of total risk specifically related to the performance of its underlying assets can be eliminated through portfolio diversification.

4. Individual securities and investment portfolios are priced or valued by the capital market according to their level or market-related (as opposed to security-specific) risk.

The first proposition needs little explanation, since it spells out the basic condition underlying all competitive markets. However, several definitions are useful. In the context of this model, risk is defined as the variability of returns or—in more precise, statistical terms—as the dispersion of negative and positive deviations from an expected return. This dispersion of returns can most usefully be thought of as a probability distribution such as the one shown in Figure 5-1.

In investment alternatives 1 and 2, return A is the most likely to occur and is therefore the expected outcome. The dispersion of outcomes around the expected outcome represents uncertainty of the investment. Since the dispersion of outcomes of investment alternative 1 is less than the dispersion of outcomes of investment alternative 2, the first alternative is considered to be less risky. We can generalize by saying that the greater the dispersion of possible outcomes around the expected outcome, the greater the risk.

The most likely outcome of an event such as an investment is known as its expected value, or $E(\ )$, while its variability or range of dispersion is known as its risk.[2] Our two investment alternatives have the same expected return, $E(R) = A$, but investment 1, whose dispersion of possible

FIGURE 5-1. Probability Distribution of Returns

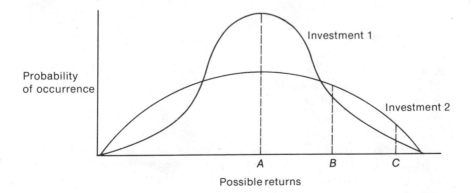

Possible returns

outcomes is less than that of investment 2, is less risky. Risk averse investors will therefore prefer investment 1 to investment 2, since it presents less risk for the same level of expected return.

The application of this concept of risk to investment decisions is straightforward. The risk of an investment is the uncertainty surrounding the future receipt of the initial value of the investment plus a return on that investment. The more uncertain this future receipt with respect to size and timing, the more risky it is. For investors in capital assets, such as corporations, risk is the variability of the capital asset's free cash flow, where free cash flow is defined as the cash remaining at the end of the operating cycle after those reinvestments necessary to maintain the asset's productivity have been made. For investors in securities, risk is the variability of the security's dividends (or interest) and capital appreciation. This variability will reflect, of course, the cash flow pattern generated by the security's underlying assets.

Since capital appreciation (or depreciation) results from a change in the present value of an asset's future free cash flow between any two points in time, the notion of present value, or discounted cash flow (DCF), deserves a brief comment.[3] The present value of a future cash flow stream can be expressed by the well-known formula:

$$PV = \sum_{t=1}^{n} D_t/(1 + R)^t$$

where PV is the present value of the cash flow stream, D_t is the cash flow received in each time period t, and R is an annualized rate of return, or discount rate. This discount rate will reflect the risk or the variability of the cash flow constituting D_t. The more risky the cash flow, the greater the discount rate. By summing the present values of an asset's expected cash flow in each time period, its total present value can be determined. A change in present value will occur if the discount rate, R, changes; if the expected cash flow, D_t, changes; or if the timing of the receipt of the expected cash flows, $t = 1$ to n, changes. For instance, if expected cash flow increases, the discount rate decreases, or the time horizon of the receiving expected cash flow increases, then the present value will increase. Conversely, if the expected cash flow decreases, the discount rate increases, or the time horizon of the expected cash flow decreases, then the present value will decrease.

As discussed above, an investor's "return" during a given time period is the cash flow he has received plus any capital appreciation (depreciation) or, more specifically, any increase (decrease) in the present value of the remaining cash flows for the asset. We can express this return either in absolute dollar terms or as a rate—that is, as a return per unit of investment per unit of time. For a security, an investor's rate of return will be the security's dividends (or interest) and capital appreciation (or depreciation) in the relevant time period divided by the security's price at the beginning of the time period.

These notions of risk and return greatly facilitate investment analysis. By using a rate of return as the basis for measuring investment attractiveness, one can determine an investment's potential for wealth creation on a comparative basis, eliminating size and timing differences of the investments included in a comparison. Similarly, by focusing on the variability of an investment's return as a measure of risk, one can compare the relative value of investments showing different expected rates of return. Finally, the notions of risk and return, as defined above, help frame two critical questions surrounding most investment decisions taken in market economies: Is the investment's expected rate of return commensurate with its apparent risk? How much additional return must be obtained for taking on an additional unit of risk?

The second proposition of the model states than an investor can alter his level of risk and return through portfolio diversification. This can be explained most easily by a simple two-security example. As shown in Figure 5-2, an investor in security *A* can increase his level of risk and return by selling some proportions of his holdings and using the proceeds to purchase some amount of security *B*. The mix of securities represented by portfolio *C* has a level of risk and a return midway between that of the two undiversified portfolios, *A* and *B*. Portfolio *C* does not, however, have a risk/return profile superior to either portfolio *A* or *B*.

The example portrayed in Figure 5-2 assumes that the returns of securities *A* and *B* are perfectly correlated, or, in other words, that when the returns of *A* change, the returns of *B* change by the *same* percentage.

FIGURE 5-2. Risk/Return Profile for the Two-Security Portfolio

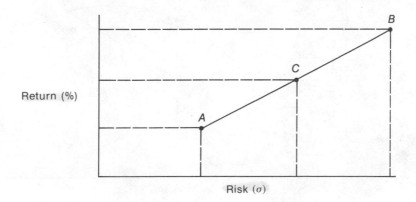

This explains the linear relationship between points A, B, and C in the figure.

More typically, however, the returns of pairs of securities exhibit less than perfect correlation. Under this more realistic assumption, we can expect that the returns of security B, for example, will not change proportionally with the returns of security A. Such a nonlinear relationship between security returns allows an investor in securities A and B to improve the relationship between risk and return in his portfolio by varying the mix of these two securities. As shown in Figure 5-3, an investor can obtain a higher return (at portfolio D) for the same risk (as portfolio C) or a lower risk (at portfolio E) for the same return (as portfolio C) than is possible with perfectly correlated securities. Because portfolios on the curve AEDB are superior in terms of risk and return to portfolios on the line ACB, they are said to be more efficient.

This notion of efficiency can be extended to the case where many securities are available for inclusion in the portfolio. The efficient frontier is defined as that set of portfolios which offers the optimum tradeoffs of risk and return to the investor. Figure 5-4 depicts such an efficient frontier in relation to the securities composing it. Because of the nonperfect correlation of returns among the securities, portfolios can be constructed that yield more efficient combinations of risk and return than is possible from holding individual securities.

This basic proposition has several important embellishments. For example, the presence of a risk-free asset, perhaps best represented by a U.S. Treasury bill, allows investors to increase the efficiency of their portfolios.

FIGURE 5-3. Impact of Nonlinear Risk/Return Relationships in the Two-Security Portfolios

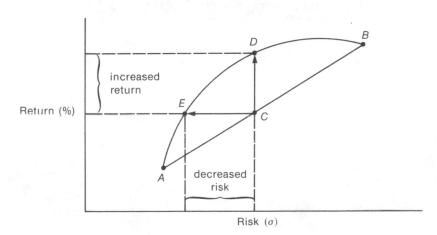

FIGURE 5-4. Individual Securities and the Efficient Frontier

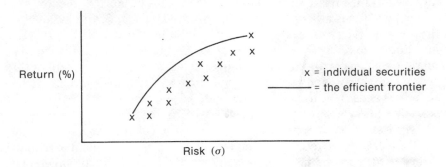

As shown in Figure 5-5, investors holding portfolio A could construct a more efficient portfolio by selling A and buying some combination of the risk-free asset R_f and portfolio B. All portfolios on line R_f–B exhibit risk/return tradeoffs superior to those of portfolio A. Similarly, combinations of R_f and portfolio C are still more efficient. The result of this process is that the efficient frontier becomes a straight line from R_f and tangent to the original efficient frontier (at P^*). All efficient portfolios, therefore, become combinations of P^* and the risk-free asset. As investors buy and sell securities to reach this frontier, P^* eventually becomes the market portfolio—that is, it will consist of all available securities in the market, weighted in proportion to their market values.

FIGURE 5-5. The Efficient Frontier and the Risk-Free Asset

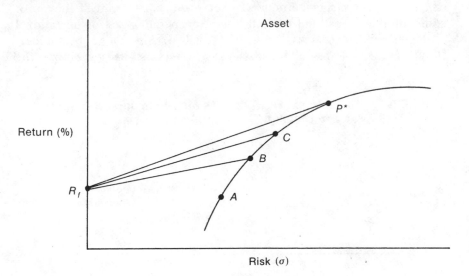

Another embellishment can be introduced when the possibility of borrowing at the risk-free rate is recognized. This means that the investor can borrow funds at R_f and invest the proceeds in P^*. Figure 5-6 depicts the new efficient frontier under this condition. To the left of P^*, the investor is investing in a combination of P^* and R_f. To the right of P^*, funds are being borrowed at R_f and invested in P^*. (The equivalent of this activity in corporations is (1) the investment of idle cash in marketable securities and (2) the use of debt for financial leverage.) The line extending from R_f through P^*, the market portfolio, is referred to as the capital market line, since it represents the most efficient way an investor can obtain incremental returns by adding risk to his investment portfolio. Every portfolio on the capital market line is a perfectly diversified portfolio, since its only risk asset is the market portfolio.

The third proposition of the risk/return model states that it is not possible to eliminate through portfolio diversification that component of a security's total risk that is related to capital market risks. This is an important proposition, since it forms the basis of a widely accepted theory of how individual securities and diversified portfolios are valued by the capital market.

We can clarify this proposition by focusing on the distinction made between security-specific and market-related risk. Market-related risk, commonly referred to as systematic risk, is that portion of a security's risk that is correlated to the market's risk or to changes in general economic conditions. Since systematic risk is that risk common to all securities (the market), it cannot be diversified away. Security-specific risk, commonly referred to as unsystematic risk, is that risk unique to the security itself. It stems from such events as changes in the specific demand for a company's products or services, changes in the behavior of competitors, strikes, and the full range of operating and organizational problems. Unsystematic risk can be diversified away. This is best understood by remembering that the market portfolio, or P^* in Figure 5-6, is the

FIGURE 5-6.   The Efficient Frontier with Risk-Free Borrowing and Lending: The Capital Market Line

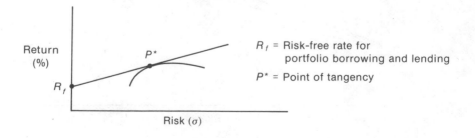

most diversified portfolio that an investor can obtain. By definition, all of its risk is market related. The market, therefore, has no unsystematic risk element. This means, then, that portfolio diversification can reduce total risk, but only by eliminating the security-specific, or unsystematic, risk component of total risk. An efficiently diversified portfolio will have only a systematic risk element.

Since only unsystematic risk can be eliminated through portfolio diversification, many professional investors concentrate their attention on evaluating the systematic, or market-related, risk of their securities or portfolios. This can be done by regressing a security's historical returns against corresponding market returns or against an appropriate market index, such as the S&P 500. The resulting linear regression measures a security's unsystematic and systematic risk elements. These measures are commonly identified by their regression coefficients, or the Greek letters "α" (alpha) for unsystematic risk and "β" (beta) for systematic risk. Figure 5-7 depicts the meaning of such a correlation.

Each dot in Figure 5-7 represents one set of security and corresponding market returns during one time period. The trend line is the best representation of this relationship over time. The slope of the trend line, or beta, relates the security's return to the market's return and thus measures the security's systematic risk. The trend line's point of intercept, where the market's return is zero, represents the security's specific, or unsystematic, return (risk). The beta of the market portfolio is, of course, 1.0, and its alpha is zero, because the market portfolio is both perfectly correlated with itself and perfectly diversified. A beta less than 1.0 indicates that the security's returns are less variable than the market's returns and therefore "less risky." The opposite is true for a security with a beta greater than 1.0.

Despite the fact that the beta of a security or capital asset reflects historical relationships, it nevertheless has a special utility in investment analysis. For short-term forecasts, historical measures of betas have been

FIGURE 5-7. Correlation of a Security's Return with the Market's Return

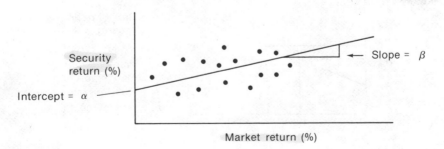

shown to be good predictors of future betas. This is because most assets' risk profiles change slowly over time. For longer time periods, however, where significant changes in a company's economic and competitive environment can occur, changes in the company's (and its security's) free cash flow and risk profile may be substantial. Where these environmental changes can be foreseen, an investor should adjust his forecasts for the company's free cash flow and systematic risk. These changes can lead the investor to believe that the market is either overvaluing or undervaluing the company.[4]

The fourth and final proposition of the risk/return model states that individual securities and investment portfolios are priced or valued by the capital market according to their level of market-related, or systematic, risk. This proposition follows directly from the argument outlined above: namely, that since investors can diversify away unsystematic risk in their own portfolios, securities will yield a return commensurate with their systematic risk instead of their total risk.

According to this proposition we can redraw Figure 5-6 to depict a relationship between return and systematic risk instead of total risk. As shown in Figure 5-8, this relationship can be represented by a line extending from the risk-free rate of return (where $\beta = 0$) through the market's level of risk (where $\beta = 1$) and return. The resulting line is identical to the capital market line in that the risk-free rate of return and the market's level of risk and return, or P^*, are the same in each case. The important difference between the two, however, is that systematic risk, rather than total risk, is used as the relevant risk measure. Therefore, a position on the line reflects the relationship between a security's systematic risk (or the level of systematic risk selected for a portfolio) and its expected return relative to the expected returns of the market and the risk-free asset.

This revised framework is much more versatile in that it can also be used to predict the rate of return of individual capital assets or securities with a given level of systematic risk, whereas the capital market line

FIGURE 5-8. Capital Asset Pricing Model

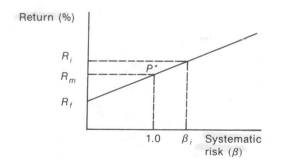

R_i = Rate of return on the ith security

P^* = Market portfolio

R_m = Rate of return on the market portfolio

R_f = Risk-free rate of return

β_i = Beta of the ith security

shown in Figure 5-6 could only be used to predict a rate of return for efficiently diversified portfolios. This expanded usage led to its being called the capital asset pricing model (CAPM).

CAPM is algebraically expressed as:

$$E(R_i) = E(R_f) + \beta_i[E(R_m) - E(R_f)]$$

where $E(R_i)$ denotes the expected value of the investment's risk-adjusted rate of return and β_i is the systematic risk level of a specific capital asset, security, or portfolio. The term $[E(R_m) - E(R_f)]$ is the market's risk premium. The expanded term $\beta_i[E(R_m) - E(R_f)]$ is the asset's risk premium. The more positively correlated the returns of that risky asset relative to the market returns, the higher its beta, and consequently the larger its risk premium. Adding an asset's risk premium to the risk-free rate of return determines the rate of return required by the market for purchasing that asset's cash flow stream. Once this rate of return is known, a price can then be established for the asset's cash flow stream. This price is the present value of the asset's future cash flows discounted at its expected or risk-adjusted rate of return.

Capital Market Rates of Return

As we have shown, CAPM provides a framework for assessing the rate of return the capital market expects an individual asset to earn. This rate of return, according to CAPM, is a function of the asset's level of systematic risk, the capital market's rate of return, and the risk-free rate of return. While we have emphasized the notion of systematic and unsystematic risk in previous sections, we have not identified what the market's rate of return, the risk-free rate of return, and the market's risk premium have been historically.

Determining the size and stability of these rates of return has been the objective of several empirical studies. The capital market's rate of return has three components: (1) a pure or real rate of interest, commonly thought of as the opportunity cost of forgoing current consumption for future consumption; (2) a purchasing power adjustment to allow the investor to obtain the same amount of goods or services in the future for his monetary assets as in the present; and (3) a risk premium for accepting an uncertain amount of future assets relative to the certain amount of the investor's current assets. The risk-free rate of return is composed of the real rate of interest and a purchasing power adjustment, or items (1) and (2) above. Since the risk-free rate of return is itself a component of the market's rate of return, we will comment on the risk-free rate before moving to a more comprehensive discussion of the capital market's risk premium and the capital market's rate of return.

The rate of return of U.S. Treasury bills is often used as a proxy for the risk-free rate of return, since T-bills have the lowest probability of default and are the most liquid of all instruments in the capital marketplace.[5] The pure or real rate of interest is normally considered to be the difference between this risk-free rate of return and the purchasing power adjustment. The purchasing power adjustment measures the amount of inflation or deflation occurring in the economy.

Economists have generally argued that the pure or real rate of interest lies in the range of 1 percent to 3 percent. At the lower end of the range are numerous historical examples, while at the upper end of the range is evidence from studies based upon "ex ante" returns or the rate of return investors expect to make. Deciding which is the relevant measure is at the root of much of the difficulty in accurately determining rates of return. A similar problem arises in determining how to measure the rate of inflation and to design an appropriate index. For the sake of convenience, the Consumer Price Index is typically used, but this index measures the inflation rate of only one segment of the U.S. economy and suffers from numerous estimation biases. Despite these problems, the rate of return on U.S. Treasury bills probably remains the best measure of the risk-free rate of return and the CPI remains the best inflation index. Since the T-bill rate usually exceeds the CPI rate of inflation, the difference is normally accepted as the pure or real rate of interest.

The difference between the rates of return earned by owning the risky market portfolio and owning the risk-free asset, or $(R_m - R_f)$, constitutes the market's risk premium. This is the third component of the market's rate of return. In theory, the market portfolio should include all risky assets, such as stocks, bonds, capital assets, and the intangible assets of investors. In practice, however, the market portfolio is usually limited to equity securities on the NYSE or a subset such as the stocks comprising the S&P 500.[6]

The volatility of returns for the stock market has raised problems in determining the appropriate time frame over which to measure the market's rate of return, and by implication, its risk premium. As investors clearly know, the decade encompassing the late sixties and early seventies was as different from the decade preceding it as they both were from the 1930s. The choice of the time period for measuring the market's return is obviously quite important. It must be long enough to include "up periods" as well as "down periods" and include enough observations to dampen the highly volatile annual returns characteristic of the stock market.

Fisher and Lorie were the first to report on long-run rates of return for investments in common stocks.[7] Their initial 1964 study and more comprehensive 1968 report established a 9.3 to 9.5 percent annual rate of return on investments in common stocks over the period from 1926 to 1965. This rate of return became widely accepted in the 1970s as the long-run expected rate of return on common-stock investments.

More recently, a detailed analysis of a broad range of capital market rates of return over the period 1926 to 1976 has been published by Ibbotson and Sinquefield.[8] Their studies measured five total rate-of-return series for investments (common stocks, long-term corporate bonds, long-term government bonds, U.S. Treasury bills, and inflation) and determined several component rate-of-return series (the market's risk premium, default premiums, maturity premiums, and real interest rates). Tables 5-1 and 5-2 present these total investment and component rates of return. The difference between the geometric mean and the arithmetic mean is that the arithmetic mean is the average of the observed annual rates of return, while the geometric mean gives effect to compounding these annual returns over time. Consequently, the geometric mean is the relevant rate of return for use in long-term decision making.

Several noteworthy conclusions can be reached from Ibbotson and Sinquefield's results. Interest rates on Treasury bills (2.4 percent) approximately match the inflation rate (2.3 percent), implying a real rate of interest near zero. More important for investors in risky assets, the risk premium on the stock market is approximately 6.7 percent over the Treasury bill rate of return (2.4 percent). One can also see the volatility of stock returns relative to returns on the other investment options; the standard deviation of the stock market's annual return is approximately 22 percent, versus standard deviations under 6 percent for the other investment returns. That equity rates of return, in particular, should be measured over relatively long time periods is seen in the fact that during

TABLE 5-1. Investment Total Annual Returns, 1926–1976

Series	Geometric Mean	Arithmetic Mean	Standard Deviation
Common stocks	9.2%	11.6%	22.4%
Long-term corporate bonds	4.1%	4.2%	5.6%
Long-term government bonds	3.4%	3.5%	5.8%
U.S. Treasury bills	2.4%	2.4%	2.1%
Inflation	2.3%	2.4%	4.8%

TABLE 5-2.   Component Annual Returns, 1926–1976

Series	Geometric Mean	Arithmetic Mean	Standard Deviation
Risk premiums (stocks-bills)	6.7%	9.2%	22.6%
Default premiums (LT corps-LT govts)	0.6%	0.6%	3.2%
Maturity premiums (LT govts-T bills)	1.0%	1.1%	5.9%
Real interest rates (T bills-inflation)	0.0%	0.1%	4.6%

Source: Roger B. Ibbotson and Rex A. Sinquefield, *Stocks, Bonds and Inflation: The Past (1926–1976) and the Future (1977–2000),* Financial Analysts Research Foundation, Charlottesville, Va. 1977. Reprinted by permission of the authors and the publisher.

34 of the 50 years studied, the stock market had an annual rate of return between −13.2 percent and +31.6 percent.[9]

It is useful to compare these capital market rates of return with the results of Holland and Myers.[10] This study aimed to determine the real rate of return on corporate assets (corporate investment in land, plant and equipment, working capital, and intangibles) and the real cost of capital faced by nonfinancial corporations. They concluded that over the period 1929 to 1976 the after-tax, real rate of return on corporate assets was between 6 and 7 percent. This rate of return is in the same range as Ibbotson's and Sinquefield's market risk premium (6.7 percent). The close correspondence between the real rate of return earned on corporate assets and the market's risk premium (the real rate of return earned by investors in corporate securities) is what one would expect for an economy in long-run equilibrium. For shorter time periods, however, significant differences between these two rates can and do occur. (Holland and Myers's study suggests that the period covering the late 1950s to mid 1960s was one period when the market was overvaluing corporate earnings.)

The close correspondence between the capital market risk premium and real rates of return on corporate assets aids in establishing long-run expected rates of return for investment decision making. Simply, in aggregate and over time, investors in corporations and corporations themselves can expect to earn approximately 6 to 7 percent per annum in real or inflation-adjusted returns on investments in risky assets. This means that nominal and expected rates of return should include both the expected rate of inflation and this risk premium. If a 6 percent plus rate of inflation is expected for the economy, as was the case in 1978, the market's rate of return is probably in excess of 13 percent. If, however, the inflation rate moderates in the future to historical rates, the 9.2 percent rate of return over the last fifty years may indicate a more appropriate rate of return level for forecasting.

These long-run rate of return studies are also useful to investors in individual capital assets. Once reasonably well-defined ranges are established for the market's risk premium and the expected rate of inflation, expected rates of return for individual assets can be estimated through CAPM. For securities or assets with systematic risks higher or lower than the market, corresponding adjustments can be made in the assets' risk premiums. (A company's equity risk premium is its systematic risk times the market's risk premium.) When this risk premium is added to the risk-free rate of return, the expected rate of return on that investment can be estimated.

As a final point, it is worth stresssing that the expected rate of return, $E(R_i)$, found through CAPM is equivalent to the discount rate, R, used in DCF valuations. Since the former is the investor's expected rate of return on capital invested, the latter must be the investment's cost of capital or, alternatively, the rate at which the investment must earn income in the future to meet the investor's minimum expectations. The capital asset pricing model merely provides a rate of return that the market determines to be appropriate for the riskiness of an investment's cash flow. The identity between CAPM's expected rate of return, $E(R_i)$, and DCF's discount rate, R, links the findings of contemporary capital market theory with more traditional approaches to asset valuation. It also enables managers and investors to understand better the underlying economic determinants of systematic and unsystematic risk.

Economic Determinants of Market Based Risk: A Technical Explanation[11]

A security's systematic risk, measured in the marketplace, is the degree of correlation between its return and the market's return. Defined as cash income plus capital appreciation over one time period, these "returns" are equivalent to a security's cash flow over its lifetime. This equivalency holds because capital appreciation merely measures the change that occurs between two time periods in the present value of future cash flows. Cash flow is a much more useful basis for analysis than current cash income plus capital appreciation, since it can be applied to capital assets as well as securities. In addition, it utilizes a multiperiod time horizon rather than the constrained one-period time frame of CAPM, as expressed in the preceding section.

Focusing on cash flow allows systematic risk to be thought of as having two components, the systematic risk of the current-period cash flow and the systematic risk arising from future cash flows (best sum-marized in their price at the end of the current period). Since current cash flow is fixed in timing and size (it cannot show any period-to-period growth), its systematic risk is exactly what one expects it to be: the correlation between itself and the economy's level of activity.[12] The more closely an asset's or company's free cash flow is correlated with the economy's level of activity, the higher the asset's or company's intrinsic systematic risk.

The future cash flow component of systematic risk, however, is not fixed. It has a variable time horizon and the possibility of growth, and its estimated size is naturally affected by changing investor expectations. The effect of varying the time horizon and growth of a cash flow on its present value is readily apparent: an increase in either results in more cash in absolute terms at some future date in time and, consequently, a greater present value than a cash flow without growth or with a more limited time horizon. The impact of changing investor expectations is not as clear. In economic language, the degree or rate at which expectations are revised over time are called elasticities of expectation. These changes in future estimates are based on the difference between what one ex-pected to happen in the current time period and what actually did happen, or alternatively, the impact of unanticipated events on current forecasts. Elasticities of expectation normally lie between 0 and 1. An elasticity of expectation of 0 means that future expectations are not revised when actual performance in the current period differs from that expected; an elasticity of 1 means that future expectations are revised by the same percentage as the difference between actual and expected performance for the current period.

These three items, elasticities of expectation, cash flow life, and cash flow growth, influence the size of the price (and therefore capital apprecia-tion) component of systematic risk. Whenever the elasticity of expecta-tion is less than one, future estimates of cash flow, and thus the price, will be less volatile than the cash flow during the current period. The relative influence of these three items on an asset's beta is seen in Table 5-3.

As one can see, the impact of asset life on beta is particularly sig-nificant for low elasticities of expectation; for assets of relatively long life, beta is approximately proportional to the elasticity of expectation. Simi-larly, growth significantly reduces an asset's beta for low elasticities of expectation. The most important conclusion from the table, however, is the impact of elasticities of expectation. A reduction in the elasticity of expectation from 1 to .5, for example, almost always leads to nearly a 30 percent reduction in beta. The power of accurate forecasting (or very stable and predictable cash flows) and therefore low elasticities of expec-tation can be easily seen.

The changing pattern of a company's future free cash flows as well as

.**TABLE 5-3. Calculated Betas**

1. Asset beta as a function of asset life (T) and elasticity of expectations (η)

	$T = 1$	2	3	10	20	40	∞
$\eta = 0$	1.438	0.737	0.316	0.177	0.110	0.080	0.058
$\eta = 5$	1.438	1.080	0.866	0.797	0.766	0.755	0.763
$\eta = 1.0$	1.438	1.438	1.438	1.438	1.438	1.438	1.438

2. Asset beta as a function of growth rate (g) and elasticity of expectations (η), for infinite-lived project ($T = \infty$).

	$g = 0$	.02	.04	.08	.12
$\eta = 0$	0.068	0.041	0.014	*	*
$\eta = .5$	0.753	0.740	0.726	0.699	*
$\eta = 1.0$	1.438	1.438	1.438	1.438	1.438

Assumptions:

$$r_f = .05; \quad \sigma_m^2 = .02; \quad \beta\sigma_{im} = .025; \quad E(\bar{R}_m) = .12$$

* Asset value not defined.

Source: S. C. Myers and S. M. Turnbull, "Capital Budgeting and the Capital Asset Pricing Model: Good News and Bad News," *Journal of Finance* 32, May 1977, p. 326. Reprinted by permission of the American Finance Association.

the changing volatility of its current free cash flow explains why betas tend to be unstable over time. For example, a young Xerox with a copying process that radically changed the business office faced almost limitless growth opportunities in the early 1960s but had a very volatile current cash flow. By the early 1970s, Xerox's current cash flow was much more stable and it still faced significant growth opportunities. However, by 1978 a mature Xerox was growing at a reduced rate and generating revenues linked to the level of the nation's overall economic activity. Consequently, Xerox's systematic risk fell from the 1.5–1.6 range in the early 1960s to the .8–1.0 range in the early 1970s and then began rising to the 1.2–1.4 range in the late 1970s. Polaroid, on the other hand, saw its systematic risk rise from a 1.2–1.4 range to a 1.8–1.9 range in the same time period. This occurred as its maturity brought a cash flow more dependent on repeating film purchases than on new equipment sales. In both cases, the importance of market-related risk relative to business-specific risk (or systematic risk relative to unsystematic risk) increased dramatically as Xerox and Polaroid matured.

Assumptions of the Risk/Return Model

The risk/return model claims that a security's expected return is related to the market's expected return by its level of systematic risk, or beta.

According to the model, the greater a security's systematic risk, the greater its required rate of return and the lower its market value relative to its cash flow. Conversely, the lower the systematic risk, the lower the risk premium and required rate of return and the higher the market value of the security, all other things being the same.

The early development of capital market theory, upon which much of the risk/return model is based, required several simplifying assumptions about the real world. These assumptions included such restrictions as (1) the absence of transaction costs such as brokerage fees, (2) free and readily available information, (3) investor indifference to the form of their future cash flows (dividends, interest, capital gains), (4) homogeneous expectations among investors in the capital market, (5) risk-free borrowing and lending rates, and (6) risk-averse investors who are single-period, expected-wealth maximizers and who choose among alternative investments on the basis of the expected value of their returns and the variability of that expected value.

While these assumptions may seem to represent an unreal capital market environment, recent research has shown that relaxing the first five constraints does not alter the conclusions of capital market theory. For example, where transaction costs exist or where information has a cost, actual market prices will be lower than those that would exist in a "costless" world. Under these conditions, it appears that investors will pay for information or make transactions just up to that point where it ceases to be profitable. Similarly, the fact that individual investors are not indifferent to the form of their future cash flows and do not have homogeneous expectations suggests that an active, trading marketplace exists. These different preferences and expectations will cause investors to search out and buy opportunities that are profitable to themselves; while pension funds might concentrate on high-yield, low-growth investments, young professionals might be acquiring high-growth, low-yield investments. In the course of this process, investors with their varying needs will drive prices toward an equilibrium where the relative attractiveness of each investment to the marketplace would be the same. At this point, the marketplace in aggregate will exhibit homogeneous expectations and indifference to the form of the cash flows. Within this overall equilibrium, however, individual investors would be continuing to alter their own portfolios. Since borrowing and lending rates are not the same for all investors and are not unlimited in quantity, individual investors will once again perceive personally profitable investment opportunities. As before, investors acting on these opportunities will drive the market toward equilibrium, but each individual investor will continue to have a different set of investment opportunities. Thus, relaxing these five assumptions allows capital market theory to describe realistic, individual investor behavior without sacrificing its overall conclusion that the capital market is in long-run equilibrium.

The sixth assumption has allowed economists to characterize the investment decisions in relatively simple terms. This assumption, we can recall, asserts that investors aim at maximizing their wealth in a single time period by choosing among alternative investments with two criteria in mind: the investment's expected return (or its mean return) and the variability of that return (or the variance of that return). Several researchers have shown that the characterization of investors as one-period wealth maximizers can be relaxed with no loss in the model's rigor.[13] In addition, it is also possible to characterize the investment decision without resorting to the mean-variance criteria mentioned above.[14] Thus, as with the other simplifying assumptions of capital market theory, the one-period, expected-wealth maximization assumption does not severely restrict the model's application to the capital market as it actually exists.

If capital market theory describes how securities are priced, then it should be testable through empirical research. Positive tests would indicate that the capital market values securities on the basis of their expected risk and return. These tests are known as tests of market efficiency.

In recent years there have been many empirical tests of market efficiency, categorized conveniently into three types: weak-form, semistrong-form, and strong-form tests.[15] Weak-form tests have sought to demonstrate that successive changes in security prices are substantially independent and that through using only historical data the currently observed price is the best estimate of the "intrinsic" value of that security. The semistrong-form tests have attempted to show that all public information is fully reflected in stock prices or, in other words, that security prices appear to adjust quickly to public announcements concerning a company. Strong-form tests of the efficient market hypothesis have tried to prove that all available information, both public and private, is reflected in the market price of a security.[16]

Weak-form tests of market efficiency are principally concerned with determining whether "profits" can be made on the basis of security price behavior. The empirical research is best described as voluminous and demonstrates that for periods of a day or longer, security returns follow a "random walk" pattern. This randomness in security returns supports the notion that current price is the best, although an imperfect, predictor of future returns. Semistrong tests, in which prices presumably reflect all obviously public information, also support the efficient market hypothesis. Among the most important tests have been studies concerning stock splits, earnings announcements, new issues, and large block secondary issues. The common conclusion is that the information embodied in these announcements is, on average, already fully reflected in the security's price.

Strong-form efficient market tests are probably best viewed as a benchmark against which market efficiency can be judged. Two important deviations have so far been found. The first is that specialists on the major exchanges do have monopolistic access to information about buy and sell orders and can profitably act on the information. The second is that corporate insiders, as one would expect, often have access to nonmarket information about their own firms. Other evidence of investors with "monopolistic information," however, has been lacking. Perhaps the most noteworthy investigation supporting the strong-form efficient market hypothesis is Jensen's study of mutual fund performance.[17] His conclusion is that despite their extensive research, wide-ranging contacts, and daily participation in the marketplace, mutual funds are unable to forecast returns well enough to even recover their own research and transaction costs.

In summary, the exceptions that apparently exist to the efficient capital market hypothesis typically relate to situations where nonmarket information would be expected to exist. While some of the methods developed to test empirically the various forms of the efficient market hypothesis are still controversial and some researchers have discovered examples of apparent imperfections in the valuation of securities,[18] the efficient capital market hypothesis has not been seriously jeopardized.[19] The strength of this hypothesis lies not in the absolute sense that every asset or security is correctly priced at all times, but rather that when viewing all securities over time, the "overvaluations" by the market and the "undervaluations" will tend to balance out.[20]

One final issue that has often arisen out of empirical research using capital market theory is the apparently low explanatory power of security betas. Typically, betas explain 30 to 50 percent of a security's return performance, while the remaining 50 to 70 percent is security specific. Critics ask how good decisions can be made on what appears to be relatively low levels of confidence. What they overlook is that once reasonable portfolio diversification has occurred, beta becomes very significant in its explanatory power. In a well-diversified portfolio of eight securities, beta explains approximately 70 percent of the portfolio's return, while at sixteen securities, over 80 percent is explained. In addition, critics forget the econometric basis from which security betas are derived. In virtually all the social sciences, including economics, the ability to explain 30 to 50 percent of an individual's behavior in terms of group behavior is quite noteworthy. The relevant conclusion for users of capital market risk measures is that while individual betas should be used with a great deal of caution, portfolio betas are quite usable.

Implications for the Diversification Decision

The financial orientation of the risk/return model tells managers that a candidate for a diversifying acquisition must be evaluated as an investment decision. The key issue to be considered is the free cash flow and systematic risk of the company to be acquired and its impact on the risk/return complexion of the acquiring company. Furthermore, since price reflects the interaction of risk and return, managers must obviously be concerned with the cost of a diversifying acquisition. Using this model, managers would ask of the acquisition candidate:

1. What is the systematic risk and market required rate of return of this company?

2. Does the price of the acquisition candidate accurately reflect its expected free cash flow discounted at its required rate of return?

3. If the acquisition is made, how would the systematic risk and expected free cash flow of the combined company change?

4. What would be the net effect of this acquisition on the market value of the combined company?

This effect can be viewed in terms of where the acquisition places the combined company on the capital asset pricing model line described in Figure 5-8. Figure 5-9 depicts the situation where company *A* acquires a riskier company *B*. The merged company *C* has a different risk/return profile from the original company *A* and will thus be valued accordingly by the market. However, since the combined company remains on the capital market line, no value has been created. Only at points above the line *AB* (such as *C'*), where for a given risk the return is increased or where for a given return the risk is decreased, will the shareholders' position be improved. Assuming the market efficiently prices risk and return, a company's position above the line *AB* will be repriced such that

FIGURE 5-9. Impact of a Diversifying Acquisition

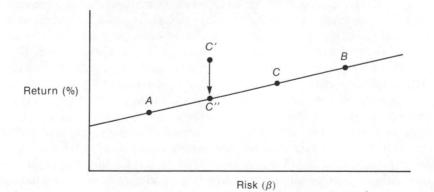

its risk/return profile once again lies on the line (such as C''). This movement from C' to C'' recognizes the improved risk/return relationships and accordingly increases the value of the company.

The market value of the combined company reflects two things: the systematic risk (β) of the combined company and the returns of the combined company to its investors. The risk/return model does not tell managers whether one level of risk and return is more desirable than another, but only how the market values various levels of risk and return. This enables managers to determine whether a combination of the two companies' risks and returns will lead to the creation of value for their shareholders.

Whether or not corporate diversification through acquisition has, in practice, created real economic value has been the focus of numerous capital market studies. These studies have attempted to test (1) whether stockholders of acquiring firms earn abnormal returns from mergers[21] or (2) whether the separation of control from ownership in the modern corporations frees managers to pursue sales growth, in contrast to profitability, as their primary goal.[22] Surprisingly, the bulk of the empirical research in the late 1960s strongly refutes the former notion. The researchers' consensus was that mergers had a negative effect on the profitability of the acquiring company and a neutral effect on the sum of the acquiring plus acquired companies. The implication was that corporate mergers occurred primarily to increase corporate size rather than for profitability.

Several recent analyses of the profitability of corporate mergers lead to more tempered conclusions. Mandelker, after adjusting returns for systematic risk, concluded that the market for acquisitions is perfectly competitive.[23] In other words, acquiring companies pay prices for acquisitions that enable them to earn a normal, or risk-adjusted, rate of return. He also found, however, that the stockholders of the acquired company earned abnormal returns in the months preceding the merger and that significant changes in beta, or systematic risk, typically accompanied corporate mergers. Following these results, Haugen and Langetieg analyzed these changes in systematic risk to determine whether "synergism," or a change in risk greater than what one could expect from portfolio diversification, occurred.[24] Their conclusion was that a statistically significant change in systematic risk beyond that of portfolio diversification did not occur. Dodd and Ruback further refined these procedures to focus on security return behavior in the month in which a tender offer is made.[25] The tender announcement is usually the first public information concerning a target company's acquisition potential. Dodd and Ruback concluded that in the month of the tender announcement, the acquisition target's shareholders earn large and significant abnormal returns (18 to 20 percent). Surprisingly, stockholders of companies making successful tender offers also seem to earn abnormal returns (less than 3 percent) in the offering month. In all cases, no abnormal returns could be found after the tender offer.[26]

These empirical studies lead to two important conclusions. First, the acquired company's shareholders, through the tender premium, receive the preponderance of any potential benefits to arise from a merger. Second, and highly important for public policy decision making, no abnormal or monopoly returns seem to accrue to acquiring companies in general.

These findings, along with the evidence cited in Chapter 1 concerning the efficiency of corporate portfolio diversification, provide an extremely difficult challenge to managers of diversifying companies. Their task is to improve their companies' risk/return profiles so that shareholder wealth is increased. Thus, in the language of the risk/return model, *diversification decisions should meet at least one of the following conditions: either they should (1) reduce the level of systematic risk below that of a comparable portfolio of securities without reducing expected returns or (2) increase returns above those of a comparable portfolio without increasing systematic risk*. More generally, top managers of diversified companies should encourage investment decisions that reduce the variability of returns or increase returns to investors to a greater extent than those available through simple portfolio diversification. The nature of these investment decisions and their underlying financial and operating logic can be deduced from the risk/return model.

Using the Risk/Return Model

The general conclusion of recent empirical research on the profitability of diversification through acquisition is that acquiring companies, on average, earn only normal or risk-adjusted rates of return on their investments in acquired companies. While this provides little apparent support for corporate diversification through acquisition, it is a strong statement about the efficiency of the capital markets. All is not lost, however, for corporations interested in diversification through acquisition.[27] An efficient capital market still allows for exceptional corporate performance and high value acquisitions; in fact, it expects instances of each as well as instances of disastrous results. What a diversifying corporation (or any investor) needs to remember is that slightly above average performance on a consistent basis will achieve spectacular long-run results. Here lies the challenge of the risk/return model to managers of diversifying companies: that of identifying and making only those acquisitions that have a greater value to the diversifying company's shareholders than the price paid for the acquisition. The risk/return model, however, also aids managers in meeting this challenge. Like the strategy and product/market-portfolio models, the risk/return model suggests certain guidelines for achieving consistent, above average performance. We can usefully begin our discussion of these guidelines by focusing first on the model's general prescriptions for management and then turning to the more specific implications for the decision to diversify through acquisitions.

The general prescriptions of the risk/return model reflect its capital market orientation. Business decisions, whether they involve expansion, diversification, or liquidation, must be analyzed in terms of the investment's expected free cash flow and the risk of that cash flow. The specific insight provided by the risk/return model is that in a competitive marketplace where assets are traded, the relevant risk is not the total volatility of that cash flow but rather its volatility relative to the volatility of all other assets in the marketplace. This risk is known as systematic risk. The more closely an asset's cash flow volatility matches the market's volatility and the greater the magnitude of that volatility, the riskier that cash flow or asset will be. The greater an asset's systematic risk is, the greater the rate of return the market expects to earn on it, and the lower the asset's market value—relative to its expected cash flow. Once free cash flow and systematic risk are quantified, alternative investments can be readily compared on the basis of how much their estimated market value, or discounted free cash flow, exceeds their investment cost.

The relationship of free cash flow and systematic risk to market value suggests how managers can increase their company's market value. Given a business opportunity producing a cash flow, the risk/return model emphasizes that market value will be affected by managing systematic risk rather than unsystematic, or company specific risks. Ironically, managers spend most of their efforts on these very real company specific risks. Managers do this because company specific risks (such as competitive retaliation, labor relations, or even bankruptcy) are both obvious and immediate, as well as being potentially disastrous to personal and organizational welfare. The risk/return model argues, however, that management strategies that lead to either stabilized cash flows relative to the level of the economy, growth in free cash flow, or improved investor confidence about future cash flows will tend to lead to reduced systematic risk and increased market value for the firm.

The logic of the risk/return model thus suggests three management guidelines:

1. Managers should develop strategies for their business aimed at generating free cash flows that have as little relationship to the level of activity of the economy as possible. The most efficient strategies of systematic risk reduction are those that "decouple" business performance from that of the economy.

2. Managers should develop strategies that extend the time horizons of their business's cash flow or improve the growth rate of their business's cash flow. Both have the impact of shifting value into the future, and thereby reducing the company's systematic risk.

3. Managers should not forget the intuitively obvious point that future cash flows that can be forecast with greater confidence than otherwise possible will be less severely discounted by the marketplace and have a higher market value.

For companies considering diversification through acquisition as a strategic option, the risk/return model offers more specific guidelines than the ones stated above. It states that value creation through corporate diversification occurs only when the combination of two companies' skills and resources leads to either an increase in the income stream or a decrease in the systematic risk of the income stream greater than that available from a portfolio investment in the two companies.

Increased returns can be achieved when:

1. Related diversification leads to more effective utilization of the company's key skills and resources, thereby leading to lower unit costs and improved margins. In the language of the product/market-portfolio model, this occurs when distinct product markets have overlapping experience curves.

2. Unrelated diversification creates a larger set of investment opportunities within the corporation, from which a greater proportion of high-return projects are selected and managed.

3. Aggressive financial management within the diversified company improves working-capital management and employs greater levels of debt than otherwise possible.

Reduced systematic risk can be achieved when:

1. Related diversification has reduced the variability of a businesses's cash flow by increasing the size of the operating margin relative to the fixed costs of the business. In the language of the product/market-portfolio model, this occurs when a company becomes the low-cost producer or the dominant competitor within a business.

2. More effective asset selection and management by the diversified corporation generates either a faster-growing or more

stable free cash flow than available in a comparable portfolio of businesses.

3. Corporate diversification enables management to adopt high-business-risk strategies for individual businesses that have, or lead to, low systematic risk. Less-diversified companies may be unwilling to employ such strategies because of the potentially high organizational and financial costs accompanying them.

Managers need to consider carefully these risk/return guidelines for corporate diversification. The guidelines suggest that the benefits actually accompanying corporate diversification are much more limited in scope and magnitude than commonly perceived. In addition, not only must the benefits of the diversifying acquisition be judged relative to portfolio diversification, but the total cost of the acquisition must be included in the analysis. Only when the discounted cash flow of the acquisition, reflecting its integration into the diversifying company, exceeds its total purchase price (or market value plus tender premium plus transaction costs plus integration costs) will value be created for the diversifying company's shareholders. This establishes a very stiff set of standards for the diversifying acquisition to meet.

Nevertheless, the risk/return model does suggest that a well-designed and well-managed diversified company can provide real economic value for investors. In such a company, low-potential, high-present-value businesses will use the size and stability of their free cash flow to "feed and protect" high-potential, low-present-value businesses. The overall portfolio of businesses will thus produce a free cash flow with a low systematic risk that is being reinvested in opportunities that promise to become high-present-value businesses. This means that effective management of a diversified company's portfolio of businesses provides not only significant cash flow recycling benefits but also opportunities to reduce the company's systematic risk. Achieving either can lead to significantly higher market values for the diversified company.

Notes and References

1. See, for example, Harry Markowitz, "Portfolio Selection," *Journal of Finance* 7, March 1952; William F. Sharpe, "A Simplified Model for Portfolio Analysis," *Management Science* 9, January 1963; John Lintner, "Valuation of Risk Assets and the Selection of Risky Investments in Stock Portfolios and Capital Budgets," *Review of Economics and Statistics* 47, February 1965; and Fisher Black, Michael C. Jensen, and Myron Scholes, "The Capital Asset Pricing Model: Some Empirical Tests," in M. C. Jensen, ed., *Studies in the Theory of Capital Markets* (New York: Praeger, 1972).

2. In quantitative terms risk is defined as the standard deviation of possible outcomes around the expected value. Economists refer to the use of expected values and standard deviations as "mean-variance analysis."

3. The importance in investment analysis of comparing future cash flows to current cost (or value) was first articulated over forty years ago. J. B. Williams, *The Theory of Investment Value* (Cambridge: Harvard University Press, 1938), pp. 55–75.

4. While it is possible to forecast with reasonable accuracy the relationship between a diversified portfolio's return and the market's return over the short term on the basis of historical data, developing an accurate forecast of the market's return over that time period is considerably more difficult. This no doubt explains why investors and financial analysts spend so much of their time trying to find more accurate ways of predicting the market's short-term returns.

5. While U.S. Treasury bills are clearly the least risky asset in the marketplace, they are not totally free of systematic risk, as CAPM would indicate. This can be seen when one considers the inverse relationship between the level of interest rates and the level of stock prices. As most investors know, rising interest rates typically accompany falling stock prices and falling interest rates accompany rising prices. The covariance embodied in this relationship has caused some capital market theorists to develop more complex capital-asset pricing models using the rate of return on the "zero-beta," or no-covariance, portfolio in place of risk-free rates of return. For example, see Black, Jensen, and Scholes, "The Capital Asset Pricing Model."

6. The biases introduced by using these subsets form part of the basis for current criticisms of CAPM. See Richard Roll, "A Critique of the Asset Pricing Theory's Tests; Part 1: On Past and Potential Testability of the Theory," *Journal of Financial Economics* 4 (March 1977): 129–76.

7. L. Fisher and J. H. Lorie, "Rates of Return on Investments in Common Stock," *Journal of Business* 37 (January 1964): 1–21; and "Rates of Return on Investments in Common Stock: The Year by Year Record, 1926–1965," *Journal of Business* 41 (July 1968): 291–316.

8. Roger B. Ibbotson and Rex A. Sinquefield, "Stocks, Bonds, Bills, and Inflation: Year by Year Historical Returns (1926–1974)," *Journal of Business* 49 (January 1976): 11–47; and *Stocks, Bonds, Bills and Inflation: The Past (1926–1976) and the Future (1977–2000)*, Financial Analysts Research Foundation, Charlottesville, Va., 1977.

9. Another recent study of long-run rates of return for the period 1910 to 1976 has found even higher rates of inflation (3.1 percent) and lower risk premias (1.6 percent) for common stocks. This undoubtedly reflects the highly inflationary decade of 1910–1919. Robert M. Soldofsky and Dale F. Max, "Stocks and Bonds as Inflation Hedges," *MSU Business Topics*, Spring 1978, pp. 17–25.

10. Daniel M. Holland and Stewart C. Myers, *Trends in Corporate Profitability and Capital Costs*, Sloan School Working Paper, #999-78, Massachusetts Institute of Technology, May 1978.

11. Much of this discussion is drawn from S. C. Myers and S. M. Turnbull, "Capital Budgeting and the Capital Asset Pricing Model: Good News and Bad News," *Journal of Finance* 32, May 1977. See also Jack L. Treynor and Fisher Black, "Corporate Investment Decisions," in S. C. Myers, ed. *Modern Developments in Financial Management* (New York: Praeger, 1976), and Joseph T. Williams, "Capital Asset Prices with Heterogeneous Beliefs," *Journal of Financial Economics* 4, May 1977.

12. Theoretically, this correlation should be between the asset's cash flow and the total cash flow of all risky assets in the economy. The economy's level of activity, however, is closely correlated to this "total cash flow" and is certainly easier to discuss and measure.

13. See, for instance, E. F. Fama, "Multiperiod Consumption-Investment Decisions," *The American Economic Review* 60 (March 1970): 163–74.

14. An example is the arbitrage pricing theory model. See S. A. Ross, "The Arbitrage Theory of Capital Asset Pricing," *Journal of Economic Theory* 13 (December 1976): 341–60.

15. A cogent statement of these tests is presented in James C. Van Horne, *Financial Management and Policy* (Englewood Cliffs, N.J.: Prentice-Hall, 1977), pp. 46–48.

16. These tests and empirical evidence are summarized in James H. Lorie and Mary T. Hamilton, *The Stock Market* (Chicago: Richard D. Irwin, 1973), chap. 4; Jensen, *Studies in the Theory of Capital Markets;* and Eugene F. Fama, "Efficient Capital Markets: A Review of Theory and Empirical Work," *Journal of Finance* 26, May 1970, among others.

17. Michael C. Jensen, "Risk, the Pricing of Capital Assets, and the Evaluation of Investment Portfolios," *Journal of Business* 42 (April 1969): 167–247.

18. See, for example, Burton G. Malkiel, "The Valuation of Closed-End Investment-Company Shares," and S. Basu, "Investment Performance of Common Stocks in Relation to their Price-Earnings Ratios: A Test of the Efficient Market Hypothesis," both in the *Journal of Finance* 32, June 1977.

19. Recently, a new problem with the capital market theory and the capital-asset pricing model, in particular, has been identified. At issue is whether or not the model can ever be accurately tested since any test must rely on an index for the marketplace. Since this index is a subset of the entire marketplace, it and all measurements based on it may well be skewed or biased. See R. Roll, "A Critique of the Asset Pricing Theory's Tests; Part 1: On Past and Potential Testability of the Theory," *Journal of Financial Economics* 4, March 1977. The development of the arbitrage pricing theory model has been spurred by this argument, since it avoids CAPM's reliance on a market index. See Ross, "The Arbitrage Theory of Capital Asset Pricing."

20. This situation is exactly what a supporter of free capital markets would hope for. While many businessmen and professionals in the financial markets strongly attack the efficient market hypothesis conclusion as being heresy, they are missing its true message. They claim numerous market imperfections and often state that efficient capital market theory implies that the work

of financial analysts and advisers is superfluous. In actuality, however, this is not what the model suggests. It concludes that these individuals as well as individual investors are doing their job so well that few additional opportunities for excess profits can be found. Furthermore, the notion of efficient capital markets is essentially Darwinian in that it allows for a few outstanding performers as well as a few miserable ones. Efficient capital market theory's warning, however, is that, in aggregate, the total performance of all participants in the marketplace must equal the market's performance *less* all those costs incurred by the participants in trying to achieve their performance goals. Since investment management costs must be subtracted from the market's return, the total performance of all investors in the marketplace will be worse than the market's performance. This implies that while some investors will do better than the market, most will do worse.

21. This is the classic rationale for corporate mergers.

22. The second option follows from arguments that date back to Berle and Means (1932) and intertwine with behavioral theories of the firm developed in the last two decades.

23. Gershon Mandelker, "Risk and Return: The Case of Merging Firms," *Journal of Financial Economics* 1 (December 1974): 303–35.

24. Robert A. Haugen and Terence C. Langetieg, "An Empirical Test for Synergism in Merger," *Journal of Finance* 30 (September 1975): 1003–14.

25. Peter Dodd and Richard Ruback, "Tender Offers and Stockholder Returns: An Empirical Analysis," *Journal of Financial Economics* 5 (December 1977): 351–73.

26. If the market for acquisitions is looked at as an auction where the acquisition targets are companies that are either undervalued or whose assets are underutilized, these conclusions are easy to explain. In such an environment, a tender offer announces the target company's underperformance to the marketplace. If more than one firm can improve the operations of the acquisition target (or recognize its investment value), a bidding process begins that will stop only when all but one potential acquirer has either run out of resources or has reached a price that no longer enables a "normal" return to be earned. Nevertheless, at this price a portion of the target's potential value to the acquirer may remain unpaid for. Shareholders of the acquisition target are the ones who obviously gain, since the bidding process leads to a price higher than the market would pay for the company's previously expected performance. Even if only one company can make these improvements or take advantage of the acquisition target's operations, the acquisition's shareholders will still reap most of the potential gains, since they must "accept" the purchase offer. Finally, even if a tender offer fails, the information concerning the target company has been disseminated into the marketplace and typically forces management to improve corporate performance.

An analysis of merger and acquisition profitability within Great Britain's brewing and distillery industries has led to similar conclusions for the United Kingdom's capital market. Once again, shareholders of acquired companies earned significant, abnormal returns prior to the merger, while the shareholders of acquiring firms earned positive though small abnormal returns. After the merger, no abnormal returns could be found. See J. R. Franks, J. E. Boyles, and M. J. Hecht, ''An Industry Study of the Profitability of Mergers in the United Kingdom,'' *Journal of Finance* 32 (December 1977): 1513–25.

27. The diversifying company may find in its analyses that even though it stands to earn only a normal rate of return on an acquisition, the acquisition may be much cheaper in terms of time, management involvement, and financial investment than attempting similar diversification efforts through internal development.

CHAPTER 6

Perspectives on Value Creation

THE INTELLECTUAL HISTORY of each of the three models discussed in the preceding chapters shows an evolution in strategic thinking from a qualitative, subjective approach to value creation to more quantitative, market-based approaches. This evolution received its impetus not only from the increasingly complex planning task faced by growth companies during the past thirty years but also more directly from the carefully worked out concepts and ideas of researchers in both universities and industry.

Initially conceived as an aid in formulating and evaluating strategies of predominantly single-business enterprises, the strategy model stresses how the broad range of relationships between an enterprise and its operating environment can be profitably managed. The product/market-portfolio model, developed in response to the special resource allocation problems facing multiproduct and multibusiness companies, focuses on the problem of what businesses to invest in heavily, which to maintain, and which to liquidate or manage for cash. In contrast to the strategy model, it is based on a set of testable hypotheses relating cash flow performance and overall profitability to the market share and market growth characteristics of companies' component businesses. The intellectual history of the risk/return model reveals over twenty years of empirical, statistically based research devoted to demonstrating how the wealth position of rational, risk-adverse, and well-informed investors operating in reasonably efficient capital markets can be maintained or improved.

The common preoccupation of each model with the creation (and maintenance) of value, whether viewed from a managerial or an investor's perspective, provides an opportunity for integrating them into a single analytical framework. Thus, the purpose of this chapter is to explain the conceptual links among the three models and show how they provide complementary perspectives on the creation of economic value. The Appendix to this chapter (p. 272) elaborates our views on the complementarity, or lack thereof, in managers' and investors' objectives implicit in each of the models. In Chapters 7 through 10 we will discuss in detail how the framework summarized in this chapter can be usefully applied to the selection of diversification objectives, the development of acquisition guidelines, the design of acquisition screening systems, and the careful analysis of diversifying acquisitions.

Conceptual Links among the Three Models

Common Underpinnings: A Fundamental Concern with Risk

Economic value is created when the price or present value of a specific asset's future returns exceeds the cost of creating or acquiring that asset. When the price of an asset increases, it reflects a revised estimate by buyers in the marketplace of either the size (greater), the life (longer), or the timing (sooner) of its future cash flows; it can also reflect an increased ability of the market to predict the size, life, or timing of an asset's future cash flows. As the predictability of an asset's future cash flow increases (or, alternatively, as the variability of expected returns decreases), an asset's level of risk decreases, all other things being equal. In managerial terms, an asset's risk level decreases when managers are successful in reducing the marketplace's uncertainty about that asset's future returns. The problem of coping with risk and the uncertainty of the marketplace is a fundamental concern of each model—although, as we will shortly see, each approaches the problem from a somewhat different perspective.

As summarized in Table 6-1, each model focuses on different levels of economic activity and therefore defines risk somewhat differently. The

TABLE 6-1. Perspectives on Risk Suggested by the Three Models

	Level of Analysis	Principal Risk Measure
STRATEGY MODEL	Operating level	Total risk (environmental, managerial, financial)
PRODUCT/MARKET-PORTFOLIO MODEL	Corporate level	Business portfolio risk
RISK-RETURN MODEL	Capital Market level	Market-related or systematic risk

strategy model focuses on predominantly single-business enterprises or operating units. We can call this level of economic activity the "operating level." Risk at the operating level can be assessed in two ways: (1) management's subjective judgment of the variability of returns in their particular business and (2) management's ability to predict future financial performance of the business through the budgeting and resource allocation process.

The two methods of assessing risk at the operating level imply very different risk measures. The so-called "judgmental approach" to measuring business risk can best be characterized by two questions that are often raised in the planning process: What factors could negatively affect this business and how likely are they? and What is the downside risk of this business? In answering these questions, the many variables that influence potential returns are typically listed and their importance evaluated. The so-called "forecasting approach" to measuring business risk is based on the budget. The business's risk can be measured by analyzing the accuracy of budgets as predictors of financial performance, the basic concept being that individual businesses whose financial performance characteristics are easiest to predict, either because of the skill of management or the basic stability of the business, will have the lowest risk. Thus, from the perspective of the strategy model, the role of the general manager is to get a measure of control over the variability of business profits by influencing its underlying determinants.

The product/market-portfolio model focuses on a company's portfolio of products or businesses. The level of analysis assumed by the model is that of corporate headquarters—or possibly a group vice president—in a diversified company. We can refer to this level of analysis as the "corporate level," recognizing that in widely diversified companies there are often intermediate levels of general management responsible for managing a portfolio of businesses.

Risk at the corporate or group level of a diversified company can be defined as the predictability and stability of cash flows associated with a portfolio of businesses that has been assigned a targeted (or expected) growth rate. This portfolio will normally include product markets in the development or "takeoff" stage as well as product markets in maturity or declining stages of their life cycle. In this context, the greater the opportunity for a diversified company to utilize internally its cash flow by subsidizing on a consistent basis less-established, high-potential businesses needing cash for growth with the excess cash throwoff of maturing businesses, the greater the chance of meeting the company's objectives and the less risk that portfolio of businesses presents to corporate level management.

The fundamental proposition of the product/market-portfolio model is that a "balanced" portfolio of businesses with a high market share and promising new ventures leads to sustained corporate growth and more sure cash flow returns to the corporate office. Thus, from the perspective of this model, top management's job is to integrate and balance cash flow streams coming from businesses at various stages in their life cycle so that overall financial objectives for the company are achieved.

The risk/return model adopts the perspective of well-informed rational investors operating in a reasonably efficient market. The level of analysis assumed by this model can therefore be called the "capital market level." The risk measure associated with this level of analysis lends itself to sophisticated statistical expression. It addresses the uncertainty of future cash flows to the investor. More specifically, since the price of an asset in an efficient market is an expression of the present value of expected future cash flows, investors are concerned with the uncertainty of an asset's future cash flows. The degree of volatility in an asset's past returns provides a basis for measuring current risk and predicting future risk. The most common measure of this volatility is the standard deviation of the returns. The more volatile an asset's historical returns, the greater the standard deviation and the less confidence the investor will probably have in predicting future returns.

This standard deviation of an asset's returns includes both systematic and unsystematic risk. Since unsystematic risk can be eliminated through efficient portfolio diversification, it is an asset's systematic risk, reflecting the response of an asset's cash flow return to broad changes in the economy, that is most important to the investor and to the risk/return model.

Each of the three models assumes a successively higher level of economic analysis, ranging from the basic operating level of business activity to the capital market level. The risk measures associated with each model naturally reflect these different perspectives on economic activity and corporate performance. Taken together, each risk measure contributes to a logical progression from an intuitive and subjective concept of risk to a more objective, market-related concept. This progression reflects the interests of three important groups of "players": operating level managers, corporate or group level managers, and investors.

The Concept of Value Creation

While focusing on the notion of risk allows us to see the common underpinnings of each model, only an examination of their relationship to the concept of value creation can reveal how the three models complement each other in a conceptual sense. We will move to such an examination after a brief commentary of the notion of value.

The value of a business, its underlying assets, or its securities can be measured in many ways. Indeed, the term value is used in economic, business, and legal phraseology with a wide variety of meanings. Some of the many kinds of value have been identified as follows:

> *assessed value* for the purposes of property taxation; *condemnation value* awarded as payment in takings by right of eminent domain; *book value*, as derived from accounting statements; *replacement value* of existing fixed tangible business assets; *going concern value* of assets of at least potentially profitable business enterprises; *liquidating value* of assets on dissolution of a business; *collateral value*, representing the amount that may be borrowed on the pledge of an asset; *fair value*, used as a base for public regulation of utility rates; *sales value*, representing the anticipated realization upon sale under various conditions; *intrinsic* or *investment value*, which is established by well informed and highly rational investors; *market value*, usually determined from actual prices, or bids and offerings in some sort of "market" (which implies the existence of potential buyers and sellers), though it may be imputed by estimate; and *fair market value* that adds to the concept of market value the assumption of the existence of a large number of buyers and sellers.[1]

Most of the methods of valuing a business, whether it be publicly or privately held, fall into two main categories: those that emphasize asset values (such as book value, replacement value, and liquidation value), and those that stress the value of an ongoing income stream (such as going concern value, intrinsic value, and market value). Both methods depend upon establishing estimates of worth in terms of cash. While no valuation approach is without its conceptual problems, the notion of market value (or, more precisely, fair market value) is the most appropriate starting point for thinking about the creation of real economic value because it is the least subjective estimate of what an asset or its income stream is worth.

Market value is that price at which informed and willing buyers and sellers exchange assets or securities, which are merely financial claims on assets. Stated in terms of the concept of present value, market value can be understood as an equilibrium point balancing buying and selling prices for future returns among investors with differing perceptions of present value. It is useful to emphasize the mundane point that investors typically have different perceptions of an asset's present value. Indeed, investors trade assets precisely because they have a differing judgment than the marketplace of the current worth of future values. Thus, the effect of a market transaction is to establish a compromise measure of investors' estimates of an asset's present value. Since buyers and sellers are presumably acting in their basic self-interest, "the bloodless verdict of the marketplace" is a practical expression of present value that should be preferred to more subjective, individual expressions of value.

If market value is a practical measure of future worth, it is also a measure of relative worth. The market price of an asset at any point in

time reflects its worth in relation to that of all other investment opportunities. The price of an asset in a free market therefore serves as an
effective common denominator of all the current ideas of the worth of an
asset or a security as compared with other investment opportunities.[2]

It is commonly presumed that the market value of a company or any
capital asset can be represented by a simple revision of the present value
(*PV*) formula presented in Chapter 5

$$MV = \sum_{t=1}^{n} D_t/(1 + R)^t$$

where *MV* is the market value of a company, D_t is the return or income
stream that is to be received by the investor in each time period, and *R* is
the discount rate or rate of return appropriate to that income stream's
risk. In converting from *PV* to *MV*, market estimates have replaced
personal estimates of *D, t,* and *R*. According to this formula, market value
will increase if the expected income stream increases, or the time horizon
of the expected income stream increases, or the discount rate decreases.

The *MV* formula or concept of market value is applicable in all market
economies and is critical to many management decisions: *investments
should be made only when the expected returns have a greater market
value than the cost of the investment*. It is also especially useful to
diversified companies. It helps strategists demonstrate concretely how
diversification can affect their companies' market value and how diversified companies can increase (or vary) their market value by seizing one
or more of their numerous investment opportunities.

We will demonstrate in the following discussion how each of the three
analytic models provides complementary perspectives on the process of
value creation as defined by market based measures. Our discussion will
proceed by breaking apart the market value formula or framework into its
component parts—cash flow and the risk-adjusted rate of return—and
showing what each of the models contributes to an understanding of these
basic determinants of market value.

Cash Flow: Impact on Market Value

The key variable to be considered in any valuation process and market
transaction is the return or income stream that will arise from an asset.
This income stream represents the future values available to the owner for
either consumption or further investment. The strategy, product/market-
portfolio, and risk/return models all help define what is meant by an
asset's income stream.

The strategy model defines an income stream in terms of business profits. Profits, before the advent of many modern accounting complexities, the extensive use of credit, and the impact of inflation, closely corresponded to the cash a company had left after paying all its bills. However, this correspondence has been greatly reduced in the last twenty years. Revenues now include business done on credit, though no cash has been received. Expenses include historical depreciation with little relevance to replacement or economic costs. The one-year accounting cycle often has no relevance to the company's operating cycle. In short, where a business's profit once had real economic meaning, today it has little correspondence to a firm's real income or the unencumbered cash it generates through its activities. It is therefore not surprising that many managers using the analytical approach suggested by the strategy model now prefer to think in terms of cash flow rather than accounting profits.

The product/market-portfolio model has helped focus management attention on the importance of cash flow to a business. The model emphasizes that cash is the only asset that can be invested in a business or paid out to its investors. Since cash is both the original asset inflow and the ultimate asset outflow from the company, it can (and should) serve as the basic measure of return.

The product/market-portfolio model also focuses on cash flow over an asset's life, where cash flow is defined as new funds actually available to the company after investments have been made to support that asset's continued existence. This means that even though an asset might be profitable in an operating sense, it is considered to be a cash user if it requires additional cash investment to sustain its productivity. Only assets generating cash that can either be paid out to investors or invested in new assets are considered truly profitable.

The risk/return model looks at returns in what appears to be a very different manner. It defines returns as dividends (or interest) plus capital appreciation over one time period, the risk/return model's time horizon. However, the price of the asset, in this case a security, at the end of period 1 will depend upon its expected cash flow in period 2 and its price at the end of period 2, the price at the end of period 2 will depend on its expected cash flow in period 3 and its price at the end of period 3, and so on. The price of an asset at any time, therefore, reflects investors' estimates of future cash returns; capital appreciation (depreciation) merely reflects changes in investor estimates of this future cash flow. The risk/return model is thus based on investor estimates of the cash a company will pay out over its lifetime to its investors. The cash paid by the company to its owners must, however, come out of the company's cash balances. This means that a strong correlation exists between the cash flow from securities and internal corporate cash flow; in fact, over the company's lifetime this correlation equals 1. The fact that cash flow to investors depends on the cash flow of a company's underlying assets explains why sophisticated investors concentrate their attention on estimating a company's cash flow.

We can see that all three models are directly concerned with a company's free cash flow, or D_t. Free cash flow can be defined as cash flow from operations after the reinvestment necessary to maintain or support the current level of productivity of existing assets has been made. Free cash flow is therefore available for (1) investments to improve a business' competitive situation (such as increased market share), (2) investments to exploit growth opportunities, and (3) payout to debt and equity investors. It is important to note that equity investors will be indifferent to reinvestment or payout when the rate of return on the company's projects equals the investors' required rate of return; if a company's new projects have a rate of return in excess of investors' required rate of return, then investors will prefer reinvestment to dividend payout, and if the rate of return is lower than required, they will prefer payout.[3] Assuming reinvestment of current free cash flow, a company's future free cash flow will come from three sources: (1) free cash flow from the company's existing business assets, (2) free cash flow from additional investment (or disinvestment) in the existing business, and (3) free cash flow from investments in new business opportunities. Since market value reflects the free cash flow available to investors, corporate managers like investors can correctly focus their attention on free cash flow.

Given this definition of free cash flow, one that is compatible with the concepts underlying each of the three models, what do the three models have to say about the creation of cash flows? As we shall see, the strategy and product/market-portfolio models have the most to contribute to an understanding of this process.

The basic economic challenge facing a business is to exploit profit opportunities with its available resources. While the initial identification of a profit opportunity and application of resources to this opportunity is typically an entrepreneurial action, the subsequent refining of this match is a basic task of general management. If the opportunity has been met successfully, a positive cash flow will develop. As the strategy model suggests, the size and nature of the cash flow will depend on the economic and structural characteristics of the opportunity and the skills and resources used in meeting it.

The strategy model provides several explicit prescriptions on how to improve the match between profit opportunities and corporate resources and thereby increase the resulting cash flow. According to the model, one of the primary objectives of management should be the development or reinforcement of the company's distinctive competence. This distinctive competence, or the ability to perform some valued function particularly well, will lead to either greater utility to the purchaser or a reduction in costs. Either way, cash flow will be increased. Alternatively, management can concentrate on developing a unique competitive position, such as exploiting limited resources or creating a new or more efficient product. Once again the effect will be an increased cash flow. In short, the strategy model emphasizes that the better the skills and/or resources of an enterprise that can be applied to its environmental opportunities, the greater its prospective returns. Managements utilizing the strategy model thus seek to identify the critical success requirements for a perceived opportunity and then to provide the required resources.

The product/market-portfolio model builds upon the strategy model in identifying means of increasing cash flows. It does this by focusing attention on certain competitive characteristics that have typically augmented cash flows. The basic goal of companies using a product/market-portfolio approach to strategic planning is to obtain a dominant market share position for as many of its products or businesses as possible. The value of a market share arises from the lower unit costs that typically accrue to the dominant producer in the market. This means that the dominant company will have the lowest costs within a product/market and the highest margins given a single product price. Since obtaining market share is most easily done during a product/market's growth period, the product/market-portfolio model naturally argues for aggressive investment in growing businesses.

The superior cost position of the enterprise with dominant market share leads to two important benefits as the industry matures. First, the achievement of lowest unit costs and highest unit sales contribute to a significantly higher cash flow than any other competitor. Second, if the relevant product market has normal "life cycle" characteristics, the dominant competitor will find that it has both an improving market share position and the longest cash flow life span as its less-efficient (higher-cost) competitors find the product market turning less attractive economically and leave.

The scenario of investing for market share during industry growth and then "milking" that position as the industry matures leaves two implementation questions unanswered: Where do the investment funds come from for aggressive market share expansion? and What should be done with the excess free cash flow that develops? This is where the concept of product/market portfolios has special relevance. First, if a business can profitably recycle its free cash flow into new opportunities, it is in a position to generate a perpetual income stream for its investors rather than one with a limited life span. Furthermore, if the company in its recycling of cash flow can exploit growth opportunities, it obtains two benefits: new dominant market share positions and an increasing free cash flow. The product/market-portfolio model therefore has a well-defined prescription for increasing a company's cash flow: Invest aggressively for market share in growing industries (those with significant opportunities) using, when available, the high free cash flow generated by mature businesses that have a dominant market share.

The methods for maximizing cash flow provided by the strategy and product/market-portfolio models complement each other closely. Both emphasize the value of aggresively exploiting market opportunities and obtaining dominant competitive positions. The roles of "distinctive competence" and "accumulated experience" in achieving market power are roughly equivalent. In addition, while the product/market-portfolio model says to invest in market share, the strategy model says how to do that investing most effectively.

The product/market-portfolio model adds an important dimension to the strategic analysis suggested by the strategy model. It emphasizes the benefits of having a portfolio of product/market opportunities, some growing and some dying. Ideally, these growing opportunities should be exploited by harnessing the company's existing skills and resources in such a way that the highest income stream possible will result. An ability to generate a sustained, growing free cash flow by this means will lead to a higher market value for the company as long as the company's new investments have a rate of return greater than the cost of investment funds. Determining this cost is the focus of the risk/return model.

Risk-Adjusted Rate of Return: Impact on Market Value

While most managers have been primarily concerned with managing the size of cash flows, investors have been concerned with managing the risks of their cash flows. This separation of concerns and functions arises from the differing responsibilities of each. Investors in most market economies have become suppliers of capital with little say in a company's management. The investor's choice is either to supply capital or withhold it. Managers, however, use the capital and produce a return for their investors, usually in the form of dividends or interest on the investment. Since corporate managers have control over both the size and timing of the cash flow their investors receive, the investor has to base his investment decision on whether that cash flow meets or exceeds his expectations. These expectations are the investor's opportunity cost for giving up current value for future value or, alternatively, his required rate of return. This required rate of return depends largely on the uncertainty or risk of the investment.

Because the capital market is composed of numerous securities or claims on real assets, the investor can choose among alternative assets with more or less risky cash flows. When the cash flows of risky assets are compared with one another, their volatility or risk can be decomposed into two parts. One risk is asset-specific and diversifiable, the other is market-related and nondiversifiable. Since the former risk can be easily eliminated from an investor's portfolio, only the latter is relevant to his investment decision as emphasized by the risk/return model. We can recall that this risk element, the measure of a cash flow's volatility relative to the cash flow of all other assets or the marketplace, is called systematic risk. Its most important characteristic is that it is not an absolute measure of risk but rather a comparative measure.

The competition by investors in the capital marketplace for the acquisition of assets (represented by securities with accompanying cash flows) has meant that a market assessment of the cost of risk is available. The cost of the market's level of risk is the incremental or additional rate of return over the risk-free rate of return obtained by investors owning the market's portfolio of risky assets. As explained earlier, this cost—commonly referred to as the market's risk premium—can be expressed as $(R_m - R_f)$. The risk premium for a specific asset in the marketplace will be its systematic risk times the market's risk premium or $B_i(R_m - R_f)$. The asset's risk-adjusted rate of return will be the risk-free rate of return plus the asset's risk premium, or $R_i = R_f + B_i(R_m - R_f)$. Where the risk/return model is used in a predictive capacity, expected values, or E( ), should be used for each of the variables.

Investors and managers who want to influence their risk-adjusted rate of return must concentrate their attention on systematic risk, because the rates of return on the marketplace (R_m) and the risk-free asset (R_f) are variables over which they have no control. Only by adjusting the level of systematic risk can they change the rate of return required for (and obtained from) owning an asset or portfolio of assets. As we have seen, managers can reduce their company's systematic risk and risk-adjusted rate of return in four ways: (1) by reducing the company's cash flow volatility relative to that of the economy as a whole, (2) by increasing the time horizon over which cash flows are received, (3) by increasing the size of the cash flows to occur in future time periods, and (4) by improving the ability to forecast future cash flows.

Turning to the first means of reducing systematic risk, we need to identify those factors affecting a company's relative cash flow volatility. Two factors are particularly noteworthy: (1) the relationship between the demand for a company's products or services and the pattern of demand throughout the economy as a whole and (2) the degree of operating and financial leverage selected by the company.

Where the demand for a company's products or services is highly dependent on the general level of economic activity, a high level of systematic risk will probably exist. Where managers can develop strategies that serve to decouple their business's level of demand from that of the economy, systematic risk will be reduced. Such "decoupling strategies" include developing a distinctive competence to service specialized demands, as suggested by the strategy model, or securing long-term contracts from customers along with equally long-term, fixed-price contracts from suppliers. In addition, the product/market-portfolio model suggests a third decoupling strategy: obtaining a dominant market share position. Market share tends to stabilize demand, while accumulated experience tends to stabilize costs. Like the first two strategies, achieving market share dominance will tend to reduce the volatility of a company's cash flow relative to that of the economy as a whole.

Much has been written on the impact of operating leverage and financial leverage on cash flow. Since both forms of leverage entail fixed supply costs that cannot be easily reduced as demand falls off, highly leveraged companies face larger swings in their cash flow than unleveraged companies as demand rises and falls. Highly leveraged companies therefore tend to have a high degree of systematic risk, which can be reduced, of course, at the discretion of management. A reduction in operating or financial leverage will not reduce the cyclical pattern of a company's cash flow; however, such action will reduce the amplitude of the company's cash flow volatility. When this volatility relative to that of the economy is reduced, the company's systematic risk and risk-adjusted rate of return will decline.

The second and third factors affecting a company's systematic risk are the timing and size of its future returns. As indicated by the risk/return model, a security's returns can be decomposed into two parts: the actual cash returns or dividends received during a time period and the capital appreciation or change in price that occurred during the time period. Generally speaking, the longer the period over which returns are expected for the future or the larger these expected future returns, the less exposed a company is to current fluctuations in the economy. Thus, if managers can develop strategies that lengthen the time horizon over which an expected return occurs and undertake projects that promise growing cash flow streams, value is transferred further into the future and the company's systematic risk is reduced.

There is an important concept underlying this plausible argument. Investors tend to revise their expectations about future returns (as reflected in a security's price) by a smaller amount than the difference between the returns expected during the most recent time period and those actually received. (These revisions were referred to as "elasticities of expectations" in Chapter 5.) In other words, if a company's returns decline by 20 percent during a given time period relative to investor expectations, it is unlikely that investors will reduce their expectations about future returns (which will be reflected in a security's price) by as great a percentage. Thus, if managers can emphasize the importance of future returns relative to current returns, they can lower their company's systematic risk.

The strategy model quite naturally presumes that long-lived and growing cash flows are desirable. The product/market-portfolio model suggests two ways of attaining this. In markets exposed to the dynamics of product life cycles, those companies achieving high market share will tend to have longer periods over which they can expect to be viable competitors generating free cash flows than their lower market share competitors. Furthermore, where companies are able to construct a portfolio of mature businesses that can fund the development of growing businesses, a perpetual and growing income stream can be created.

The product/market-portfolio model also suggests how a "balanced" portfolio can affect a company's systematic risk. When multiple cash flows with different risks exist within a company's asset portfolio, the present value of each income stream increases as the time horizon increases but not at the same rate. The lower risk income streams are discounted less severely so that their importance to the portfolio relative to higher risk income streams increases as the time horizon increases. In other words, the longer the time horizon, the greater the impact of safer income streams and the lower the composite systematic risk, or beta, for the portfolio. In addition, as time passes, those growing cash flow streams that were initially quite volatile tend to mature and become less volatile. Because of their increasing size and decreasing volatility, these cash flow streams have the effect of becoming the portfolio's highly weighted, low-risk investments.

The fourth factor influencing systematic risk is the degree to which investors change future expectations when the results for the current time period differ from those originally expected. The degree to which investors change their expectations is closely related to the accuracy of their forecasts. The more accurate an investor's forecasts, the more likely that deviations from forecasts will be considered random and the less likely the investor will revise his forecasts for the future. When an investor's forecasts are more accurate for a specific asset's cash flow than for the economy's cash flow or returns, that asset will tend to have a lower systematic risk than otherwise.

This has two important aspects for managers of assets. First, the company that can accurately forecast its product market can better control its cash flow and thereby reduce its systematic risk. Second, if the marketplace is to improve the accuracy of its forecasts for the company, thereby reducing the risk premium demanded, it must have good information about the company's activities. This information includes competitive, strategic, and economic assessments of the company's businesses as well as current profitability reports. The difficulty the market has in getting this information for many widely diversified firms may explain why they appear to have high risk-adjusted rates of return despite relatively attractive economic performances.

We can now summarize how management can influence a firm's risk and thereby its risk-adjusted rate of return. The basic risk of any cash flow will depend on how well corporate skills and resources have been matched to environmental opportunities. The extent to which the firm's product demand is dependent on the general level of economic activity will determine its basic level of systematic risk. Once a cash flow has been established, management can influence its systematic risk through several strategies. First, the increased utilization of financial and operating leverage with their fixed costs will tend to increase systematic risk. Second, market share can be valuable in reducing risks, since accumulated experience and high market shares often combine to stabilize cash flows. In addition, as market share increases for a product with a life cycle, the prospective free cash flow stream from it will lengthen, decreasing current systematic risk. Furthermore, since better control over product market risks often accompanies high market share, companies pursuing high market share strategies are often in a good position to forecast their cash flows more accurately and to reduce their exposure to unexpected events. Third, a company with a balanced product/market portfolio can invest its free cash flow in growth opportunities. Both the increased time horizon and the potential growth of the firm's cash flow, which may occur from this strategy, act to reduce the firm's current systematic risk. Finally, accurate forecasting by investors and managers reduces the uncertainty about future returns and thereby reduces current levels of systematic risk.

While the notions of systematic risk and the various business strategies that may influence it may appear rather complex, they are actually quite similar to many of the classic concepts of risk management. A low risk asset is basically one with a stable and predictable income stream, preferably growing, and with a very long time horizon. The risk/return model shows, however, that the risks that matter are much more subtle than often believed. Most important, systematic risk or asset risk relative to the risk of the economy is what matters and what determines an asset's risk premium and required rate of return. In addition, it is the size and volatility of free cash flow rather than accounting measures of performance that is most relevant to the market's valuation of an asset or security. Finally, perceptions of future value and risk often have significant impact upon investors' current measures of value and risk. In short, many of the classic arguments about the attractiveness of growing, predictable income streams are misleading in that they treat the subject too simply. The marketplace is a competitive environment that assesses risk and establishes value on a relative basis. It will only value an asset in excess of its economic or replacement value when its management can generate performance that the marketplace cannot otherwise duplicate.

Market Value as an Integrating Concept

Our discussion of cash flow and risk, the two critical variables considered by the market in assessing value, shows how closely the three models are related to each other. All three models are useful in defining and measuring the attractiveness of future value. All three models treat return in an absolute sense and risk in a relative sense. Each is concerned with the difficult problem of managing future cash flows so that current market value can be maximized.

This last point is particularly important. Each model is useful to the manager interested in reducing the impact of unforeseen events on the specific assets he manages. The key insight provided by the risk/return model is that asset managers should focus their attention on the relationship between an asset's returns and those of the economy as a whole. In addition, the model implies that managers of assets should develop strategies aimed at increasing their control over their assets' future returns or cash flows. The strategy and product/market-portfolio models provide a methodology and body of concepts that have proved to be helpful to managers with precisely these objectives.

A major value of the integrated framework presented here is that it helps establish a quantitative market-based relationship between risk and return. It also demonstrates that company-specific risks are immaterial to the valuation process; rather, it emphasizes that those risks with the greatest effect on market value concern the relationship between the company's and the economy's returns. In addition, by showing how the marketplace values a company's future cash flows and risks, the framework enables managers to compare the potential increase in market value stemming from various strategies with the costs of implementing them. Finally, managers familiar with the related set of concepts presented here are in a position to develop strategies that promise the greatest opportunity for creating real economic value for their investors and ensuring the firm's long-run competitive viability.

Conclusion

We have argued that the three models stress compatible risk measures and provide complementary views on how a company's market value can be affected by its business policies. Because of their basic compatibility, the three models can be readily applied to the basic question posed in our introductory chapter: How can real economic value be created through diversifying acquisitions? The purpose of the following chapters is to address this question in detail.

It is worth emphasizing at this point, however, that the power of the three models, taken as a complementary package of concepts, lies in their ability to assess the benefits and costs of diversification as well as other strategic options. The three models not only help to clarify how a company can benefit from diversification through acquisition but they also help identify who pays the cost of uneconomic diversification and what the nature and size of these costs may be. Thus, it should not be surprising that viewed from the perspective of our analytical framework the economic and strategic logic underlying many common arguments for diversification through acquisition is open to question.

For example, managers concerned with ensuring the perpetuity of their companies often argue that corporate diversification has value even if the diversifying company's systematic risk/return profile remains unaffected. This argument typically has strong appeal where wide-ranging diversification can reduce the risk of bankruptcy or mitigate the effects of dying businesses and thereby preserve employment and other rewards for both management and other members of the enterprise. It can be buttressed with the observation that many investors do not hold diversified portfolios and that companies would be remiss if they failed to diversify on behalf of their shareholders.

Our analytical framework suggests, however, that corporate diversification in the context of efficient capital markets offers little value unless the company can improve upon the risk/return relationship available in the marketplace. A fully diversified investor can all but eliminate the unsystematic risk associated with the bankruptcy of one of the companies in his investment portfolio and is therefore only compensated for the unavoidable, systematic risk inherent in his portfolio. Various studies have shown that as few as eight to ten unrelated investments are sufficient to eliminate over 80 percent of a portfolio's unsystematic risk.[4] The investor does not need an operating company to diversify away this unsystematic risk on his behalf. Indeed, we will argue later on that there may be real costs to the investor associated with various forms of corporate diversification.

As we will point out in the next chapter, there are many ways that companies can create value through diversification for their investors. But where capital markets are reasonably efficient, a diversification program aiming primarily at the reduction of risk is not economically justifiable. It is, of course, understandable that many managers would want to pursue diversification strategies aimed at reducing company specific risk. In fact, many companies during the 1960s, aided by a booming stock market, investor naïveté, and favorable accounting rules, did justify their diversification programs on precisely these grounds. Even today, many advisers advocate unrelated diversification to reduce a company's exposure to declining or risky businesses. However, our discussion of the three complementary models should serve to warn the strategist not to confuse past and current practice with appropriate practice.

If our set of concepts challenges common presumptions about the potential benefits of diversification through acquisition, so too does it reinforce other presumptions that have long had intuitive appeal to experienced businessmen. For example, there is a common presumption that related diversification is safer than unrelated diversification. Despite the oversimplification (which we will discuss later on), the logic of all three models strongly supports this belief. The strategy model treats the relatedness of businesses in terms of requirements for competitive success. It implies that value will be created for the shareholders of an acquisition-minded company where the reinforcement of skills and resources critical to the success of one of the combined company's businesses leads to increased profitability. This transfer of skills and/or resources between businesses has been characterized by the term "synergy." The creation of value is the realization of potential synergy.

While the product/market-portfolio model only indirectly addresses the question of relatedness, its emphasis on "accumulated experience" suggests that investments in markets closely related to current fields of operation can lead to a reduction in long-run average costs and increased returns on capital. This will occur where the similarities of the related businesses lead to either scale effects, rationalization of production and other important managerial tasks, or new opportunities for technological innovation.

The risk/return model provides a third perspective on the benefits of related diversification. For example, where the operations of two businesses can be integrated, the return of two combined companies can often be increased without any increase in systematic risk. In addition, if a related acquisition brings information or skills that help the combined company to control its internal and external environment, forecasting can be improved, enabling more effective strategies to be employed. Under either of these two conditions market value and shareholder wealth will be increased.

Thus, we can see that the true value of the set of ideas developed in the past four chapters is that the partial models constituting it provide complementary perspectives on the creation of value and suggest complementary criteria for analyzing corporate strategies. While the purpose of this chapter has been to reveal the basis of this complementarity, we will discuss in detail in Part III how these complementary perspectives on value creation and complementary criteria for analysis can be applied to the strategic and economic problems facing diversifying companies.

Notes and References

1. Adapted from Pearson Hunt, Charles M. Williams, and Gordon Donaldson, *Basic Business Finance,* 4th ed. (Homewood, Ill.: Richard D. Irwin, 1971), p. 550.
2. Ibid., p. 557.

3. Investors with differing tax characteristics or marginal tax rates will clearly have different preferences for the use of a company's free cash flows.

4. See Fischer Black, Michael C. Jensen, and Myron Scholes, "The Capital Asset Pricing Model: Some Empirical Tests," in Michael C. Jensen, ed., *Studies in the Theory of Capital Markets* (New York: Praeger, 1972); and William F. Sharpe, *Portfolio Theory and Capital Markets* (New York: McGraw-Hill, 1972).

Application of Strategic and Economic Concepts

Introduction to Part III

In contrast to Part II, this section of the book is applications oriented. Our principal concern in Part III is the challenge of creating real economic value through corporate diversification. While many of the notions stressed in the next four chapters are applicable to internal diversifiers as well as acquisitive diversifiers, we will focus on the latter class of companies, since the market transaction accompanying a diversifying acquisition allows us to accent the economic issues more clearly.

The past and current importance of corporate diversification in American and European industry forces us to develop and apply more advanced techniques for analyzing the potential costs and benefits of diversification. Certainly the financial record to date of acquisitive diversifiers as a group suggests that traditional concepts have not had a constructive influence on the strategies of many diversifying companies.

Our framework for strategic and economic analysis is, of course, not without its shortcomings. Like almost every other analytical framework addressing a complicated problem—be it economic, social, or political—our framework leaves several abstractions unattended to. Referring back to the contribution of the strategy model, we have not (and the model itself does not) defined clearly what a distinctive competence actually is. Similarly, the product/market-portfolio model never defines in precise terms what constitutes a market. This, strange as it may appear, remains a complex issue, which industrial economists continue to debate with some energy. The risk/return model contributes its measure of ambiguity as well. What, for example, is the best measure of systematic risk, or beta, for a privately held company or a division of a large, diversified company? Are so-called "proxy betas" from comparable companies or assets adequate reflections of the systematic risk?

Despite these abstractions and unresolved conceptual questions, we intend to show in this section of the book that the framework developed in Part II is a powerful aid in developing economically sound strategies of diversification through acquisition. We intend to demonstrate the framework's power in two ways: first, by addressing a related set of administrative issues such as selecting diversification objectives, developing acquisition guidelines, screening acquisition candidates, and so on, and second, by examining in varying degrees of detail the histories of several well-known diversifiers. These include such companies as Heublein, Genstar, Continental Group, General Cinema, Ciba-Geigy, Rockwell International, and INCO (International Nickel).

CHAPTER 7

Diversification Objectives

A CAREFULLY FORMULATED STRATEGY for diversification through acquisition has its roots in an explicit decision to pursue either related or unrelated diversification and an articulation of acquisition guidelines consistent with this choice of diversification objectives. In the present chapter we will discuss the options of related and unrelated diversification in some detail. After a review of some basic definitions, we will identify and discuss the potential benefits of both related and unrelated diversification. This will be followed by a discussion of those corporate conditions that appear to facilitate successful related and unrelated diversification.

Our discussion of diversification objectives will not address the question of why companies diversify. (Many of these reasons are summarized in Chapter 1.) Neither will we address questions of who should be responsible for formulating diversification objectives and acquisition guidelines. We are assuming that the chief executive has the ultimate responsibility for all strategic decisions and that the organization of activities related to the diversification process will reflect both the unique talents and interests of top-level decision makers and the bureaucratic traditions that have characterized the company's strategic decision making in the past. Thus, it should be clear that our principal interest is not to record administrative behavior and practices with respect to diversification decisions. Rather, our intent is to assist whoever may be responsible for a diversification program to think through what diversification objectives and guidelines are appropriate.[1]

Definitions of Related and Unrelated Diversification

In the most general sense, the notion of "relatedness" depends upon how managers define their businesses. From an operating point of view, no single set of categories—such as the U.S. Government's Standard Industrial Classification codes—is useful in discriminating between related and unrelated businesses. Businesses are related, in the final analysis, if operating managers perceive them to be related in an important way. Thus, a manufacturing manager, for example, may perceive the manufacture of zippers to be closely related to the manufacture of watchbands, even though the marketing and distribution of these two products could be quite different. Similarly, while Merck & Company and Marion Laboratories are both pharmaceutical companies, their activities may be perceived quite differently by their operating managers. Insiders may well perceive Merck as a research intensive company, while the managers of Marion Laboratories probably perceive their company as concentrating on distributing and marketing pharmaceutical products developed by others. As such, Marion's managers probably feel their business is unrelated to Merck's business in terms of key management tasks and critical success factors.

With this caveat in mind it is nevertheless useful for us to make as fine distinctions as possible between related and unrelated diversification. As we pointed out in the introductory chapter, businesses are commonly considered related if they either share common functional skills and "critical success factors" or operate at different stages in the same commercial chain, thereby possessing complementary skills and resources. Diversification can thus be considered related if at least one of the following four characteristics are present. The first three characterize related-supplementary diversification, while the fourth characterizes related-complementary diversification.

First, diversification can be said to be related if it involves businesses serving similar markets and/or using similar distribution systems. The businesses of the large consumer product companies such as Gillette and Procter & Gamble are appropriate examples. Gillette historically concentrated on the production and marketing of disposable personal care items. One strength Gillette developed was an extensive distribution system to supply such retail outlets as supermarkets, drugstores, and mass merchandisers. Gillette's recent acquisition of companies in the writing instrument, lighter, small appliance, and plant care businesses can thus be considered related diversification moves, since products of these businesses could be easily integrated into Gillette's existing marketing and distribution system.

Diversification can also be said to be related if the businesses employ similar production technologies. According to this criterion, Ralston Purina's move into such grocery products as pet foods and the Chex cereals can be considered as closely related to its original business, comprising over 100 basic rations of animal feed for livestock and poultry, since grain purchasing and processing is basic to both businesses. One indicator of these commonalities is that in 1976 Ralston Purina still maintained centralized purchasing and engineering staffs at the corporate level despite its reorganization in the mid-1960s into several divisions, each with profit and loss responsibility.

Third, diversification can be considered related if the businesses exploit similar science-based research. Many of Du Pont's numerous businesses, such as industrial chemicals and synthetic fibers, can therefore be considered related to one another by virtue of their common link to organic chemistry and to Du Pont's continuing research in organic chemistry. Similarly, to return to a previous example, pharmaceutical companies often generate new chemical products from the same research programs that give rise to new drugs. Many pharmaceutical companies, therefore, consider themselves related business diversifiers. Kodak's diversification from photographic products into office copiers can be seen in the same light.

Finally, diversification can be considered related even if the businesses involved do not share the same functional skills or "critical success factors," as long as they operate at different stages of the same commercial chain. Thus, the expansion of Hart Schaffner & Marx into the retail business (through both acquisition and internal development) must be considered a related diversification move, since both businesses operate in the apparel industry. To the extent Hart Schaffner & Marx's retail division provides assured distribution for the products of the company's six manufacturing divisions, it also involves a degree of vertical integration.

Unrelated diversification involves a move into businesses that do not share any one of these four characteristics. The acquisition of a paint company and a publishing company by International Silver Company (now Insilco), formerly a flatware company, is a good example of a pair of unrelated diversifying acquisitions. So, too, is Mobil Oil's more dramatic acquisition of Marcor, even though Mobil is considered a premier marketer of petroleum products in the United States. Clearly, quite different marketing and distribution skills are required for petroleum products than for general merchandise and containers. Mobil's production and supply operations are another obvious point of differentiation.

Potential Benefits of Related Diversification

Benefits accruing to shareholders from related or unrelated diversification can either be of a long-run, continuing nature or of the short-run, essentially cosmetic variety. Short-run changes that generally result in no increase in market value for the company can accrue from such items as a change in tax treatments (more deferrals) or a change in accounting (such as a switch from FIFO to LIFO methods of inventory valuation).[2] Of much greater interest are the potential benefits of the long-run, continuing variety, which relate to the ongoing operating and financial characteristics of the diversifying company.

The perspectives on diversifying acquisitions provided by the strategy, product/market-portfolio, and risk/return models all suggest that the more related a diversifying acquisition is to the activities and management skills of the acquiring company, the greater the potential benefit of that acquisition to the acquiring company's shareholders. This suggestion reflects, in part, a notion derived from financial economics: value is created for shareholders when the combination of two companies' resources leads to either (1) an income stream for the combined company greater than that which could be realized by an investor owning the shares of the two companies or (2) a reduction in the variability of the income stream for the combined company greater than that which could be realized from a portfolio investment in the two companies.

The concepts underlying the corporate strategy model help amplify this notion of value creation. The strategy model implies that benefits can occur in a diversification move when there exists the possibility of transferring resources and/or functional skills between the acquiring company and a recently acquired related business. Such a transfer of functional skills and/or noncapital resources between related businesses can increase the productivity of an investment in the combined company and thereby create value for the original shareholders of the diversifying company. The productivity of the combined company's capital is most likely to increase when the special skills and industry knowledge of one business can be applied to the competitive problems and opportunities facing the other. Where the reinforcement of skills and resources critical to success of one of the combined company's businesses leads to increased profitability, value will have been created for the shareholders of an acquisition-minded company. This transfer of skills and/or resources between businesses has been characterized by the term "synergy." The creation of value is the realization of potential synergy.[3]

The case of Heublein's acquisition of United Vintners in 1968 provides an example of the benefits of related diversification implied by the strategy and product/market-portfolio models. The basic strategy of Heublein, Inc. during the 1960s was to market high-quality consumer products that would provide the high margins necessary to support intensive, innovative advertising. The company's liquor products division accounted for over 80 percent of Heublein's 1965 sales. Its principal product was the premium-priced Smirnoff vodka, the fourth-largest and fastest-growing liquor brand in the United States. The division also sold a low-priced vodka, gin, whiskey, tequila, a collection of sherries, ports, and cordials, and bottled cocktails. In addition to liquor products, Heublein sold beer and specialty food items. The 1968 acquisition of United Vintners, the marketing arm of a large grape growers' cooperative that owned two of California's best wine brands, provided the opportunity for Heublein to increase its investment in an industry where it had some experience (it was the U.S. distributor for Lancer's wine) and to broaden the range of application of its proven skills in marketing and promoting consumer products. Since wine was perceived to be another type of alcoholic beverage, Heublein apparently felt that it had a certain amount of expertise transferable to the wine industry.

Several additional things attracted Heublein to a major investment in the wine industry. From its position as a wine importer, the company could see that wine consumption was growing steadily. In addition, the relatively low per capita consumption figures (less than 2 gallons a year versus 17 for beer) augured well for greater future wine growth. Also important was the fact that the drinkers between twenty-five and thirty-five, who were responsible for most of the growth in wine consumption, were showing a marked shift in preference away from traditional wine varieties toward brand new, lighter-bodied products.[4] Here is where Heublein's expertise at promoting specialty products came into play. As Heublein's CEO, Stuart D. Watson, a former advertising agency (Interpublic) executive vice president, pointed out at the time of the acquisition, Heublein's skills stemmed from its consumer orientation and skill in new-product introductions. Heublein's marketing skills were in marked contrast to its competitors, who typically had been production and distribution oriented.[5] Watson saw a great opportunity for Heublein to exploit United Vintners' business base by bringing its special expertise to bear on United Vintners' marketing programs. The most tangible evidence of this assistance was the installation of Victor Bovonomo, an experienced marketing executive with General Foods, as United Vintners' CEO in 1969. In so doing, Heublein hoped to increase significantly the return on investment United Vintners had been earning. In point of fact, by first identifying and then exploiting an emerging consumer preference for brand new, lighter-bodied, often slightly flavored products, Heublein was able to assist United Vintners in launching two new products: Cold Duck (a champagne–sparkling burgundy combination) and Bali Hai (a fruit flavored wine). By the end of 1969, one year after its acquisition of United Vintners, Heublein had increased sales by over 2.5 million cases while increasing the subsidiary's profitability.

Heublein's marketing strategy was so successful that it was able to lift sales from $103 million to $583 million during the 1960s and increase earnings per share from 37 cents to $1.45. In the early 1970s the marketplace valued Heublein's performance, best summarized by an average return on equity exceeding 30 percent for the preceding ten years, at over thirty-five times earnings. Subsequent diversification efforts by Heublein into brewing (via the acquisition of the Theodore Hamm Brewing Company) and fast foods (via the acquisition of Kentucky Fried Chicken) were not as successful, however.[6] By 1977, Heublein saw its price/earnings ratio fall to 10 and its stock price decline to one-third of its previous high.

Other benefits of related diversification through acquisition stem from the effects of business expansion and increased investment in an industry similar to current fields of operation. Business expansion in an area of competence can lead to the generation of additional resources that can be used to develop competences equal to or even superior to those of the competition. In many industries, managers claim that companies have to achieve a certain size or critical mass before they can compete effectively with their competition. In the laboratory instrumentation field, for example, the only way many small companies can hope to offer sustained competition against such entrenched companies as Hewlett-Packard, Tektronix, Beckman Instruments, and Technicon is to attain a size where they have sufficient cash flow to fund competitive research-and-development programs. One of the ways of attaining this required size is through closely related diversification.

Related diversification or expanded investments in markets closely related to current fields of operation can also bring benefits to an acquiring company's shareholders if such investments lead to a reduction in the acquiring company's long-run average costs. A reduction in average costs can accrue from scale effects, rationalization of production and other important managerial tasks, and new opportunities for technological innovation. For example, a marketing department's budget as a percentage of sales will decline if existing resources can be used to market new or related products. Similarly, a company like Procter & Gamble can expect to see its per unit distribution costs decline if the existing distribution system can be used to move more products to the marketplace. In another example, the Head Ski Company's manufacturing organization, oriented toward precision metalworking on a high-volume basis, had an opportunity to increase its manufacturing efficiencies by adding the manufacture of contraseasonal metal tennis rackets to its ski fabrication activities. There was also the opportunity for more cost-effective brand advertising if Head could field a product line with year-round appeal to the sports-minded consumer.

Finally, related diversification can also benefit the diversifying company's shareholders where an acquisition results in a reduction in the variability of the acquiring company's income stream to a greater extent than that which its shareholders could obtain from simple portfolio diversification. Although there is no evidence that General Motors' strategy was developed with this notion in mind, an important effect of G.M.'s diversification within the motor vehicle industry is that it can absorb changes in demand for any one automotive product more easily than, say,

Chrysler. G.M.'s extensive related product line allows it to maintain manufacturing efficiencies as the market changes while more specialized and narrow line competitors cannot. In addition, since G.M.'s automotive diversification reduces the company's marketing risk, it has enabled G.M.'s managers to concentrate on production efficiencies, which reduces G.M.'s costs and improves its margins. As a result, G.M.'s income stream tends to be less volatile than that of many of its competitors. General Motors is thus in a better position to generate a more stable, less risky income stream for the investor than a portfolio of investments in several unassociated, though automotive-related, companies.

Potential Benefits of Unrelated Diversification

By far the most commonly articulated benefit of unrelated diversification is that it enables a company's income stream to be stabilized. For decades, proponents of unrelated or conglomerate diversification have argued that when a company diversifies into an industry with a business cycle or set of economic risks different from its own, the "safety" of that company's income stream is enhanced. In essence, this is a very simple form of the risk pooling concept underlying insurance. Supposedly, when one industry is "down," another will be "up"; and the average will remain much more stable than its parts.

By now it should be obvious that this argument is a very superficial one. First, given the complex interactions of the U.S. and world economies, it is very hard to find clearly countercyclical businesses. At best, what one observes are industry cycles that either lead or lag the general economy (housing and capital goods, respectively) or which are not as cyclical as the economy in general (such as consumer goods and tobacco products). More importantly, however, the benefits of stabilizing an income stream can be attained by the investor through simple portfolio diversification. Modern financial economics shows that moderating earnings variability through corporate diversification merely duplicates what the investor can easily do for himself.[7] Still the argument for moderating earnings volatility through diversification lives on and is reiterated annually in many reports to shareholders and in the recommendations of many consultants and investment bankers.

While simple risk pooling through unrelated diversification does not produce any direct shareholder benefits other than those already available from portfolio diversification, it can lead to several indirect advantages. These indirect advantages stem primarily from capital efficiencies, or efficiencies that effectively reduce the corporation's total cost of funds. Perhaps the most important and most obvious is the ability to improve cash management. Many large companies can achieve significant savings from centralized cash management. The potential benefits are particularly great in the unrelated diversified firm. With its operations at different levels of production and in different stages of seasonal or business cycles, the diversified corporation through centralizing cash balances can act as the banker for its operating subsidiaries. By being the banker, the corporate office can route cash from units with a surplus in relation to their operating needs to those units in deficit and, in doing so, reduce the need of the diversified company (relative to the needs of its component businesses) to purchase working capital funds from outside sources. It should be emphasized that this type of cash management is an operating benefit and completely separate from the recycling of cash on an investment basis.

Closely related to improved cash management are two debt-related capital efficiencies that can result from unrelated diversification. As the number of businesses in the portfolio of the unrelated diversifier increases and the overall variability of its operating income or cash flow decreases, the diversified company's risk as perceived by its lending institutions will decrease.[8] This altered risk perception leads to two benefits. First, the lower perceived risk will result in a smaller risk premium on the funds borrowed by the diversified company than by its nondiversified, more volatile components. In addition, since the overall variability of the diversified company's cash flow is reduced, it is in a position to borrow funds to a greater extent than otherwise possible. This ability to incur a greater amount of financial leverage enables a company's shareholders to shift some of the corporation's risk to the government (since interest, in contrast to dividends, is deductible for tax purposes, the government shoulders a portion of the cost of capitalizing a business venture) and, thereby, reduce the company's total cost of capital. These benefits—reduced risk premiums and increased borrowing ability—only become significant factors, however, when the diversifying company aggressively manages its financial risks by employing a high debt/equity ratio or having several highly risky, unrelated projects within its portfolio of businesses.[9]

Next to the claimed benefits of earnings stability, probably the most widely cited benefit of unrelated diversification is that it can help a company develop a capacity for self-financing. This capacity is thought to be particularly important for rapidly growing or highly capital intensive companies. While these companies should be able to raise capital in the securities marketplace, a strong argument has been made for doing this internally. This argument is built upon the notion that capital raised from investors in the marketplace comprises doubly taxed (corporate and personal) dollars. Where a corporation can bypass the securities market and directly invest its "free" dollars, which would otherwise be paid out to its shareholders, it can make investments at a lower total cost than can its shareholders on their own. While this argument is valid on financial grounds, a question remains as to whether or not the corporation's investment decision would be the same as its stockholders'. Where stockholders do wish a specific corporation to make further investments and to diversify on their behalf, then the internal recycling of funds between alternative businesses may make financial sense. However, in many instances the economic advantages may also be more apparent than real.

Consider, for example, the recent argument for unrelated diversification made by Donald J. Donohue, the Chief Financial Officer of the Continental Group (formerly Continental Can) in an interview with *Forbes* magazine.[10] The focus of the interview was Continental's proposed acquisition of a life insurance company. Donahue explained that Continental's packaging business (1975 revenues of $3.1 billion) was both highly cyclical and highly capital intensive. To meet the industry's capital requirements, Continental had, during the previous five years, poured $1.2 billion into new plant and equipment. Despite the relatively favorable economic environment, Continental found that its combined depreciation and earnings after dividends were barely sufficient to finance its capital spending. With every intention of continuing to invest heavily in capital projects, it feared that internal cash flow alone might not be able to cover projected expenditures of $1 billion over the next four years. Since the company was already leveraged at 32 percent of total capital, a conservative Continental did not want to increase its debt ratio. Here is where the Richmond Corporation, a slow-growing $1.4 billion (assets) life insurance company, came into the picture. Richmond had close to $300 million in equity capital with little debt. With Richmond's capital, Donahue explained, Continental could comfortably do some extra borrowing without stretching its debt ratio. "The more I thought about it," said Donahue, "the more I became convinced that Richmond was the best means of achieving a broader capital base." Donahue went on to add that he felt the ideal marriage between businesses involved putting a capital intensive business together with a more stable business having low capital requirements.

While the "buying cash" argument has been articulated as the reason underlying many diversifying acquisitions, it is our opinion that it is valid in only a few situations. Taking the Continental Group's acquisition of Richmond as an example, one should ask just what sort of "excess" cash flow Continental expected. Specifically, attention must be focused on whether or not Richmond would be able to generate more cash than that necessary to carry the $200 million worth of securities and $100 million in cash Continental was offering to complete acquisition. With annual payments exceeding $30 million, we find it difficult to see where the extra cash to invest in capital projects or to support additional debt would come from, unless Continental intended to liquidate Richmond's investment portfolio. The argument that the acquisition of Richmond would improve

Continental's borrowing capacity by adding equity capital is also irrelevant. If Continental had just sold those securities that were to be offered for Richmond in the equity market, there would have been a similar impact on Continental's capitalization. (Thus, the interesting financial question is whether or not Continental would be better off with the cash obtainable from selling those securities instead of using them to purchase Richmond.) In essence, the claimed benefits of buying cash through unrelated diversification are not always real ones. One explanation for this may be that many managers are much more concerned with their cost of capital on a cash basis instead of that cost on an opportunity basis. This attention to the cash cost of capital is particularly evident when equity securities or equivalents are involved. However, once the "opportunity" cost of equity is added to its "cash" cost, it is doubtful that it is ever possible to justify "buying cash" through an acquisition.[11]

Closely related to the "buying cash" argument (and, perhaps, implicit in the statements of its defenders) is a less familiar and much more contemporary argument, which has conceptual links with the product/market-portfolio model.[12] This model implies that unrelated product/market diversification can be used as a means of recycling the excess cash flow from mature businesses into new businesses currently in the cash-using stage of their life cycle. This notion represents a major expansion in scope of the previously articulated benefits of so-called cash management. In addition to managing the cash flows of many businesses over one economic cycle, it is also possible to manage cash flows over a single business's life span (and, by extension, over several businesses' life spans). According to this framework, cash is no longer viewed in solely a banking perspective but is also viewed in terms of being an investable asset.

The argument claims that long-run profit maximization is best achieved by a corporation comprising a large number of operationally independent, dissimilar businesses managed as a single financial entity. The basis of this claim is the notion that the shareholders of a diversified corporation are in the unique position of being able to achieve a balance of businesses, each in different market-share/market-growth environments and, therefore, in different stages of the net cash flow cycle. To ensure a long-term, high net cash flow for the whole corporation, management can use the currently high net cash flow businesses to provide the investment funds for those businesses where net cash flow is presently zero or negative but where the expectation is that positive cash flow will develop in the future. This process of recycling earnings and cash flow balancing (often labeled cross-subsidization) is claimed to be the key to the long-run profitability of the modern corporation.[13,14] Underlying this argument is the implicit assumption that shareholders cannot as easily reap the economic benefits of recycling earnings and balancing cash flows through the development of a portfolio of investments comparable to that of the widely diversified corporation.[15]

This argument was recently made by Genstar Limited (of Canada) in its Submission to the Royal Commission on Corporate Concentration.[16] In this testimony, which was aimed at demonstrating the contributions of large diversified companies to the Canadian economy, Genstar argued that the well-managed, widely diversified company could call on its low growth businesses to maximize net cash flow and profits so that funds could be reallocated to those high-growth businesses needing investment. By so doing, the company could reap long-run benefits from improved return on investment, and the public, as a whole, could benefit from lower costs and, presumably, prices.

An examination of Genstar's cash flow patterns during 1971–1974 demonstrates how a diversified company might choose to manage internal cash flows. As shown in Table 7-1, two of Genstar's major business areas, cement and chemicals and fertilizers, utilized far less cash than they generated. The excess cash generation from these businesses was utilized to fund the cash needs of the housing and land development, construction, and marine activities. By recycling excess cash flow into those industries

TABLE 7-1. Relationship between Cash Utilized and Cash Generated by Business Area, Genstar, Ltd., 1971–1974[a]

Area	Cash Utilization Ratio[b] (Excluding cost of acquisition)
Building supplies	1.01
Cement	.31
Housing and land development	1.72
Construction	1.67
Chemicals and fertilizers	.38
Marine	1.87
Import/export	.46
Investment	.52
Total	1.02

[a] From *A Submission to the Royal Commission on Corporate Concentration,* November 3, 1975, page 24. Reprinted by permission of Genstar, Ltd., Montreal, Canada.

[b] Cash utilized represents the increases in capital investment and working capital required by the business area. Cash generated is defined as net income after tax plus depreciation and deferred tax. The business area's cash utilization ratio is determined by comparing its cash utilized to its cash generated. A cash utilization ratio greater than 1 indicates that the business area is a net cash user while a ratio of less than 1 indicates a net cash generator.

with cash needs, Genstar claimed that it was able to utilize its assets more productively than would otherwise have been possible.

Other benefits of unrelated diversification can accrue from capital allocation procedures, which can be more rigorous in diversified companies than in single-business companies. This rigor stems from two factors. Each business will have its own set of investment alternatives with varying risk/return characteristics. When these businesses are managed as a single financial entity, the scope of potential investments naturally expands, and tradeoffs among the risk/return characteristics of one business and another can be made. As they do so, capital can be transferred from those businesses showing less favorable characteristics to those with more favorable characteristics. This is impossible to do in single-business companies faced with a limited number of related investment projects. In addition, since diversified companies have operating subsidiaries in several businesses, they have access to information that is often unavailable to the investment community. This information is the internal market data of each industry in which it operates—data that include intelligence on the competitive position and potential of each company in the industry. With this inside information, diversified companies are often in a significantly better position than individual investors to assess the investment merits of both specific projects and entire industries. In short, the exposure of diversified companies to a greater number of investment opportunities than single-business companies enables them to choose more attractive investment projects while their access to internal market data enables them to allocate capital among industries more efficiently than the capital markets. Using the language of the financial economist, we can say that the internal capital market of the diversified company can be more "efficient" than that of the external capital market.

A Summary Comment on the Benefits of Diversification

Diversification offers potentially significant benefits to the firm's shareholders. In general, the operating benefits of related diversification have the greatest potential for improving corporate performance. As one moves from related diversification toward unrelated diversification, the nature of potential benefits changes, as does their potential impact. Operating "synergies" related to integrating functional activities fade into benefits stemming from general management efficiencies. Eventually, when the totally unrelated diversifying acquisition is made, only financial benefits can be achieved. Where the capital market is reasonably efficient, the benefits of unrelated diversification will simply be portfolio ones. The scale and type of benefits achievable through diversification is shown in Table 7-2.

TABLE 7-2. Potential Benefits of Diversification

	Related Business Diversification	Unrelated Business Diversification
Product-market orientation	Diversification into product markets with similar marketing and distribution characteristics, or similar production technologies, or similar science-based research activities.	Diversification into product markets with key success variables unrelated to the key success variables of the acquirer's principal business.
Transferable resources with greatest potential for creating value	Operating and/or functional skills; excess capacity in distribution systems, production facilities, or research operations.	General management skills; surplus financial resources.
Nature of potential benefits	Increased productivity of corporate resources through operating efficiencies, improved competitive position accruing from increased size of business, and reduction in long-run average costs can lead to a reduction in the variability of a company's income stream and/or a larger income stream than that available from simple portfolio diversification.	More efficient cash management and allocation of investment capital, reduced cost of debt capital, and growth in profits through cross-subsidization can lead to a larger income stream than that available from simple portfolio diversification. Reduction of systematic (market-related) risk is unlikely.
Relative ease of achieving potential benefits	Relatively difficult because of organizational problems associated with integrating formerly self-sufficient companies into the acquiring company.	Relatively easy to achieve capital efficiencies and benefits of cross-subsidization.

145

Unfortunately, those benefits of diversification that offer the greatest potential are usually those least likely to be implemented. Of the synergies usually claimed possible in a diversifying acquisition, financial synergies are often unnoted while operating synergies are widely trumpeted. Yet, the overwhelming evidence is that the benefits most commonly achieved have occurred in the financial area.[17] It is not hard to understand why this is so. All one has to do is to reflect on the nature of the corporation. Most managers will agree that the greatest impediment to change is the inflexibility of the organization itself. Ironically enough, the realization of operating benefits accompanying diversification usually requires significant changes in the company's organizational format and administrative behavior. These changes are typically slow to come; so are the accompanying benefits of changes in bureaucratic practices.

In the context of this summary, it is important to comment on a separate issue commonly raised by diversification. This is the claim that the diversified corporation can improve the management performance of its acquisitions. Often this is described as invoking "the discipline of the corporate office" or introducing "modern" management systems and responsive managers into stodgy companies.[18] In fact, these and many similar claims are not benefits of diversification per se but simply the benefits of good management. To achieve these benefits, a company needs only to allow those managers with the requisite skills to implement their desired improvements in the organization. However, it is a rare organization that willingly embarks on changes which could drastically affect its traditional administrative and managerial practices. In many instances change will only occur when forced from the outside, and diversifying companies often represent such a force. Still, the benefits achieved are not, strictly speaking, benefits of diversification.

Enabling Conditions for Successful Related and Unrelated Diversification

Given the potential benefits of related and unrelated diversification, what conditions should be present in the acquiring company to increase the likelihood of successful diversification into related or unrelated business areas? If these conditions can be explicitly recognized, it will help managers decide whether or not their companies should pursue a diversification strategy, and if so, whether it should be related or unrelated. This decision is the first step in developing strategic guidelines for a diversifying company.

Several conditions for successful diversification in general have previously been identified by Myles Mace and George Montgomery in their research conducted in the early 1960s on the management problems of corporate acquisitions.[19] These include:

1. The existence of a venturesome, risk-taking management point of view in the acquiring organization.

2. Competent management in the acquiring organization who are motivated to perform well in the new product field.

3. Competent management in the acquiring organization who can quickly adjust to being responsible for doing business in new industries, or the employment of executives from other companies who have experience in the new field.

4. Recognition by the acquiring management of the different requirements for success in different industries; and

5. A willingness by the acquiring management to include newly acquired top management executives in company policymaking.

To this list we think it is important to add several more enabling conditions. Two of these can have a direct impact on the performance of both related and unrelated diversification. Other conditions are more specific to each diversification alternative.

The basic financial logic of any successful acquisition program requires that the future returns of the acquisition exceed, at a minimum, the risk-adjusted cost of capital for the acquisition.[20] Beyond this minimum, every acquisitive company searches for returns in excess of this rate. The most direct means of achieving this result is to locate and purchase undervalued assets that can be revitalized with minimum investment.[21] The ability to recognize assets as being undervalued (relative to potential value) when other judges of value (such as the equity market) do not view the assets in the same light is a rare talent. Companies intent on diversification through acquisition can benefit greatly from individuals who possess such skills—assuming, of course, that these companies also possess the capacity to develop such acquisitions into properties earning returns in excess of those expected by the equity markets at the time of acquisition.

Another, though less critical, enabling condition of a general nature is access to financial resources. The ability of many rapidly growing and even mature businesses to exploit their market opportunities is often constrained by capital shortages. Where an acquisition-minded company has excess cash or access to financing on favorable terms, the opportunities for helping incoming companies reach their full profit potential can be significant.

Turning now to related diversification, it is useful to recall that the principal benefits of related diversification stem from opportunities to increase the profitability of the incoming or acquiring company by more effectively utilizing each company's core skills and resources. In the context of related-supplementary diversification, such an application typically requires a transfer of core skills and resources between merger partners. In order for this transfer to take place without an increase in overall costs, there has to be a surplus of these special resources and skills in either one of the two new partners. Obviously, if such a surplus does not exist, bringing in a team of experienced managers with functional skills related to the needs of one company or increasing in-house research efforts in areas relevant to that company's business development efforts will not lead to any reduction in total management costs. To return to the Heublein example cited above, the full benefit of the United Vintners acquisition could not have been realized unless the Heublein management was able to put its top marketing talent to work with United Vintners on its program of new-product development and introduction. If there had been no "excess capacity" in Heublein's marketing group, low-cost, direct assistance to United Vintners would have been difficult. In the context of related-complementary diversification, increasing the profitability of the merged companies is, of course, more dependent on integrating each company's different resource structure rather than on transferring common functional skills and resources between companies.

A second essential condition for successful related diversification through acquisition is suggested by the first. There must be a strong commitment on the part of acquiring management to exploit the potential benefits of related diversification. Such a commitment typically involves developing the capacity to create organizational relationships between subsidiaries or divisions that facilitate the exploitation of potential synergies. This involves the extremely difficult task of creating structures that both encourage interdivisional cooperation and focus the attention of divisional management on the performance of their semiautonomous operating unit.[22]

While it is unrealistic to overdraw distinctions between enabling conditions for successful unrelated diversification and those most relevant to related diversification, a few additional observations on unrelated diversification are useful. A common argument heard during the 1960s was that acquisitive conglomerates could improve the profitability of acquired companies by revitalizing management, and introducing "modern" administrative practices. The testimony of Harold Geneen, chairman and president of ITT, before the House Antitrust Subcommittee on November 20, 1969, strongly echoed this argument. In commenting on how ITT provided "constructive bases for merger," Geneen stressed that "we can afford to price fairly and to exchange our own equity stocks with the shareholders of an incoming company. We can improve operating efficiencies and profits sufficiently to make this valuation worthwhile to both sets of shareholders".[23] This point was reinforced in a document submitted to the subcommittee outlining ITT's basic acquisition philosophy. Here Geneen wrote that from 1960 to 1965 the company had "developed the ability through management skills, routines and techniques to set and progressively meet higher competitive standards and achieve them in practically every line and product that we have undertaken.[24]

Writing in 1968, David N. Judelson, President of Gulf + Western Industries, told how his corporation was able to revitalize and supplement the productive forces of acquired companies that had been relatively dormant.

> Gulf + Western acquired a small manufacturing company that had reached just $1,000,000 in sales in the twelve years of its existence, lacked funds to open another plant, and needed to have access to a broader top management team in order to expand. Gulf + Western provided the capital and the necessary management specialties, so that today, seven years later, the company is doing $12,000,000 a year in sales and has a total of seven plants. In another instance, G+W acquired a company that had taken 45 years to reach $18,000,000 in sales. In just two years, sales more than doubled to $38,000,000. Still another company that had been recording profits of 5% on sales raised this to 12 percent within a short time after joining Gulf + Western.[25]

Judelson claimed that Gulf + Western was successful in revitalizing relatively unproductive assets because of its versatile and talented management experts in such areas as "advanced business systems development; cost measurement and control; short- and long-term market planning, including new product analysis; distribution logistics; electronic data processing; management recruitment; inventory management; factory management; and mathematical quantitative techniques." In the same article, Judelson noted that Gulf + Western's internal growth record (for example, an after-tax increase in internal earnings of 18.5 percent from fiscal 1966 to 1967) was as remarkable as its record of growth through acquisition.

Lynch's findings from a 1967 study of the widely diversified Walter Kidde & Company reinforces the claims of Geneen and Judelson. Lynch found that operating managers in Kidde's subsidiaries felt that the most significant postacquisition influence from the corporate office affecting the operating performance of the subsidiaries came in the area of planning and control. Specifically, Lynch found that these influences centered on (1) how the chosen sets of goods and services are produced and distributed to their markets and (2) how the process of planning, decision making, reporting, reviewing, and controlling is structured and managed.[26] These processes no doubt reflected the kind of management skills, routines, and techniques that Geneen mentioned to the Antitrust Subcommittee and Judelson relied upon from his team of management experts.[27]

The successful application of operating influence from an acquiring company requires, of course, that managers skilled in advanced management techniques exist in the company's organization. Where management resources of this kind do not exist or are either overburdened or not well developed, conditions for the successful management of unrelated diversification will typically not exist. While an acquiring company could conceivably develop additional resources of this kind or hire general management talent from other companies, the cost and more importantly the time required by these options can make them unattractive.

In addition to the advantages of having surplus managers skilled in the techniques of improving a company's operating performance, unrelated diversifiers have a special need for senior executives with skills in forecasting and planning for the financial requirements of a wide range of business activities. If the objective of unrelated diversification is to build a widely diversified company with the capability of calling on its profitable low-growth businesses to provide cash flow for its high-growth businesses that require significant infusions of cash, then the corporate office of the diversified company must have experienced managers possessing both the financial and administrative skills required by such a program.

As can be seen by studying companies like Genstar, Ltd. or other well-managed conglomerates like Textron, the financial management skills required by unrelated business diversifiers need to be supplemented by corporate officers capable of performing systematic strategic analyses of a wide range of industries and individual businesses. The corporate office in a widely diversified company needs to recognize the fundamental differences among its businesses in terms of competitive position and key success variables of the various product markets in which it participates. Genstar management, for example, develops a medium-term to long-term view about each of its major businesses and determines:

- which businesses show promise for future long-term growth in profits.
- in which [geographic] directions successful businesses can be extended.
- which complementary or related activities might be entered in order to increase the stability of operations and/or reduce the costs of existing businesses.
- which poorly performing businesses show no sign of successfully reversing competitive and cost positions.
- what kinds of acquisitions might make sense from both operating and financial points of view.

This analysis enables Genstar management to move internal cash flows from slower-growth businesses to areas of high growth and promising investment prospects.

A final condition for successful unrelated diversification also relates to management resources. Widely diversified companies require general managers at the corporate and group levels who can build and administer an organization that is responsive to the multitude of demands created by businesses with differing operating characteristics, problems, and opportunities. As companies become more diverse, it often becomes increasingly difficult to rely on uniform structural and administrative arrangements. Corporate-wide operating policies of all kinds often tend to become less valid. The history of Insilco (formerly known as the International Silver Company) is a good case in point.[28] Having initiated an aggressive diversification-through-acquisition program in 1957, the company consisted of twenty-four subsidiaries organized into seven diverse product groups by 1971. In commenting on the role of the corporate office and the seven group vice presidents in managing Insilco's collection of businesses, one group vice president commented that "as Insilco has become diversified, it has become increasingly difficult to formulate uniform policies." Apart from some control over incentive compensation and the allocation of capital, this group vice president and his six colleagues stressed that the corporate office exerted few controls over the subsidiaries. This tended to place, of course, a considerable amount of pressure on the seven group vice presidents and the corporate headquarters to work out informal arrangements with each of the twenty-four subsidiaries. As a result of these informal working arrangements, each reflecting to some extent the special needs of the subsidiaries and their top managers, Insilco had to develop the ability to live with (and even promote) corporate divisional relationships and administrative systems that varied significantly from one part of the company to another.

The poor operating records of many widely diversified companies during the late 1960s and early 1970s suggest, however, that the ability to release operating units from the constraints of uniform administrative practices without sacrificing accountability and control may be an extremely rare management talent.[29] This record also suggests that experienced general managers at all policy levels, willing and able to develop unique concepts of managing diversity, may well turn out to be the critical precondition for successful diversification into many unrelated fields.

Conclusion

While future research into the management of diversified companies will inevitably contribute more to our understanding of those conditions most likely to foster successful diversification, our preliminary observations can be of some help. If a company does not have a surplus of financial and general management resources, the risks of unrelated diversification may turn out to be very high. Similarly, if neither partner in a related-business merger possesses functional or industry related skills and resources that can be transferred to the other partner, the chances are that no benefits will accrue to shareholders above those available from an investment in the securities of each company.

Put more positively, when a diversifying company has an ability to export (import) surplus functional skills and resources relevant to its industrial or commercial setting to (from) an acquired company on a continuing basis, it should consider related diversification as an attractive strategic option. On the other hand, when a diversifying company possesses the capacity to analyze the strategies and financial requirements of a wide range of business, the ability to tolerate and, indeed, encourage a lack of uniformity in the structure and administrative systems within the organization, and the ability to transfer surplus financial and general management skills to recently acquired subsidiaries when necessary, it is in a position to exploit the potential benefits of unrelated diversification. Finally, where a diversifying company can satisfy the enabling conditions of both related and unrelated diversification, the selection of diversification objectives will then have to rely heavily on the personal inclinations of its top managers and their perceptions of shareholder interests.

While the personal preferences or inclinations of top managers may reflect idiosyncratic aversions to either capital intensive or high-technology or government regulated businesses, they need not be arbitrary. Indeed, our experience indicates that what often appears as arbitrary preferences for either related or unrelated diversification turns out, upon inspection, to be based on one or two common perceptions of the transferability of corporate resources and the risks of diversification. Managers who profess a preference or inclination for related diversification will often argue that successful companies develop distinctive competences and skills that are transferable to companies operating in allied businesses. They will also argue that risks of diversification can be reduced if companies apply their skills and resources to businesses they can understand and in which they can exercise informed judgment. In contrast, managers who show an interest in unrelated diversification often argue that the existence and transferability of distinctive corporate skills is irrelevant as long as one acquires a strong company and that operating risk can be reduced by integrating a recent acquisition into the company's planning and control system. They will also argue that portfolio diversification, not portfolio specialization, reduces investment risk. Such propositions by themselves are not sufficiently rigorous to support a major commitment of capital and management time to a diversification program, but we have seen from the preceding discussion how they can form the basis of a set of working hypotheses about what kind of diversification makes sense for a given company and its inevitably unique package of corporate resources.

Once a company has made a decision to pursue either related or unrelated diversification, there is still the task of establishing acquisition guidelines consistent with the company's diversification objectives. In the next chapter we present examples of diversification objectives and demonstrate how useful acquisition guidelines can be developed for companies pursuing either related or unrelated diversification.

Notes and References

1. We approach this task well aware that there is a small but growing body of evidence suggesting that managers do not habitually behave as the rational decision makers that our analytical framework implicitly assumes. See, for example, E. Eugene Carter, "The Behavioral Theory of the Firm and Top-Level Corporate Decisions," *Administrative Science Quarterly* 16, December 1971, and Henry Mintzberg, "The Manager's Job: Folklore and Fact," *Harvard Business Review* 53, July–August 1975.

2. See, for example, Nicholas J. Gonedes, "Efficient Capital Markets and External Accounting," *The Accounting Review* 47, January 1972; T. Ross Archibald, "Stock Market Reaction to the Depreciation Switch-Back," *The Accounting Review* 47, January 1972; and Eugene F. Fama, Lawrence Fisher, Michael C. Jensen, and Richard Roll, "The Adjustment of Stock Prices to New Information," *International Economic Review* 10, February 1969.

3. Of course, synergy can also be realized through the addition of new skills and resources, as in related-complementary diversification.

4. Forbes, Nov. 1, 1970.

5. Ibid., Nov. 1, 1968.

6. Following Heublein's decision in 1974 to dispose of Theodore Hamm, it admitted that it had misread the key success variables in the beer industry. While marketing was important, scale economies in production and distribution were even more important. Achieving these economies required skills and resources that Heublein was unable, or at least, unwilling to commit. Shortly thereafter, quality control problems arose at Kentucky Fried Chicken, destroying much of the consumer franchise that had been previously built. Since 1974 Heublein has been working to overcome this problem and to rebuild a positive consumer impression about Kentucky Fried Chicken.

7. As shown in the Appendix to this chapter (p. 283), a risk/return analysis of Gulf + Western Industries suggests that this conglomerate, despite its attractive rate of earnings-per-share growth, has little to offer investors with

respect to risk reduction over a diversified portfolio of comparable securities. One might also note that a company pursuing this strategy may actually lose value for its shareholders by overpaying for an asset whose countercyclical value has already been factored into its market price. Readers who have difficulty accepting this proposition might like to review our discussion in Chapter 5 of the theory underlying the risk/return model and the extensive body of empirical evidence supporting this notion.

8. This is risk pooling in its truest sense. The most obvious example would be a diversified company supporting a weak division that, if independent, would face high risks of bankruptcy. Academic discussion of this benefit began with Haim Levy and Marshall Sarnat, "Diversification, Portfolio Analysis, and the Uneasy Case for Conglomerate Mergers," *Journal of Finance* 25, September 1970, and Wilbur O. Lewellyn, "A Pure Financial Rationale for the Conglomerate Merger," *Journal of Finance* 26, May 1971. The subject of risk pooling has generated intense, albeit indecisive debate. Recently, E. Han Kim and John J. McConnell, in "Corporate Mergers and the Co-Insurance of Corporate Debt," *Journal of Finance* 32, May 1977, undertook an empirical test of risk pooling benefits. Their conclusion was (1) that a coinsurance effect did exist and (2) that the wealth transfers to debt holders that accompanied this benefit were typically negated by the merged company's increased use of debt financing.

9. The capital efficiency benefits of diversification should not be confused with the capital efficiency benefits stemming from increased corporate size. These latter benefits, which may be significant, arise because transaction costs do not increase proportionately with the size of a financing and because the risk of a large company is typically less than that of a smaller company in the same business. While diversification can also provide these benefits, they are fully available to nondiversified companies of similar size, possessing similar financing needs.

10. *Forbes,* Sept. 15, 1976.

11. To expand this example, assume that a common stock sells for $20 and yields $1 annually in dividends. The cash cost of the dividend is 5 percent. Since the common stock is clearly more risky than the company's bonds yielding 9 percent, the shareholder must be expecting an additional return. This additional return is the expected price appreciation of $1 to occur over the next year. The shareholders' total expected return is therefore 10 percent. As explained in Chapter 5, the shareholders' expected rate of return must be, through an identity, equal to the company's cost of equity. The difference between the actual cash cost of the equity and its total cost is the opportunity cost of selling the share now, instead of one year later. The opportunity cost represents the shareholders' future expectations for the company. If those future benefits are *fixed,* any expansion in the number of claims upon those benefits will result in a decrease in the value of each claim. This is "dilution" in its truest sense.

12. See Chapter 4 for a full discussion of this model.

13. While cross-subsidization can be seen as the key to long-run profitability of

the diversified corporation, opponents of conglomerate mergers and diversifying acquisitions have argued that conglomerates have "the special capacity to circumvent and subvert the forces of the marketplace through the practice of cross-subsidization," among other activities. In brief, it has been asserted that the large, multibusiness company has open to it "the possibility of dissolving the nexus of product cost and revenue functions on which economic models of firms and markets . . . have been erected." Thus, cross-subsidization continues to be one of the focal points of current antitrust debates. See, for example, Jesse W. Markham, *Conglomerate Enterprise and Public Policy,* Division of Research, Graduate School of Business Administration, Harvard University, 1973.

14. The variety of meanings of cross-subsidizations and their implications for management and public policy are discussed in Chapter 11.

15. It should be noted that the economic benefits assumed by the product/market-portfolio model are principally a result of the U.S. Tax Code, under which capital returns to shareholders are taxed. By recycling these earnings rather than distributing them to shareholders, the diversified company defers the tax shareholders would have to pay on these funds. It therefore has more funds to invest than tax-paying shareholders would have, if they received their return on capital, paid taxes on it, and then reinvested their remaining funds.

    The economic benefits of recycling earnings and balancing cash flows should not be confused with the notion that conglomerate mergers benefit shareholders by dampening swings in corporate earnings through ownership of one or more countercyclical businesses. Presumably, whatever benefits accompany this corporate strategy can also be obtained by an investor through simple portfolio diversification.

16. Submitted on November 3, 1975.

17. See for example William W. Alberts and Joel Segall, eds., *The Corporate Merger* (Chicago: University of Chicago Press, 1967), and Ronald W. Melicher and David F. Rush, "Evidence on Acquisition-Related Performance of Conglomerate Firms," *Journal of Finance* 29, March 1974.

18. This argument, presented by Harold Geneen of ITT and David N. Judelson of Gulf + Western Industries, is discussed below as one of the enabling conditions of unrelated diversification.

19. Myles L. Mace and George C. Montgomery, Jr., *Management Problems of Corporate Acquisitions,* Division of Research, Harvard Business School, 1962, p. 21.

20. The risk-adjusted cost of capital for a company reflects both its business risk and its financing risk. The greater the business and/or financing risk, the higher the risk-adjusted cost of capital will be.

21. Of course, one should recognize that the potential value of the acquisition must exceed the total cost of the acquisition in order for it to be financially justifiable. This total cost should include, in addition to the acquisition's original market value, any planned investments by the acquiring company in

the acquisition as well as the transaction costs and purchase premium necessary to effect the acquisition.

22. See Jay W. Lorsch and Stephen A. Allen III, *Managing Diversity and Interdependence,* Division of Research, Graduate School of Business Administration, Harvard University, 1973, for an extensive discussion of this organizational problem.

23. Hearings Before the Antitrust Subcommittee of the Committee of the Judiciary, House of Representatives, Ninety-first Congress, pt. 3, p. 250.

24. Ibid., p. 269.

25. "A Philosophy for a Conglomerate Company," *Business Horizons* 11, June 1968.

26. Harry H. Lynch, *Financial Performance of Conglomerates*, Division of Research Graduate School of Business Administration, Harvard University, 1971.

27. As noted above, these conditions could help make related acquisitions succeed, too. Good management can have an impact on all classes of companies. However, it is much more critical for unrelated diversifiers than related diversifiers, since they cannot count on exploiting the potential synergies and operating efficiencies stemming from a cluster of similar product market commitments or functional skills. Once again, we want to emphasize that improved corporate performance stemming from better management practices is not, strictly speaking, a benefit of diversification, even though such improvements often accompany diversification through acquisitions.

28. Insilco Corporation (A) and (B), Harvard Business School Case #2-373-121 and 2-373-120.

29. See Chapter 1 for recent statistics on the performance of widely diversified companies in the United States.

CHAPTER 8

Acquisition Guidelines

WHEN A COMPANY DECIDES TO PURSUE either related or unrelated diversification through acquisition, it must draw up precise acquisition guidelines. Where it prefers some form of related diversification, the preparation of acquisition guidelines can usefully focus on a careful analysis of what strengths and weaknesses the company has in personnel, product line, manufacturing and distribution facilities, and research and development. Where it prefers unrelated diversification, the preparation of acquisition guidelines can usefully focus on a careful analysis of both the company's risk/return profile and the cash flow characteristics of its existing product/market portfolio.

While an audit of corporate strengths and weaknesses and an analysis of a company's risk/return profile and cash flow characteristics can usefully be undertaken by all diversifying companies, we will argue in this chapter that the process of developing acquisition guidelines for unrelated diversification should differ in focus from the process employed for related diversification. Our argument and recommended method of developing acquisition guidelines is summarized briefly in this introduction and then further developed in subsequent sections, which discuss situations faced by Ciba-Geigy Corporation, a related-business diversifier, and General Cinema Corporation, an unrelated-business diversifier.

As a preface to a discussion of acquisition guidelines, it is useful to recall the concepts underlying our discussion of diversification. Taken together, the three analytic models presented in Part II can provide a guide for a company's self-analysis, which is the critical first step in developing specific acquisition guidelines. Such guidelines can help focus attention upon those acquisition candidates possessing the greatest potential for fulfilling a company's diversification objectives and creating value for the company's shareholders.

The Comprehensive Framework

The fundamental issue underlying every business transaction is the relationship between risk and return; the higher the risk of a business venture, the higher that venture's expected rate of return. A company's managers must deal with this relationship in two ways. First, they must constantly manage the tradeoffs between risk and return in the company's everyday business decisions. In addition, since a company is an asset with a market value related to its risk/return characteristics, its managers must try to undertake only those projects whose value (when included in the company's portfolio of projects) is greater than the cost of the project.

To create value in this manner, managers of a public company must not only make their own assessment of risks and returns but also know how the market assesses these tradeoffs. More specifically, management must determine the company's risk/return profile and understand how the market values it before they can determine whether a particular project or a change in the company's total risk/return profile will have the potential for creating value for its shareholders.

For a company intent upon diversification, knowledge of its own risk/return characteristics and the market's assessment of those tradeoffs (in addition to those of potential acquisitions) is particularly important. Current financial theory, which assumes reasonable efficient capital markets, shows that the market prices each asset (or company) on the basis of its cash flow and the volatility of that cash flow (risk/return characteristics) relative to all other assets in the marketplace. However, since an asset (or company) may have more than one use, each with different risk/return characteristics, assets can and do have values different from their market price in the eyes of different investors. For example, a diversifying company may acquire another company and by changing the use of that company's assets achieve a better risk/return profile than had previously existed. Thus, the diversifying company could create value for its shareholders by varying the use and/or improving the performance of what were previously underutilized assets.

Since the actual marketplace may not be perfectly efficient (over either time or all assets), some assets may be either over- or undervalued.[1] For a diversifying company to take advantage of these situations, it must be able to assess the extent of the market's over- or undervaluation of potential acquisitions relative to the market's valuation of the diversifying company.[2] Where a company can acquire another company at a price below its intrinsic value (irrespective of whether or not it can improve the utilization of the acquired assets) and then have the marketplace recognize the wisdom of this move, it can create value for its shareholders. This will only occur, however, if the diversifying company can effectively communicate to the market its strategy and other information needed by the market to assess the potential benefits of an acquisition.

While the risk/return model can help managers assess the relative value of assets, it does not greatly help managers explain why an asset or company has the cash flow characteristic that it does. The product/ market-portfolio model helps managers do this by focusing their attention on a company's relative competitive position. The key variables of the model—market growth and relative market share—can be used to explain the cash flow position of a company relative to that of its competitors. When measures of capital intensity are added, comparisons of market-share/market-growth positions among different industries can be made. By using all three measures or variables, the model helps to explain why businesses exhibit the cash flow characteristics that they do. The model enables diversifying companies to identify the market characteristics and investment requirements of their present product/market portfolio and, by implication, the characteristics of acquisitions that will improve their existing product/market portfolio.

As useful as this level of analysis can be, it does not answer why a company is in its particular competitive position. This requires a strategy analysis that focuses on identifying the skills and resources of the company that have lead to its competitive success. This analysis helps re-define such corporate characteristics as capital intensity, market share position, and growth in terms of key success factors. For example, does a company with dominant market share owe its success to its marketing skill or its production efficiency? If production efficiency is the key, what underlying factors are the reason: logistical experience, plant design, or the utilization of a unique resource input?

Kenneth Andrews, in his book on corporate strategy, provides some useful hints for identifying and analyzing corporate resources and special competences. Andrews warns that it is important to remember "that individual and unsupported flashes of strength are not as dependable as the gradually accumulated product and market-related fruits of experience."[3] The implication is clear. The identification of corporate skills and resources that might be transferred between merger partners must begin with an examination of the internal factors that have contributed to whatever success or failure an acquiring or target company has achieved in the market.

In summary, these three models provide a comprehensive, practical framework for corporate self-analysis and the subsequent development of detailed acquisition guidelines. As will be demonstrated in our discussion of General Cinema, concepts drawn from the risk/return and product/ market-portfolio models should dominate the initial effort to develop acquisition guidelines for companies pursuing unrelated diversification. This is because the benefits of unrelated diversification correspond closely to capital investment decisions where risk/return tradeoffs are of paramount importance and where the expectation of transferring functional skills and resources between merging companies is low. In contrast, our discussion of Ciba-Geigy will show why companies pursuing related diversification should base their efforts to develop acquisition guidelines principally upon concepts drawn from more traditional strategy models. This follows from the fact that so many benefits of related diversification depend on the operating synergies achievable by two merging companies possessing marketing, manufacturing, or R&D resources that either complement or supplement each other.

This is not to say, however, that the strategy model is inapplicable to unrelated diversification or that the risk/return and product/market-portfolio models do not aid in analyzing a related diversifying acquisition. In fact, using each model significantly aids any diversification decision. For instance, developing a comprehensive understanding of an industry and a business's competitive position within it, a critical step in planning for an unrelated diversifying acquisition, is impossible without the in-depth analysis offered by the strategy model. Similarly, the product/market-portfolio model, through its use of experience curves and relative cost positions, helps quantify the potential operating synergies identified in related diversifying acquisitions. Finally, only the risk/return model offers an analytic procedure for comparing future benefits, or cash flow, with their current cost, or investment. No matter how attractive or unattractive an acquisition may seem, there is always some price at which the analysis changes. Our development of different sets of acquisition guidelines for different diversification objectives merely reflects the fact that the usefulness of each model is relative to how and when each model is used in the analysis of diversifying acquisitions.

Developing Acquisition Guidelines for Related Diversification

The most significant shareholder benefits from related diversification accrue when the special skills and industry knowledge of one merger partner can be applied to the competitive problems and opportunities facing the other. It is worth stressing that not only must these special skills and resources exist in one of the two partners, but they must also be transferable to the other. Since the transferability of functional skills and resources related to a particular industrial setting is so critical to successful related diversification, the acquisitive diversifier can usefully delineate its corporate strengths and weaknesses as a first step in establishing its acquisition criteria. Once transferable skills and resources and corporate weaknesses are identified, the diversifying company can then establish specific objectives for related diversification (related-supplementary or related-complementary) and a profile of the kinds of companies or businesses that is compatible with these objectives. Such a profile can usually serve as the diversifying company's basic set of acquisition guidelines.

The Case of Ciba-Geigy Corporation

Lest the identification of corporate strengths and weaknesses and the articulation of related diversification objectives appear too obvious or elementary, consider the case of Ciba-Geigy Corporation, the principal U.S. subsidiary of Ciba-Geigy Limited (a publicly owned Swiss corporation with sales in excess of $2.6 billion). Although Ciba-Geigy Corporation did not issue public financial statements, 1973 sales were known to be in excess of $550 million. The company's products were almost entirely specialty chemicals and pharmaceuticals. Madison Laboratories, a small consumer products division accounting for less than 2 percent of total sales, sold such items as breath spray, dental cream, and skin care products. The company did not sell commodity chemicals like sulfuric acid, caustic soda, or benzene.

Ciba-Geigy Corporation's diversification objectives were to continue to improve its long-term profits through new products derived from its research program and from acquisitions in related fields. It was expected that acquisitions would be financed primarily with Ciba-Geigy Corporation's own cash flows. The company was willing to invest up to $250 million in new acquisitions. As explained by Don MacKinnon, a vice president of the company:

> We wish to remain a very research-oriented organization with vigorous and on-going internal growth. However, we also look to our acquisition program as a means of complementing this growth. I should emphasize that we have no interest in becoming a vast conglomerate. We are not making acquisitions merely to become bigger. We are interested only in those companies which would complement our current business or put us into related new business areas.[4]

The first step in implementing the acquisition program was the creation of an Acquisitions Task Force in September 1973. This group, chaired by Mr. MacKinnon, had the responsibility of establishing basic guidelines for Ciba-Geigy's acquisition program. A Task Force memorandum spelling out the characteristics of attractive acquisition candidates and identifying areas of acquisition interest included the following acquisition criteria:

1. The candidate should participate in growing markets.

2. The candidate should have a proprietary position in its markets.

3. The candidate's operations should be favorably affected by Ciba-Geigy's knowhow in the fields of research and development and the manufacture and marketing of complex synthetic organic chemicals.

4. The candidate's business should be product rather than service oriented.

5. The candidate should have sales of $50 million or more.

6. The candidate should earn a good gross profit margin on sales.

7. The candidate should have the potential to yield a return on investment of 10 percent or more.

8. The probable purchase price should not exceed $250 million.

The memorandum stressed that the company was particularly interested in companies that could offer a potential for substantial growth outside the United States through the efforts of the parent company's worldwide organization.

In addition to these acquisition criteria, areas of acquisition interest were also identified in the Task Force's memorandum. These included specialty chemicals, proprietary pharmaceuticals, cosmetic and toiletry products, animal health products, proprietary household and garden products, medical supplies, products and services related to air, liquid, and solid waste treatment, and photochemicals and related products.

To implement its search for acquisitions, Ciba-Geigy circulated its criteria among investment and commercial banking firms so that these organizations could refer acquisition candidates to Ciba-Geigy. In addition, the Task Force reviewed approximately 10,000 publicly held companies (from Standard & Poor's and Moody's industrial directories) and 8,000 additional companies (using Dun & Bradstreet computer types), which were primarily privately owned. A computer review by industry, conducted by an investment banking firm, supplemented this manual review. At the same time that this massive screening was going on, the Task Force worked with all the company's divisions to identify any companies or divisions of companies in which they might have had an interest.

After several months of screening, about one hundred companies emerged as meeting Ciba-Geigy's general criteria. The Task Force then prepared a two-page summary on each for review by Ciba-Geigy's Corporate Managing Committee. Among these companies was Airwick Industries.

The Dilemma Posed by Airwick Industries, Inc.

In fiscal 1973 Airwick Industries had sales of $33.5 million, net earnings of $2.7 million, and return on shareholders' investment of 22.5 percent. The company's principal products consisted of odor-counteracting air fresheners together with a full line of sanitary maintenance items, including disinfectants, cleaners, and insecticides with odor counteraction features, and certain swimming pool products. These products were marketed through four divisions—Consumer, Institutional, International, and Aquatic—with the assistance of food brokers and franchised dealers. Three air fresheners—Airwick Solid, Airwick Liquid, and Airwick Spray—accounted for 97 percent of the Consumer Division's net sales and 72 percent of total corporate sales.

In addition to having experienced rapid growth (in excess of 15 percent per year for the last five years), the air freshener market had become extremely competitive. Many manufacturers and distributors were trying to stake out a position in the market for room deodorants. Major competitors of Airwick included Bristol-Myers with its Renuzit brand (which had recently eclipsed Airwick as the number one brand), American Home Products with its Wizard brand, Home Products Corporation with Days-Ease, and S. C. Johnson & Company with Glade. Intense competition developed in 1973 in the "solid" segment of the household air freshener market. While the market was expanding significantly, competitive products proliferated. American Home Products was a new entrant, and it was believed that Gillette was preparing to enter the market. Thus, Airwick's principal competition came from large marketing-oriented companies whose size and financial strength enabled them to expend large sums in packaging, advertising, and promoting their products.

After two weeks of interviewing and analysis, a special Airwick Task Force concluded that if Ciba-Geigy had a strategic interest in entering the household products business, Airwick could be an attractive way of doing it, assuming the price was not excessive.

The detailed findings of the Airwick Task Force included the following points:

1. Airwick is a profitable company whose earnings may have temporarily plateaued due to severe competition in the consumer segment of their business.

2. Competition in the consumer segment of the business will definitely restrict growth and reduce profitability of this segment in the immediate years ahead. Indeed, without a more carefully prepared marketing plan, a well-conceived new-products program, and additional advertising expenditures, it

will be difficult to achieve an increase in sales of much more than 5 or 6 percent annually.

3. The Institutional segment of Airwick (Airkem Institutional Division) is in excellent shape. They have good management, good products, and a good marketing program. They participate in a large, fractured market where the leading competitor is estimated to have only 8 percent of the market, as compared with an estimated 5 percent for Airwick. There is good potential for this division.

4. The International segment appears to be a profitable part of Airwick in terms of contribution as a percent of revenues. Current growth rates can most likely be maintained.

5. While the Acquatic segment appears to be healthy, it does not appear to be the kind of business that would normally be attractive for Ciba-Geigy.

6. Airwick's present financial position is difficult because of a need for cash. At the end of 1973 the company had only a minimum of debt outstanding, but as of May 7, 1974, it had $8 million in short-term loans outstanding, paying prime interest rates. The cash shortage seems to have been caused by the recent acquisition of the Seablue Corporation for $4 million in cash; the necessity of building seasonal inventories for the Aquatic segment of the business; and the turndown in Airwick's consumer business over the last nine months.

7. Production is relatively simple and efficient. While the new St. Peters plant is impressive, the Carlstadt, N.J., plant is overcrowded and needs immediate relief.

8. The research-and-development activity appears to be suffering from understanding and a lack of direction.

9. Airwick appears to be highly people-oriented. The president addresses a substantial number of employees by their first name and seems to know a great deal about them. This personal attention is reflected in their benefit programs, which appear to compare favorably with those of Ciba-Geigy.

10. Potential synergisms:

    a. Madison Laboratories has personnel with marketing skills that may help Airwick; Airwick has the sales organization that Madison Laboratories lacks.

    b. Ciba-Geigy has money, which Airwick needs to grow.

    c. Ciba-Geigy has available space and equipment, which may be useful to Airwick.

    d. Ciba-Geigy's chemical ability and research facilities could improve Airwick's products and provide Airwick with a better research-and-development effort with little increase in incremental costs.

    e. Ciba-Geigy's Agricultural Division has products that could be marketed by Airwick.

11. A savings of $1 million in Airwick's overhead could be achieved, which would add to the return of any contemplated investment in Airwick.

The tentative nature of the Airwick Task Force's conclusions are significant. The Airwick Task Force concluded that Airwick Industries, at the "right" price, could be an attractive acquisition *if Ciba-Geigy had a strategic interest in entering the household products business.* But what was Ciba-Geigy's "strategic interest"? Why didn't the Airwick Task Force know what it was? Why did the Airwick Task Force show such little faith in their own conclusions on potential synergisms between the two companies? Was this uncertainty due to acquisition criteria that failed to provide practical guidelines for identifying businesses related to Ciba-Geigy's distinctive competences and serving the company's strategic interest?

These questions had special importance in the spring of 1974, since Ciba-Geigy was just completing a tender offer for Funk Seed International and was holding discussions with two other acquisition candidates closely related to other areas of Ciba-Geigy's business. While these diversifying acquisitions, if consummated, would not eliminate the possibility of further acquisitions, there was concern that postmerger problems would consume more top management time and corporate funds than currently expected.

The possible acquisition of Airwick posed a "fish or cut bait" decision for Ciba-Geigy with respect to consumer products in general and household products specifically. The fact that Ciba-Geigy was seriously considering divestiture of the small Madison Laboratories Division added to the decision's immediacy. By the time the Airwick acquisition study was presented, Ciba-Geigy had already held three sets of discussions with companies interested in acquiring Madison. Airwick's acquisition would mean not only that household products was an appropriate business for Ciba-Geigy but also that Airwick was the best vehicle for developing a position in this field.

In the course of analyzing both Madison and Airwick, Mr. MacKinnon and his colleagues began to question whether or not their company's special strengths were relevant to the long-run success of consumer product companies. The underlying motivation was simple enough. If Ciba-Geigy thought it could help these companies improve their competitive position, then the investment could be a potentially profitable one. It also became apparent that by identifying the company's special strengths, they would not only be able to structure the "go/no-go" decision regarding Airwick Industries, but they would also have the basis for developing meaningful acquisition criteria for the continuing work of the Acquisitions Task Force. In essence, the thinking which Mr. MacKinnon and his colleagues were led to do *after* the report of the Airwick Task Force was exactly what the Acquisitions Task Force could have usefully done before establishing and circulating Ciba-Geigy's acquisition criteria.

The questions posed by the conclusions of the Airwick Task Force and the resulting problem faced by Ciba-Geigy Corporation are not an isolated incident in the history of acquisition-minded companies. Many companies face similar dilemmas, which, more often than not, are intensified by investment bankers who inevitably (and understandably) bring brilliant "deals" to acquisition-minded clients. The case of Ciba-Geigy Corporation provides a convenient vehicle for demonstrating not only the dilemma faced by many companies but also how more useful acquisition criteria or guidelines can be developed for companies interested in related diversification through acquisition. It is a particularly useful example precisely because it is not a case of pathology. Indeed, Ciba-Geigy's approach can be cited as a model of intelligent acquisition behavior, as far as it goes. While Ciba-Geigy's extensive screening of industries and companies reflects acquisition guidelines that can be readily associated with propositions underlying both the product/market-portfolio and risk/return models, the company apparently did not pursue the line of analysis suggested by the strategy model. As demonstrated below, this line of analysis provides the most useful guidelines for successful related diversification.

Rethinking Ciba-Geigy's Acquisition Guidelines

Related diversification requires that new businesses or activities have a coherence, or "fit," with the existing businesses of the acquisition-minded company. Achieving this fit involves exploring a range of possible choices. At one extreme, where a company wishes to diversify by expanding its existing competences in its key functional areas, a related-supplementary diversification objective exists. At the other extreme, where a company wishes to diversify by adding skills that complement existing functional skills, a related-complementary diversification objective exists. Acquisition guidelines for related diversification should reflect either a related-complementary or a related-supplementary diversification objective. If a company wishes to pursue both objectives, then it should have two sets of acquisition guidelines. Since related diversification involves expansion of an existing business, preparation of acquisition guidelines should focus on the operating and management aspects of the diversifying acquisition rather than on its purely financial and economic characteristics. This procedure recognizes that the benefits of related diversification stemming from operating synergy are much greater than those stemming from improved financial management or capital efficiencies.[5]

With this in mind, one can see the deficiency in Ciba-Geigy's rather extensive list of acquisition guidelines. Instead of concentrating on its unique skills and resources and the operating requirements of potential acquisitions, Ciba-Geigy's guidelines focused on financial and investment criteria. Of the eight guidelines, only two embodied any notion of strategic fit. Since the fourth guideline principally concerned product definition, only the third acquisition guideline provided operating or management criteria for analyzing how a related acquisition could create value for shareholders.

What were Ciba-Geigy's distinctive skills and resources, and what were the characteristics of businesses that could benefit from these skills and resources? Like many specialty chemical companies, Ciba-Geigy's special strengths stemmed from its sophisticated science-based research skills (reinforced by patent protection for new discoveries or formulations) and its ability to control product quality. From a management point of view, ensuring a fruitful research-and-development program was the critical task. Once effective new products were developed, successful product launching and market development was highly probable. The continual development and introduction of specialized products also meant many of the problems associated with managing an undifferentiated product in a competitive market were deferred until competitors were able to duplicate the company's research-and-development efforts, often many years later. Thus, relative to many other companies, Ciba-Geigy did not require (nor perhaps, encourage) the development of marketing skills. For industrial, agricultural, and pharmaceutical products, successful marketing involved a combination of technical documentation and sales management. Ciba-Geigy's need for consumer product marketing was low, and using the performance of Madison Laboratories as an indicator, the company's skills in this area were marginal.

The major risk points in Ciba-Geigy's business and, by implication, the company's key functional skills lay in areas of organic chemical research and the manufacture of quality-assured products. If Ciba-Geigy's diversification objectives had been to build upon these skills, a strategy of related-supplementary diversification, attractive acquisition candidates would have been companies whose critical success variables were the same as Ciba-Geigy's. More specifically, attractive acquisition candidates would have the following characteristics:

1. Business requiring high levels of chemically based research-and-development skills.

2. Businesses whose products are manufactured by chemical processes requiring a high degree of engineering or technical knowhow.

3. Businesses whose principal products are sold on technically based performance specifications.

4. Businesses not requiring heavy advertising or expensive distribution systems that would take resources away from the maintenance of distinctive R&D and manufacturing capabilities.

5. Businesses whose products served distinctive market segments though closely related in terms of production requirements and/or technology.

According to these criteria, Ciba-Geigy would have steered away from businesses that were either marketing-intensive or involved in the production of commodity products. Indeed, many businesses concentrating on household and personal care products, garden products, and waste treatment products—all businesses included on Ciba-Geigy's initial list of areas of acquisition interest—would not have met these criteria. On the other hand, such business areas as proprietary pharmaceuticals, animal health and veterinary products, chemically based diagnostic aids, and specialty chemicals like biocides, molding compounds, coatings, and chemicals for pretreating and finishing textiles—all related to Ciba-Geigy's existing commercial activities—would most likely have qualified.

If, however, Ciba-Geigy had wished to pursue related diversification through adding key skills or resources in new functional activities, a strategy of related-complementary diversification, a very different set of acquisition guidelines would have been necessary. In this situation, acquisition guidelines could have usefully identified companies that utilized the same basic resources as Ciba-Geigy but whose skills complemented those of Ciba-Geigy. Since science-based chemical research and high-quality, low-volume chemical production were Ciba-Geigy's strengths, related complementary businesses would have been organizations with skills in large-scale manufacturing, marketing, and distribution. Attractive related-complementary acquisition candidates would therefore have the following characteristics:

1. Businesses whose resource inputs could include Ciba-Geigy specialty chemicals.

2. Businesses whose success is highly dependent on chemical usage or application.

3. Businesses involved in the production and/or distribution of chemically based products.

4. Businesses whose key success factor is marketing-oriented. This may include, but is not limited to, companies with extensive distribution systems, well-known brand names, and/or customer acceptance.

According to these guidelines Ciba-Geigy would have been looking at high-volume and marketing-intensive businesses related to its existing chemical base. These guidelines do not suggest that Ciba-Geigy produce commodity chemicals such as benzene but rather high-volume products that use specialty chemicals as part of their formulation. Businesses meeting these guidelines might have included household care products, garden products, waste treatment products, cleaning compounds, and photographic supplies. These businesses were included on Ciba-Geigy's initial list of areas of acquisition interest, but their critical success factors differ significantly from those of Ciba-Geigy's traditional businesses.

The Source of Ciba-Geigy's Dilemma

Viewed through the filter of related-supplementary acquisition guidelines, guidelines reflecting Ciba-Geigy's strengths, Airwick does not look like an attractive acquisition. While air fresheners and odor counteractants were made from chemical solutions, their formulation depended on "blind testing" and their production on batch mixing. This does not qualify as the kind of sophisticated research-and-development or high-technology manufacturing where Ciba-Geigy excelled. In addition, while Ciba-Geigy sold its products on technical performance characteristics, Airwick relied heavily on promotion-oriented marketing strategies. Airwick's consumer products required advertising, sales promotion, and packaging expenses in excess of cost of goods sold. Ciba-Geigy had little experience in dealing with this type of product. In short, Ciba-Geigy and Airwick shared few critical success factors, and the opportunities to reinforce each other's basic strengths were limited.

The analysis of Airwick significantly changes, however, if one assumes Ciba-Geigy wanted to follow a related-complementary diversification objective, a strategy of adding key functional skills to its existing resource base. The related-complementary acquisition guidelines outlined above suggest the merits of moving down the commercial chain toward individual consumers. In particular, the guidelines suggest that marketing-oriented companies with chemically based products would be desirable. Viewed in the context of these guidelines, Airwick looks much more attractive. While Airwick's consumer business was weakening, its reputation was well established and offered Ciba-Geigy an important channel to consumer markets and an introduction to consumer marketing. In addition, Airwick's institutional business could offer a new marketing channel for products from Ciba-Geigy's Agricultural Division (pesticides, for example) as well as industrial cleaners, coatings, and adhesives that could be formulated from Ciba-Geigy's specialty chemicals.

These conflicting conclusions—stemming from different guidelines for analysis—help us identify why the Acquisitions Task Force was so ambivalent about Airwick. The Task Force's difficulty in grasping Ciba-Geigy's "strategic interests" and coming to a final judgment on Airwick resulted from the failure of its acquisition guidelines to distinguish between two quite different objectives for related diversification. In the absence of precisely defined objectives, the Task Force fell into analyzing Airwick according to a related-supplementary diversification objective. This led the Task Force to feel more comfortable with companies requiring skills similar to those of Ciba-Geigy. However, since (1) Airwick's key success factors were quite different from Ciba-Geigy's and (2) Ciba-Geigy's functional strengths were largely irrelevant to the future of Airwick (a substantial bankroll notwithstanding), the Task Force quite naturally felt the need to hedge its recommendations. Similarly, Mr. MacKinnon quite naturally felt the need to develop more meaningful acquisition guidelines for marketing-oriented companies. Both the Task Force and Mr. MacKinnon sensed that Airwick offered an acquisition opportunity, but they were unsure about what standards should be used in judging its potential benefits to Ciba-Geigy.

The lesson of the Ciba-Geigy case is simple but fundamental. Companies pursuing related diversification through acquisition need to pursue a rigorous identification and analysis of both their distinctive skills and resources and their points of weakness. Such an "audit" provides the basis for defining diversification objectives (related-supplementary diversification, related-complementary diversification, or both) and formulating acquisition guidelines that provide meaningful criteria for evaluating acquisition candidates. Poorly defined related diversification objectives or a preoccupation with financial criteria can confuse managers responsible for executing a strategy of related diversification or force them, by default, to reject their guidelines as a practical decision-making tool.

Epilogue

After some urging by the Swiss parent, Ciba-Geigy Corporation tendered for Airwick's stock in June, 1974. The tender offer was successful at a total transaction value of $44 million, a 50 percent premium over Airwick's market value prior to public knowledge of Airwick's willingness to entertain a takeover. Whether or not Airwick will be able to generate sufficient returns to compensate Ciba-Geigy for such a large premium is, of course, uncertain. But it is noteworthy that the greatest potential for value creation lies in Airwick's ability to bring new functional skills and resources to Ciba-Geigy's existing resource base. Accordingly, Ciba-Geigy's management should direct Airwick's consumer marketing expertise toward those Ciba-Geigy chemical products with the highest potential for finding a profitable niche in consumer markets. Such a consumer business would not only complement Ciba-Geigy's existing businesses and resource structure but also represent an important shift in Ciba-Geigy Corporation's overall corporate strategy.

Developing Acquisition Guidelines for Unrelated Diversification

Shareholder benefits from unrelated or conglomerate diversification can occur where more efficient capital management and/or growth in profits through cross-subsidization leads to a larger return for corporate investors than that available from a diversified portfolio of securities of comparable systematic risk.[6] Additional benefits, not strictly due to diversification, can be created where an acquiring company can obtain undervalued assets or can successfully revitalize previously underutilized assets. Since value can only be created for a company's shareholders by undertaking projects that improve its risk/return profile, a company pursuing unrelated diversification can usefully identify its own risk/return characteristics as an aid in determining what kind of financial characteristics acquisition candidates should have so that the potential for value creation will exist for its shareholders. Following this, the development of additional acquisition guidelines focusing on the desired cash flow characteristics of companies can help narrow the field of acquisition candidates. As a final step in developing acquisition guidelines, additional economic and strategic characteristics of high-potential acquisitions should also be articulated. The following discussion will show how concepts drawn from the risk/return model, the product/market-portfolio model, and the strategy model—used in that order of analysis—can help structure this process.

The Case of General Cinema Corporation

A situation that lends itself to the kind of analytic procedure suggested above is provided by the General Cinema Corporation. In 1975 General Cinema was the largest operator of multiple-auditorium theater complexes (328 locations) and the largest soft-drink bottler (21 beverage plants) in the United States. Revenues in 1975 totaled $358 million. Earnings growth had been at a 23.4 percent compounded rate over the previous ten years, providing a 20 percent return on equity. By 1976 the company had successfully reduced the large amount of debt incurred while General Cinema was an active acquirer of soft-drink bottlers, and the company began to search for what was referred to as "the third leg of the stool."

General Cinema's acquisition guidelines indicated a preference for high-potential, medium- to-large-sized companies ($5 to $20 million in pre-tax earnings); companies requiring significant cash infusions; consumer- and leisure-oriented companies with unique characteristics that serve to protect them against potential competitors; companies run by good operating managers; and companies whose primary orientation was toward the U.S. market. In discussing these qualitative objectives, General Cinema's managers spoke of bringing the company's existing competences to bear on any new business that they might acquire. General Cinema's president, Richard Smith, noted that he "didn't want to be dependent on the specialized skills of a few individuals." His executive vice president echoed a similar sentiment when he said, "Rather than becoming dependent on acquired management, I would feel more comfortable if we could do their job as well if the need arose." All this suggests that General Cinema was looking for some vaguely defined, related business.

Other evidence, however, indicates a high degree of ambivalence about related business diversification. General Cinema's soft-drink bottling business cannot be said to be closely related to the multiple-auditorium theater business in either a product market sense or an administrative sense. Neither can several of General Cinema's earlier attempts at diversification: bowling alleys, FM radio stations, and furniture retailing. In the case of General Cinema's diversification efforts, the difference between espoused theory and the company's actual behavior is both clear and notable. Assuming, therefore, a realistic interest in unrelated diversification (as well as continued expansion of its present businesses), the question arises as to what additional acquisition guidelines could usefully structure General Cinema's search for an attractive unrelated acquisition candidate.

Risk/Return Analysis

As suggested above, the first step in developing acquisition guidelines for a company intent on pursuing unrelated diversification is analyzing the company's risk/return profile. In January 1976 General Cinema's beta, or level of systematic risk, was a relatively high 1.80.[7] Underlying this high beta was not the inherent cash flow volatility of General Cinema's businesses but rather its policy of financial leverage. With a debt-to-equity ratio in excess of 3 to 1,[8] General Cinema's unlevered, or equity, beta would be approximately .8. This is confirmed by an industry risk analysis, since unlevered betas for the bottling industry are in the .9 to 1.0 range while unlevered betas for movie theater operations are in the .6 to .7 range.[9] When the unlevered betas are combined in proportion to General Cinema's (probable) investments in each business, the portfolio beta is somewhere between .7 and .8.

With these data one can see how General Cinema was attempting to create value for its shareholders. Management's preference was apparently for businesses with relatively stable, predictable cash flows. In order to increase these returns to meet their goal of 20 percent return on equity, General Cinema's management was willing to increase its risk profile by taking on more debt. Since interest, unlike equity returns, is tax deductible, financial risk taking in General Cinema's case created value for its equity owners.[10] In addition, by combining two industries with somewhat different cash flow patterns General Cinema had a new, more stable cash flow than previously existed. This, in turn, enabled General Cinema to take on either more debt than the two businesses, as separate entities, could most likely have done or the same amount of debt at a lesser cost.[11] General Cinema's unrelated diversification therefore had the potential of creating value for shareholders by enabling the corporation to take on a greater amount of debt at a potentially lower cost than could its component businesses as separate entities.

Using concepts drawn from the risk/return model, three different approaches to unrelated acquisition (and therefore three sets of acquisition guidelines) can be generated. The three options can be differentiated according to (1) assumptions about how much risk General Cinema's stockholders are willing to bear and (2) the means by which that risk is to be achieved. The first option would be to acquire a company with relatively low systematic or market-related risk in an effort to reduce General Cinema's overall level of systematic risk. This option would be justified if General Cinema's managers felt their shareholders preferred a lower risk company or that a better risk/return tradeoff was available at lower levels of systematic risk.[12] The principal benefit achieved, that of risk pooling, would be of questionable value to shareholders unless General Cinema releveraged itself. Furthermore, if General Cinema wanted to reduce its overall riskiness, it could best achieve that objective by reducing its debt burden. A second option would be for General Cinema to acquire an unrelated company with high systematic risk. This option is consistent with management's apparent belief that General Cinema's shareholders wanted a high-risk, high-return company. Since the opportunity for aggressively leveraging this type of acquisition is probably minimal, the potential benefits are limited primarily to improved capital management.[13]

A third option would be for General Cinema to acquire a company with a low business risk which, when included in General Cinema's portfolio, could benefit from both risk pooling as well as the ability to use increased financial leverage. Since this option appears to be the most attractive of the three, acquisition guidelines reflecting it can be articulated. In general terms, a highly attractive unrelated diversifying acquisition would be a company with low systematic risk and the capacity to carry a high level of debt. In other words, using the language of risk/return model, the acquisition candidate should have an unlevered beta under 1.0, preferably beneath .8, and be capable of supporting a debt-to-equity ratio in excess of 2 to 1. The candidate's levered beta, after acquisition, should be in excess of 2.0. In addition, the acquisition candidate's unsystematic or business specific risk should be relatively large, implying significant risk pooling benefits.

Product/Market Portfolio Analysis

The second step in the process of developing practical acquisition guidelines for a company pursuing unrelated diversification should focus on the market share status and cash flow characteristics of a diversifying company's product/market portfolio. Since General Cinema's divisions were the largest competitors in industries with real growth rates between 2 percent and 4 percent, they were classic "cash cows" as defined by the product/market-portfolio model. If one refines the notion of market share to reflect restricted geographic areas due to the "franchise" nature of each industry, General Cinema's competitive position appears even stronger. In addition, since both bottling and movie theaters were not capital-intensive businesses, General Cinema's cash flow was, relative to many industries, already high. This economic strength was likely to increase as growth in revenues and continued financial leverage interacted to generate an increasing surplus of cash funds.

A cash flow analysis of General Cinema based on a consideration of the company's product/market portfolio suggests two types of high potential unrelated acquisitions. One would be to acquire a relatively large, maturing company generating a minimal excess cash flow and using General Cinema's surplus cash to provide the incremental funds necessary to fund the purchase. The second, more commonly articulated alternative, would be to acquire a smaller, rapidly growing, cash-using business. In this scenario, the acquiring company would make significant cash infusions into the acquired company, thereby enabling the acquired company to maintain or increase its growth rate. Ideally, this strategy would lead to market dominance and the higher return on investment that such a position typically brings. One should note that both alternatives could involve the same capitalized value, but the investment and payout patterns would be significantly different.

While both would be viable alternatives, acquiring a growth company probably fits General Cinema's characteristics and management goals more closely. In particular, a growth situation could make better use of General Cinema's increasing cash flow. It would also not require the significant "up-front" investment typically associated with purchases of well-established companies. Assuming this choice, acquisition guidelines should emphasize growth situations where significant market share could be obtained. More specifically, the acquisition candidate should be growing in excess of 10 percent per year and offer a potential operating return in excess of 25 percent. The acquisition should be asset-intensive or have barriers to entry suitable for employing financial leverage. This would enable General Cinema to increase its rate of investment in the subsidiary and lead to earlier profitability.

Strategic Analysis

A broad strategic analysis of General Cinema generates further guidelines for a successful unrelated acquisition. There are three key success factors in operating movie theaters: site location, film selection and procurement, and management of geographically decentralized operations. Management of geographically dispersed operations is common to many service businesses, and film selection and procurement at attractive terms is primarily a function of size and market share; only site location is a highly specialized skill. With respect to soft-drink bottling, there are two key success factors: good distribution and marketing, and efficient production. Both industries are similar in that they deal with the final consumer and require high volumes to achieve efficient operations. This indicates that General Cinema had most likely developed functional skills closely related to the distribution and marketing of consumer products and services. In contrast, since General Cinema had only recently emerged from an entrepreneurial stage of corporate development, it did not appear to have a surplus of general managers in either the two operating divisions or the corporate office. The corporate office did, however, utilize extensive planning and control systems and disciplined resource allocation procedures.

A brief assessment of General Cinema's strengths and weaknesses leads to several additional acquisition criteria. Since the most important weakness was General Cinema's lack of surplus general managers, any unrelated acquisition had to have good, top-level operating managers who would stay with the company. The acquisition also had to be adaptable to General Cinema's extensive control system, which enabled the company's relatively small headquarters office to monitor performance and allocate resources. Finally, a high-potential, unrelated acquisition would be a company whose principal activities involved the marketing and/or distribution of goods or services from a large number of relatively small, geographically dispersed units.

Acquisition Guidelines

These three sets of acquisition guidelines, each reflecting concepts drawn from the risk/return, product/market-portfolio, and strategy models, can be combined into a more comprehensive list. These guidelines, expanding upon those originally developed by the company,[14] can help General Cinema's management identify acquisition candidates that offer their shareholders the greatest potential for value creation. They are:

Risk/Return Characteristics

1. Industries/companies with high levels of unsystematic or business-specific risk.

2. Industries/companies with relatively low levels of systematic or market-related risk when financed on an all-equity basis. Unlevered betas under .8 would be preferred, though the .8 to 1.0 range is acceptable.

3. Industries/companies that can be debt financed so that the levered beta is in excess of 2.0. This would imply debt to equity ratios of 2 to 1 or greater.

4. The ideal acquisition candidate should be one whose high level of business-specific risk either greatly increases the cost of debt financing or prevents it from being used extensively. These characteristics would present General Cinema with the potential to benefit through risk pooling.

Product/Market Portfolio Characteristics

1. Industries that are relatively capital intensive and capable of absorbing significant infusions of cash.

2. Industries experiencing sustained levels of above-average growth (10 percent or greater).

3. Industries where a strong competitive position is obtainable through either aggressive growth or entry barriers.

4. The interaction of guidelines 1, 2, 3 imply that the more capital intensive the acquisition is, the lower its growth rate needs to be in order to absorb General Cinema's surplus cash.

Strategic Characteristics

1. Companies with proven products and proven management. Startups or ventures requiring extensive involvement of the corporate office are to be avoided.

2. Industries/companies where planning, cost, and investment controls can be established and easily integrated into General Cinema's existing control system.

3. Companies whose products and/or services are sold directly to the general population.

4. A high-potential acquisition candidate would share similar key management skills with General Cinema's existing businesses. These skills include marketing and distributing products or services to consumers in multiple geographic areas.

Once articulated, these acquisition guidelines can be used to identify attractive acquisition candidates. Direct usage of these guidelines requires both that extensive data banks be available and that exhaustive analysis be done. Even with its own acquisitions staff, the diversifying company will often rely on outside professionals, including investment bankers, management consultants, and data compilation companies to accomplish this. In addition, analysis of such nonquantitative guidelines as desired management characteristics will require careful thought and significant amounts of time on the part of managers responsible for implementing a program of diversification through acquisition.

These acquisition guidelines can be used to develop less technical descriptive statements about attractive acquisition candidates. These statements should embody more readily observable industry and company characteristics than the acquisition guidelines. Such statements for General Cinema would include the following:

1. The acquisition candidate should have a minimum return on invested capital of 16 percent. Total invested assets (working capital, debt, leases, and equity) should be at least three times the equity investment. Reflecting this leverage, the before-tax return on equity should be at least 30 percent.[15]

2. Since General Cinema's surplus cash flow is increasing, significant growth potential over an extended period of time must exist. The industry growth rate should be in excess of 10 percent; a 20 percent growth rate should be achievable by the acquisition in order to absorb General Cinema's surplus cash flow.

3. The acquisition candidate should be asset intensive. These assets may either be fixed assets such as buildings and equipment or intangibles such as trademarks, franchises, or goodwill.

4. Since high levels of debt will be used, the acquisition's assets must create high barriers to entry. If these assets are intangibles, they must be well established with significant ongoing value in order to be "bankable." This implies products relatively immune to market change or technological obsolescence.

5. The requirements for relative immunity to market change and a high growth rate imply that the acquisition will be service oriented rather than technology based.

6. For General Cinema's management to feel comfortable with the acquisition, it should market or distribute products or services to the consuming public.

7. Since General Cinema lacks surplus general managers, the acquisition must have good operating managers. Successful integration into General Cinema requires that the acquisition be adaptable to intensive planning and financial controls.

8. A highly attractive acquisition candidate might operate a large number of geographically dispersed units where site location contributes directly to unit profitability.

While the acquisition guidelines developed here do not conflict with General Cinema's original set, our procedure has produced more specific guidelines which indicate those conditions that must be met in order for value to be created for General Cinema's shareholders.

Conclusion

The discussion of the Ciba-Geigy and General Cinema cases shows how the process of developing acquisition guidelines for unrelated diversification should differ in focus from the process employed for related diversification. In conjunction with the argument presented in the introduction to this chapter, our discussion also indicates why the process of developing such guidelines should differ from companies pursuing different strategies of diversification through acquisition.

In essence, our rationale for a strategy-specific approach to developing acquisition guidelines stems from the simple notion that related and unrelated diversification imply very different means of creating value for shareholders. While the former approach requires that the special skills and industry knowledge of one merger partner be applied to the competitive problems and opportunities facing the other, unrelated diversification depends on improving the risk/return profile of the diversifying company through either more efficient asset management or more efficient capital management. Given these differences in the conditions necessary for creating value, it is logical to expect that the self-analysis and subsequent development of acquisition guidelines should differ for related and unrelated diversification.

The Ciba-Geigy and General Cinema cases also demonstrate how closely tied acquisition guidelines should be to overall corporate strategy.

Effective acquisition guidelines must reflect carefully thought-out diversification objectives. These objectives, in turn, should be consistent with the long-run strategic orientation of the enterprise. In situations where the diversification objectives lack specificity, as was the case with Ciba-Geigy, acquisition guidelines will be vague and have limited utility as a decision-making tool. This is as true for unrelated diversification as it is for related diversification. Diversification objectives and acquisition guidelines expressed in terms of countercyclical businesses possessing certain size, profitability, and growth characteristics cannot help companies like General Cinema identify high-potential acquisitions. More detailed objectives and acquisition guidelines, reflecting a careful analysis of the current characteristics of the business and management's designation of an appropriate relationship between risk and reward, are necessary to ensure that acquisition candidates will possess the potential of creating value for the shareholders of unrelated diversifiers.

While we have demonstrated in this chapter how the process for developing acquisition guidelines for related-business diversifiers should differ from that appropriate for unrelated-business diversifiers, we have not fully addressed the issue of how such guidelines can be built into formal systems for identifying and screening acquisition candidates.

Notes and References

1. There are several reasons why this might occur, but probably the most significant is the unevenness of information and analysis concerning future economic events.

2. This implies that an acquisition's potential for value creation must be compared to the potential of all of a company's investment opportunities, including the reacquisition of its own equity, to create value. If, for example, a potential acquisition was undervalued by 20 percent and the diversifying company was undervalued by 30 percent, the diversifying company could create more value for its shareholders by reacquiring its own stock rather than making the acquisition, assuming the competitive investments were of equal size. If, however, the diversifying company was undervalued by only 10 percent, then the acquisition would provide a relatively greater potential for value creation. While a company should undertake all projects that show a return in excess of their risk-adjusted required rate of return, capital constraints imply that projects with the highest risk-adjusted potential for value creation be undertaken before those with a lesser potential.

3. Kenneth R. Andrews, *The Concept of Corporate Strategy,* Dow Jones–Irwin, 1971.

4. In connection with the 1970 merger of Ciba, AG, and JR Geigy, AG, Ciba-Geigy Corporation was constrained by a consent decree with the Justice

Department from making acquisitions in its existing lines of business for a period of five years.

5. See Chapters 3 and 7 for a more detailed discussion of the potential benefits of related diversification.

6. Since investors can diversify away unsystematic or security-specific risk, the market can be said to compensate investors for only systematic or market-related risk.

7. Company betas, or level of systematic risk, are reported by several organizations, including Value Line and Merrill Lynch. The data presented here are based on Merrill Lynch's January 1976 Security Risk Evaluation report. Industry betas can be compiled as a weighted average beta of the industry's component companies.

8. Current financial theory implies that in an efficient market, leases have the same impact on a corporation's risk/return profile as its debt. This implies that leases should be capitalized and added to the corporation's debt in determining a company's debt-to-equity ratio.

9. Unlevered, or pure equity, betas are determined by eliminating the impact of financial leverage on an asset's risks and returns. This enables the risks and returns of similar assets to be compared regardless of their financing and their managers' or owners' total risk preference. For a description of how to determine the unlevered systematic risk of a company, see the Appendix to Chapter 7, pp. 283–288.

10. One should remember, however, that financial leverage is available to all companies and their equity holders and that much of the value created by General Cinema through its financial policies was not specifically due to diversification.

11. While a direct relationship between such business risks as potential bankruptcy and market based risk measures has not been established, it is safe to say that high business-specific risks indicate a potential for risk pooling. Risk pooling provides benefits for equity holders where altered perceptions of risk by lenders lead to improved borrowing abilities.

12. This implies that General Cinema's managers felt that the market is inefficient in that it values lower-risk/lower-return companies more highly than higher-risk/higher-return companies.

13. If this highly risky acquisition happened to have a volatile cash flow pattern that was negatively correlated with General Cinema's cash flow pattern, the risk pooling benefits and ability to use leverage could be significant. However, since General Cinema's businesses are relatively stable, it is hard to conceive of a cash flow pattern that would, in fact, complement it.

14. See page 172.

15. Rates of return can be computed using the capital asset pricing model, which relates risk and expected return through the following formula: $R_i = B_i(R_m - R_f) + R_f$, where B_i is the beta or level of systematic risk of the ith asset, R_m is the expected market return, and R_f is the expected risk-free rate of return. A beta of .8 implies a return on equity of approximately 8 percent given

long-run market and risk-free rates of return of 9.5 percent and 3 percent respectively. An after-tax return on equity (ROE) when debt is utilized can be found through the equation $ROI = [(D/D + E) \times ROD] + [(E/D + E) \times ROE]$ where $(D/D + E)$ and $(E/D + E)$ reflect the relative amounts of debt and equity in the capital structure and ROD is the after-tax return on debt. Assuming a 2-to-1 debt-to-equity ratio, an interest cost of 8 percent (an after-tax cost of 4 percent), and an 8 percent after-tax ROI, the after-tax return on equity is approximately 16 percent. This return is equivalent to the expected return for a systematic risk (or beta) of 2. Before-tax returns can be determined by dividing the after-tax returns by the corporate rate. One should note that all these returns should be adjusted to reflect the expected rate of inflation over the time horizon under consideration.

CHAPTER 9

Acquisition Screening Systems

THE PROCESS OF SCREENING potential acquisitions involves identifying companies with characteristics that fit the needs of the diversifying company and assessing their appropriateness for acquisition. Companies that successfully pass through a preliminary screen then merit the detailed examination suggested in Chapter 10. The final step in the screening process is determining the relative attractiveness of the leading acquisition candidates.

Effective screening systems have four important properties. First, an effective acquisition screening system must provide measures of the potential for creating value for the diversifying company's shareholders. Without such measures, managers responsible for a program of diversification through acquisition are in no position to discriminate between high- and low-potential companies. Second, an effective screening system must be able to reflect the special needs of each company using the system. Relying on checklists and/or priorities claiming to have universal applicability is the surest possible way of placing an entire acquisition program in jeopardy. Third, an effective screening system must be easy to use but not overly rigid. Since most structured frameworks of analysis run the risk of promoting mechanical solutions to complicated decision problems, formal screening procedures must not be allowed to crowd out more informal and spontaneous contributions to the decision-making process. Finally, an effective screening system must serve as a mechanism for communicating corporate goals to the parties involved in the diversification and acquisition process. The analytic concepts and language inherent in such a system can significantly aid managers in implementing a diversification strategy that reflects corporate and investor goals.

The purpose of this chapter is to present a structured approach for selecting potential acquisitions that possesses these properties. In the following discussions we will identify a group of measures, drawn from the conceptual framework and analytical procedures developed in previous chapters, which provide an overview of the potential for value creation. In addition, we will show how these measures can be tailored to a particular company's diversification objectives and acquisition guidelines. If employed with discretion and judgment, our formal screening system can assist managers in casting a wide net for potential acquisitions and reducing the catch to a small enough population so that an intensive analysis of acquisition options can be profitably undertaken. We will then present a method for quantifying an acquisition's potential for value creation as an aid in the final evaluation and ranking of acquisition candidates.

Measures of the Potential for Value Creation

Measuring the potential for creating value is the key function of our acquisition screening system. Understandably, this requires explicit measures that can help identify the potential for value creation. The screening grid, shown in Table 9-1, comprises twenty-three measures that summarize the key factors contributing to the value creation potential of acquisitions. These measures are divided into three broad groups dealing with risk characteristics, return characteristics, and integration potential. The first two groups of measures principally reflect the conceptual orientation of the risk/return and product/market-portfolio models. The third group corresponds more closely to the analysis suggested by the strategy model. We will comment in this section on each of these measures and indicate how the concepts underlying each measure can be used to assess the value of a specific industry or company to an acquisitive diversifier. How companies pursuing different diversification objectives should use these measures in the screening process will be discussed in a subsequent section. We only want to stress at this point that each measure will have a different value for each diversifying company and that the analysis of industries and companies will require many qualitative assessments of industry and company attributes.

Risk Characteristics

Risk characteristics cluster into three subgroups: capital market risk measures, microeconomic risk characteristics, and political and legal characteristics. Each measure has the potential of providing a diversifying company with important insight about the merits of an industry or an individual company.

TABLE 9-1. Acquisition Screening Grid

	Scoring Range	Industry A (Company A)	Industry B (Company B)	Industry N (Company N)
I. Risk Characteristics				
A. Capital Market Measures				
1. Financial risk				
2. Systematic (market-related) risk				
3. Unsystematic (business-specific) risk				
B. Microeconomic Measures				
4. Vulnerability to exogenous changes in supply and demand				
5. Ease of market entry and exit				
6. Potential of excess productive capacity				
7. Gross margin stability				
8. Strength of competitive position				
C. Political and Legal Measures				
9. Degree of government intervention				
10. Societal liabilities				
11. Antitrust risk				
Subtotal, Risk Characteristics				
II. Return Characteristics				
A. Nature of the Investment				
1. Size of the investment				
2. Period of the investment				
3. Liquidity of the investment				
4. Noncapitalized strategic investments				

	Scoring Range	Industry A (Company A)	Industry B (Company B)	Industry N (Company N)
B. *Nature of the Return*				
5. Size of the return				
6. Period of the return				
7. Return due to unique company characteristics				
Subtotal, Return Characteristics				
III. *Integration Potential*				
1. Supplementary skills/resources				
2. Complementary skills/resources				
3. Financial fit/ risk-pooling benefits				
4. Availability of general management skills				
5. Organizational Compatibility				
Subtotal, Integration Potential				
Grand Total				

Financial Risk: Financial risk refers to the burden of fixed payments stemming from the assumption of debt or other long-term contractual arrangements requiring a steady commitment of financial resources in the future. The most common and important of such contractual arrangements is long-term leases. The higher the fixed burden stemming from such financing or contractual arrangements, the higher the risk. The lower the fixed burden, the greater the opportunities for the acquirer to increase equity returns (and risk) through increased leverage. Generally, the less risky an asset is, the greater the amount of financial risk that can be incurred in its ownership. Industries can often be characterized by their financing practices, and individual companies can use financial risk as an integral part of their corporate strategy.

Systematic and Unsystematic Risk: A security's or asset's total risk and return can be decomposed into two parts: that which is specific to each company and called "unsystematic," since it can be diversified away, and the other known as "systematic," since it is common to all securities and hence nondiversifiable. Systematic risk, which capital market theory identifies as the most relevant measure of risk, refers to the variability of a security's return relative to the returns of all other securities in the market. A security's systematic risk/return characteristic is often referred to as "beta" (β), from the term in the correlation formula that relates a security's return to the market return. The more volatile a security's returns relative to the market's returns, the more risky it is and the higher its beta is. Betas are computed for many public companies by Merrill Lynch and the Value Line Investment Service, among others. Industry betas are also available through these sources.

In thinking about a company's systematic or market-related risk, it is useful to distinguish between (1) the risk due to the inherent characteristics of the company's underlying assets and (2) the financial risk, which stems from how those assets are financed. The unlevered systematic risk, or pure equity beta, measures the volatility of a company's returns relative to that of the market, assuming no financial risk has been incurred to finance the security's underlying assets. This measure eliminates financial risk and is the most fundamental risk measure of a company (or any other asset). It is also the most important market-related risk measure for an acquisitive company, since the acquirer will most likely change the acquired company's financing structure along with the usage of the acquired company's assets. In addition, an asset's systematic risk influences its required rate of return and therefore the asset's price or value in the marketplace.

Recent financial research, discussed in Chapter 5, has helped identify the economic determinants underlying systematic and unsystematic risk. These economic determinants include the volatility, timing, growth, and predictability of an asset's cash flow and the covariance of that asset's cash flow with the economy's level of activity. Assets with relatively nonvolatile cash flows, growing or long-lived cash flows, or predictable cash flows will tend to have lower systematic risk than otherwise. The pattern of cash flow generated by the assets of a specific business typically depends upon that business's microeconomic characteristics and its strategy for using its assets. Therefore, an analysis of these characteristics can help one better understand the factors contributing to a company's systematic and unsystematic risk. Several microeconomic measures particularly relevant to the diversification decision are discussed below.

Vulnerability to Exogenous Changes in Supply and Demand: This measure focuses on a company's supply and demand functions. In examining the risks affecting both supply and demand, careful attention should be devoted to identifying environmental factors subject to changes outside the company's control. Such factors may include resource vulnerability, changed social mores, or a greatly altered government presence. The risk faced by a company depends on how critical the specific environmental factor is to the company, how readily available substitutes are to the company, and how specialized the company's internal resources are. In addition, a company's risk depends on its ability to pass on or "lay off" these risks in the marketplace (such as through price increases). Where demand for a company's products or services is highly elastic (sensitive to price changes), the impact of changes in the availability and price of key factors of production on cash flow is high and implies significant risks.

Ease of Market Entry and Exit: The greater the ease of market entry or exit, the more one can expect competitors to enter a profitable market or leave an unprofitable one. This entry and exit by competitors will drive rates of return in that market toward "normal" or risk-adjusted levels. Ease of market entry and exit depends on so-called "barriers," which tend to insulate a market or company from economic competition. The nature and size of these barriers will greatly differ from market to market and company to company.

Entry and exit barriers can include capital needs (both fixed and working capital), specialized skills and resources, such as technology, patents, trademarks and distribution systems, and government licenses and permits. In addition, organizational strength and management skill may be the most effective entry barrier of all. Management commitment may also be the most pervasive exit barrier, since leaving a market often connotes management failure.

The impact of entry and exit barriers on the cash flow and profitability of competitors within a specific market can be significant. For example, where high entry barriers exist in a market characterized by high rates of profitability, entrants by acquisition will be limited to a more normal rate of return by having to pay a substantial acquisition premium. This acquisition premium amounts to the capitalized value of the candidate's "excess" return over "normal" or risk-adjusted rates of return.

Tendency toward Excess Productive Capacity: The risk of excess capacity is directly related to the nature of capital investments in a particular market or industry and the market's perceived and "real" rate of growth. If it is most efficient to add new capacity in large increments and if this new capacity is principally fixed investment (representing a fixed cost), there will be significant incentives to maintain volume through price cutting. (If market demand is relatively price inelastic, this strategy eventually leads to reduced total revenues for the entire industry.) In addition, if demand growth can be reasonably anticipated or forecasted, several competitors will often simultaneously add capacity to meet that projected demand, thereby risking the development of excess capacity for the industry as a whole. Finally, where market growth rates are low and capital assets are long-lived and suited to productivity improvement (for example, paper-manufacturing machines), there will also be a tendency toward surplus capacity, as companies can easily increase the output of existing facilities through technological upgrading. The fertilizer, paper, petrochemical, and aluminum industries have all experienced similar problems in the last decade.

Gross Margin Stability: The stability of gross margins is clearly related to production capacity and the ease of market entry and exit. Gross margins are the best indicators of industry profitability and the availability of cash flow to support administrative overhead, technological or market development, and new business ventures. In addition, the stability of gross margins indicates the relative attractiveness of substituting capital investment with its fixed costs for variable costs in the production process as a means of increasing long-run profitability.

Strength of Competitive Position: A leading indicator of competitive strength is market share. Its associated risk measure is vulnerability of market share position. Market share risks can be separated into two broad categories: those primarily internal to the market, involving competitive interactions, and those external to the market, involving environmental changes. While the separation of these two categories cannot be perfectly delineated, externally oriented risks generally include such events as technological obsolescence, radical changes in consumption patterns, and new distribution systems associated with changing demographics or technology.

Internal market risks include the degree of market turbulence (including growth) and the way competitors choose to modify their products and strategies in response to this turbulence. The market environment can provide either competitive opportunities or risks for an individual company, depending on the company's relative strength, the direction of market change, and the ability of the company to use its strengths to exploit opportunities or minimize risks created by market change. A company with a strong consumer franchise supported by a well-established distribution and marketing system, for example, can often offset the threat of rapid technological change. Similarly, a company can improve its competitive position in a mature, "commodity-type" market by radically improving the production technology.

Political and legal risks can be as important in evaluating an industry and its members as economic risks. Indeed, they are closely related, as the energy crisis has demonstrated. Three major clusters of political and legal risks can be useful for screening industries and companies of interest to an acquisitive diversifier: government intervention, societal liabilities, and antitrust policy.

Government Intervention: Forms of government intervention range from outright nationalization to the regulation of so-called "competitive" markets. Nationalization is most relevant when screening foreign investments in such politically vulnerable businesses as mining, steel, and banking. At the other extreme, government intervention takes the form of less dramatic legislation, such as regulating the advertising and labeling of many products.

Regulated businesses are best described as businesses that exist through government franchises. In the United States they include, for example, transportation, public utilities, and broadcasting. Government regulation principally affects the "regulated" company by erecting artificial entry barriers and establishing non-market-based return-on-investment targets. A diversifying company may want to move either into or out of a business subject to government regulation, depending on the skills it has acquired in dealing with government bodies and whether it perceives that certain benefits of regulation (such as reduced competition) outweigh the costs.

Societal Liabilities: The most pervasive form of government intervention occurs through the continual flow of legislation dealing with social issues. Societal liabilities typically include issues of public concern before they attract specific government involvement. A current list of such potential liabilities includes environmentalism, consumer protectionism, employee safety (OSHA) and benefits (ERISA), and other issues of comparable social importance.

Antitrust Policy: The risks of antitrust action in a particular industry or accompanying a particular kind of merger are spelled out in Chapter 11. It is worth mentioning here, however, that the risk of antitrust action following a merger is directly proportional to the strategic fit of related partners and to the size of an unrelated acquisition. The more attractive the acquisition is from a strategic standpoint, the greater the antitrust risks. In addition, it is useful to note that antitrust risks increase wherever a very successful corporate strategy has been employed. A successful corporate strategy typically leads to improved market share position; antitrust policy has been designed to prevent companies from exploiting superior market share positions.

Return Characteristics

Return characteristics principally concern the size and timing of cash flows associated with an acquisition. Investment refers to cash outflows; returns refer to cash inflows. Taken together, they enable an acquirer to assess the cash flow that can be expected from its acquisition in each relevant time period. While return characteristics are typically thought to be more company-specific than industry-specific, most industries do exhibit readily identifiable cash flow and financial patterns.

Size and Period of Investments and Returns: The purpose of identifying the investment and return characteristics of a potential acquisition is to help diversifying companies judge whether or not a particular cash flow pattern is attractive. In assessing these characteristics, it is important to remember that the size and timing of cash flows will depend on an acquisition's capital intensity, its growth rate, and its stage of maturity. Generally speaking, the more rapid the growth rate, the greater the investment needs. Similarly, the more capital intensive a business is, the greater its investment requirements (and the larger its operating cash flow). One should note that a company's competitive position will also influence the pattern of cash flows. Trying to improve market share in a mature, capital intensive industry, for example, can be very expensive and will dramatically affect the size and timing of cash flows. Finally, the stage of a company's products in their cycle of development, growth, and maturity will help indicate when a changeover from negative to positive cash flow or from positive to negative cash flow is likely to occur.

Liquidity of the Investment: An investment's liquidity depends to a large extent on the marketability of its underlying assets. Generally, the more easily an asset can be converted to cash, the greater its liquidity and the less risk involved. Working capital assets may be more or less liquid depending upon their nature (accounts receivable versus inventory) and their degree of specialization. When assets such as inventories have few alternative uses, they tend to be more illiquid and riskier than assets with multiple uses. In the course of normal operations, investments in working capital can be recovered relatively quickly through liquidation, whereas investments in fixed assets are recovered over a longer period through depreciation. Expensed investments, represented by goodwill on or off the balance sheet, are typically highly illiquid, although they may have high ongoing value to the company.

Noncapitalized Strategic Investments: An important aspect of every company's investment program is those investments that are not reflected on the company's books. The intangible assets created by these investments are often the most effective competitive weapons and market entry barriers a company can have. Noncapitalized strategic investments include such intangibles as trademarks, technology, established distribution systems, and advertising presence. Since investments in such intangible assets are expensed for tax purposes, they significantly improve a company's cash flow. The returns from investments in intangible assets can also be high, since along with specialized management skills they often represent the distinctive competences of a company.

Return Due to Unique Company Characteristics: Not only can unique company characteristics affect ongoing cash flow patterns, as indicated above, but such characteristics often command a high capitalized value if purchased. Offsetting this cost, investments in certain unique characteristics can lead to significant strategic advantages and often provide relatively safe returns. The geographical franchise of newspapers or the broadcast license of TV and radio stations are obvious examples. On the other hand, unique returns due to the skills or services of individuals such as entrepreneurs are relatively uncertain. One should differentiate between company characteristics that can be developed (noncapitalized strategic investments) and those which are truly unique, like entrepreneurial talent, exploitation of unique natural resources, or the granting of exclusive licenses by political bodies.

Integration Potential

Assessing integration potential involves an analysis of both the strategic fit (or potential synergy) and the organizational compatibility between the diversifying company and the potential acquisition. Different measures of strategic fit should be stressed in the screening process, depending, of course, on the objectives of the diversifying company. Whereas measures of strategic fit (the first four measures discussed below) can be useful in screening industries as well as companies, the measure pertaining to organizational compatibility is principally limited to screening individual companies.

Supplementary Skills/Resources: For companies pursuing a related-supplementary objective, it is important for one of the merger partners to possess surplus functional skills or resources that can be used by the other partner to its competitive advantage. In order for this productive transfer of functional skills and resources to take place, the potential merger partners must share critical success factors.

A key analytical task for companies pursuing related-supplementary diversification is assessing whether or not an industry or company possesses relevant functional skills or resources, whether or not they are transferable, and the degree to which those skills or resources provide a competitive advantage. This last point is particularly important. If all competitors within an industry rely on the same key skill, that skill must be exceptionally well developed within one partner to provide a competitive advantage for the merged company. Another point to keep in mind is that, generally speaking, the potential advantages of a merger to the partners concerned tend to increase as the shared skills and resources constitute an increasingly larger element in the cost of doing business or are of increasingly critical strategic importance.

Complementary Skills/Resources: For companies pursuing a related-complementary objective, it is important that one merger partner's skills complement or add to the other's. For example, combining the skills and resources of a steel distribution company and a steel mill could provide the basis for a productive related-complementary merger. Ideally, this type of diversification leads to more effective utilization of skills and resources through stabilized demand, improved logistics, and more efficient production. In addition, such a strategy can also reduce strategic risks by expanding the market base for products (downstreaming) and/or securing captive sources of supply (upstreaming). A key analytical task for companies pursuing related-complementary diversification is assessing the extent to which the integrated skills or resources provide an improved competitive advantage by reducing the costs (risks) associated with volatile supply and demand functions.

Financial Fit–Risk-Pooling Benefits: Financial fit is closely related to the risk and return characteristics discussed above. The most direct analysis of financial fit should focus on the balance of cash flows between the acquiring company and the potential acquisition, given the constraints of capital availability and cost. Attention should be paid to whether or not the acquisition requires a large up-front investment or series of smaller investments continuing over several years. Similarly, it is important to distinguish between acquisitions that are made for the purposes of securing cash flow (and profits) in the future and those that aim at harvesting existing cash flows.

In addition to the fit, or "balance," achieved between the cash flows of the diversifying company and the acquisition candidate, attention should be paid to potential risk-pooling benefits. These benefits principally arise from improved cash management techniques and decreased cash flow volatility. They enable the diversifying company to increase its debt capacity while decreasing its relative needs for working capital. While reducing cash-flow variability is the most important impact of risk pooling, secondary benefits also arise. For example, geographic diversification can reduce the risks of operating in unstable political climates, while technological risks can be reduced through "windows on new technologies." Even commercial risk, in particular the undertaking of large business ventures, can be reduced in its relative impact by increasing the size and diversity of the portfolio supporting the particular business entity undertaking the risky project. Measuring the potential for risk pooling requires an analysis of the compatibility of the merger partner's capital market risks as well as the underlying microeconomic risk characteristics.

Availability of General Management Skills: Where a merger, be it related or unrelated, depends on creating value for shareholders through the regeneration of underutilized assets in one of the partners, the other partner must possess a surplus of general management skills. While the transfer of general management skills can move in either direction between the acquired company and the acquirer, it is difficult to conceive of a company with deficient general management acquiring a very successfully managed company. Indeed, a surplus of general management skills in the acquiring company may be the critical success factor for unrelated diversification through acquisition. Still, given the widely acknowledged shortage of effective general managers, a surplus of general management resources in a potential acquisition must always be considered as an extremely positive feature.

Organizational Compatibility: Measures of strategic fit, such as those discussed above, are indicators of the potential for creating value through merger. This potential, however, can only be realized by an organization that exploits those opportunities. Where two merged companies fail to exploit potential economies because of irreconcilable differences in administrative inheritances and practices, shareholders will be denied their expected rewards. While it is very difficult for an acquisition-minded company to judge the compatibility of a potential acquisition's administrative systems and personnel policies from the outside, it is useful to pursue answers to the following cluster of questions:

Does one merger partner possess certain administrative systems (such as purchasing or inventory management) that can help upgrade the performance of the other partner? Are the planning and control systems in the acquiring and target companies compatible, or does the approach used in one appear either threatening or superfluous to the other? Is there compatibility in the design and administration of executive compensation systems, or are the reward systems so different that successfully integrating administrative units or transferring personnel between companies is highly unlikely? Is there compatibility in the work rules, wages, and benefits of the respective labor forces? Do the companies share common values with respect to product quality, risk taking, and social responsiveness? Can the acquisition be successfully managed without being closely integrated into the diversifying company?

Using the Acquisition Screening Grid

Adapting the Grid to Individual Corporate Needs

For each measure or line item in the acquisition screening grid it is useful to develop detailed statements that reflect the diversifying company's objectives and acquisition guidelines. As an example, a cash rich company which expects to face substantial capital demands in five years might begin the statement for the line items referring to the size and period of investment: "The most favorable investment pattern (purchase price plus subsequent infusions of funds into the acquisition) is a maximum of $100 million over the next three-year period. The acquisition should become financially self-sufficient by the end of the third year." Alternatively, a pharmaceutical company with a highly productive R&D effort in biochemistry might begin its statement about related-complementary integration potential: "The acquisition candidate should have a well-established identity and distribution system in the agrichemical industry.

This presence should be particularly strong with commercial farmers as opposed to the retail/consumer sector."

Composing such statements is the means by which a company can tailor the criteria constituting the screening grid to its previously articulated acquisition guidelines and diversification objectives. Where such guidelines or criteria are perceived as being complex or especially important to the acquiring company, a particular measure may require more than one statement, or an additional entry might be suggested for the screening grid. The desired characteristics of industries and companies with respect to the measures outlined in the acquisition screening grid may be expressed in either positive or negative terms, depending on the company's existing resources and its diversification objectives.

All members of the group or task force responsible for formulating and implementing a strategy of diversification through acquisition should generate their own descriptive statements based on their understanding of the company's objectives and needs. Subsequent discussions between these key individuals should then lead to a single set of widely accepted, explicit screening criteria.

Development of a Weighting, or Scoring, System

Once formal statements reflecting each of the key measures have been made, weightings, or scoring ranges, need to be established. In designing the scoring system, it is not necessary that the same maximum number of points be set for each measure. Indeed, each line item may have a different maximum score. These maximum scores, relative to one another, will reflect the perceived importance of each item to the acquiring company. After maximum scores have been set, scoring ranges within each item can then be established.

As an example of how maximum scores and scoring ranges can be established, consider the cases of two acquisitive diversifiers, one relatively risk averse and the other an aggressive risk taker. In the case of the former company, a mature, low-technology manufacturing company, a maximum weight of 10 points might be assigned to an industry or a company with a low beta—say, less than .7. This indicates a preference for assets whose returns tend to vary significantly less than that of the economy taken as a whole. In the case of the latter company pursuing, for instance, a strategy similar to that of Gulf + Western Industries or United Technologies, a maximum weight of 18 points might be assigned to an industry or company with a beta greater than 2.0. This indicates an extremely strong preference for highly volatile companies that promise high returns. Utilizing these maximum points, which reflect different corporate objectives, two quite different ranges can be established, as shown in Table 9-2.

TABLE 9-2. Sample Scoring Ranges for Risk-Averse and Risk-Taking Companies

Betas	Risk-averse Company	Risk-taking Company
<.7	10	1
.7–.9	8	3
.9–1.1	6	5
1.1–1.5	4	8
1.5–2.0	2	12
>2.0	1	18

The differences in the scoring ranges reflect important differences in the implicit weightings used by each company. By changing the maximum value and the internal distribution of points within the scoring range for each line item, a company can establish both the absolute importance and the orientation of that measure relative to its needs and objectives.

The process of establishing maximum scores and their scoring ranges is a critical step in the screening system. If the maximum score for a particular item does not accurately reflect the perceived importance of that item, overall confidence in the system will be reduced. Similarly if the scoring range is not accurately established, the system will be perceived by managers as being rigid and unadaptable to the (changing) needs of the company. Much more important, however, establishing weights or scoring ranges forces managers to discuss the entire acquisition program in terms of corporate objectives and the company's resources and skills. Such a discussion serves as a selfcheck on the internal consistency and merits of the program. When wide discrepancies occur, it may signal differing perceptions about the company's objectives, strategy, or existing distinctive competences. Alternatively, it may signal that certain key elements in the diversification strategy have either been overlooked or remain totally implicit in the thinking of the company's strategists. Facing up to these discrepancies enables a company to check out its own logic and establish a high degree of goal congruence among its top managers.

Both the explicit statements of the desired characteristics of industries or companies and the scoring ranges for each such characteristic should be modified as new information about the acquirer and/or the environment emerge. It may also be useful to make the statements more detailed as the screening process narrows attention down to fewer potential acquisitions. Generally, the need to revise statements will be less for related diversifiers than for unrelated diversifiers, since they typically have a clearer idea of what conditions need to be satisfied in order for value to be created through merger.

The Screening Process

After descriptive statements and scoring ranges have been established for the acquisition screening grid, the acquisition task force should prepare itself to screen industries, industry subgroups, and individual companies. The screening process will typically be an iterative one, reducing the potential acquisition universe to a smaller and smaller size. Industry subgroups (companies sharing the same key success factor or similar product/markets) will replace industries, and companies will replace industry subgroups until a limited set of candidates exist.

In practice, the search process for an unrelated acquisition can be much more time-consuming than that for a related acquisition. In place of a few, high-potential acquisitions for the related diversifier that are relatively easily identifiable, the unrelated diversifier's universe of potential candidates is literally the entire business world. The unrelated diversifier's search process must therefore, first and foremost, narrow down that enormous number of candidates to a set that can be explored within reasonable limits of time and management resources.

As the screening process progresses and several industries or clusters of companies are identified as high-potential areas, the weighting of various measures, as well as their degree of explicitness, might be modified as needed. During the final stages of the screening process, one or more screening measures may even be eliminated and attention focused on what is considered to be the most important or critical industry or company characteristics.

At each iteration in the screening process, the managers involved in formulating and implementing the diversification strategy should individually fill out the scoring sheet. Once the results have been tabulated, these managers should meet to analyze the point scores and discuss any major differences that exist. At each step, managers need to ask: Do the results make intuitive sense? Why is there such a wide/narrow spread in the point scores? Has some critical element been overlooked?

The function of this procedure is to stimulate the flow of information and judgments among those responsible for an acquisition program. Such a process can lead to a questioning of assumptions and a critical analysis of differences of opinion and can improve the consistency between corporate objectives and resources. Just as the capital budget or the operating budget can be used as a communications tool, so too can the acquisition screening grid serve an important communication function. Clear communication of objectives and differences of opinion is a particularly important aspect of the acquisition process, since once an acquisition decision has been made, a company can reverse its decision only at high financial and organizational costs.

The final output of the screening process will be a limited set of acquisition candidates ranked according to a largely qualitative set of criteria. At this stage, it becomes practical to conduct an intensive study of each candidate along the lines suggested in Chapter 10. Such a detailed study will provide the information necessary for an acquirer to identify explicitly a candidate's potential for value creation.

Assessing an Acquisition's Potential for Value Creation

The last step in the acquisition screening process is determining the potential for value creation of a select number of acquisition candidates. This involves quantifying the potential value of an acquisition to the shareholders of the acquiring company and then comparing that amount to the total cost of the acquisition.

Essentially, this procedure is similar to capital budgeting exercises relying on the notion of net present value or discounted cash flow.[1] In order to determine whether or not to undertake a project (or make an acquisition), a company needs to know three items: the cost of the project, the risk of the project and the required rate of return associated with that risk level, and the project's expected cash flows. Knowing the project's required rate of return and expected cash flows, a discounted cash flow analysis can be done to determine the project's present value. When this value is compared with the project's cost, the relative attractiveness of the project or its potential for value creation can be ascertained.[2]

While the basic methodology is the same, the analysis of an acquisition is much more complex than typical capital budgeting decisions. Whereas the typical investment project involves assets with risks reasonably similar to those already in the company's portfolio and under the control of familiar managers of known quality, this is not the case with diversifying acquisitions. Not only are the acquired assets' risks different, but the managers of an acquired company are typically strangers of unknown quality. Even where some familiarity exists, their attitudes and motivation are subject to radical change after the acquisition is consummated. Predicting the degree and direction of this change is uncertain business.

Another significant difference between an acquisition and the typical investment project is that the capital markets act as a pricing mechanism to equate the value of a company with its risk/return characteristics. Since the capital markets are not perfectly efficient, an acquisitive company may find a bargain—or, in more precise words, a company whose discounted cash flow is greater than its market value plus the transaction costs necessary to acquire it. This, of course, makes for an attractive investment. Much more likely, however, is the case where an acquisition candidate is not undervalued relative to its existing risk/return characteristics but undervalued relative to the risk/return characteristics projected by the acquirer. In this case, the acquirer will want to make changes in the acquired company's management and/or asset utilization. These changes, which will reflect the acquirer's diversification objectives and include the transfer of functional skills and resources, general management talents, or financial resources between the two companies, will typically result in a business whose risks and expected returns are significantly different from what they previously were. These changes further complicate the valuation process.

Since most acquisitions are of the latter sort, the acquiring company needs to identify the operating cash flows and risks associated with integrating the acquisition into the acquirer. This requires the detailed analysis suggested in Chapter 10. In addition, the potential benefits of the acquisition must be identified and then evaluated. *This requires a comprehensive plan of integration detailing how, when, and at what cost the potential benefits will be achieved.* Once these items have been identified, the diversifying company can then determine the acquisition's potential value by discounting the acquisition's expected cash flows at a rate of return commensurate with the acquisition's systematic risk level. This valuation can then be adjusted to include the specific impact of the financing choice on the potential value of the acquisition. (In particular, the more debt used to finance an acquisition, the greater the risks, potential returns, and equity value accruing to the diversifying company's shareholders.)

If the acquisition is likely to affect the diversifying company's risks and expected returns, an effort should also be made to quantify that impact. An acquisition, for example, may improve the strategic position of the acquirer or provide favorable risk-pooling benefits. In addition, one might also want to consider the potential losses that could occur if a competitor acquired the candidate rather than the diversifying company. When such returns or risk adjustments are integrated into the analysis, the total potential value of the acquisition to the diversifying company can be estimated.

Offsetting the total potential value of the acquisition is its total cost. The explicit economic cost of an acquisition comprises two basic elements. The first is the acquisition investment, or the acquisition's market price plus tender premiums and transaction costs incurred to make the acquisition. The second is the integration cost, or the present value of the additional capital investments (or liquidations) necessary to achieve the cash flows and risk levels identified in the detailed strategic and operating analysis of the acquisition. The total cost of an acquisition therefore measures the total present value of the investment to be made in the acquisition.

Managers should also be aware of a host of other "implicit costs," some real and some perceived, that can accompany diversification. Learning costs can arise in the diversifying corporation as senior management seeks to understand the new business. During this learning process, a misallocation of resources can occur. This misallocation of resources can lead to opportunity costs arising from either over- or underinvestment in the new or existing business. All too often, a company committing resources to a diversification program discovers that the strategic and competitive position of its existing businesses unexpectedly erodes. Economically successful reallocation of resources within the diversified corporation requires an internal allocation process at least as efficient as the external capital marketplace. Finally, the host of issues surrounding corporate overhead and its costs are relevant. For example, will the handling of the diversifying company's internal books after the acquisition be on the same basis as the analysis leading to the acquisition? If not, what does this imply about the continuity of strategic and operating analyses? The size and allocation of corporate overhead charges (as many operating managers know) can greatly influence the analysis of, decisions about, and perceived viability of a business or division within a company's portfolio.

This information enables the diversifying company to determine the acquisition's potential for value creation by subtracting the total cost of the acquisition from the present value of its expected cash flow returns, according to the following expression:

$$PVC_{\text{acquisition}} = PV_{\text{acquisition}} - TC_{\text{acquisition}} + \Delta PV_{\text{acquirer}}$$

where PVC signifies the potential for value creation, PV the present value or discounted cash flow stemming from the operating income and financial structure of an acquisition, TC the total cost (present value) of the acquisition investment plus any additional costs of integration, and ΔPV the present value of any incremental benefits accruing to the acquiring company through the acquisition. If the result is a positive figure, there is a potential for value creation, and a sound argument exists for acquiring the candidate.

However, since capital constraints always exist, capital projects, including acquisitions, should be compared with each other. Therefore, a comparative analysis of an acquisition candidate's attractiveness relative to other acquisition candidates should be made. Furthermore, the acquisition candidate's potential for value creation should be compared with the company's other investment opportunities, since expansion through acquisition is only one element of a company's strategy and one component of a diversifying company's capital budget. Perhaps the most instructive investment alternative for a diversifying company (or any company) is an analysis of the benefits or costs accompanying the repurchase of its own stock. A company will have the best information with the least probable forecasting error about the risks and future cash flow of its existing operations. A comparison of this cash flow's present value with the company's market value can provide a standard against which the relative attractiveness of a new or diversifying asset can be measured.

A careful application of this methodology will force an acquisitive diversifier to be as concrete as possible about its assessments of future returns and costs of an acquisition as well as the risks involved. No one formula or methodology, least of all this simplified one, should be expected to reveal by itself the best option or decision. This methodology's value will vary according to the quality of information utilized and the ability of managers to use this tool as a way of structuring a decision problem without eliminating the intuitive judgments required in all business decisions, particularly those of diversification. Such judgments are necessary because assessments about such items as the compatibility of corporate cultures, the quality of an acquisition candidate's management, and long-term strategic viability are impossible to quantify.

The room for error in making these judgments is great. The perceived benefits of an acquisition are often greater than those that are realized, just as actual costs often exceed those initially identified. Realizing diversification benefits, especially those stemming from operating synergies, requires considerable time and management effort. Knowing which benefits are achievable and at what costs stems from both prior experience and a strong sense of administrative feasibility. These personal characteristics of decision makers, along with the ability to value future returns accurately, lie at the base of a successfully applied acquisition screening system.

Conclusion

Executives occasionally ask why they should have an elaborate screening process when acquisition decisions must often be made without sufficient time for detailed, comprehensive analysis or when the acquisition candidates best suited to their company's needs are not available. Answers to this question are scattered throughout the foregoing discussions, but are worthy of summary.

Formal acquisition screening systems can help companies prepare themselves for swift action in many ways: First, working through a formal process in periods of relative calm tends to reinforce a broad understanding among executives of the company's diversification objectives and acquisition guidelines. Given the complexities of organizational life in the modern corporation, this benefit is not a trivial one. Second, experience with a structured screening process, such as writing descriptive statements for the measures constituting the acquisition screening grid, can lead to widely shared assumptions about the company's strengths and weaknesses and its special needs. These shared assumptions can contribute to a general agreement on what is most important for future profitability and corporate development. Third, working within a formal screening system develops a common language or set of concepts relevant to the diversification decision. This language system, the analytical methodology it represents, and a mutual understanding of the company's objectives and special needs all serve to ensure that key decision makers follow similar logics when acquisition opportunities suddenly appear and the rush of events requires quick acquisition decisions. Confident action, whether taken in relative leisure or in crisis, requires both relevant information and a system for processing that information in a conceptually meaningful way. The acquisition screening system described in this chapter meets these conditions. Just as important, however, a comprehensive acquisition screening process forces the diversifying company's managers to analyze thoroughly the consistency between the acquisition opportunity and the company's resource structure, overall strategy, and diversification objectives. Managers should never forget that diversification is not an end in itself but only a means to achieve the corporation's goals and objectives.

The issue concerning the availability of acquisition candidates is often overemphasized. Most assets, especially publicly owned companies, are always available at a price. In the capital markets, where there is a continual auction of corporate securities, assets change hands every day according to this principle. The real question is not whether attractive acquisition candidates are available but whether the acquisition's potential for value creation for the acquiring company's shareholders is sufficient to justify the required purchase price. Here again, a formal acquisition screening system has a key role to play when employed by experienced and sensitive managers.

Notes and References

1. A discussion of the notion of discounted cash flow and net present value is found in Chapter 5. In addition, texts such as J. Fred Weston and Eugene Brigham, *Managerial Finance* (New York: Holt, Rinehart & Winston, 1978), James C. Van Horne, *Financial Management and Policy* (Englewood Cliffs, N.J.: Prentice-Hall, Inc., 1977) or Harold Bierman Jr. and Seymour Smidt, *The Capital Budgeting Decision*, (New York: Macmillan Publishing Co., 1971) discuss the concept in depth along with its advantages and limitations.

2. It should be noted that present-day capital-budgeting analyses can be and often are much more complex than the approach presented here. These analyses of risky projects, utilizing numerous techniques for simulation modeling, can be usefully applied to the acquisition analysis. Not only does a manager obtain a better feel for the project or acquisition from using these techniques, but the sensitivity analysis typically accompanying them enables the manager to determine both the critical variables affecting the project and his margin for error.

CHAPTER 10

Analysis of Diversifying Acquisitions

IN PREVIOUS CHAPTERS WE DEMONSTRATED how carefully prepared diversification objectives and acquisition guidelines, along with a conceptually sound acquisition screening process, can increase the probability of selecting a merger partner that will create real economic value for the combined company's shareholders. We also demonstrated how the three models constituting our analytic framework contribute to a rigorous process of corporate self-analysis, goal setting, and targeting of high-potential acquisition candidates. In this chapter we will push one step further and show how our framework can contribute to a detailed strategic and economic analysis of companies that have been identified as candidates for a diversifying acquisition.

We will proceed by examining Rockwell International's acquisition of Admiral Corporation and INCO's takeover of ESB, Inc. Each of these recent cases highlights different ways in which our conceptual approach can help decision makers enrich their analysis of diversification opportunities. Equally as important, our review of these two diversifying acquisitions shows the kind of insights that are obtainable from a structured analysis of publicly available information. It should be kept in mind, however, that our intent is not to provide a definitive evaluation of each transaction or to give the final word on why each acquisition was made. This would require, of course, supplementing the published information upon which our analyses are based with confidential information from each of the parties involved.

Rockwell International's Acquisition of Admiral Corporation*

Rockwell International is one of the nation's leading aerospace manufacturers. In 1975 two of its best known projects were the space shuttle and the B-1 bomber. Rockwell had also diversified into several other areas, including automotive components, electronic components and systems, utility products, textile machinery, and, with the acquisition of Admiral, home entertainment products and household appliances. Table 10-1 shows the breakdown of Rockwell's 1973 (pre-Admiral) sales for these operations.

The history of Rockwell International portrays a classic picture of aggressive diversification through internal development and acquisition. In 1967, North American Aviation and Rockwell-Standard merged to become North American Rockwell. This merger was a strategic move on the part of North American Aviation to diversify into commercial markets, and Rockwell-Standard became the commercial products group of the new company. In 1973 North American Rockwell merged with Rockwell Manufacturing to form Rockwell International. Table 10-2 outlines the key acquisitions and mergers that led to the creation of Rockwell International.

This aggressive diversification program produced substantial growth for Rockwell International. From 1971 to 1975, sales increased from $2.2 billion to $5 billion, an annual growth rate of approximately 22.6 percent. After-tax profits hovered around 3 percent of sales to return 9 to 10 percent on stockholders' equity.

In 1973 Rockwell announced its intention to acquire Admiral as part of its continuing diversification program. The resulting merger was consummated in April 1974 through a stock transaction valued at $86 million.

Prior to its acquisition by Rockwell, Admiral Corporation manufactured consumer electronics products and home appliances. Its main products included black-and-white and color televisions, radios, clock radios, stereos, cassette tape recorders, refrigerators, freezers, room air conditioners, electric ranges, and home laundry equipment. Admiral's products were marketed both under its own name and through private label arrangements with Montgomery Ward and other retail chains.

Admiral's 1973 sales of $515 million made it about one-sixth the size of Rockwell. While sales had been growing at nearly 12 percent a year since 1970, profitability was low, and Admiral had lost money in 1970 ($14.3 million) and 1971 ($1.5 million).

* This analysis was prepared during the fall of 1976 before President Carter canceled the B-1 bomber program and Rockwell's entry into consumer products became the subject of intense discussion by the business press.

TABLE 10-1. Rockwell International 1973 Sales by Product Line

	Sales ($ Million)	Percentage of Total
Automotive Operations		
Automotive Components	$ 883	27.8
Electronics Operations		
Guidance and Control, Avionics, and Telecommunications Equipment	364	11.5
Calculator Products and Components	84	2.6
Total	$ 488	14.1
Aerospace Operations		
Aircraft (including General Aviation)	$ 620	19.5
Space Systems and Rocket Engines	325	10.2
Other	74	2.3
Total	$1,019	32.0
Utility and Industrial Operations		
Utility Products	$ 170	5.4
Textile Machinery, Graphic Arts, and Industrial Components	551	17.3
Total	$ 721	22.7
Consumer Operations		
Power Tools	108	3.4
Total	$3,179	100.0

Source: 1973 Rockwell International Annual Report.

Rockwell and Admiral: A Business Strategy Perspective

Use of the strategy model in an analysis of Rockwell's acquisition of Admiral in 1974 leads to such questions as why were policymakers at Rockwell considering such a diversifying acquisition in the first place and what was the stimulus for further diversification of Rockwell's business portfolio. While we can only speculate on the answers, since Rockwell has not disclosed its thinking on the matter, the strategy model provides insight to one line of argument. According to the logic of this model, Rockwell's managers would have asked: "What are the business risks faced by the company's current mix of businesses?" Their answer may well have paralleled the following explanation.

Rockwell's Automotive Operations served primarily two markets in 1973: passenger vehicles and commercial trucks, and off-the-road vehi-

TABLE 10-2. Key Diversifying Acquisitions That Created Rockwell International

1967	North American Rockwell (NAR) created by merger of North American Aviation and Rockwell-Standard.
1967	NAR merges with Draper Corp., large manufacturer of textile machinery.
1968	NAR acquires five more companies with combined sales of over $100 million.
1969	Acquisition of Miehle-Goss Dexter Co., manufacturer of printing and graphic arts equipment with annual sales of $162 million.
1969	Acquisition of Morse Controls (cable control systems) and Whittaker Marine & Manufacturing (fiberglass houseboats).
1971	Investment in Collins Radio with 1971 sales of $262 million. Acquisition completed in 1972 as a diversification into high technology electronics.
1972	NAR and Rockwell Manufacturing merge to become Rockwell International.

cles (for example, construction). With 28 percent of its sales in this area, Rockwell was vulnerable to the cyclic nature of passenger car sales and construction activity.

Rockwell's Electronics and Aerospace Operations, which constituted the bulk of its remaining sales (see Table 10-1), also faced market-related risks. Sales to the government, which were over 40 percent of Rockwell's total 1973 sales, were dependent on the level of defense spending. While development risks on long-term defense and space programs were largely underwritten by the government, profit margins on later production runs were lower for this reason. The development of general aviation aircraft was, however, company funded. This forced Rockwell to bear the risk of expensive development efforts for aircraft that would have to compete in a highly competitive market. In addition, the market for general aviation aircraft was very sensitive to the general cycle of business conditions.

In this context, the stimulus for further diversification by Rockwell's managers was to reduce the company's vulnerability to both the general business cycle and the company's heavy dependence on a government sales. Managers following the precepts of the strategy model would have examined alternate ways of achieving this objective. Most probably they would have asked: "What strengths and resources does the company have that can help reduce the company's vulnerability in the marketplace?" A realistic answer to this question might have included the following observation.

The three companies that became Rockwell International (North American Aviation, Rockwell-Standard, and Rockwell Manufacturing) shared an important resource: the ability to exploit technology. This was

Rockwell International's distinctive competence, which ran through its various businesses.[1]

With this corporate strength or distinctive competence in mind, decision makers following the methodology of the strategy model would then have examined the Admiral opportunity by pursuing three related questions: "Does Admiral help us minimize the risks associated with our current customer base? If so, how do companies successfully compete in Admiral's business, and what resources do we have that could help Admiral compete more effectively?"

Answers to these questions may well have centered on the observation that Admiral presented Rockwell with a chance to enter the less cyclical consumer electronics and home appliance markets in a big way. While Admiral's appliance business was linked to construction activity, as was Rockwell's sales to manufacturers of off-the-road vehicles, an acquisition of Admiral would mean a diversification of Rockwell's products away from capital goods. The effect of acquiring Admiral would be an increase in consumer market sales from 6 to 18 percent of total corporate sales and a reduction in government sales from 40 to 34 percent of total sales.

A logical response to these questions would have continued by noting that in consumer electronics advanced technology was quickly becoming a significant element in competition, both in terms of design features offered the consumer and cost reduction stemming from integrated circuit technology. The argument would most probably have continued by noting that in the home appliance sector of the market, continued product development based on electronics was a key element of success, as shown by the constant parade of new features being introduced on recent models of refrigerators and laundry equipment. Rockwell managers would not have failed to emphasize that they had significant skills in developing and manufacturing new products based on advanced electronic technology.

At first cut, then, the strategic framework of analysis would probably have led decision makers at Rockwell to see a fit between the Admiral opportunity and Rockwell's capabilities—a fit based on the notion of technology transfer. This idea no doubt looked plausible, since similar technology transfers had worked before. Raytheon, for example, was a high-technology–based company that had entered the home appliance industry with acquisitions of Amana (1965) and Caloric (1967). Through these acquisitions, Raytheon introduced radically new technologies to the industry. By 1971 Raytheon had gained a substantial share of the new microwave oven market—a market that it had pioneered.

Apparently, something similar to this line of reasoning was followed, since Rockwell's public announcements on the 1974 merger stressed the logic of technology transfer. In its 1974 annual report, Rockwell revealed that a task force with representatives from Admiral's Home Entertainment Division and Rockwell's Collins Radio and Microelectronics Groups

was at work developing plans to strengthen, technologically, home entertainment products for both the short and long term. The group was
reported to be studying "technology transfer applications as far ahead as
10 years." The 1975 annual report continued this same theme:

> During the past 18 months Rockwell and Admiral management thoroughly
> analyzed the group's problems and made numerous changes to improve opera-
> tions. The full impact of these actions, embracing virtually every aspect of the
> business, will be felt over a long period of time. . . . Here are some of the
> year's highlights and achievements:
> With help from Electronics and Aerospace Operations in design, production
> procedures and test techniques, product quality and product performance
> were improved significantly during the year. For example, the 1975 models of
> Duplex refrigerators have been designed to decrease energy consumption by
> 30 percent from the 1974 models.
> New product development programs were initiated, making extensive use of
> Rockwell's broad technology, for a series of consumer electronics products to
> be marketed in the future.

While the opportunities for technology transfer from Rockwell to
Admiral may have appeared compelling and, in fact, may have formed
the basis of the decision to acquire Admiral, managers employing the logic
of the strategy model would also have asked whether or not Rockwell
possessed sufficient (financial) resources to help Admiral through what
was clearly a period of rebuilding. Although Admiral had shown increasing sales through 1973, profitability had been poor in recent years. Losses
had been registered in two of the previous four years. Margins had to be
improved, and to the extent that higher margins depended on investments
in increased market share and cost reduction programs, Admiral was
faced with a significant demand for funds. If Admiral's full line of products was to be retained, major investments would have to be made on
several fronts at once. A reduction in Rockwell's investment in Admiral
(over and above the purchase price) could theoretically be achieved by
thinning out Admiral's product line, but this would most probably mean
that fewer economies in warehousing, transportation, and marketing services would accrue to Admiral on a per unit basis—thereby slowing its
profit recovery.

A quick estimate of Rockwell's free cash flows for 1974 would have
warned managers that Rockwell's financial resources were not in excess
of current needs. Assuming a 15 percent increase in sales for 1974 to $3.6
billion, maintenance of current margin levels at 4 percent of sales, depreciation cash flow of approximately $75 million, new investment in fixed
and current assets of $136 million for growing businesses already owned
by Rockwell (based on 1972–1973 incremental sales/assets ratio), a constant dividend payout ratio yielding $64 million in dividends, and debt

repayment of $10 million (a very conservative estimate), Rockwell could have expected a maximum of $10 million in uncommitted cash flow for 1974.

An astute manager would have pointed out to his colleagues that a mere 0.3 percent increase in cost of goods sold or operating expenses could wipe out these excess funds. So, too, could a modest increase in business activity over estimates or slight decline in prices (such as that which afflicted calculators). While Rockwell probably had access to additional debt capital, its current debt/equity ratio of .36 and recent long-term borrowings signaled that limits were being approaches on this source of funds. Similarly, with working capital in 1973 down by $34 million over 1972 and a current ratio slightly under 2 to 1, Rockwell was not excessively liquid, despite its $108 million in cash and short-term securities.

Additional attention to the demands that the Admiral acquisition would put on Rockwell's resources would have brought up the issue of top management time. Successful technology transfer between divisions requires careful coordination by group-level and corporate-level management under the best of conditions. Where the receiving division is a recent acquisition with different bureaucratic traditions and values than those of the acquiring company, major commitments of time by senior executives would be required over a substantial period. Furthermore, since Admiral was a weak competitor in each of its markets, Rockwell's top management would undoubtedly have wanted to invest time in developing their own opinions about how Admiral could improve its marketing strategy, internal operations, and overall performance. This would be the inevitable result of a new division like Admiral coming to corporate headquarters for additional funds. All this would add up to a major investment of Rockwell's management resources in order to convert the potential for technology transfer into a reality. A manager following the logic of the strategy model might well have concluded that there was a less attractive fit between Rockwell's resources and the Admiral opportunity than first met the eye. As we shall see, the logic of the product/market-portfolio model and the risk/return model would have reinforced any doubts about the wisdom of acquiring Admiral.

Rockwell and Admiral: A Product/Market Portfolio Perspective

Use of the product/market-portfolio model leads one step further in the analysis of Rockwell's acquisition of Admiral. This model suggests that managers focus their attention on the competitive strength and cash flow patterns in their company's present and prospective portfolio of businesses.

In assessing Rockwell's 1973 portfolio of businesses, managers using the product/market-portfolio model would have asked: "What are the cash flow characteristics of the existing businesses? Where is the portfolio financially weak or unbalanced?'' Figure 10-1 presents a rough estimate of Rockwell's portfolio of businesses in 1973 as categorized under the market-share/market-growth matrix. At first glance, the portfolio seems fairly well balanced. About 17 percent of Rockwell's sales (graphic arts machinery, textile machinery, and industrial components) were clearly in the ''cash cow'' category.[2] Twenty-seven percent of sales (calculators, heavy duty auto components, and general aviation) were in high-growth markets. However, 17 percent of sales (passenger auto components,

FIGURE 10-1.   Rockwell International 1973 Product/Market Portfolio Chart[a]

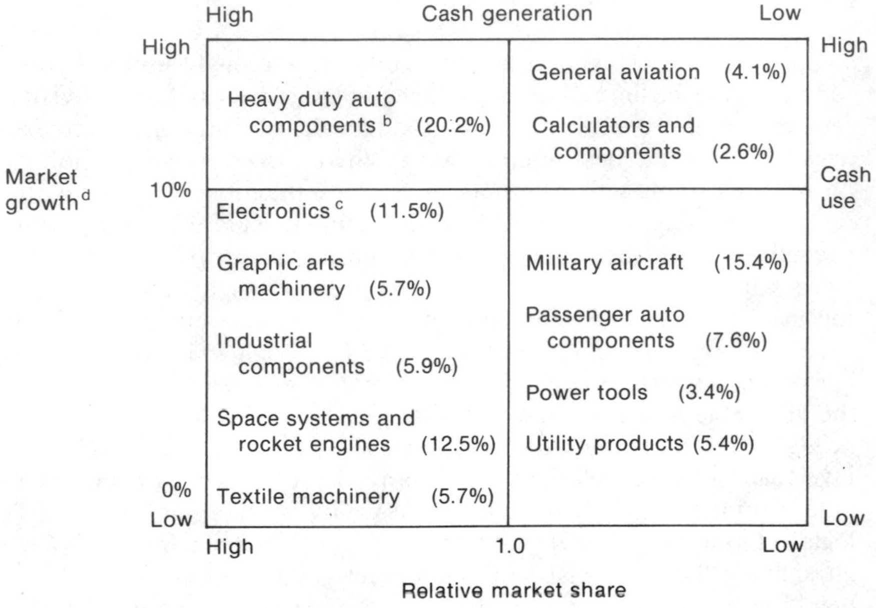

	High	Cash generation	Low	
High	**High**			**High**
	Heavy duty auto components [b] (20.2%)	General aviation (4.1%) Calculators and components (2.6%)		
Market growth[d] 10%	Electronics [c] (11.5%) Graphic arts machinery (5.7%) Industrial components (5.9%) Space systems and rocket engines (12.5%)	Military aircraft (15.4%) Passenger auto components (7.6%) Power tools (3.4%) Utility products (5.4%)		Cash use
0% Low	Textile machinery (5.7%)			Low
	High	1.0	Low	

Relative market share

[a] Numbers in parentheses indicate percentage of 1973 sales in that business. Total 1973 sales = $3,179 million.

[b] Primarily components for trucks, off-the-road construction vehicles, and farm equipment vehicles.

[c] Includes avionics, guidance and control, and communications systems. Does not include calculators and components.

[d] Estimates of market growth and market position are based on dollar rather than unit sales.

Sources: 1. Product-line breakdown from annual reports and 10-K forms.
2. Market growth estimates from trade publications and U.S. Department of Commerce reports.
3. Market position (dominant or not dominant only) estimates from trade publications and competitors' annual reports.

utility components, and consumer power tools) were in the cash trap category, meaning that previous investments in this cluster of businesses were probably not generating surplus cash flow. The 40 percent of sales contracted by the government (military aircraft, space systems, rocket engines, and electronics) would have been difficult to categorize as either cash generators or cash users because of the complexities of government contracting. While Rockwell's cash traps could have been viewed as candidates for liquidation or divestiture, since they represented neither growth opportunities nor sources of surplus cash flow, moving out of Rockwell's government contracting business, in particular, was unthinkable. Put simply, this business had provided Rockwell with much of its technological capability. In addition, it was a low-risk business when cost-plus contracts could be signed with the government.

Management of Rockwell's stars and questionable ventures would have involved increasing market share in order to maintain or augment rates of return on invested capital.[3] According to the logic of the product/market-portfolio model, an aggressive market share strategy encompassing 27 percent of the company's business would have required substantial cash commitments. This requirement for investment capital could have represented a serious weakness in the company's existing portfolio of businesses. With this weakness in mind Rockwell's managers would have asked: "What are the cash flow characteristics of the Admiral portfolio? How well do these characteristics fit Rockwell's needs?"

Figure 10-2 gives an estimate of Admiral's 1973 portfolio as categorized by the market-share/market-growth matrix. One aspect is immediately obvious: Admiral was not the dominant competitor in any of its businesses. In fact, in terms of 1973 market share, Admiral was number eight in color TV, number four in black-and-white TV, fourth in freezers, and fifth in refrigerators. Admiral faced growth markets only in the color television segment of the home entertainment business and, to a lesser extent, in the freezer and electric range segments of the home appliance market. These businesses were potential candidates for the success sequence shown earlier in Chapter 3, but a substantial cash commitment would have been required. If this investment did not take place before market growth declined, these businesses would join the rest of Admiral's products in the "dog" category as cash traps.

These characteristics of Admiral's portfolio of businesses could have given Rockwell's managers reason to pause, if they had the product/market-portfolio model in mind. They would have understood that Admiral's cash traps should be liquidated and the proceeds invested along with Rockwell's own cash in (1) market share for the growth businesses and/or (2) new product development (like Raytheon's introduction of the Amana microwave oven) to put some "stars" in the portfolio. The implications would have appeared profound: Admiral could not remain a full-line

FIGURE 10-2. Admiral Corporation 1973 Product/Market Portfolio Chart[a]

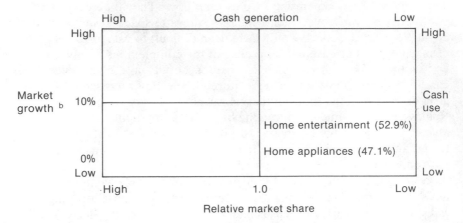

[a] Numbers in parentheses indicate percentage of 1973 sales in that business. Total 1973 sales = $515 million.

[b] Estimates of market growth and market position are based on dollar rather than unit sales.

Sources: 1. Product-line breakdown from trade publication estimates of Admiral market share and size of markets.

2. Competitive position estimates from trade publications.

3. Market growth estimates from trade publications and U.S. Department of Commerce reports.

manufacturer, and its mix of businesses would have to be fundamentally altered. This would have appeared particularly disturbing to the managers of Admiral's appliance business since marketing and distribution advantages typically accrued to full-line producers. Most important from Rockwell's point of view, however, the acquisition of Admiral would have meant that Rockwell would end up investing heavily in businesses where other companies had dominant market positions and, most likely, cash flow patterns favoring further investment in market share in the appliance business. Rockwell would, therefore, risk being dragged into large cash investment where opportunities for business growth and market dominance were limited.

If the estimates and the assumptions underlying this argument are correct, the product/market-portfolio model would have intensified the concerns raised by the strategy model. While the strategy model would have raised questions about the fit between Rockwell's resources and the opportunities presented by Admiral, the product/market-portfolio model would have raised additional questions concerning the financial compatibility and strength of the two companies. Since it would have appeared that Admiral would require additional infusions of cash over the short run and that Admiral could not provide a substantial source of surplus cash over the long run, the wisdom of the Admiral acquisition could have been seriously challenged.

Rockwell and Admiral: A Risk/Return Perspective

The application of the risk/return model to corporate diversification leads managers to consider the potential effect of the acquisition on the market value of both the acquiring company and its investors' portfolio of securities.

According to the risk/return model, the capital market prices securities according to (1) the income stream available over time to the shareholders and (2) a rate of return determined by that income stream's level of risk. Managers adopting this viewpoint would have been led to consider the effect that the diversifying acquisition would have on the income stream and required rate of return of the acquiring company. In addition, since the model assumes that the market correctly values the securities of each company as a separate business entity, managers using this model to assess an acquisition would have asked, "What does this acquisition do for our shareholders that they could not do for themselves?"[4] This question implies that many of the motives for corporate acquisition, such as adding countercyclical businesses, are not particularly relevant decision criteria. While such reasons should not be ignored, the model's goal is to differentiate between the benefits achieved by diversifying a portfolio of securities and the benefits achieved through corporate diversification. This differentiation is necessary because a company's shareholders, should they decide to, could easily achieve any portfolio diversification benefits by investing part of their personal portfolio in the securities of the proposed acquisition. For an acquisition to create value, it should either reduce the (systematic) risk or increase the income stream of the combined entity to a greater extent that that which would occur in an investment portfolio containing the securities of those businesses.

As such, the risk/return model implies that a corporate acquisition is justifiable whenever "synergy" exists. By providing a method of quantifying the amount of synergy needed, the risk/return model goes beyond both the business policy model, which directs managers to look for synergy in a general way, and the product/market-portfolio model which focuses on the compatibility of cash flow patterns.

One can estimate how much synergy is needed to create value for the shareholders of a diversified company by using the discounted cash flow method of valuation along with concepts of risk and return. Our expanded discounted cash flow framework states that the market value of the firm, *PV*, is equal to the return, or income stream, the shareholder can expect in each time period, D_t, discounted at a rate appropriate to the income stream's risk in a diversified portfolio, R. This valuation model is expressed as:

$$PV = \sum_{t=1}^{n} D_t/(1 + R)^t$$

If any two variables are known, the third can be determined. Furthermore, if the value of these variables for the diversifying company and the potential acquisition are known (or estimatable) for the periods preceding and following the acquisition, the incremental benefit or value created by the acquisition can be determined. This benefit will be the difference between (1) the costs incurred to effect the acquisition and to achieve the synergies possible and (2) the capitalized value of the income stream resulting from the synergies obtained. More simply, this benefit (or newly created value) should equal the difference between the market values of the portfolios before and after the acquisition.[5]

Unfortunately, it is difficult to predict accurately (over time) the extent of changes in risks or returns available to the investor resulting from the merger. What can be done with relative ease, however, is to work backwards from the costs incurred in the acquisition to determine what level of "synergy" is required to maintain the market wealth of the acquiring company's investors. The only information that the manager needs to estimate is the investment required to effect the transaction (the acquisition premium and transaction costs) and the investment that the acquiring company will have to make in the acquired company after the transaction has been completed. The "synergy" necessary to maintain the acquiring company's shareholders' wealth can then be estimated by (1) letting the acquiring company's investment in the acquisition premium, transaction costs, and postacquisition expenditures equal the change in market value of the combined companies, (2) varying either the size of the incremental income stream or the level of systematic risk (and, therefore, the required rate of return) and (3) solving a discounted cash flow equation for the third variable. This analysis is most easily done by holding the level of systematic risk equal to that of an investment portfolio comprising the two companies and solving for the incremental income stream. With subscript P referring to the combined company, such an analysis can be expressed mathematically as follows:

$$\Delta PV_P = \sum_{t=1}^{n} \Delta D_{tp}/(1 + R_P)^t$$

This analysis, as applied to the Rockwell-Admiral merger, is shown in Table 10-3. Given the $30 million premium Rockwell paid to acquire

TABLE 10-3. The Return on Admiral Necessary to Maintain Rockwell Shareholders' Wealth

	Rockwell	Admiral	Portfolio
Market Value ($ million)[a]	750	50	800
Beta (Value Line)	1.03	1.62	1.07
Required Rate of Return[b]	9.5%	11.2%	9.7%
Implied Income Stream ($ million)	71.2	6.5	77.6
Acquisition Premium ($ million)		30.7	

Assume $20 million in investment by Rockwell in Admiral to achieve the full benefits of the combination. Holding risk constant, the incremental return required for Rockwell's shareholders to be no worse off is:

$$30 + 20 = \sum_{t=1}^{n} \Delta D_{tP}/(1 + R_P)^t$$

Assuming further that Admiral's incremental return will be both level and perpetual, this formula simplifies to:

$$50 = \Delta D_{tP}/.097$$

$$\Delta D_{tP} = \$4.85 \text{ million}$$

For Rockwell's managers this incremental cash flow is equal to a 24 percent after-tax return on their "tangible" investment in Admiral of $20 million.

---

[a] Before announcement of acquisition.

[b] The required rate of return can be found by using the algebraic description for the capital market line presented in Figure 5-6. The algebraic description is $E(R_i) = R_f + \beta_i(R_m - R_f)$, where $E(R_i)$ represents the expected rate of return on the investment; R_f, the risk-free rate of return; R_m, the market rate of return and β_i, the investment's systematic risk, or beta. Our calculations assume long-run risk-free and market rates of return of 3.0 and 9.3 percent, respectively.

[c] Implied income stream is that income stream which then capitalized at the required rate of return equals market value.

Admiral and assuming that $20 million in additional investment would be required to achieve the potential synergies, an incremental annual return of approximately $4.85 million is required to maintain Rockwell's shareholders' previous level of wealth.[6]

For the Rockwell-Admiral merger, the risk/return model indicates that Rockwell's shareholders would not be any better off from the Admiral acquisition until the synergies achieved either provide an increased annual return of $4.85 million, holding systematic risk constant, or reduce the combined company's systematic risk (beta) by over 9 percent, holding the returns constant. If synergies of this magnitude did not seem possible,

Rockwell's managers could have once again seriously questioned whether the acquisition should have been made.

Rockwell and Admiral: A Summary

As emphasized above, we have not tried to present a final judgment on the merits of the Admiral acquisition by Rockwell International. Our purpose has been more narrow in scope: to demonstrate how the integrated use of three conceptual models can help structure and enrich an analysis of diversifying acquisitions.

In the case of the Rockwell-Admiral merger, the strategy model would have helped Rockwell managers recognize not only the potential benefits of technology transfer but also the potential strain on Rockwell's resources if such a transfer to Admiral were to be attempted. A product/market-portfolio analysis would have reinforced any doubts about the wisdom of the acquisition by suggesting that the Rockwell mix of businesses needed more cash generators while the Admiral mix of businesses was at best a break-even operation on a cash flow basis. A risk/return analysis would have carried Rockwell's managers one step further in their analysis. Given the price that Rockwell would have to pay for Admiral, this model suggests that (rational) Rockwell shareholders would have wanted a 24 percent return on Rockwell's tangible investment or a 16 percent return on the total Admiral investment. These levels of returns— far above Admiral's recent returns and even those of General Electric, the industry leader—would have provided a clear indication of how difficult it would have been for Rockwell to make the Admiral acquisition a success.

Epilogue

In light of this analysis, one would expect that Rockwell's relationship with Admiral would be a stormy one. Indeed, the relationship soured very early. During 1974 and 1975, new management was brought in and a major revamping of Admiral's entire product line was undertaken. "Advanced technology" was emphasized in both production and marketing. Nevertheless, Admiral's market position continued to deteriorate, and by 1977 its poor health was well known both within and without the industry. Quality control problems in its home entertainment sector, in particular, were further exacerbated by the continued onslaught of high-quality, low-price imports. In early 1978, the business press described Admiral as Rockwell's sorest thumb.[7] The situation continued to deteriorate until September 1978, when Rockwell announced that Admiral was abandoning the television business and taking an estimated $30 million writeoff. Even with this massive retrenching, considerable doubt remained as to whether or not Admiral was a viable entity.

INCO's Acquisition of ESB, Inc.

Maintaining a realistic perspective on value during a fast moving bidding contest is always difficult, and when a corporation is the target, even a minor mistake can involve large sums of capital. The conceptual models suggested in Part II can be of great assistance to decision makers who find themselves in this situation, as an analysis of the takeover of ESB, Inc. by INCO (formerly the International Nickel Company of Canada, Ltd.) demonstrates.

In July, 1974, INCO launched a tender offer for all the outstanding shares of ESB. With 1973 sales of $1.2 billion, INCO was the world's largest producer of nickel and a major producer of copper and platinum-group metals. In addition to mining and refining operations, INCO also manufactured nickel alloys into a variety of rolled, forged, and machined products for general engineering applications. The target, ESB, Inc., was one of the world's major manufacturers of power storage systems (batteries) and related products. With over a hundred plants in seventeen countries, ESB had shown a sound record of growth and had reported sales of $436 million in 1973.

INCO's initial tender offer for the shares of ESB stock was announced on July 17. The $28-a-share offer amounted to a total purchase price of $157 million in cash and, assuming all of ESB's shares were tendered, a premium of $50 million (44 percent) over ESB's market value.

ESB management quickly denounced the offer, calling it a "hostile bid from a foreign company." They also termed the offer undervalued and urged shareholder rejection. Seeking a friendlier partner, ESB management set about reviving dormant merger discussions with United Aircraft (now United Technologies). On July 23 United entered the contest with a $34-a-share counteroffer. INCO bumped the price to $36 the next day, only to be matched by United. On the morning of July 25, INCO went to $38 and was matched a few hours later by United. By the end of the day INCO jumped its bid to a decisive $41 level. INCO's final offer was valued at $225.5 million, excluding an estimated $8 million in soliciting fees, legal costs, and other related expenditures. This was 46 percent above its original bid and 110 percent higher than the price of ESB when the bidding started.

When it bowed out of the competitive bidding at the $38 level, United's only comment was that the price was too high to justify to its shareholders. It was natural in this context for many observers to ask why INCO had exhibited such confidence in the competitive bidding, since its management carried the same responsibility for its shareholders' interests as United. In fact, one investment banker was quoted: "At $38 a share, it's antitrust. At $41, it's not. This is a new standard."

Simple models, however, provided only simplistic answers. Since the market was valuing ESB's shares at a discount to net working capital, INCO's offer had to be substantially above the market price for the offer not to be dismissed out of hand by ESB shareholders. Also, with the market averages reflecting investors' uncertainty stemming from mounting economic concerns and President Nixon's apparent decision to drag out impeachment proceedings, a 10-times-earning multiple (based on 1973 earnings) seemed like a realistic starting point. If INCO's tender offer at $28 per share (which approximated ESB's book value) was successful, it would have fit these rules of thumb. Even at $34 a share, no standard rules of thumb would have been violated. One could expect to pay about 12 times earnings for an industry leader with a solid track record. Indeed, at $41 the offer was still below 15 times 1973 earnings.

At this point the superficial explanation breaks down under the pressure of additional information. In July 1974, the average price/earnings ratio for the Standard & Poor's 500 was about 9.5 times earnings. With inflation at double-digit rates and the United States in the midst of its worst recession in twenty-five years, the outlook for equities was dismal. Few economists were confident about the long run. Given these conditions, whose evaluation of ESB was most realistic? Was the equity market's valuation at $19.50 a share "correct"? Was United's at $38 or less? Was INCO's at $41 or more? How could anyone be sure? In short, how could INCO's directors defend this diversifying acquisition as a prudent business decision? Considerable insight into these questions can be gained by examining the takeover from the combined perspectives of the strategy model, the product/market-portfolio model, and the risk/return model.

INCO and ESB: The Business Strategy Perspective

Why did INCO decide to embark on a major diversification effort, when in its previous history it had concentrated its skills entirely within the nickel mining, refining, and processing industry? While INCO had not made any public statements regarding diversification prior to the ESB acquisition, a strategy analysis reveals a fairly clear picture of the strategic alternatives facing INCO's management and the rationale behind their diversification effort.

INCO's origins date back to the 1880s, with the discovery of large nickel deposits in the Sudbury region of Ontario. After a period of growth and then consolidation, the International Nickel Company emerged in the early 1920s. In many ways analogous to Morgan's U.S. Steel or Rockefeller's Standard Oil, INCO dominated the nickel industry with over 60 percent of the world's production in the 1920s and 1930s and approximately 50 percent of the free world's production during the decade 1965 to 1975.

Mining and refining have always been highly capital intensive businesses, where two dollars of fixed investment are often needed to generate one dollar of sales. An operation's profitability depends greatly upon the quality of the ore mined and how easily it can be refined. In these respects, INCO was blessed. Its Canadian nickel ore bodies were among the richest in the world and their sulfide composition meant that the nickel was relatively easy to extract. INCO's competitors typically had lower mining costs (open pit mines) but much higher refining costs.

INCO's rather unique position meant that it was consistently profitable, good times or bad, whereas many of its competitors were only marginally so. However, INCO still remained exposed to wide swings in sales and earnings. These swings typically lagged the business cycle, following the sales of the stainless steel and capital goods industries. The magnitude of INCO's swings in sales and earnings could be seen in the most recent cycle. In 1970, a banner year, sales increased 54 percent, to $1.05 billion, and earnings per share almost doubled. One year later, though, sales fell to $789 million, and return on equity fell over 50 percent, to 10.4 percent. The improving economy and increased prices in 1973 and early 1974 carried INCO's sales through the $1 billion mark to $1.6 billion in 1974, and earnings per share tripled from their 1971 low. The impact of the rising economy in 1973 and 1974 on INCO's cash flow was dramatic. For the first half of 1974, INCO's effective cash income was $242 million. With capital expenditures of only $97 million, $145 million was left to swell its cash and marketable securities accounts to $330 million and working capital to over $700 million.

In addition to the wide swings in INCO's sales and earnings and a substantial buildup of cash, the company faced an additional problem. Its high-grade Canadian ore bodies had a reported life span of only twenty-five years. This meant new deposits had to be discovered and developed if INCO was to maintain its dominant position in nickel mining and refining. INCO undertook the expansion with an $850 million project in Indonesia and a $300 million project in Guatemala. While these projects could have consumed INCO's internal cash flow, INCO decided to follow recent industry practice of using project financing. This enabled the substantial political and economic risks of each new project to be localized and allowed INCO to raise over $750 million in capital without incurring any liability. However, by employing project financing INCO was left with significant surplus funds.

This situation was apparently recognized in 1972 when two teams were established to scout for acquisitions, one in the natural resources area and one for all other areas. (It was only after the ESB acquisition that the existence of these two teams came to light.) As 1974 progressed, INCO's cash surplus continued to grow by over $5 million per week while the world's stock markets moved toward their lowest levels in a decade. This created an ideal acquisition climate for a cash-rich company like INCO. On July 18, 1974, INCO launched its tender offer for ESB, Inc.

While ESB was the world's largest battery manufacturer, it was not the dominant company in any of the market's three distinct segments. In dry cells it was second to Union Carbide, and in both the automotive and special purpose areas it was number three. All three segments were highly concentrated, with the top six producers in each segment controlling over 90 percent of the market's sales. ESB was a major market force, however, selling its products under its own trademarks (Ray O Vac, Willard, Exide) and private brand names. In addition to batteries, ESB also produced specialty electrical equipment, safety and health products, and specialty chemicals and plastics. A breakdown of both INCO's and ESB's sales is shown in Table 10-4.

The power storage industry had been a relatively profitable one, with 10 percent pretax margins. ESB had been able to achieve this margin on its power storage activities, but had a much lower margin in its other businesses. Despite the industry's profitability, ESB was in a break-even to negative cash flow position because of the capital requirements of the industry's 10 to 15 percent growth rate, a growth rate that industry

TABLE 10-4. INCO and ESB 1973 Sales by Product Line

	Sales ($ Million)	Percent of Total
INCO		
Nickel Processing		
Primary Nickel	$656	56
Rolling Mill Products	227	19
Total	$883	75
Copper	$222	19
Other Metals	68	6
Total	$1,173	100
ESB		
Batteries and Related Equipment		
Dry Cells	$138.2	32
Automotive	151.6	35
Special Purpose	69.8	16
Total	$359.6	83
Other	$ 76.4	17
Total	$436	100

specialists expected to increase in the next decade as alternative energy sources and pollution control became more important.

The stage was thus set for INCO's diversification move. Its strengths were an awesome surplus cash flow and a superior metallurgical expertise. INCO's managers probably perceived the company's risks as stemming from cyclical sales and high fixed costs, on the one hand, and the political exposure of its highly visable assets, on the other. If a more stable, consumer-oriented business utilizing similar technological skills could be acquired for cash, then INCO's strengths could be leveraged and its weaknesses diminished.

ESB apparently fit the bill from this point of view. Although INCO was basically in the metals-processing business, it had done extensive research and development in electrochemistry, the field on which batteries are based. Nickel also had the potential of being a significant battery component and was already used extensively in other segments of the energy field. Furthermore, the acquisition of ESB by INCO would significantly increase INCO's direct consumer sales and, thereby, reduce its exposure as a commodity producer. Since ESB's consumer market was much less cyclical than INCO's metal sales and was growing faster, INCO's managers probably perceived the acquisition as stabilizing and improving INCO's growth rate. In short, a limited strategic fit existed between ESB and INCO. Both had significant experience in electrochemistry, and nickel had the potential of being a major battery component. Through ESB's acquisition INCO hoped to expand significantly its consumer-related sales utilizing ESB's acknowledged management and marketing expertise.

INCO and ESB—A Product/Market Portfolio Perspective

An assessment of INCO from the perspective of the product/market-portfolio model involves asking two key questions: "What are the cash flow characteristics of our existing businesses? What is the competitive strength of our business units?" A detailed answer to these questions is difficult to prepare because of the vertically integrated structure of INCO's business. While there were three distinct segments of INCO's nickel operations (mining, refining, and processing), the mining and refining stages were intricately intertwined at the mine site. And while processing included such distinct processes as rolling and milling, they were also an integral part of INCO's business. Breaking apart this vertical production chain, therefore, does not appear either practical or conceptually sound.

However, in addition to nickel production, INCO was involved in two other businesses: the production of copper and precious metals. The application of the market-share/market-growth matrix to these three businesses results in a picture like that presented in Figure 10-3. At first

FIGURE 10-3.   INCO 1973 Product/Market Portfolio Chart[a]

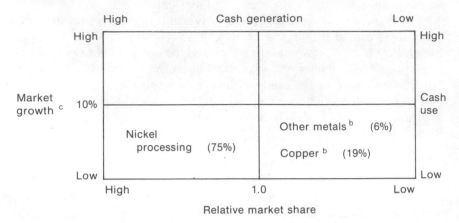

Relative market share

[a] Numbers in parentheses indicate percentage of 1973 sales in that product line. Total 1973 sales = $1,173 million.

[b] These metals are not specifically mined by INCO, but are by-products of its nickel processing facilities. Nevertheless, INCO's sales of copper were almost 30 percent of that of the world's largest producer.

[c] Estimates of market growth and market position are based on unit sales.

Sources: 1. Product line breakdown and competitive position from 1974 *World Mineral Survey Yearbook.*
2. Market growth estimates from U.S. Bureau of Mines estimates.

glance, INCO seems to have 75 percent of its business in the "cash cow" quadrant. Indeed, this was the case, since (1) INCO's nickel operations were over five times larger than those of its nearest competitor and (2) the industry's real growth rate was predicted to remain in the 4 percent range for the foreseeable future. However, it also appears that approximately 25 percent of INCO's sales were in the low-growth/low-market-share quadrant, typically characterized as "dogs." According to the market-share/market-growth matrix, these businesses should be candidates for divestment or liquidation.

Further analysis, however, shows that this is an oversimplification of the situation. Even though INCO's copper and precious metals operations were only one-third to one-sixth of the size of the largest producer in each industry and the industries were growing at 4 to 6 percent, INCO's operations were not "dogs." If anything, they were cash generators. This occurred because INCO's Canadian ore bodies contained not only a high percentage of nickel but also substantial quantities of copper and precious metals. These metals were not distinct businesses but joint products of INCO's nickel mining and refining operations. This situation was not unusual within the mining industry; often the profitability of a mine was as dependent on the production of secondary metals as it was on the primary product.[8]

There are several reasons in addition to those relating to market-share/market-growth characteristics that help explain INCO's substantial cash flow. First, while INCO's mines had higher operating costs than many other nickel mines in the world, they produced relatively high-value ore. Second, INCO had not invested a lot of money differentiating its product through elaborate marketing programs. Instead, the company concentrated on joint R&D with customers to meet and expand its customers' needs for nickel. Third, INCO had initiated the use of project financing (where each operation is independently financed on its own merits) for its new operations in order to minimize political and economic risks. Project financing meant that a relatively small percentage of equity capital was needed, and once operating and financial commitments were met, a free cash flow developed. The effects of INCO's increased use of project financing can be seen in examining the period from 1972 to 1978, when INCO planned to "invest" $1.1 billion in mine development using only $300 million in equity and incurring no liability at the parent level for the rest. As a result of this financing choice, INCO was faced with a surplus cash flow from its present operations, which ranged between $2 million and $7 million per week depending upon the conditions of the world economy.

The one weakness, therefore, in INCO's portfolio of businesses was the lack of opportunities in which it could invest its surplus cash flow. With this weakness or imbalance in mind, INCO's managers probably asked, "What are the cash flow characteristics of the ESB portfolio? How well do they fit INCO's needs?"

Figure 10-4 gives an estimate of ESB's market share/market growth portfolio. Virtually all of ESB's products were in or near the "question mark" category, where they enjoyed high market growth but not market dominance. Despite being the largest battery manufacturer, ESB was either number two or three in each of its three major market segments. ESB was a strong competitor in each, however, and was known for its technological competence, marketing skill, and management experience. In short, ESB had a continuing, significant need for capital in order to grow with the industry and to increase market share.

These characteristics of ESB's portfolio ideally matched the requirements of INCO's cash-rich, investment-poor portfolio. Assuming that our estimates are fairly accurate, a product/market-portfolio analysis confirms that there were probably significant cash flow advantages in combining the two portfolios. ESB, in a rapidly growing industry, needed significant capital investment in order to expand its market share and achieve high returns on investment. Its surplus cash flow was minimal. INCO, on its

FIGURE 10-4.   ESB 1973 Product/Market Portfolio Chart [a]

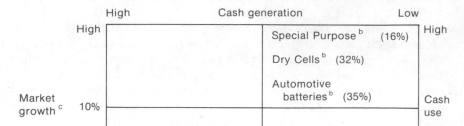

[a] Numbers in parentheses indicate percentage of 1973 sales in that product line. Total 1973 sales = $436 million.

[b] Although ESB is the largest "stored power" manufacturer in the world, it is either the second or third largest competitor in each of these fields.

[c] Estimates of market growth and market position are based upon dollar rather than unit sales.

Sources: 1. Product line breakdown from Annual Reports and 10-K forms.

2. Competitive position estimates from 10-K forms.

3. Market growth estimates from trade publications and U.S. Department of Commerce reports.

side, had a continuing surplus of cash with no foreseeable investment needs. An INCO-ESB merger would give INCO a place to invest its surplus funds and allow ESB to grow to its fullest possible extent.

INCO and ESB: A Risk/Return Perspective

As explained earlier, the risk/return model assumes that capital markets price a security by discounting its expected income stream over time at a rate of return determined by that income stream's systematic or market-related risk. This model suggests that managers be concerned with the impact of a diversifying acquisition on the income stream and required rate of return of the acquiring company. In addition, the model suggests that managers ask, "What does an acquisition do for our shareholders that they could not do for themselves?" The risk/return model implies that the only time diversifying acquisitions can create value for the shareholder is when an improved risk/return tradeoff is obtained. (This does not exclude, of course, the possibility that a significantly undervalued company could be acquired.) These conditions provide further guidelines for an analysis of INCO's acquisition of ESB.

The INCO acquisition of ESB was notable from many standpoints. ESB was the first acquisition INCO had undertaken and one of the first of several major American acquisitions made by foreign companies in the 1970s. In addition, INCO's tender offer marked a return to the use of cash instead of the "creative" securities packages which had characterized the acquisition spree of the 1960s. Third, INCO's offer for ESB spawned a serious and determined counteroffer by United Technologies (then United Aircraft), an uncommon situation even in the "go-go" conglomerate days of the mid-1960s. Finally, and perhaps most noteworthy, was the astounding 110 percent premium over market price that INCO eventually had to pay to win ESB. Tender premiums of 40 to 50 percent were rare, and one investment banker commented that the INCO offer created "an entirely new ball game."

As can be seen in Table 10-5, both ESB and INCO have the same level of systematic risk despite being in different businesses. In addition, one can observe that ESB's market value is significantly smaller than INCO's. Since the levels of systematic risk of the two companies are very close and the acquisition a relatively small one, a risk/return analysis can determine what incremental income stream is necessary to justify the acquisition premium paid by INCO.

Assuming INCO planned no additional investments in ESB, the $120 million acquisition premium suggests that an annual incremental return of $11.2 million is required in order to maintain INCO's shareholder's wealth

TABLE 10-5. Capital Market Data on INCO and ESB

	INCO	ESB	Portfolio
Market value, July 1974 ($ millions)	$2,088.	$104.	$2,192.0
Beta (Value Line), July 1974	1.0	1.0	1.0
Expected Rate of Return[a]	9.3%	9.3%	9.3%
Dividends paid in 1973 ($ millions)[b]	$ 119.0	$ 7.0	
Acquisition Premium ($ millions)		$120.0	

[a] The expected rate of return for a company with a $\beta = 1$ is the same as the market's historic rate of return, often taken to be 9.3 percent.

[b] Dividends paid is the sum of dividends paid by the company in the preceding four quarters.

(incremental return = .093 × $120 million). This return is significantly greater than the $7.0 million in dividends ESB paid in 1973. One should remember, however, that the power storage industry was experiencing significant growth. This implies that ESB's future dividends (cash flow) could be significantly greater than present dividends, assuming that ESB's growth could be internally financed and that ESB maintained a constant payout ratio.

This situation also lends itself to the discounted cash flow method of valuation. However, instead of solving for incremental changes in value, income streams, or risks, the discounted cash flow equation can be solved for a growth rate in dividends based upon existing levels of dividends, risks, and prices. One form of a discounted cash flow equation with a growth term (which assumes perpetual growth) is

$$PV = \sum_{t=1}^{\infty} D_0(1 + g)^t/(1 + R)^t$$

where D_0 represents current dividends. The growth rate, g, necessary to equate ESB's 1973 dividends of 7.0 million and a rate of return of 9.3 percent with its total acquisition price of $225.0 million is 6.2 percent. This growth rate is significantly lower than the industry's present growth rate (12 percent), though greater than the economy's long-term rate of growth (4 percent). This indicates that ESB at $225.0 million was probably fairly priced because of its above-average rate of growth.

An alternative approach using the risk/return model provides a much better understanding of the dynamics surrounding the bidding war for ESB. This approach utilizes the more general discounted cash flow formula. Its purpose is to establish a range of prices, given various income streams and risk adjusted rates of return. In essence, the approach determines whether an asset or security is under or overvalued relative to its expected cash flows and risks.

The discounted cash flow valuation formula, in its

$$PV = \sum_{t=1}^{\infty} D_0(1 + g)^t/(1 + R)^t$$

format, includes an explicit growth term $(1 + g)^t$ and has an infinite time horizon. These are both serious constraints. The basic discounted cash flow formula

$$PV = \sum_{t=1}^{n} D_t/1(1 + R)^t,$$

however, does not have either of these problems. This enables both the period and rate of growth, which are implicit in D_t, to be varied. In general, the greater the income stream's growth rate and/or the greater the time period over which growth occurs, the greater the corresponding present value. This valuation has been applied to ESB in Table 10-6.

In preparing Table 10-6 several assumptions were made. First, ESB's systematic risk and required rate of return was assumed to remain at 9.3 percent. Second, the growth rate that will follow the period of high growth will be that of the economy, or about 4 percent per year. Finally, the initial cash flow consists of ESB's 1973 dividends of $7.0 million. Based on these assumptions and forecasted growth rates over specified periods, the range of present values shown in Table 10-6 can be calculated.

As indicated by Table 10-6, if ESB could maintain its present market position over the period of the industry's exceptional growth (ten to fifteen years), then ESB was clearly a bargain at INCO's original offer of $28 per share ($157 million). Even by the time the bidding had escalated to $38 per share ($209 million), the price remained within reasonable estimates of ESB's present value. However, when INCO raised its offer to $41 per share, or $225.5 million, United Technology backed down. At this price ESB was clearly approaching the upper limit of any reasonable value based on its existing characteristics and the possibility that substantial capital investments might be required. If, however, INCO's management felt that it could enable ESB to expand its market share or maintain its high growth rate over a longer period of time (or, more simply, create synergy), then ESB's potential value was still greater. In the context of the risk/return model, this synergy would be reflected in either (1) an income stream for the combined company greater than that which could be realized if INCO's shareholders merely took an investment position in ESB, or (2) a reduction in the variability of the income stream available to INCO's shareholders greater than that which could be realized from investing in ESB. Even if INCO had to invest an additional $20 or $30

TABLE 10-6. Present Value of Alternate Income Streams for ESB

Annual Growth Rate	Growth Period	Approximate Present Value ($ Millions)
10%	10 years	$200
12	10 years	228
15	10 years	280
10	15 years	205
12	15 years	250
15	15 years	330

million to obtain this synergy, ESB's acquisition at $41 per share could still have a net positive impact on INCO and its shareholders' wealth.

ESB at $225.5 million does not appear to be a "bad deal" for INCO. However, the risk/return model shows that this price is very near the upper limit that could be prudently paid for the company as a separate entity. While we have no evidence that INCO's managers used this analytical framework, it indicates that INCO's managers probably felt that they were buying many years of above-average growth that would require little or no additional capital resources from INCO. It also indicates, however, that if growth did not materialize or if significant additional investment was required to achieve that growth, ESB's potential for value creation could be significantly reduced.

INCO and ESB: A Summary

As in the case of the Rockwell-Admiral merger, we have not tried to present a final judgment on INCO's acquisition of ESB. Instead, we have hoped to show how the three models can help structure the analysis of diversifying acquisitions.

The strategy model shows the fundamental soundness of the ESB acquisition. Both companies relied on related technological skills. ESB provided INCO with both a means of expanding its product base utilizing ESB's consumer market orientation and a way of dampening the effects on sales and profits of the cycles associated with nickel mining and processing. The product/market-portfolio model further confirms a financial fit by showing that INCO, on the one hand, was a heavy cash generator with limited investment alternatives, while ESB, on the other hand, needed cash to grow and expand its market share to a position of dominance. The risk/return model goes an additional step and shows that even at the enormous premium that INCO paid, the deal does not appear unreasonable, though it was not a bargain. This stems from the point that given ESB's systematic risk, its potential return could justify the price that INCO had to pay. In addition, if technological skills could be shared or surplus cash invested in ESB's market share, there would exist the potential for significant synergies and value creation. In summary, all three models give a green light to INCO's acquisition of ESB, although it appears doubtful that it will be an outstanding financial success.

It reviewing this acquisition, it is realistic to acknowledge that there may have been reasons for INCO's move that were not highlighted in this discussion. In particular, INCO may have been concerned by the fact that mining projects in general, and its operations in particular, were highly visible and could offer ready targets for expropriation. ESB, with its widely dispersed operations and consumer orientation, provided no such target. Furthermore, the changing risks of mining meant that it was no longer prudent to invest large sums of equity capital into any one project, even if a company had the funds. This uncertainty existed even in Canada, INCO's home base, with its increasing socialistic and nationalistic economic policies. INCO's long-term prospects in the nickel mining industry may have appeared uncertain at best. By making the diversifying acquisition of ESB, however, INCO was not only reducing its exposure to mining but also effectively transferring assets and future potential to a more stable political and economic environment.

Conclusion

The epilogue to INCO's takeover of ESB was written by the courts. On January 19, 1976, the U.S. Government filed an antitrust suit against INCO in connection with the acquisition of ESB. The suit asked the court to order INCO to divest itself of "all ownership and control" of ESB. The suit was settled out of court during the fall of 1977, when INCO signed a consent decree in which the company promised to cross-license with ESB's competitors any major technological breakthrough achieved by ESB with INCO's support.

This event is particularly noteworthy in the context of our analysis of diversifying acquisitions. Where our analytical framework raised serious questions about the merits of an acquisition, as in the case of Rockwell's acquisition of Admiral, no resistance was voiced by the Justice Department. However, where our framework pointed to considerable advantages of an acquisition from the point of view of the acquiring company, as in the INCO-ESB merger, the Justice Department found that the acquisition was not serving the public interest. Herein lies a basic conflict between business policy and emerging public policy. Since this conflict is important enough to merit separate attention, Chapter 11 will summarize the current status of antimerger law and comment on recent attempts to extend the reach of antitrust legislation to diversifying companies.

Notes and References

1. While certain of the businesses, such as automotive components, do not fit our usual notion of high technology, product development resulting from technology transfer is certainly one determinant of competitive success in those areas.
2. While aerospace operations required large investments in both research and development and capital equipment, most of this was financed by government sources.
3. A close relationship between market share and profitability is the major assumption of the product/market-portfolio model. This assumption has been

    validated by extensive research. See for example R. D. Buzzell, B. T. Gale, and R. G. M. Sultan, "Market Share—A Key to Profitability," *Harvard Business Review* 53, January–February 1975.

4.   Where the acquisition candidate is a privately held company or a division of another company, this portfolio analysis should begin by identifying comparable, publicly owned companies that can be used as proxies for the specific acquisition candidate. This is the typical procedure for valuing privately held companies for sale and tax purposes.

5.   There is no reason, of course, why this value has to be a positive figure. If the costs incurred exceed the value of the benefits obtained, then the market value of the combined company should be less than the sum of its constituent parts.

6.   The $30 million acquisition premium represents the price of the *option* paid by Rockwell to Admiral's shareholders for the chance to improve Admiral's profitability. It's interesting to note that the $4.85 million income stream is equal to a 24 percent after-tax return on Rockwell's $20 million investment in tangible assets for Admiral and leads to a 16 percent after-tax return on the preacquisition market value of Admiral *plus* the $20 million investment.

7.   "Rockwell's Surprising Growth Targets," *Business Week,* May 29, 1978, pp. 60–66.

8.   This example shows the danger of relying on simplifying frameworks of analysis. It also reveals a major weakness of the product/market-portfolio model. Where joint facilities or resources exist, the true competitive strength and profitability of a product may be significantly different from those implied by the product/market-portfolio model.

PART IV

Barriers to Diversification through Acquisition

CHAPTER 11

The Antitrust Challenge

ANTITRUST LAW RELEVANT TO diversifying and diversified companies is frustratingly unclear. Whether pursuing related or unrelated diversication, managers of large, diversifying companies must act without the benefit of confident legal counsel regarding their vulnerability to antitrust attack.

As a general rule, the more related a diversifying acquisition is to the acquiring company's core skills and competences, the more vulnerable it is to antitrust attack. The INCO-ESB merger discussed in Chapter 10 is a good case in point. In addition, totally unrelated large-scale acquisitions are becoming increasingly vulnerable to attack. Given this state of affairs, it is important for managers of diversifying companies and their advisers to be able to justify a particular diversification strategy and diversifying acquisition in terms of the public interest as well as more specific stockholder interests. In preparing such a justification, however, there can be no substitute for a general awareness on the part of management of the legal issues involved, since the Supreme Court has stated flatly that "possible economies cannot be used as a defense to illegality."[1]

Section 7 of the Clayton Act

The current law relevant to merger activity is grounded in Section 7 of the Clayton Act, which prohibits any company from acquiring another "where in any line of commerce in any section of the country, the effect may be to substantially lessen competition, or to tend to create a monopoly."[2] It is noteworthy that prosecution under the Clayton Act requires proof that competition in an identifiable "line of commerce" may be inhibited. The act does not address itself explicitly to the alleged dangers of aggregate economic concentration.

The origin of the Clayton Act of 1914 lies in the will of Congress to impose stricter standards with respect to certain classes of mergers than the Sherman Act[3] had provided. The Sherman Act, although couched in very general language, addressed itself to three basic concerns: (1) that the economic power of contemporary trusts resulted in higher prices to the consumer and lower prices to such suppliers as farmers; (2) that control by a few corporations of a substantial share of the nation's economy was a threat to the opportunities of individuals and smaller businessmen to compete on an equal basis in a competitive system; and (3) that concentrations of economic power might seek to preserve dominance through political influence. While mergers could be attacked under the Sherman Act as illegal combinations in restraint of trade or as attempts to monopolize a specific market, the merger sections of the statute could only be applied successfully where the merging companies were on the verge of attaining monopoly power.[4] Sponsors of the Clayton Act thought that competitive market structures could only be maintained by blocking mergers before there was an imminent danger of monopoly. Thus, they drafted the principal provision concerning mergers, Section 7, to give the government more power in blocking mergers by replacing the imminent danger of monopoly test with the less constraining test of whether or not a merger stands "to substantially lessen competition" in "any line of commerce."

The language used in Section 7 specifically prohibited stock acquisitions, the principal method of making major acquisitions during that period, but said nothing about the purchase of a competitor's (or any other company's) assets. This omission created a large loophole in the law that had the effect of permitting many "purchases of assets" that would have been blocked had the acquisition been structured as a purchase of stock. This loophole was closed in 1950 when Congress, moved by an extremely controversial Federal Trade Commission (FTC) Report claiming that "the giant corporations will ultimately take over the country,"[5] passed the Celler-Kefauver Act. This act amended the original Section 7 of the Clayton Act, removing the asset-acquisition loophole, among other changes. The Celler-Kefauver Amendment of the Clayton Act was followed by a flurry of antimerger complaints. From December 29, 1950, through December 31, 1965, for example, the Justice Department and the FTC initiated a total of 173 antimerger complaints under the new law. Out of these 173 complaints, 133 progressed to final resolution by 1965. Of these, 83 percent are considered victories by the government by virtue of (1) a final court or Federal Trade Commission decision barring the merger, (2) consent decrees restraining past or future acquisitions, or (3) mergers voluntarily abandoned after challenge.[6]

As in the Sherman Act monopolization cases, the courts' action on many Section 7 merger cases hinges on how the relevant geographic market and product market is defined. Generally speaking, the courts have blocked mergers wherever a reasonable argument could be supported for defining a geographic and product market in such a way to demonstrate substantial anticompetitive effects. Similarly, the courts have typically accepted product market definitions that favor action preventing mergers with possible anticompetitive effects. For example, in 1964 the Supreme Court struck down a merger between the Continental Can Company, the nation's second largest producer of tin cans, and the Hazel-Atlas Glass Company, the third-largest bottle manufacturer. A district court found cans and bottles to be separate lines of commerce and concluded that competition was not substantially reduced by the merger. The decision was overturned by the Supreme Court, holding (1) that tin cans and glass bottles were closely competitive in such applications as beer, soft drinks, and baby food packaging and (2) that given Continental's 22 percent share of the combined market for cans and bottles and Hazel-Atlas' 3 percent share, the merger was anticompetitive. Representing the majority of the Court, Justice White wrote:

> In defining the product market . . . we must recognize meaningful competition where it is found to exist . . . though the interchangeability of use may not be so complete and the cross-elasticity of demand not so immediate as in the case of most intraindustry mergers, there is over the long run the kind of customer response to innovation and other competitive stimuli that brings competition between these two industries within Section 7's competition-preserving proscriptions. . . . That there are price differentials between the two products or that the demand for one is not particularly or immediately responsive to changes in the price of the other are relevant matters but not determinative of the product market issues. . . . Where the area of effective competition cuts across industry lines, so must the relevant line of commerce.[7]

The result of court action on cases initiated under the Celler-Kefauver Amendment of Section 7 is that horizontal mergers between companies with substantial shares of a market or vertical mergers likely to foreclose to competitors an appreciable share of some market are now clearly prohibited (except where one of the merger partners is on the brink of financial disaster or where some other extenuating circumstances exist). In reviewing the leading Celler-Kefauver Act court interpretations, Scherer concludes that "when one company acquires a competitor with 3% or more of sales in some relevant market, and when the combined market share exceeds 20%, the probability of judicial disapproval approaches unity. And mergers may be prohibited when they involve much smaller market shares . . . if the industry has a history of rising concentration."[8]

The problems posed by what the law considers conglomerate mergers—mergers between companies operating in separate and distinct markets—are much more complex than those posed by horizontal or vertical mergers. First of all, diversification into numerous fields or markets can affect competition in several subtle ways. Since 1950, decisional law under the amended Clayton Act has identified and focused on several potentially anticompetitive effects of mergers in which diversifying companies might be involved. Among the most important are:

- The elimination of future competition
- The elimination of the present threat of future competition
- Cross-subsidization[9]
- Disciplinary pricing[10]
- Reciprocity[11]
- Heightened barriers to entry

Second, the law on conglomerate mergers is much less clear than the law concerning horizontal and vertical mergers. Indeed, there is still sharp disagreement among lawyers and economists over whether or not Section 7 is applicable to mergers when there is no discernible functional link with prior operations.

In the following discussion, we will be concerned with only two of the three types of conglomerate mergers customarily distinguished by the law: (1) product line extension mergers that add to the acquiring company's portfolio new products related in some way to existing production processes and marketing channels and (2) "pure" conglomerate mergers between companies in completely unrelated businesses. We will refer to the former as related mergers (acquisitions) and the latter as unrelated mergers (acquisitions) to conform with the language system used in previous chapters. The third type of conglomerate merger identified by the law, market extension mergers in which the partners sell the same products to geographically separate markets, will not be directly addressed, since they predominantly involve issues of horizontal integration. Neither will we discuss mergers leading to vertical integration. Our attention will be more narrowly focused on product market diversification.[12]

The Appendix to this chapter (p. 289) provides a copy of the Department of Justice's "merger guidelines" as an indication of the standards currently being applied in determining whether a merger will be challenged under Section 7 of the Clayton Act. The guidelines relate to horizontal, vertical, and conglomerate mergers. While our interest is focused primarily on so-called conglomerate mergers, the full set of guidelines has been included in the Appendix because the conglomerate nature of a merger does not change the standards to be applied in judging its legality. As the Supreme Court pointed out in the historic Procter & Gamble case "all mergers are within the reach of the statute [Section 7 of the Clayton Act], and all must be tested by the same standard, whether they are classified as horizontal, vertical, conglomerate or other." The reader should note, however, that the guidelines relating to conglomerate mergers have been very cautiously phrased.

Antitrust Aspects of Related Diversification

The company that pursues a policy of related diversification is likely to confront more severe antitrust challenges than one whose goal is simply to build a portfolio of unrelated enterprises and who stands ready to make any acquisition that looks promising. The theory of related diversification[13] can lead a company astray of the antitrust law by directing its attention toward acquisitions by holding out the promise of operating efficiencies, or "synergy." The same technological, marketing, and production strengths on which an acquiring company would rely in increasing the productivity of acquired assets may well persuade litigious competitors, federal prosecutors, and the courts that the acquisition will have a detrimental impact on the line of commerce entered via acquisition. Where synergy is such that the acquirer can be viewed as a likely potential competitor of the acquiree, the probability of a legal blocking action increases. Just such a set of conditions lay behind the adverse decision handed to the Procter & Gamble Company in its legal battle to hold onto Clorox.[14]

In 1957 Procter was a marketer of a wide range of low-priced, high-turnover household consumer items sold by its aggressive, well-trained sales force through grocery, drug, and department stores. These items were divided into four major categories: food products, toilet goods; paper products; and soaps, detergents, and cleansers. Soaps, detergents, and cleansers (referred to below as household cleansing agents) accounted for almost 55 percent of its total domestic sales of $900 million in 1957.

Procter was the largest buyer of television time in the nation. It spent $80 million on domestic television advertising and another $47 million on "miscellaneous sales promotion." The company received the highest volume discounts available on its advertising and sales promotion dollars. Allegedly, it received as much as 25 to 30 percent discounts on its expenditures in television advertising.

Procter acquired Clorox in August, 1957, after a thorough study of the liquid bleach market by its promotion department. The report indicated that Procter's entry into this market would require "a very heavy investment" in order to achieve a satisfactory market share for a new brand of liquid bleach and that the acquisition of an existing company, such as Clorox, was a more attractive alternative. It predicted that Procter's "sales, distributing and manufacturing setup" could increase Clorox's share of the market in certain areas where it was low and effect a number of savings that would increase the profits of the business considerably.[15]

In addition to the potential operating efficiencies that could accrue to Procter, several other aspects of the acquisition caught the attention of antitrust prosecutors. First, although Clorox was a relatively small company, with $40 million in sales, it commanded an important 49 percent share of the U.S. liquid bleach market. Second, the Federal Trade Commission (FTC) noted that the bleach industry was highly concentrated. The six leading companies accounted for more than 80 percent of total industry sales in 1957, despite the fact that two hundred companies operated on the industry's fringe.[16] Another red flag for the FTC was the success that some companies had in building up strong brand preferences for their products through heavy advertising and promotional expenditures. Clorox, it was noted, was able to command a 10 to 20 percent price premium over many of its rivals because of the strength of its brand name.[17]

It did not take long for the FTC to challenge the Clorox acquisition, and after six years of hearings and investigations, Commissioner Philip Elman delivered the opinion of the FTC on November 26, 1963, indicating that the acquisition would "tend to lessen competition" and thus would be in violation of Section 7 of the Clayton Act. In 1966 the Court of Appeals for the Sixth Circuit disagreed and dismissed the Commission's complaint. On April 11, 1967, the Supreme Court announced that the Court of Appeals had erred, confirmed the Commission's findings, and ordered Procter to divest Clorox.

Since Commissioner Elman's findings were supported by the Supreme Court and have subsequently become the basis for guidelines governing the legality of similar acquisitions or mergers, they are worth noting in full[18]:

1. The household liquid bleach industry is highly concentrated and oligopolistic, strongly characterized by product differentiation through advertising. Clorox is the dominant and only national seller in this industry. It enjoys a decisive competitive advantage and has succeeded in creating a definite consumer preference for the Clorox brand, enabling it consistently to be priced at or above the level of any competing brand. In point of either market share or financial strength, no firm except Purex can be regarded as a significant competitive factor in the industry, and Purex does not compete with Clorox at all in about one-half of the nation.

2. At the time of the merger, even though entry or slight market expansion on the part of very small neighborhood bleach producers was possible despite Clorox's dominant position, the industry was concentrated and barricaded to new entry to a degree inconsistent with effectively competitive conditions. Clorox can selectively prevent entry of new rivals and

expansion of its existing rivals regionally or nationally. It is an inhibitor of vigorous competitive activity.

3. Clorox's merger with Procter only intensifies the characteristics of the liquid bleach industry mentioned earlier. Clorox, by being a part of a multi-product national advertiser of tremendous financial reserves, can further dominate the industry and markedly heighten the barriers to entry by (a) obtaining substantially larger discounts on its advertising expenditures (particularly TV) than what it received prior to the merger and than that received by its nearest rival, Purex, because Procter's very high volume advertising expenditure enables it to receive the highest discount—33⅓% on television; (b) using Procter's direct aggressive sales force which can, if necessary, use the leverage of other Procter products in obtaining shelf space for Clorox; (c) obtaining 'wider consumer exposure' when advertised on television with other Procter products; (d) being able to get 'choice television spots' when necessary; and (3) tying-in with other Procter products as loss leaders.

    As a result of the merger and consequent enormous financial power available to the Company, Clorox could have sufficient price flexibility to undercut a competitor's price and incur a loss on a sustained basis in order to drive the rival out and/or to improve its market share.

    In addition, Procter is an even more feared competitor than was the pre-merger Clorox. Since market behavior is determined by the state of mind of the firms in the market, Procter's history of success, its general size and its prowess, which loom large in the eyes of the small liquid bleach firms, must for that reason alone be reckoned significant factors.

4. The Commission rejects the argument that it should not proscribe a merger that is productive of 'efficiencies' for the sake of protecting the 'inefficient' small firms in the industry. In this case, the cost savings resulting from the scale of advertising, distribution, and marketing do not promote competition; they serve only to increase the barriers to new entry into the relevant market, and thereby impair competition. . . . In short, the kind of 'efficiency' and 'economy' produced by this merger is precisely the kind that—in the short as well as the long run—hurts, not helps, a competitive economy and burdens, not benefits, the consuming public.

5. Large advertising expenditures in the liquid bleach industry have not resulted in a lower unit price to the consumer. (Clorox, the most extensively advertised liquid bleach, is also the most expensive for the consumer.) Thus we have a situation in which heavy advertising is not beneficial to the consumer, who pays for such advertising in the form of a higher price for the product.

Commissioner Elman added:

If we consider . . . not what Procter will in fact do to exploit the power conferred on it by the merger, or has done, but what it can and is reasonably likely to do in the event of a challenge to its dominant market position in the liquid bleach industry, we are constrained to conclude that the merger has increased the power of Clorox, by dominating its competitors and discouraging new entry, to foreclose effective competition in the industry.

What is important for related business diversifiers to learn from the Clorox case is that when a market entry acquisition is the dominant competitor in a highly concentrated industry, as was Clorox, the case for disallowing the acquisition or forcing divestiture becomes a strong one. Equally as important, where the Commission or a court determines that business judgment suggests the feasibility of market entry through internal growth, no evidence presented by an acquirer is likely to be of much use in defending its disinclination to diversify and enter new markets other than by acquisition. This follows from the findings by both the Commission and the Court that (1) the operating efficiencies Procter stood to realize by entering the household cleanser market were so apparent that Procter was likely to pursue independent entry had the acquisition route been foreclosed, (2) the likelihood of entry by Procter into the home cleanser field was perceived by members of the industry before the fact, and (3) Procter's brooding presence at the edge of the market served to discipline the industry and keep it more competitive than it otherwise might have been.

Of course, not every related acquisition is as vulnerable to attack on the grounds of eliminating future competition and the present threat of future competition as was Procter's in the Clorox case. The government retains the burden of demonstrating that the acquiring company is the most likely entry into the market and that the number of potential entrants is limited. This is not an easy (or appropriate) case to argue in most circumstances. Indeed, while the Procter-Clorox merger may have been especially vulnerable to antitrust action, since both companies were dominant competitors in their respective (and related) markets, most other related mergers are less clear cut for the government. Still, all large-scale, related acquisitions will be reviewed by the government, since, according to the Hart-Scott-Rodino Antitrust Improvement Act of 1976, companies with total assets or annual sales of $100 million intending to acquire other companies with total assets or annual sales of $10 million or more are required to notify the Antitrust Division of the Justice Department at least thirty days prior to consummation. With the Clorox case indicating a widely accepted line of judicial logic, one can readily identify what kind of related acquisitions run the highest risks of provoking antitrust action.

Antitrust action aimed at blocking or rescinding a related acquisition is most likely where competition in the target company's market stands to be adversely affected by (1) diminished competitive rigor stemming from the inability of competitors to match the new resources available to the acquired company from its parent, (2) increased barriers to market entry, or (3) the new-found competitive power of the acquired company arising from either greatly reduced costs or the elimination of an actual or perceived competitor. As can be seen from Table 11-1, the impact (and potential impact) of these factors on competition depends to a large extent on the market share positions of both the acquiring and the acquired companies.

Most related acquisitions by companies currently commanding market shares of 20 percent or more are high-risk ventures from a legal point of view, whether or not the target company operates in an oligopolistic or classically competitive market. Only where a dominant competitor acquires another company in a related line of business with a low share of a concentrated market are the chances for government review or intervention low. This poses a paradox for companies pursuing related diversification through acquisition from a strong competitive position. Just those factors that go to prove the antitrust case against a synergistic acquisition also make that acquisition especially interesting from a strategic point of view.

Economic logic implies that the very elements of product, market, and technological synergy that make a potential acquisition especially appropriate for a particular company should provide that company advantages that other potential acquirers would not be able to realize. The special nature of the opportunity for the acquiring company, in turn, should permit it to calculate a price for the acquisition especially advantageous from the perspective of both buyer and seller: by foreseeing a more productive utilization of acquired assets, the buyer should be able to project higher earnings for the acquired firm than would any other potential buyer, thus enabling him to lead the bidding for the seller while still anticipating the realization of his required rate of return. These same characteristics, however, constitute red flags for antitrust authorities on the lookout for acquisitions that eliminate potential independent entrants and perceived threats to entry that discipline the market. The conclusion appears inescapable that the more attractive a related acquisition appears to a strong competitor from the standpoint of operating (as opposed to purely financial) efficiencies, the more vulnerable it is likely to be to antitrust attack. In marked contrast, related acquisitions by companies with low market shares are less likely to provoke antitrust attack.

Antitrust Aspects of Unrelated Diversification[19]

In the case of an acquisition that has no discernible link with the acquiring company's prior operations, the Clayton Act currently poses no great

TABLE 11-1. Antitrust Risks for Related Business Diversifiers

Acquiring Company	Target Company	Structure of Target Company's Market		Antitrust Risks
		Few Competitors	Many Competitors	
D[a]	D	x		High: threat of increased market concentration; potential for predatory pricing.
D	D		x	High: threat to present and future competition (forbearance) by establishing new entry barriers; potential for predatory pricing.
D	S[b]	x		Low: acquisition should increase competition.
D	S		x	High: forbearance; potential for predatory pricing.
S	D	x		High: potential for reverse predation.
S	D		x	High: potential for reverse predation.
S	S	x		Low: no antitrust problems.
S	S		x	Low: no antitrust problems.

[a] D signifies a dominant competitor with at least 20 percent share of market.
[b] S signifies a subordinate competitor with 3 to 5 percent share of market.

obstacle to management. The acquiring company in this context would not be perceived as a likely independent entrant to the market (and thereby as a restraining influence on that market). Nor would it be perceived as one of a few likely entrants standing at the edge of the market whose entry through acquisition would diminish the competitive stimulus that its expected entry would otherwise provide. The issue of cross-subsidization is also not likely to block a proposed merger between companies pursuing separate and distinct business activities. Cross-subsidization is a violation of the Clayton Act and the Sherman Act if it leads to prolonged sales at prices below out-of-pocket (variable) costs; if prices do not drop to that level, the law presently considers cross-subsidization inconclusive and noninvidious. However, it is unlikely that a court operating under current interpretations of the law would predict such extensive cross-subsidization in the absence of such behavior in the past on the part of the two merger partners.[20] Indeed, a recent study by Jesse W. Markham suggests that because of the decentralization of pricing and advertising decisions in widely diversified companies, the potential (or even the incentive) for cross-subsidization leading to below-cost pricing practices in one or more lines of business after unrelated, or "pure," conglomerate mergers take place is very low.[21] It is also doubtful that the practice of reciprocity would be viewed as an inevitable result of "pure" conglomerate mergers.[22]

Objections to an unrelated, or "pure," conglomerate merger based on anticipated increases in barriers to entry and potential price leadership and disciplinary pricing practices could conceivably be more troublesome to managers of diversifying companies than the issues mentioned in the preceding paragraph. Although a court pursuing this line of argument would be setting precedent rather than following it, it is conceivable that a merger involving a widely diversified company and a dominant company within an industry characterized by a loose oligopoly structure might be struck down as involving a substantial danger to competition. It could be argued that in an industry in which the number of sellers is large enough to allow some price competition but small enough so that each is aware of the identity of its competitors, the entry of a large, diversified company might inhibit competitive pricing (from fear of disciplinary pricing by the diversified company in the future) and deter subsequent entry by a potential competitor unwilling to invest in an industry dominated by a major conglomerate.

Where a market is already uncompetitive, however, this argument is unlikely to prevail. Indeed, it can be argued that in such circumstances entry by a diversified company could have a pro-competitive impact by challenging the existing price structure. Similarly, where the market entered is sufficiently competitive so that price and output decisions are reached without explicit consideration of competitive reactions by individual competitors, price leadership and disciplinary pricing would be extremely difficult for a court to predict with any confidence.

Since the current position of the courts and many economists is that mergers do not influence competition as long as they do not result in (1) the dominance of a well-defined market or (2) the consolidation of companies in competition or potential competition with each other, truly conglomerate mergers should not cause insurmountable legal difficulties for most companies.[23] However, suits brought by the Justice Department between 1969 and 1971 against ITT, Northwest Industries, and Ling-Temco-Vought (based on broad definitions of "lines of commerce"), proposals aimed at inhibiting economic concentration through conglomerate mergers, and recent antitrust legislation all suggest that mergers among the top two hundred manufacturing companies, acquisitions by one of the top two hundred manufacturing companies, or acquisitions by one of the top two hundred companies of any leading producer in any concentrated industry will generate careful government scrutiny at the very least.

Effect of the ITT Cases

In 1969 Richard W. McLaren, then head of the Justice Department's Antitrust Division, sought to test his conviction that Section 7 of the Clayton Act was intended to apply to all kinds of mergers that contributed substantially to aggregate concentration, including purer forms of conglomerates. Of the five conglomerate merger cases he filed, three involved attempts to block ITT's acquisitions of Canteen Corporation, the nation's largest food vending company, Grinnel Corporation, the leader in automatic sprinklers and sprinkler installation, and Hartford Fire Insurance Company, the nation's sixth largest property and casualty insurer. In its ITT-Grinnel complaint the Antitrust Division charged that if the court were to allow the merger, "the current trend of acquisitions of dominant firms in concentrated markets by large companies [would] be furthered and encouraged, thereby (1) increasing the concentration of control of manufacturing assets, (2) increasing the barriers to entry in concentrated markets, and (3) diminishing the vigor of competition by increasing actual and potential customer-supplier relationships among leading firms in concentrated markets."[24] A federal district court rejected the Division's argument and, in doing so, upheld the view that mergers which leave the structures of specific markets intact cannot be said to promote monopoly power or to lessen competition. In essence, the court reaffirmed the theory that Section 7 did not apply to "pure" conglomerate mergers.

As the Grinnel decision was being handed down, the trial of the government's case against ITT's acquisition of Hartford Fire Insurance was getting under way. Shortly thereafter the government appealed the

Grinnel case to the Supreme Court. However, since the government stood to lose its basis for continued attacks on economic concentration if it lost its appeal and ITT stood to lose a substantial amount of assets through forced divestiture if it lost its defense, both parties decided to compromise and settle the three pending cases out of court. As part of the settlement, ITT won the right to retain Hartford. In return, ITT agreed to divest itself of five of its companies completely, spin off a portion of a sixth, and sell its interest in yet another. These dispositions represented about $1 billion in sales. In addition, ITT was also barred from acquiring any significant U.S. corporation for ten years.

One important result of the consent judgments entered into by the government and ITT was that McLaren was not able to test his theories on competition or to receive a ruling from the high court on whether or not the Clayton Act can be applied to large-scale, conglomerate mergers. While no new interpretations of the law were written, the settlement of the government's cases against ITT nevertheless pleased many in the Justice Department, since it provided the basis for a broader interpretation of Section 7 in the future. However, in the decade following the ITT judgment, not much progress has been made in clarifying the ambiguous rules governing conglomerate mergers. Indeed, in 1974 the Justice Department found no basis to block the large Mobil Oil–Marcor merger, nor in October, 1976, to intervene in the proposed merger between General Electric Company (the nation's eighth largest company with over $16 billion in sales) and Utah International ($686 million in sales), a mining and natural resources company unrelated to General Electric's main lines of business. With the value of the exchange of shares totaling $1.9 billion, the G.E.–Utah International merger was the largest in the nation's history.[25]

Proposals for New Legislation and Enforcement Policy Governing Conglomerate Mergers

Since Section 7 does not explicitly address itself to the alleged dangers of aggregate economic concentration, it was perhaps inevitable that several legislative proposals designed to block increased economic concentration accompanying conglomerate mergers appeared during the late 1950s and the 1960s.[26] Carl Kaysen and Donald Turner proposed that conglomerate acquisitions by companies above a specified size be accompanied by a spinoff of assets of comparable size.[27] A White House Task Force on Antitrust Policy (chaired by Phil C. Neal) proposed that large companies be prohibited from acquiring leading companies in major concentrated industries.[28] The so-called Campbell-Shephard proposal sought to bar mergers that would bring into the same corporation leading companies in two or more major concentrated industries.[29] While each proposal was widely discussed, no legislative initiatives developed until 1979, when the FTC, the Justice Department, and Senator Edward Kennedy (in his new role as Chairman of the Senate Committee on the Judiciary), each drafted proposals aimed at large-scale, conglomerate mergers. While the proposals differed in some important respects, they all placed a dollar limit on the ability of the largest U.S. companies to grow through mergers. For example, according to the FTC and Kennedy proposals, which appear to have been influenced by the Kaysen–Turner proposal first presented in 1958, a giant company with over $2 billion in assets could only acquire another company if it was willing to sell an equivalent amount of assets. Efficiency and market share tests, along with divestiture rules, were also proposed for mergers of smaller companies.[30]

Following, in part, from his assessment of the low probabilities of new legislation governing conglomerate mergers being passed by Congress, Harlan M. Blake, a leading proponent of more imaginative enforcement and statutory interpretation of existing antitrust laws, argues that existing legislation provides sufficient grounds for blocking anticompetitive conglomerate mergers. According to his historical analysis, none of the sections of the Clayton Act, including Section 7, were intended to require elaborate market analysis or proof of probable impairment of the structure, performance, or competition in precisely defined markets.[31] Rather, Blake argues that the intent of the antitrust laws, including Section 7, since their beginnings have been, more generally, to prevent the destruction or erosion of "a form of economic organization in which economic power in any form should not be permitted to limit the freedom of equally efficient smaller entrepreneurs to compete, on fair and equal terms, with larger firms or groups of firms."[32] For Blake the special economic power of the conglomerate stems from its vast financial resources, which can be quickly deployed "wherever in the corporate structure greatest gains, including those from the suppression of outbreaks of competition, can be realized." Since Blake's argument represents an important theme in the current debate on antitrust policy and conglomerate mergers and in many ways complements the concerns of the FTC, the Justice Department, and Senator Kennedy about economic concentration, it is useful to summarize how he views the financial power of conglomerates as being injurious to competition.

The core of Blake's argument is that corporate financial power is a significant antitrust consideration over and apart from market power, the traditional basis of antitrust action. Blake argues that the capital at the disposal of conglomerate managers is insulated to a large degree from the competitive discipline of the public market for capital funds. Administered at the discretion of management, it can be transferred quickly from one area of corporate activity to another without many of the costs inherent in mobilizing resources in the competitive capital markets. "Its privileged status," says Blake, "provides the larger firm with a cheaper and more flexible competitive instrument than any available to an equally efficient smaller firm."[33]

The financial power of conglomerates derives, in Blake's view, from corporate and tax laws that give management total discretion in declaring dividends. Since most taxpayers find realized or unrealized capital gains on equity investments to be more advantageous than realized dividend income and since the pressure on conglomerates is primarily for "flashy growth in reported earnings," low cost pools of internal capital are inevitably generated. Blake argues that these internal pools of capital cannot be regarded as equivalent to external capital, since its amount and rate of return can be, and often is, intentionally or unintentionally concealed. In addition, Blake claims that these pools of capital are typically immune from takeover threats because of the size and diversity of the conglomerate company.

With pools of capital that are low cost, inconspicuous, and protected from takeover threats and with a wider range of investment alternatives than single-product companies, conglomerates are in a position, according to Blake, to use their financial power and whatever monopoly power they enjoy in discrete markets to maximize profits. This constitutes an inequality in competitive opportunity, in Blake's view, and is therefore inconsistent with the tenets of existing antitrust policy.[34] In addition, Blake argues that the power inherent in the discretionary use of extensive pools of capital insulated from market forces tends to extend or perpetuate itself by seeking political advantage and protection. Such action, Blake believes, can create, if it is successful, a "political-industrial complex" that may frustrate democratic processes or invite, if it is unsuccessful, reprisals such as extensive bureaucratic regulation or socialism.[35] Blake concludes his argument with the suggestion that the Justice Department pursue litigation with the intent of establishing, once and for all, the "presumption that any substantial acquisition by a large firm would probably result in an injury to competition or tend to create a monopoly."[36] Such a prescription would have the effects of (1) reinforcing the notion that "internal growth is the normal, and usually most socially efficient, means of industrial expansion,"[37] and (2) validating the theory that once a firm reaches a certain size, "the probability it will injure competition by means of integration or certain business practices is so great that the firm should carry the burden of justifying its desired course of conduct."[38] In a practical sense, this would mean that any of the leading two hundred firms in the nation acquiring another corporation would be required to rebut this presumption of illegality.

It is difficult to predict how far enforcement policy will evolve in coming years toward the position argued by Blake. However, at least one antitrust case suggests that certain aspects of Blake's argument are not alien to the Federal Trade Commission or the courts. In the Reynolds Metals case the Commission objected to Reynolds' acquisition of Arrow Brands, a company with sales of only $500,000 in 1957 that decorated aluminum foil for resale to the florist trade.[39] Importantly, the Commission did not imply a vertical theory of foreclosure. Rather, it argued that the acquisition was illegal because it gave Arrow new financial strength, financial strength demonstrated by Arrow's low prices from October 1957 to mid-1958 and its building a new plant valued at $500,000. While Arrow was not charged with predatory pricing, the Commission did complain that "Arrow could lower its prices and maintain them at low levels for an extended period which it could not have done before the merger." In short, the Commission found that this new-found financial strength was anticompetitive and therefore illegal. Subsequently, the Court of Appeals for the District of Columbia affirmed the Commission's findings.[40]

While the Commission's argument in the Reynolds Metals case does not parallel the full position put forth by Blake, it does suggest that enforcement policy and the courts will seek in coming years to clarify the conditions under which large-scale conglomerate mergers will be prohibited. In the absence of such clarifications, most companies need not defer pursuing a conglomerate acquisition on the basis of current law. Such a company should be prepared, however, to rebut arguments similar to those put forth by Blake.[41]

An Examination of the "Financial Power" Argument

Blake argues that the financial power of large, widely diversified companies stems not only from the absolute amount of their available financial resources, but also from their ability to obtain financial resources at the lowest possible cost and to transfer them quickly from one corporate activity to another. The conceptual problem facing both government prosecutors and representatives of companies pursuing growth through conglomerate mergers is to determine whether the threat to competition and the public interest posed by conglomerates is so great that all conglomerate mergers over a certain size should be presumed illegal and, therefore, subject to Justice Department review and approval before consummation.

A large part of the problem in resolving the debate over conglomerate mergers is the lack of agreement on what constitutes the public interest. To move this debate forward it is useful to start with fundamental concepts. One such concept suggests that the public interest requires the lowest prices and costs consistent with a mix of products and services responsive to public demand. If we can accept this position, then it is logical to expect that widely diversified companies pursuing growth through conglomerate mergers can contribute to the public interest, provided that:

1. predatory pricing for the purpose of displacing competitors and monopolizing the market does not result from the cross-subsidization process, and

2. concentration in an industry does not exceed a level where competitors cease to vie for increased shares of the market, and

3. prices reflect the low cost positions attained, and

4. public financial statements report results on a "line of business" basis.[42]

As long as these conditions are met, corporate size and cross-subsidization practices of diversified companies are not in conflict with the public interest. Indeed, the cross-subsidization practices that concern Blake can be seen to serve the public interest. Furthermore, the capital efficiencies presumed by Blake should be seen only as a possible and by no means an inevitable result of unrelated diversification through acquisition. We will discuss both these points in the following sections.

Cross-subsidization[43]

Cross-subsidization can serve the public interest when a diversified company uses its financial resources to make capital investments leading to greater efficiencies in production or other economies of scale in a specific industry or product market. Greater operating efficiency typically means that variable costs (such as raw materials and direct labor) are replaced by new fixed costs. When new fixed costs are less than the variable costs replaced on a per unit of output basis, total costs will decline and a company will be able to price at a lower rate than before while still being able to cover its variable costs and to contribute to its overhead costs. This public benefit of corporate cross-subsidization should be differentiated, however, from the short-run price effects of predation. One potentially destructive form of predatory behavior occurs when a diversified company uses its financial resources to cover declining margins (or actual operating costs) in one of its businesses that seeks to punish or drive out competition by pricing below its competitors' break-even points or below its own average variable costs.[44] Although the consumer benefits in this situation from reduced prices over the short run, the stage is set for unchallenged price escalation in the future. In this instance no new cost structure is likely to be established for the benefit of consumers. Rather, a diversified company's assets are merely squandered in attempting to drive out competition.

Cross-subsidization, when unassociated with predatory pricing, can also further the public interest by contributing to the efficient allocation of capital throughout industry. The widely diversified company has the unique ability to allocate capital from low-growth businesses with more cash than they require to high-growth businesses in need of large amounts of cash and thereby promote innovation. For example, IBM's entry into computers in the 1950s was heavily financed by its office equipment division, and G.E.'s light bulb and appliance businesses have helped fund the company's jet engine and nuclear reactor businesses. Often the widely diversified company is in a position to do this more efficiently than the capital markets because it (1) avoids the transaction costs associated with raising external capital, (2) reduces the tax consequences of paying dividends and (3) typically possesses more detailed information about the prospects of its existing businesses and closely related businesses than do suppliers of equity and debt capital. Most investors and creditors must rely on information that is prepared either by companies, always fearful of losing competitive advantages because of unnecessary disclosure, or by financial analysts and economists who are at least one step removed from current operating data and evolving market conditions. In contrast, the corporate headquarters of well-managed, diversified companies have both the information and the experienced personnel necessary to identify and evaluate emerging areas of opportunity.

In addition, the control systems of well-managed diversified companies can ensure economic use of resources allocated throughout the company. On this dimension, the attention paid to capital investments in widely diversified companies can be more disciplined than in less diversified companies. Since the diversified company possesses such a large range of internal investment opportunities, effective rationing of capital forces both a rigorous examination of all capital requests and a disciplined monitoring of performance after capital allocations have been made. The experience of many well-managed diversified companies in improving the performance of corporate assets, long underutilized prior to acquisition, suggests that many independent companies are treated less vigorously by investors and creditors than the divisions of successful conglomerates by their corporate office.[45]

Two final points regarding cross-subsidization need emphasis. First, where cross-subsidization significantly alters the relationship between costs and prices, as in the case of using cross-subsidization to push out competitors by selling for prolonged periods of time at prices below average variable costs, such practices can be prosecuted under the Sherman Act and the Clayton Act. That diversified companies may have a greater opportunity to use cross-subsidization for illegal purposes than single business companies should not be used as a basis for regulating the growth of widely diversified companies. Existing law is sufficiently clear to prosecute all offenders, be they single- or multibusiness companies.

Second, there is no question that the cross-subsidization practices of large, diversified companies tend to preclude individual investors from participating fully in the allocation of financial resources from one sector of the economy to another. Whether or not this is detrimental to the public interest is as much a question of ideology as it is of reconstructing the intent of Congress in passing legislation in bygone eras. However, it is important to recall that diversified companies are not alone in this intermediary role. Large commercial banks perform the same function in reallocating capital from industrial sector to industrial sector. Indeed, the investing public and the government both expect and desire such reallocation of financial resources to take place. Insurance companies, through their large-scale long-term investment activities, provide an even more dramatic example of resource allocation without the direct participation or guidance of individual investors. While various aspects of bank and insurance company activities are regulated by the government, decisions to switch funds from one industrial sector to another clearly are not. In addition, mutual funds and pension funds—and, in effect, all financial intermediaries—tend to preclude the participation of individual investors in the allocation of capital from one sector of the economy to another. To the extent that antitrust reformers picture conglomerates as financial intermediaries, their argument needs to address the role of financial intermediaries as a group in the capital markets, not simply conglomerates, which probably play the least important role in allocating investment capital.

Cost of Capital

While cross-subsidization can contribute to the efficient allocation of resources throughout industry, the practice is nevertheless viewed by some critics of conglomerate mergers as anticompetitive even where there is no intent of predation. These critics argue that large, widely diversified companies can finance new businesses (or even mature businesses) with cheaper capital than that available to undiversified competitors since (1) their average cost of capital may be lower than that of smaller, less diversified companies and (2) they can transfer capital among businesses without paying any of the transaction costs required by external capital markets. The argument implies that divisions of large conglomerates have a lower cost of capital than that of undiversified competitors and that these lower capital costs place equally efficient smaller companies at an unfair competitive disadvantage.[46] Presumably, the lower capital costs of large, diversified companies are anticompetitive and, therefore, not in the public interest because these companies would possess a competitive weapon not available to other members of the industry.

This argument is questionable on several grounds. First, as Donald Turner has pointed out, "the continued numerical significance of small businesses indicates that capital costs are not an important factor in many lines of endeavor."[47] Second, the assumption that widely diversified companies have "low cost" pools of internal capital is based on poor economic thinking. Any pool of capital, invested or uninvested, carries an opportunity cost to investors and corporations alike. This opportunity cost reflects the return on that investment that could have been earned by placing the capital elsewhere. Thus, no pool of capital can be considered low cost in a true economic sense. Third, it is inappropriate to assume (1) that the cost of capital of a large, diversified company is inevitably lower than that of a smaller, less diversified company operating in the same industry or profit market, and (2) that the cost of capital for a division of a large diversified company is identical to that of the company as a whole.

The "low cost of capital" argument, as it relates to large, diversified companies, has two serious flaws. Once companies reach a size that affords access to professional investors (say, in the $5 million to $15 million sales range), they will typically incur costs of new capital that accurately reflect their risks and opportunities. The risks and opportunities perceived by professional investors depend on both the amount and the clarity of the information available. However, since there are practical limits to the amount of information that investors can effectively process, investor uncertainty with respect to a company's risks and opportunities tends to increase as companies become more diversified and the nature of their business becomes less clearly defined. As most experienced investors would expect, the greater the uncertainty concerning the risks and opportunities of a company, the greater the return or risk premium demanded by the investor.[48] (In the equity market this risk premium translates into the rate at which future earnings are discounted.) Since there are often high levels of uncertainty concerning the specific risks and opportunities facing widely diversified companies, the cost of equity capital for diversified companies can well be higher than that of less diversified companies of comparable size. The extremely low price/earnings multiples of many conglomerates may well reflect investor uncertainty about the size, timing, and volatility of these companies' future returns. This uncertainty leads to high required rates of return for investors and therefore high costs of equity capital for companies.[49] These is also no evidence at present showing that conglomerates' absolute cost of long-term debt is lower than that for other classes of companies.[50]

Even if the average cost of capital of a widely diversified company is presumed to be lower than that of one of its many competitors (because of the lower risk of its business portfolio, greater use of debt, or greater reliance on internally generated funds), it is improper to assume that the average cost of capital for a diversified company represents the true cost of capital for each of its divisions. In fact, a division's true cost of capital reflects its own risk profile, which may be quite different from that of a sister division or the company as a whole. Thus, a division of a diversified company may have a real cost of capital (or required rate of return) that may be quite different from the cost of capital (or required rate of return) of a sister division or the diversified company as a whole.[51]

Finally, the special ability of large, diversified companies to eliminate or reduce the transaction costs associated with public offerings and private placements is easily overrated. While it is well known that transaction costs tend to decline as offering size increases, this reduced cost has an insignificant impact on a corporation's total cost of doing business. Indeed, if corporate size brings an advantage as far as financing is concerned, it will stem more from the availability of external financing during periods of capital market illiquidity than from its cost. The experience of many companies during the credit crunch of 1974–1975 appears to substantiate this judgment.

In light of these arguments, it should be apparent that sweeping statements about the anticompetitive effects of the lower cost of capital available to large, diversified companies cannot be accepted as inevitable facts of economic life. In many cases the true cost of capital for a division of a well-managed, diversified company will be similar to that of an independent competitor and therefore not anticompetitive at all. In addition, what a division of a diversified company may save in transaction costs when asking for capital from the corporate treasury (as opposed to the marketplace) has to be balanced against the division's share of the premium demanded by investors in the diversified company because of their relatively high level of uncertainty about the specific risks and opportunities facing the company. Whereas several capital based economic benefits of unrelated diversification do exist (as discussed in Chapter 7), their successful capture is by no means certain.

One final comment is needed to complete our discussion of the cost of capital and corporate diversification. It is often argued that well-managed diversified companies are in a privileged position vis-à-vis their undiversified companies since the U.S. tax laws, which encourage companies to retain earnings, enable them to obtain a portion of their equity needs from internally generated funds and, thereby, to reduce their cost of capital below that of competitors who are required to raise all their capital from stockholders, whose returns from equity investments are severely taxed. While the preceding section should serve to warn readers of the oversimplifications implicit in this argument, it is important to remember that all companies, whether widely diversified or not, are in a position to treat certain expenditures in developing new product lines or businesses as an expense to be offset against other profits. To the extent, however, that it is believed that the U.S. tax laws favor certain classes of companies over others, the issue is one of tax policy and not one of antitrust policy.

Conclusion

As large diversifying companies pursue acquisitions that present the opportunity to make especially productive use of acquired assets, both operating efficiencies and risks of antitrust attack grow correspondingly. It is all very well, and it may even be entirely correct, to argue, as Jesse Markham does, that the divisions of multimarket companies are disciplined to behave as if they were independent because of profit center management practices and organizational patterns that allow profit centers to rely on corporate headquarters for only such functions as financial planning, accounting, and legal services.[52] On the other hand, as the operational, marketing, and managerial linkages among the divisions of diversified companies become more apparent, it is predictable that both antitrust authorities and the courts will grow increasingly skeptical of arguments that the benefits of corporate diversification do not give rise to anticompetitive behavior. Antitrust's attack on diversified companies in the foreseeable future may focus not on the crude device of predatory pricing as an instrument for expanding market share, but instead on their ability to finance favored divisions during their formative stages of development on uniquely favorable terms. Without having to compete for funds in the capital markets as aggressively as nondiversified companies, these divisions may be viewed as possessing a unique (and perhaps, unfair) competitive weapon. The argument that actual corporate practice fails to support this hypothesis may not prevail against the issue that mere possession of potential anticompetitive cross-subsidization capability is deleterious to public welfare.

The extent to which new legislation will alter the direction of antitrust law looms as an enormous question mark on the planning horizon for the managers of diversified firms. Attempts to link antitrust enforcement to aggregate concentration have not, as yet, found widespread support, but proponents of such legislation could grow legion as the dimension of current merger activity, summarized in Chapter 1, becomes widely known. A matter equally pertinent to managers' immediate attention is the probable evolution of decisional law under the Clayton Act. Unless managers who find themselves in the dock can persuade the courts that corporate diversification is in the public interest, the law is likely to evolve in the most uncongenial manner possible for managers committed to improving their companies' competitive and economic strength.

Notes and References

1. Federal Trade Commission v. the Procter & Gamble Co., et al., 386 U.S. 568 (A67).

2. 15 U.S.C., 12–27 (1970).

3. 15 U.S.C., 1–7 (1970).

4. U.S. v. Northern Securities Co. 120 Fed 721 (April 1903), 193 U.S. 197 (March 1904).

5. U.S. Federal Trade Commission, *The Merger Movement: A Summary Report,* Washington, 1948.

6. F. M. Scherer, *Industrial Market Structure and Economic Performance* (Chicago: Rand McNally, 1970), p. 475. Total complaints filed between December, 1950, and June, 1967, numbered 199.

7. U.S. v. Continental Can Co. et al. 378 U.S. 441, 449, 455, 457 (1964). Cited in Scherer, *Industrial Market Structure,* p. 479. For an excellent summary of market definition precedents and their implications see Scherer, pp. 478–82.

8. Scherer, *Industrial Market Structure,* p. 481. In reversing the judgment of a District Court that had approved a merger between the Philadelphia National Bank and The Girard Trust Corn Exchange Bank, the Supreme Court held that "without attempting to specify the smallest market share which would still be considered to threaten undue concentration, we are clear that 30 per cent presents that threat" (United States v. Philadelphia National Bank, 374 U.S. 321 [1963]). The court noted other tests of market concentration, ranging from the suggestion by Keysen and Turner [*Antitrust Policy* (Cambridge, Mass.: Harvard University Press, 1959)] that 20 percent market share should be the line of prima facie unlawfulness to Bok's principal test that an increase in market concentration of 7 to 8 percent should be considered unlawful ["Section 7 of the Clayton Act and the Merging of Law and Economics," *Harvard Law Review* 74 (1960):226.] In light of these proposed tests, the Court added a footnote to its opinion, asserting that "the fact that a merger results in a less-than-30% market share, or in a less substantial increase in concentration than in the instant case, does not raise an inference that the merger is *not* violative of Section 7." Justice White, writing the Continental Can opinion one year later, clearly agreed with this view.

9. Cross-subsidization involves the recycling of earnings and cash flow from one business (division) to support the activities of another. In its antitrust context, cross-subsidization is associated with the ability of diversified companies to sell product A at a price below full economic costs, supporting the forgone profits from revenues earned in product lines B, C, ... N, and to use this form of predatory pricing as a means of increasing its market share. Opponents of conglomerate mergers have thus argued that large, multibusiness companies have the special capacity to circumvent and subvert the market—specifically, the relationships between marginal costs and prices—through the process of cross-subsidization.

In a capital budgeting context, cross-subsidization involves the recycling of earnings and cash flow from low-growth businesses generating cash in excess of their investment needs to high-growth businesses requiring additional funds.

10. Disciplinary pricing refers to a company punishing its competitors by reducing prices to a point at which competitors can no longer make a profit. Disciplinary pricing is a form of predatory pricing behavior that, according to many legal commentators, can be easily facilitated (financed) in diversified companies through cross-subsidization.

11. Reciprocity is said to exist where a company (or one of its divisions) promotes the sale of its products (or the products of a sister division) by offering reciprocally to purchase potential customers' products.

12. The reader should also be aware that many challenges addressed to market extension mergers have been carried over to challenges of both product line extension and so-called "pure" conglomerate mergers.

13. See Chapters 3 and 7.

14. FTC v. Procter & Gamble (see note 1 above).

15. This summary of the Procter & Gamble–Clorox acquisition appears in Harvard Business School case #9-372-076.

16. Scherer, *Industrial Market Structure,* p. 485.

17. Ibid.

18. See F.T.C. Docket No. 6901. Cited in full in Harvard Business School case #9-372-076.

19. The adjectives "unrelated" and "conglomerate" will be considered synonymous in this discussion. Both terms refer to what legal commentary calls "pure conglomerate." Pure conglomerate acquisitions involve companies that are unrelated both in a product market sense and in terms of the functional skills critical to their success.

20. In the absence of prior or postacquisition evidence, "only a rather progovernment trial judge is likely to be satisfied that a decent showing of probability in any specific line of commerce has been made. Courts should not, and need not, be asked to make such dubious findings." See Harlen M. Blake, "Conglomerate Mergers and the Antitrust Laws," *Columbia Law Review* 73 (1973): 568. Blake's position reflects the view that "present knowledge does not permit predictions as to the effects of most mergers." For a full discussion see Derek C. Bok, "Section 7 of the Clayton Act and the Merging of Law and Economics," *Harvard Law Review* 74 (1960): 226, 269, 271.

21. Jesse W. Markham, *Conglomerate Enterprise and Public Policy,* Division of Research, Graduate School of Business Administration, Harvard University, 1973.

22. The "reciprocity" theory is currently not a threatening one for either unrelated or related acquisitions, since it requires the compound finding that reciprocity would probably occur and that it would occur in sufficient degree to inhibit competition. See United States v. International Tel. & Tel. Corp.

(Grinnel), 324 F. Supp. 19,24 (D. Conn., 1970) and United States v. International Tel. & Tel. Corp. (Canteen), 1971 Trade Cas., 73,619 at 90, 545–59 (N.D. Ill., 1971).

23. If the anticompetitive effects of most conglomerate mergers are in fact speculative or minimal, there are other reasons for leaving them outside the reach of antitrust law: conglomerate mergers provide liquidity at a fair price for entrepreneurs when they wish to sell their companies; the threat of takeovers by conglomerates provides an incentive and discipline for corporate managers and directors of companies in imperfectly competitive product markets to keep on their toes; and when a conglomerate acquires a poor performer and helps it become a more efficient operation, competition in the acquired company's product markets can be increased. See Blake, "Conglomerate Mergers," pp. 562–63.

24. Complaint 24 (f), United States v. International Tel. & Tel. Corp., 324 F. Supp. 19 (D. Conn., 1970).

25. The merger between General Electric and Utah International was originally announced in December, 1975. At that time the Justice Department was concerned that the planned merger could have anticompetitive effects, since Utah produced uranium and General Electric purchased uranium for its nuclear steam-supply systems. To erase any impression that General Electric was interested in reaping the potential benefits of vertical integration, the company revised its original merger agreement with Utah International. Under the revised merger agreement General Electric was to transfer all of Utah International's uranium operations to a newly formed company. While General Electric would retain ownership in the new concern's stock and would receive substantially all its profits, the stock was to be deposited in a trust until the year 2000. The new concern would be prohibited from selling uranium to General Electric or any of its affiliates (*Wall Street Journal*, Oct. 4, 1976, p. 4). It is noteworthy that modifications in the merger proposal resulted from concerns voiced by the Justice Department relating to vertical integration, rather than concentration of economic power, by large, widely diversified companies.

26. These proposals have been summarized by Blake, "Conglomerate Mergers," p. 590.

27. C. Kaysen and D. Turner, *Antitrust Policy: A Legal and Economic Analysis* (Cambridge, Mass.: Harvard University Press, 1959), p. 131.

28. Task Force Report on Antitrust Policy, 115 *Congressional Record*, 1969, p. 13890.

29. James C. Campbell and William G. Shephard, "Leading-Firm Conglomerate Mergers," *Antitrust Bulletin* 13 (1968):1361.

30. *Wall Street Journal*, Dec. 29, 1978, and Jan. 18, 1979. See also Alfred F. Dougherty, Jr., Director, Bureau of Competition, FTC, "Statement before the Senate Committee on the Judiciary on the Merger Act of 1979," March 8, 1979; and John H. Shenefield, Assistant Attorney General, Antitrust Division, "Statement before Senate Committee on the Judiciary, Concerning Conglomerate Mergers," March 8, 1979.

31. Blake, "Conglomerate Mergers," p. 570.

32. Ibid., p. 571. See also Eugene Singer, *Antitrust Economics* (Englewood Cliffs, N.J.: Prentice-Hall, 1968), pp. 259–69. Source cited in Blake, note 55.

33. Ibid., p. 572.

34. It is worth noting that in several recent Sherman Act decisions the Supreme Court has gone far in adopting analyses that accept financial power as a source of market power carrying antitrust consequences. See United States v. Grinnell Corporation, 384 U.S. 563 (1966); Fortner Enterprises, Inc. v. United States Steel Corporation, 394 U.S. 495 (1969); and United States v. Griffith, 334 U.S. 100 (1948); all cited by Blake at pp. 586–90. According to our definitions of conglomerates, none of these companies can be considered as such, although Blake clearly does. Herein lies a conceptual problem involving definitions used by the law. Since the first two cases cited above are not pure conglomerates but rather what we would call related-business diversifiers—a distinction we think has strategic and managerial importance—it is difficult to accept the notion that these cases have implications for unrelated business companies or conglomerates. Indeed, it is difficult to accept the third case of United States v. Griffith as involving a diversified company at all, since Griffith was not operating in multiple product markets; rather it was a motion picture exhibitor chain with theaters in numerous cities (which the courts, according to their concepts of diversification, considered to be distinct and separate markets).

35. Blake, "Conglomerate Mergers," p. 574.

36. Ibid., p. 560.

37. Ibid., p. 591.

38. William James Adams, "Market Structure and Corporate Power: The Horizontal Dominance Hypothesis Reconsidered," *Columbia Law Review* 74 (1974): 1292. See Adams, pp. 1276–97, for an economic analysis and argument that complement the legal analysis and argument of Blake.

39. Reynolds Metals Co., Docket 7009, 56 F.T.C. 743, 776 (1960).

40. For a more extensive discussion of the Reynolds Metals case see Robert H. Bork, *The Antitrust Paradox* (New York: Basic Books, 1978), pp. 209, 250–52.

41. It is worth noting again that under rules established by the 1976 Hart-Scott-Rodino Antitrust Improvement Act of 1976, companies with over $100 million in assets or sales participating in mergers are now required to notify the Antitrust Division at least thirty days prior to consummation.

42. For a discussion of these conditions see "Submission to the Royal Commission on Corporate Concentration," Genstar, Ltd. (November 1975), at para. 11 and following. The "line of business" reporting condition is an extremely important one, since it puts pressure on companies to comply with the third condition in the series.

43. The term "cross-subsidization" is being used in the present context in its capital budgeting sense—that is, where surplus cash generated in one busi-

ness is used to finance the development of another. This notion of cross-subsidization is developed more fully in Chapter 4.

44. Professors Areeda and Turner have proposed that "a price below reasonably anticipated average variable costs should be conclusively presumed unlawful" under Section 2 of the Sherman Act. They argue that at a price less than the average variable cost, the firm is earning no return and would incur fewer losses by ceasing operations. See Phillip Areeda and Donald F. Turner, "Predatory Pricing and Related Practices under Section 2 of the Sherman Act," *Harvard Law Review* 88 (February 1973): 733.

45. For evidence pertaining to this point see *Hearings before Antitrust Subcommittee of the Committee on the Judiciary, House of Representatives, Ninety-first Congress* (1969), pt. 1, p. 215; pt. 3, pp. 254–55; and pt. 3, pp. 156–57. Also Harry H. Lynch, *Financial Performance of Conglomerates,* Division of Research, Harvard Business School (1971), and Gulf + Western Industries, Inc. (B), Harvard Business School case #1-377-221.

46. See, for example, Blake, "Conglomerate Mergers," p. 572.

47. Donald F. Turner, "Conglomerate Mergers and Section 7 of the Clayton Act," *Harvard Law Review* 78 (1965):1338.

48. Even if there were sufficient information available on the diversified company to allow investors to make as complete an assessment of it as of a nondiversified company, the cost of processing that information would be significantly greater. Under these conditions investors would require a higher return to compensate them for these costs (and companies would be required to pay a higher price for their capital).

49. Contrary to common suppositions, the capital marketplace is unwilling to lower its price or required rate of return on capital for a widely diversified company simply because the company has acquired a well-balanced or purportedly countercyclical collection of businesses. Whatever nonmarket or company-specific risks an acquisitive conglomerate is able to diversify away, the equity investor could have diversified away for himself through simple portfolio diversification. See Chapter 5 for further discussion of this point.

50. Theoretically, a conglomerate's cost of debt should only be lower than that for other classes of companies to the extent that it has minimized bankruptcy risks. See Chapter 7, pp. 139–146 for a further discussion.

51. If a diversified company overinvests in a business because it has underestimated the industry's true cost of capital, the business's asset base will inevitably become too large and its return on investment too low compared with that of its competitors. On the other hand, if the diversified company underinvests in a business because it has overestimated its true cost of capital, the company's asset base will inevitably become too small and its return too low (because of loss of market share) compared with those of its competitors. This investment behavior would amount to "disguised liquidation."

52. Markham, *Conglomerate Enterprise and Public Policy.*

APPENDIX TO CHAPTER 1

TABLE A1-1. Company Composition Underlying Indices of Unrelated Business Performance

FORBES MULTICOMPANIES— MULTI-INDUSTRY	*FORBES* MULTICOMPANIES— CONGLOMERATES	*BUSINESS WEEK* CONGLOMERATES
Company[a]	Company[a]	Company[a]
Vulcan Materials	Teledyne	Teledyne
Minnesota Mining & Manufacturing	Northwest Industries	Northwest Industries
Gulf + Western	Textron
General Electric	Industries	Avco
Koppers	White Consolidated	Studebaker-
Union Carbide	Ogden	Worthington
National Distillers	Scott & Fetzer	Southdown
Martin Marietta	Raytheon	Martin Marietta
American Brands	Alco Standard	Signal
Bendix	Lear Siegler	Colt Industries
Sperry Rand	TRW	Whittaker
Eltra	Avco	Bliss & Laughlin
Allegheny Corp.	United Technologies	Industries
FMC	Tenneco	Tenneco
General Tire & Rubber	American Standard	Chromalloy American
Esmark	Chromalloy American	Gulf + Western
Olin Corp.	Textron	Industries
N L Industries	Dayco	Fuqua Industries
PPG Industries	National Service	Kidde (Walter)
Borg-Warner	Industries	City Investing
Allis-Chalmers	Dart Industries	IU International
Westinghouse Electric	Signal Companies	U.S. Industries
Sperry & Hutchinson	W. R. Grace	IC Industries
Curtiss-Wright	Transamerica	Litton Industries
Dillingham	Kidde (& Walter)	LTV
GAF	Rockwell International	
	Sybron	
	A-T-O	
	AMF	
	Amfac	
	Brunswick	

TABLE A1-1. *(Continued)*

FORBES MULTICOMPANIES— MULTI-INDUSTRY	*FORBES* MULTICOMPANIES— CONGLOMERATES	*BUSINESS WEEK* CONGLOMERATES
	SCM	
	IU International	
	ITT	
	City Investing	
	Zapata	
	Whittaker	
	IC Industries	
	Fuqua Industries	
	US Industries	
	Bangor Punta	
	LTV	
	Allied Products	
	Litton Industries	
	Singer	
	National Kinney	

[a] Listed in order of average return on equity.

Variants of the Product/Market-Portfolio Model: Their Characteristics and Common Difficulties in Use

TO HELP CORPORATE OFFICERS ANALYZE increasingly diversified product/market portfolios, several approaches in addition to that of BCG have been developed.[1] The planning model developed by G.E. and McKinsey and the so-called PIMS model both deserve special attention.

The G.E.-McKinsey Variant

Attempting to overcome the somewhat narrow focus of the BCG model on market share and market growth, the General Electric Company and McKinsey & Co. devised a more complex, though less rigorous product/market-portfolio model. This approach primarily differs from the BCG model in its use of subjective measures rather than relative quantitative measures. For instance, there is much less emphasis on relative costs and considerably more emphasis on factors other than relative market share to assess the business's competitive position in a given industry. In addition, factors other than growth rate are used to assess the attractiveness of a market. Although the list of variables considered depends upon the particular user, a representative sample includes:

263

*Factors Influencing Industry
Attractiveness*

- market size
- market growth
- number of competitors
- strengths/weaknesses of
  competitors
- characteristics of product
  life cycle
- position in product life
  cycle
- rate of change in
  technology
- profitability
- entry and exit barriers

*Factors Influencing Business
Position*

- research emphasis
- product technology
- product quality
- manufacturing scale
- experience
- physical distribution
- marketing
- intangibles (patents,
  trademarks, goodwill, etc.)

Including these additional variables resolves many of the shortcomings of the market-share/market-growth matrix. In particular, where cash flow is associated with industry elements other than just market growth, such as entry barriers or characteristics of the product life cycle, these elements can be included. Furthermore, the inclusion of company variables such as relative technical capability, product quality, and marketing orientation in addition to market share improves the ability to predict actual competitive strength. Advocates of the resulting matrix, shown in Figure A4-1, claim that a more useful evaluation of a particular product/market portfolio can be made with this framework than with the BCG model.

The additional variables employed by the G.E.-McKinsey model typically require users to make many subjective evaluations. For example, since only two dimensions, industry attractiveness and business position, are typically included in a final display of a business portfolio, it is necessary to weigh the various determining factors. In some cases, equal weights are given to each major element of "industry attractiveness" and "business position"; in others, heavier weight is given to the factors believed to be particularly important in a given situation.

The PIMS Variant

The PIMS (or Profit Impact of Market Strategy) model is based on the premise that businesses with similar product/market and industrial organization characteristics should have similar profitability regardless of differences in the name of the industry. Thus, the approach of the Marketing Science Institute was to develop a large product/market data base and

FIGURE A4-1. Industry-Attractiveness/Business-Position Portfolio Chart

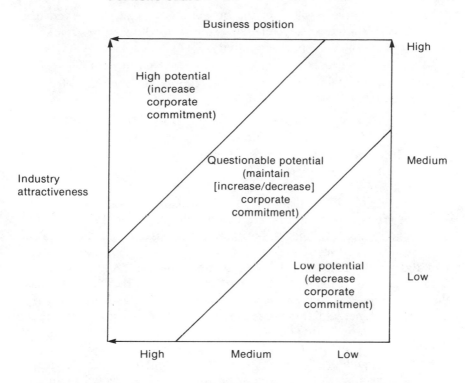

describe empirically based relationships among factors influencing profitability. The specific product/market characteristics of an individual business could then be substituted into empirically based regression equations to determine an expected outcome or standard for the particular business under analysis. This standard, or expected outcome for businesses facing equivalent market and industry conditions and occupying similar market positions, is called a "PAR report." In essence PIMS offers a rigorous market-share/market-growth analysis by utilizing the great explanatory potential of the industry-attractiveness/business-position framework.[2]

To date, PIMS has identified over 30 distinct factors which have an impact on profitability. Taken together, these factors account for over eighty percent of the observed variation in profitability for the 800 businesses in the data base. The explanatory factors may be grouped under five major headings:

1. Characteristics of the business environment (long-run growth rate, short-run growth rate, rate of inflation of prices and

      costs, purchase frequency, number and size of end users and customers).

2. Competitive position of the business (share of the served market, relative share, relative product quality, price, marketing effort, and new product activity).

3. Structure of the production process (capital intensity, degree of vertical integration, capacity utilization, productivity of capital equipment and people).

4. Discretionary budget allocations (R&D budgets, marketing budgets).

5. Strategic moves (patterns of change in any of the controllable variables above).

It should be noted that this list of explanatory variables includes industry growth rate and relative market share, as well as many variables underlying the industry-attractiveness/business-position matrix. The result is a reduction in the variance between the expected and the actual cash flow of a particular business. All those factors contributing to a disparity between actual cash flows and the cash flows expected by users of the BCG framework (for example, strategic change, fundamental differences in industry characteristics, and nonprice aspects of relative competitive strength) are dealt with explicitly by PIMS. PIMS' principal problem, however, is that by employing a large variety of explanatory factors in the regression equation, multicollinearity inevitably results. In other words, the impact of individual factors on profitability is not easily determined.

In addition to the employment of many more independent variables, PIMS also differs from the other two product/market-portfolio models in its selection of dependent variables. PIMS utilizes two separate regression equations, one based on thirty-seven factors for predicting ROI, and the other based on nineteen factors for predicting cash flow. Some factors are used by both models, others are specific to one model.

The most important characteristic of PIMS is that it is empirically based. The independent variables have been isolated through multiple regression techniques based on data collected from a large variety of businesses. In effect, PIMS replaces many of the subjective evaluations and weightings required by the G.E.-McKinsey framework with empirically derived assessment. At the same time, the PIMS regression formulas expand and improve the assumed empirical relationships underlying BCG's experience curve and market-share/market-growth matrix. Furthermore, the differences between actual and expected cash flow or profit are made explicit in the form of expected outcome or PAR reports. Since most of the major strategic variables that might be expected to affect performance are included in PIMS' regression model, differences between PAR and actual performance can be attributed to nonstrategic variables (such as operating management). This is in sharp contrast to the BCG and G.E.-McKinsey approaches, where wide differences between actual and expected performance are likely to occur and explicit bases for comparison are nonexistent.

Relative Advantages of the Various Approaches

The portfolio charts of the market-share/market-growth matrix and the industry-attractiveness/business-position matrix allow the simultaneous comparison of portfolios with several different businesses or product/markets, however defined. This comparison emphasizes the balance (or lack of balance) between growth (industry attractiveness) and cash flow. Portfolio chart analysis also focuses attention on the dynamics of cash flow among businesses and allows "good, balanced" portfolios to be quickly distinguished from "bad, unbalanced" ones.

In contrast, PIMS focuses on a single business. There is no easy way to represent the interrelationship between the various business components of a corporation, group, or division. While a PIMS analysis can be carried out at several different levels of business aggregation or definition, its extensive and detailed data requirements mean that such an analysis is both time-consuming and expensive, even where relevant market data are available.

The relative advantages of the three approaches shift when one is analyzing changes in the strategy of a single business within a portfolio. In the analytical approach suggested by the market-share/market-growth matrix, the only actionable variable is market share, which is actually more of an objective than a variable directly under the control of management. Various success or disaster scenarios drawn from the matrix involve movements of cash and businesses from one quadrant to another. Plotting this movement can indicate probable cash flow performance. Nevertheless, the conclusions drawn from the market-share/market-growth matrix are relatively coarse and lack strategic detail. The industry-attractiveness/business-position approach reduces the problem of coarseness and lack of strategic detail by including many "controllable" variables that influence market share. However, the conclusions reached by following the G.E.-McKinsey approach remain largely based on qualitative assessments.

Being empirically based, PIMS allows the manager of an individual business to explore the impact of a variety of strategic moves in terms of cash flow, ROI, net income, and a variety of other derived measures. The manager using PIMS relies not on a typology of situations, but rather on the experience of other businesses in similar industry situations making similar strategic moves from similar starting points. PIMS specifies the profit (or loss) likely to be achieved by such projected changes, along with the associated investment and cash flow.

The relative advantages and disadvantages of the three approaches shift again when the analytical task becomes the assessment of competitive dynamics. Using the BCG or G.E.-McKinsey portfolio chart, a strategist can plot the position of competitive products and businesses. This information can be used in three different ways. First, it can provide useful data, in visual form, of the relative size and strength of each major competitor in a market. Second, changes in competitive position may be plotted and competitive dynamics explored. Third, and perhaps most important, a plot of a competitor's total portfolio often provides considerable insight into where he is relatively weak or relatively strong. Offensive strategies may then be launched against positions of relative weakness and not against positions of strength.

PIMS, however, was not designed to provide insights on individual competitors. Users of PIMS can only relate their own market share position, product, quality, price, marketing efforts, and the like to the averages for companies operating in similar markets or market segments. PIMS does not provide users of its service with individual profiles of competitors. Quite apart from the confidentiality aspect, PIMS was also not designed to help strategists assess the impact of competitors' moves over time or to evaluate the overall balance of a competitor's portfolio in terms of strong or weak market positions.

Common Difficulties with Product/Market-Portfolio Models

Probably the most significant difficulty encountered in analyzing a company's product/market portfolio concerns the definition of a business in economically meaningful terms. Users of all three models must inevitably confront the dilemma of determining:

1. at which level and in which way the "product" or "business" should be defined, and
2. how the market in which the business operates should be defined.

Both questions are central to any attempt to analyze an individual business unit, its strategy, and its market environment.

A variety of factors bear upon such decisions; a few of the most important are discussed below.

Organizational Factors

The initial factor affecting the choice of business and product/market definition has to do with the organizational structure of the institution involved. Typically, the unit chosen will correspond to a unit within the organization, whether or not that unit reflects the boundaries of an economically self-sufficient business. Correspondence between the organizational unit chosen for analysis and an economically self-sufficient business is important for three reasons. First, data are typically collected and organized around major units of activity. Second, in order to make any approach actionable, organizational realities have to be considered. Third, to the extent the analytical unit chosen does not reflect the true economic situation, any conclusions reached may not be especially meaningful.

Resource Efficiencies

Efficiencies in the use of many corporate resources stem from "experience" effects and lead to lower costs and higher margins. Resource efficiencies commonly arise in the areas of research and development, production and manufacturing, or distribution and marketing and can take the form of complementary research programs, scale effects in manufacturing and marketing, and the like. Since market share is sometimes used as a surrogate measure for cumulative experience, it is important to define the business and market broadly enough to reflect such resource efficiencies. In making decisions about how and to what extent to aggregate product/markets, it is useful to consider each major functional activity separately.

Strategic Market Sectors

Even though resource efficiencies may be achieved as a result of broad product participation, it is often the case that these products, related in a resource sense, are sold in quite different strategic sectors of a market. Definitions of strategic sectors are influenced by demand-side rather than supply-side factors and may reflect closely related sectors with significantly different growth rates, competitors, or market share positions. In addition, one should note that a suitable definition in one time period may be totally inappropriate at another. A good example of strategic market sectors and their evolution is the calculator industry. During the industry's high growth phase in the early 1970s, Texas Instruments dominated the high-volume, low-price consumer market, while Hewlett-Packard dominated the low-volume, high-price special applications market. As industry growth slowed in 1976, both companies began making incursions into the other's markets, thereby blurring the boundaries between the industry's strategic market sectors.

The presence of "resource" relationships cutting across different strategic market sectors and managed by different organizational entities implies that no single definition of a "business" unit is likely to be completely satisfactory. Even when it is reasonably satisfactory at one period, competitive and market dynamics typically render it less so over time.

This problem is often resolved by working with the models at several different levels. Generally speaking, the coarser the level of definition of a business and market, the more likely the planner or manager is to be dealing with truly independent units. The problem with this approach is that most divisions are themselves aggregates of activities in several markets or market sectors. On the other hand, the finer the level of definition of a business and market, the more likely the planner or manager is to be dealing with shared resources. The problem here is that decisions to change strategy in any one "business" inevitably impact other businesses within the portfolio.

Another common difficulty with the several product/market-portfolio models is their restricted time horizon. Changes in business strategy are usually made for one of two reasons:

1. The strategy currently employed is unsuitable given the existing characteristics of the marketplace in which the company operates, or

2. Changes are occurring in the marketplace that require adaptation in the future. In some cases the company may want to be proactive, anticipating change or even promoting it; in other cases the company may be reacting to change already taking place.

All three analytical approaches have more to do with the first of these reasons for strategic change than the second. Their principal focus is assessing the viability of current strategy and the consideration of ways to improve it. While these changes can only take place in the future, the model's emphasis is not on adjusting to future changes but on realigning current strategy. In this aspect, these methods are much more important as diagnostic tools than prognostic tools. All three tend to phrase strategy in terms of "high-level" descriptive variables, rather than actionable, operating variables. Implementing these "high-level" strategies is a major problem facing most operating managers.

Notes and References

1. An in-depth discussion of the product/market-portfolio model, its variants, and its usage in management decision making is Derek F. Abell and John S.

Hammond, *Defining the Business: The Starting Point of Strategic Planning* (Englewood Cliffs, N.J.: Prentice-Hall, 1979).

2. See Sidney Schoffler, Robert D. Buzzell, and Donald A. Heany, "Impact of Strategic Planning on Profit Performance," *Harvard Business Review* 52, March–April 1974, and R. D. Buzzell, B. T. Gale, and R. G. M. Sultan, "Market Share: A Key to Profitability," *Harvard Business Review* 53, January–February 1975.

APPENDIX TO CHAPTER 6

Managers' and Investors' Objectives

ALTHOUGH WE HAVE STRESSED how management-oriented concepts (such as business strategy and product/market portfolios) and investor-oriented concepts (such as systematic risk and return) provide complementary perspectives on the creation of economic value, we have *not* argued that managers' and investors' objectives are always identical nor that managers typically act in the interests of investors. Indeed, evidence accumulated over the past twenty-five years suggests that this may be an easier proposition to contest than to support.

Adolf Berle and Gardiner Means pointed out over forty-five years ago that as equity ownership in the largest two hundred corporations became increasingly dispersed, the effective control by shareholders over the use of company assets declined. They argued that professional managers had in their possession the unusual combination of security in office and relative freedom in the choice of corporate goals.[1] Berle expanded this thesis in the mid-1950s and concluded that corporate managers were virtually free of control from capital markets that had been traditionally relied upon to ensure the best possible allocation of resources in the economy and the best possible satisfaction of the owner's legitimate rights and interests. He pointed to the fact that from 1947 to 1956 three-fifths of industrial capital in the decade of its greatest expansion came from retained earnings and depreciation allowances, while another one-fifth had been borrowed chiefly from banks. The remaining one-fifth came from the capital market.[2] Berle argued that this trend had served to increase the freedom of the corporate manager and had fundamentally altered the historically important property rights of owners, thereby weakening the traditional legal constraints on management discretion.

272

Whether corporations and their managements are, in fact, free from shareholders' influence and capital market constraints—or, more precisely, whether they act as if they are—remains an open question. Some argue that the concentration of authority in the nucleus of corporate management has benefited shareholders, since it has resulted in an unprecedented rate of industrial growth and technological innovation. Others have argued that through the 1950s, at least, the managements of most large companies paid smaller dividends than shareholders would have preferred.[3] Consistent with this observation is a large body of recent management literature devoted to explaining how and why the behavior of managers does not conform to profit-maximizing norms that presumably reflect the interests of investors.[4]

While our intention has not been to resolve the question of whether or not managerial and shareholder interests have diverged over the years or what the effect of the alleged divergence has been on business policy, we have provided theory-based support for the notion that *legitimate* business policy is essentially economic in purpose. Our emphasis on returns to investors and the market value of assets reflects the normative proposition that investor (owner) interests should dominate the interests of corporation managers, other employees, and the public at large. We should be clear, however, that our emphasis on the interests of suppliers of capital should not be interpreted as a rejection of the notion that managers should conduct their business in a socially responsive manner. Rather, we are suggesting that pursuing a policy of abstaining from the creation of economic value for investors is neither the essence of corporate statesmanship nor tenable for extended periods of time. As long as corporations need to finance their future growth from external sources of capital, they need to pursue policies that over the long run serve to increase returns to investors and the market value of their financial assets.

Managerial Discretion and Stockholder Interests: The Continuing Debate

Ours is not, of course, a new position. Many have argued this before us, some on different grounds. At base, however, the debate and related commentary over what constraints, if any, should be imposed on management's freedom of action have been fired by two issues: (1) the fear that professional managers may pursue strategies and policies that serve to perpetuate their tenure in office or increase their relative influence and rewards vis-à-vis stockholders, and (2) the failure of the management literature to justify how the social service activities of corporations fit with the traditionally defined role of corporate managers and directors as trustees with fiduciary responsibilities for the corporation's stockholders. Over the past thirty-five years the context of the debate has shifted between these two issues several times.

In the early 1930s Berle devoted considerable efforts to establishing a legal control that could more effectively prevent corporate managers from diverting profit into their own pockets from those of stockholders. To this end, he argued that the fiduciary responsibilities of directors of incorporated companies could be deduced from the legal principle of trusteeship.[5]

One of Berle's specific concerns was the trend, clearly visible to students of corporation law by the early 1930s, that corporation charters were including immunity clauses and waivers of stockholder "rights" to an increasing extent. Of the many examples provided by Berle, the power of management to acquire stock in other corporations is particularly illustrative of the new freedoms left to managers of large corporations. Almost from the beginning of corporate history, Berle explained, the courts have limited the use of this power to acquisitions tending to benefit the corporation as a whole. According to legal precedents through the first third of this century, the power to acquire stock in other corporations was not to be used to forward the interests of individuals or to subserve special interests within or without the corporation.[6]

For example, in a turn of the century case cited by Berle,[7] the Prudential Insurance Company proposed to buy a majority of the stock of the Fidelity Trust Company, which already owned a majority of stock in the Prudential Insurance Company. The transaction was enjoined by the court, which found that the result of the proposed scheme was to create a situation in which the management could maintain itself perpetually in office. The court observed that the purchase was not for the purpose of making an investment (which the insurance company could do) but for the purpose of carrying out a scheme of corporate control of advantage to the management individually. Berle also cited a series of cases from 1847 through 1930 that demonstrate that acquisitions have historically been steadily enjoined unless the corporation can justify its purchase on the ground that "the controlled corporation may furnish facilities or materials in carrying out its objects, or is engaged in substantially the same enterprise, or that the purchase aids a corporation usefully to the buyer's business."[8] Thus the notion that a reasonable connection had to be found between the purposes of the combining companies and that an identifiable advantage to the corporation and its stockholders had to result from linking two companies has strong legal precedent.

In light of this case law, Berle questioned the motives of businessmen who collected aggregations of capital from the public sale of stock in corporations with paper powers broad enough to permit them to rove the world at will. What were advertised as "investment" or "trading" companies in the 1920s and 1930s Berle saw as vehicles for managers (and their bankers) to forward their control of assets in widely dispersed fields and to reinforce the security of their positions in high office. In addition, whereas many of these corporations were defined as investment companies, Berle saw managers using their powers to purchase stock to become holding or management companies. In questioning whether this development reflected the original objective of these corporations, and their initial investors, he suggested that many directors had failed to fulfill their role as trustees for investors and that management discretion with respect to stock acquisitions had become practically unlimited despite restrictive corporate charters and almost a century of legal precedents disallowing stock acquisitions unrelated to the identifiable purpose of the corporation. (Berle explained the trend toward unconstrained, diversifying stock acquisitions with the observation that courts have become less inclined to tell the directors of an enterprise that another area of business lay outside the scope of reasonable and proper connection with their enterprise.)

While we share Berle's concern over the freedom of corporation managers to make stock acquisitions without any apparent economic justification, this is of course not the central point of the Prudential and other similar cases. Rather, the issue is the potential conflict between management power and discretion, on the one hand, and stockholder interests, on the other. Another form of the debate surrounding this potential conflict stems from the question of whether or not the business corporation has a social-service as well as a profitmaking function. As we have seen, Berle argued strongly that all corporate powers are powers in trust for the benefit of the stockholders. This proposition sparked off a twenty-year debate between Berle and E. Merrick Dodd, Jr., both law school professors.[9] Dodd, while accepting that corporate powers are powers in trust, argued that (1) the use of private property is deeply affected with a public interest and (2) corporate directors should therefore be viewed as trustees for the enterprise as a whole—that is, as an institution with several constituencies. Berle replied that lawyers and the courts should not abandon the view that business corporations exist for the sole purpose of making profits for their stockholders until a clear and reasonable enforceable scheme of responsibilities can be developed. Berle noted that no such scheme existed and that, as a consequence, the effect of Dodd's position would be to hand the control of corporations entirely to management.

In 1954 Berle finally accepted Dodd's initial position, apparently as a result of his increasing confidence in the wisdom and conscience of businessmen. But by 1959 Eugene V. Rostow, also a law school professor, was challenging the notion of directors' obligations first propounded by Dodd and subsequently accepted by Berle.[10] This challenge opened a second round of debate, which has lasted to the present day. The debate lingers not because of clouded minds or slow wits but rather because it strikes at the heart of the theory of the firm and notions about the efficient allocation of resources in a capitalist system.

From a point of view of legal and economic orthodoxy, Eugene Rostow found the argument that management's duties to employees, customers, suppliers, and the public at large are equal to management's duties to stockholders "bewildering balderdash." He noted that the lawbooks have always said that the board of directors owes a "single-minded duty of unswerving loyalty to the stockholders." In addition, he noted that many economists have demonstrated "with all the apparent precision of plane geometry and the calculus that the quest for maximum revenue in a competitive market leads to a system of prices, and an allocation of resources and rewards, superior to any alternative, in its contributions to the economic welfare of the community as a whole." [11] He therefore was greatly troubled by concepts that appeared to encourage managers with motivations different from those of the owner-capitalist and with limitations on their areas of discretionary action markedly different from those of an earlier capitalism, to emphasize a diffuse and often undefined responsibility to employees, suppliers, customers, and the general public. Rostow asked what this new concept of "managerialism" implied:

> Does it mean that the management of a great corporation should not bargain very hard in negotiations over wages or the prices paid to suppliers? Does it mean that a statesman-like and well-run company should charge less for its product than the market would bear, less than the prices which would maximize its short-term revenues, or what it conceives to be its long-term profits? Should it regard its residual profits, not as "belonging to" its stockholders in some ultimate sense, but as a pool of funds to be devoted in considerable part to the public interest, as the directors conceive it—to hospitals, parks, and charities in the neighborhood of its plants; to the local symphony or the art museum; to scholarships for the children of employees, or to other forms of support for the educational system of the nation at large? If what is good for the country is good for General Motors, as is indeed the case, does this view of managerial responsibility set any limit upon the directors' discretion in spending corporate funds for what they decide is the public good?[12]

Rostow's interpretation of managerialism led him to identify two general classes of difficulties, one economic, the other legal and political. Managerialism, and the new corporate morality that it suggests, could lead in Rostow's opinion to prices and wages that sabotage the market mechanism and systematically distort the allocation of resources. Secondly, Rostow feared that the new theory of managerialism and corporate responsibility may produce patterns of corporate expenditure that could "disturb the present equilibrium of opinion about corporations, and invite public restrictions on the present freedom of corporate management."[13]

Rostow also argued that the basic service for which society looks to business and labor is the production of goods and services at the lowest possible cost, and at prices that measure the comparative pressure of consumers' choices. He found that the literature on managerialism (or managers as unfettered trustees for investors), as represented by Berle, Dodd, and even Peter Drucker, provided "no criteria to replace the standards for judging the propriety of wages and prices which the economists have painfully developed during the last century or so."[14] He thus concluded that contemporary notions of directors' responsibilities require redefinition:

> It may give us a warm and comfortable feeling to say that the director is a trustee for the community, rather than for his stockholders; that he is a semipublic official, or some other kind of hyphenated public officer. It would be more constructive, however, to seek redefinition in another sense: to restate the law of corporate trusteeship in terms which take full account of the social advances of this century, but which direct the directors more sharply to concentrate their efforts on discharging their historic economic duties to their stockholders. The economic job of directors and management is quite difficult enough to absorb the full time of first-rate minds, in an economy of changing technology, significant general instability, and considerable competition, both from rival firms in the same industry and from those which steadily offer rival products.[15]

Rostow's argument that the objectives of business policy should not become an ambiguous amalgam of economic and noneconomic themes was echoed by other academics during the late 1950s and early 1960s, perhaps most notably by Milton Friedman and Theodore Levitt.[16] It was Gordon Donaldson, however, who brought the debate down to the operating levels of management by demonstrating how the divergence of attitudes between managers and stockholders toward corporate profits could affect financial and business policy decisions within a company.[17] This opened a third perspective in the continuing debate of management versus stockholder. Donaldson summarized his view as follows*:

> To say that management and the shareholder have much in common is only to state the obvious. So do management and the labor force, consumers, or any

* The following excerpts from Gordon C. Donaldson, "Financial Goals: Management vs. Stockholders," *Harvard Business Review* 36, May–June 1963, have been reprinted by permission. Copyright © 1963 by the President and Fellows of Harvard College.

other group having a vested interest in the corporate entity. But to extend this by saying that management, in pursuing corporate objectives as it sees them, necessarily serves the best interests of the stockholders, in either the short or long run, misstates the facts in certain important respects. It also leads to confusion in and misinterpretation of financial policy.[18]

The issue raised by Donaldson was not whether or not management is deliberately frustrating the objectives of the stockholder, but rather whether or not professional management, in pursuit of the best interests of the corporation as it sees them will be led to the same standards for financial decision as would be proposed by an informed professional investor. Donaldson assumed that this professional investor is active in the organized securities market and pursues personal financial gain via dividends and/or capital gains with great singleness of purpose. In addition, he assumed that this investor has access to a wide variety of investment opportunities and takes advantage of this through a diversified and shifting portfolio of financial assets. He wrote that for the professional investor there is

> a complete absence of the sort of identification with a single company which management feels. The concept of "loyalty," if it can be used in this context, is loyalty to superior financial performance and to nothing else. Consequently, the [professional investor] is very willing to consider the question that management is incapable of asking: Is there another company and another management which can make better use of the available funds?[19]

Donaldson argued that because of different decision criteria used by management and stockholders, potential conflicts exist in such areas as measuring financial performance, evaluating investment proposals, determining which sources of funds should be tapped to finance growth, and deciding how best to accommodate risk through product/market diversification and balancing the proportions of debt and equity. For example, Donaldson observed that management and stockholders tend to use different risk standards; whereas management measures risk in terms of preserving the individual corporate entity and its goals as management sees them, stockholders measure risk in terms of a portfolio of investments spread over many companies. These differing views of risk, Donaldson argued, naturally suggest quite different strategies for minimizing its potentially dangerous impact.

The case of companies finding themselves with a heavy concentration in a single industry provides a good example of Professor Donaldson's point. Such companies, when facing industrial instability or a potentially unstable customer like the federal government, often seek to diversify so as (1) to stabilize earnings and cash flow over time and (2) to reduce the threat to the corporate entity posed by "errors in judgment or occurrence of an unpredictable or unpredicted adverse event." As Donaldson observed, what is at stake here is "the survival of the corporate entity, its financial strength and future potential, and, no doubt, the kind of business environment within which management prefers to operate." [20] It is therefore natural, he argued, for professional managers whose present and future is intimately tied up with that of the corporation to reduce the riskiness of their own positions through product/market diversification, which serves to minimize the risk derived from unstable cash flows and errors of judgment. However, Donaldson also noted that such defensive efforts to preserve the corporate entity can lead to financial loss for investors.

> New funds will be pumped in and stock values diluted in efforts to shore up sagging sales and profits, develop product or market diversification, and so on when from the point of view of stockholders (and the economy as a whole) the funds might be better diverted to other, more promising investment opportunities. Investment standards will be lowered when they should be raised, dividends will be reduced when they should be increased, stock will be used in acquiring new businesses to extend the rule of inefficiency or incompetence, and defensive conservatism will thwart bold moves which are essential to survival.[21]

He could have usefully added that whatever business-specific risk a company experiences can be diversified away by the investor through efficient portfolio diversification.

Donaldson's observations on the practical implications of the differing objectives and attitudes held by managers and stockholders provide a fresh incentive to develop concepts or guidelines on which managers can rely when trying to balance their own interests with those of the investor and the society at large. In the tradition of practitioner-oriented finance professors, Donaldson suggests one such concept, which, happily enough, is consistent with the conceptual underpinnings of our framework for strategic and economic analysis. It is called "the concept of relative priorities."

The Concept of Relative Priorities

The concept of relative priorities has its roots in bankruptcy law. In reorganizing a bankrupt company, the courts have often determined that the interests of common stockholders and others with vested interests must be considered alongside those of certain creditors who have the legal right to all residual values. According to the concept of relative priorities, creditors have "a dominant, but by no means exclusive, claim on the assets and earnings of the newly formed company, and this in spite of prior ironclad legal contracts to the contrary."[22]

Apparently, this concept played an important role in the resolution of the recent Penn Central bankruptcy case. Creditors' claims of $3.5 billion were settled by an agreement with the U.S. Railway Association (established by Congress in 1973 to develop a rescue plan for the Penn Central and other Eastern railroads) that gave creditors USRA "certificates of value" estimated to be worth $450 million plus Conrail common and junior preferred stock with a highly uncertain market value. Despite the provisions of various indenture agreements, the creditors of the Penn Central were prevented by the federal government from seizing the assets of the company, which were judged by the creditors to be worth $7.5 billion.[23]

Donaldson explains how the concept of relative priorities can be useful to managers of our large, publicly owned companies:

> This concept of relative priority may be employed by professional management in relating the conflicting interests of stockholders, employees, customers, the general public, government, and so on to each other. Having abandoned the idea of *absolute* priority of the stockholder interest which existed only when management and ownership were one (and perhaps not even then), management continues to attach more weight to its responsibility to owners than to any other vested interest. This means, of course, that where a conflict of interest develops, management must determine how much of the stockholder interest will be sacrificed in order to behave "more responsibly" toward other interests such as the labor union or the customer. It does not mean, however, that either the direction of financial policy or the criterion by which achievement is measured has changed—only that the rate of progress in improving the rewards to the stockholder has been retarded in response to a greater awareness of other interests.[24]

The notion of relative priority allows for the socially responsive corporate behavior that many of us have come to expect while not requiring us to discard carefully developed theories of prices and resource allocation. In addition, it helps us preserve the idea of property rights, which, although undergoing considerable redefinition in recent years,[25] remains one of the foundations of market exchange. (Such exchanges cannot take place unless people "own" the assets and money they wish to exchange for other assets and services.) More parochially, it also helps explain why the models underlying the framework presented in Part II of this book are not conceptually incompatible with each other. While it is true that the risk/return model stresses the investor's perspective (maximizing return for the level of systematic risk he chooses to bear) and the strategy and product/market-portfolio models adopt a more management-oriented perspective (ensuring corporate perpetuity through continued growth in sales volume and profits), our framework accepts the reality of alternate conceptions of value and provides the means for determining who pays for the costs of uneconomic diversification and what the size and nature of these costs may be. There may indeed be compelling social and political reasons for perpetuating the life of an uneconomic enterprise. However, if this involves pursuing strategies and operating policies that cause market values to decline, it should be clear that investor interests have been subordinated to other interests. Over the short run the rate of progress in improving the rewards to the company's investors will clearly be retarded. If the interests of management, employees, and other parties consistently dominate those of the investor, long-run stability of the capital markets and our economy will be permanently eroded.

We therefore have assumed throughout our conceptual discussion of diversification the relative priority of investor interests in the long run. Failure to do so would have left too many important questions unanswered. Paraphrasing Edward S. Mason, if investor interests and the creation of real economic value is not the directing agent, how are resources to be allocated to their most productive uses, what relation will prices have to relative scarcities, and how will various factors of production get remunerated in accordance with their contribution to output?[26] And repeating our oft-sounded alarm, will not the subordination of investor interests to the interests of managers and other groups with respect to corporate diversification lead to a further destruction of economic value? As Donaldson pointed out fifteen years ago, the investing public and their advisers arc becoming more and more informed. If the economic logic of many diversifying companies is not improved, it is extremely doubtful that their market value will be maintained (or will increase) in proportion to that of other companies pursuing economically justifiable strategies.

Notes and References

1. Adolf A. Berle, Jr., and Gardiner C. Means, *The Modern Corporation and Private Property* (New York: Macmillan, 1932).

2. Adolf A. Berle, Jr., *Power without Property* (New York: Harcourt, Brace and World, 1959).

3. John Lintner, "Distribution of Incomes of Corporations among Dividends, Retained Earnings and Taxes," *American Economic Review,* May 1956, pp. 97–113. Summarized in "The Financing of Corporations," in Edward S. Mason, ed., *The Corporation in Modern Society* (Cambridge, Harvard University Press, 1959), pp. 172, 183–84.

4. See, for example, Herbert A. Simon, *Administrative Behavior* (New York: Macmillan, 1945), and Richard M. Cyert and James G. March, *A Behavioral Theory of the Firm* (Englewood Cliffs, N.J.: Prentice-Hall, 1963).

5. Adolf A. Berle, Jr., "Corporate Powers as Powers in Trust," *Harvard Law Review* 44, 1931, pp. 1049–74.

6. Ibid., p. 1063.

7. Robothan v. Prudential Ins. Co., 64 N.J. Eq. 673, 53 Atl. 842 (1902).

8. Berle, "Corporate Powers as Powers in Trust," p. 1065.

9. E. Merrick Dodd, Jr., "For Whom Are Corporate Managers Trustees?" *Harvard Law Review* 45 (1932):1145; Adolf A. Berle, Jr., "For Whom Corporate Managers Are Trustees," *Harvard Law Review* 45 (1932):1365; E. Merrick Dodd, Jr., "Is Effective Enforcement of the Fiduciary Duties of Corporate Managers Practicable?" *University of Chicago Law Review* 2 (1935):194; Adolf A. Berle, Jr., *The Twentieth Century Capitalist Revolution* (New York: Harcourt, Brace, 1954).

10. Eugene V. Rostow, "To Whom and for What Ends Is Corporate Management Responsible?," in Edward S. Mason, ed., *The Corporation in Modern Society* (Cambridge: Harvard University Press, 1964), p. 46.

11. Ibid., p. 63.

12. Ibid., pp. 63–64.

13. Ibid., p. 64.

14. Ibid., p. 67.

15. Ibid., pp. 68–69.

16. Milton Friedman, *Capitalism and Freedom* (Chicago: University of Chicago Press, 1962), and Theodore Levitt, "The Dangers of Social Responsibility," *Harvard Business Review* 36, September–October, 1958.

17. Gordon C. Donaldson, "Financial Goals: Management vs. Stockholders," *Harvard Business Review* 36, May–June 1963, p. 116.

18. Ibid.

19. Ibid., pp. 124–25.

20. Ibid., p. 127.

21. Ibid., p. 129.

22. Ibid., p. 119.

23. Jensen, Michael C. and William H. Meckling, "Can the Corporation Survive?," *Financial Analysts Journal,* January–February 1978.

24. Donaldson, "Financial Goals," p. 119.

25. See, for example, George C. Lodge, *The New American Ideology* (New York: Knopf, 1975).

26. "The Apologetics of 'Managerialism,' " *The Journal of Business* 31 (January 1958):7.

A Risk Analysis of Gulf+Western Industries

ACCORDING TO PORTFOLIO THEORY, a security's total return (yield plus price appreciation) can be decomposed into two parts: one specific to each company, the other market-related. Similarly, a security's risk (or variability of returns) can be decomposed into two parts: risk specifically related to each company and its fortunes, referred to as "unsystematic" (or diversifiable) risk; and market-related risk, referred to as "systematic" (or undiversifiable) risk, since it is common to all securities. According to the theory, a security's systematic risk/return characteristics can be represented by the correlation between a security's return and the market's return. This correlation is referred to as "beta" (β), technically the term in the correlation formula that measures the degree of relationship between a security's return and the market's return.[1]

An implication of portfolio theory is that securities of an unrelated diversifier can only be superior investment vehicles to comparable portfolios of securities if they reduce either "systematic" or "unsystematic" risks to a greater extent than comparable portfolios of securities or provide a higher expected return. Since investors can reduce "unsystematic" or security-specific risks for themselves through portfolio diversification, they do not need to hold the securities of unrelated diversifiers for this purpose—although they might logically want to hold such securities as an alternate investment intermediary to managed portfolios or mutual funds. In line with this argument, the following risk/return analysis of Gulf + Western Industries suggests that this conglomerate has little to offer investors with respect to risk reduction over a diversified portfolio of comparable securities.

To perform a risk/return analysis of a conglomerate such as Gulf + Western Industries, four sets of information are needed. First, it is neces-

283

sary to determine the industries in which the conglomerate participates. This definition can greatly affect the analysis, for if the industries are too narrowly defined (for example, helicopters, ball bearings, and nuclear reactors), there might not be any comparable companies for comparison; or if too broadly defined (transportation, food processing, and mining), no meaningful comparison can be made. To avoid these problems and to maintain consistency, the industry groupings defined by Standard and Poor for their 500 index can be used.[2] If unrelated diversifiers claim "special" characteristics or uniqueness for their investments in an industry, any consistent difference should be highlighted by a comparison of their risk/return profile with the profile of the comparable portfolio.

After determining the unrelated diversifier's industry participation, the amount of its investment in each industry must be determined. This can be achieved either by determining the company's book investment in various industries or by capitalizing the earnings of its divisions participating in these industries. Conceptually, the capitalized earnings approach is superior, since contemporary financial theory uses market valuations (which are equated to capitalized cash flows). This procedure requires the capitalization of a division's free cash flow at an industry average discount rate (or a risk adjusted rate of return). Alternatively, a division's book investment can be obtained directly from annual reports if the company reports by product line or can be estimated by dividing the conglomerate's sales in a specific industry (reported in the company's 10-K report to the SEC) by the industry's average sales to assets ratio. Both procedures have methodological and conceptual difficulties, but the very formation of portfolios will reduce the statistical impact of computational errors and poor industry analyses.

Next, the amount of financial risk common to the industries in which the conglomerate participates must be determined. Once again, this can be done in either book or market terms, with a market valuation approach conceptually stronger. An industry's financial risk is the summation (and hence the weighting) of the appropriate debt and equity market values of the companies in that industry. Financing tools, such as convertible debt and preferred stock, have to be analyzed on a case-by-case basis to determine whether they are debt or equity equivalents. Financial risk is then expressed as a leverage ratio, or the amount of debt used divided by the sum of the debt and equity invested.

Finally, systematic risks or betas must be determined for each industry. This can be done two ways. Either the industry's performance can be regressed against the market's performance, or an index of the betas of the constituent companies in the industry, weighted by their market value, can be used. For multiperiod comparisons, an industry regression is probably easier to do; for individual time periods, a weighted portfolio of company betas is probably preferable. As virtually all companies use debt in their capital structure, these systematic risk measures (betas) will reflect both the underlying risk of the assets and the financial risks incurred in the assets' ownership.

With this information, one can then determine the unlevered systematic risk (or pure equity risk) of each company and industry. This is achieved by using the Hamada argument that the unlevered beta equals the levered beta multiplied by the market value of the levered equity divided by the market value of the unlevered equity[3] or

$$\beta_u = \beta_1(E_1/E_u).\qquad(1)$$

In efficient capital markets, the advantage of using debt is its tax shield. This means that the issuance of D amount of debt (to replace an equivalent amount of equity) will decrease the total market value of the equity outstanding by only $D(1 - T)$.[4] Since equity market values are usually determined on leveraged securities or E_L, E_u is equal to $E_L + D(1 - T)$. Hamada's comparison then becomes

$$\beta_u = \beta_l[E_l/(E_l + D(1 - T))].\qquad(2)$$

The required rate of return for this investment, R_{iu}, can then be determined by relating the unlevered beta, β_{iu}, the market return, R_m, and the risk-free rate R_f, through the capital asset pricing model:

$$R_{iu} = \beta_{iu}(R_m - R_f) + R_f + e.\qquad(3)$$

TABLE A7-1. Gulf + Western Portfolio Statistics

G + W's Leverage[a] = .37		
G + W's Beta—Merrill Lynch[b]	1.15	$\sigma \approx .2$[d]
G + W's Beta—Value Line[c]	1.35	$\sigma \approx .2$[d]
Comparison Portfolio Statistics		
Portfolio's Weighted Average Leverage[e]	.30	
Portfolio's Weighted Average Beta[f]	1.15	
Portfolio's Beta when Leverage = .37[g]	1.26	$\sigma \approx .15$[d]

[a] Market value of debt divided by the sum of the market values of debt and equity.

[b] Merrill Lynch's market determined β using a five-year regression of monthly returns.

[c] Value Line's market determined β using a two-year regression of weekly returns.

[d] The determination of a β results in distribution with the β value being the mean of that distribution; σ gives an idea of the variability of that distribution around the mean.

[e] From Table A7-2, using industry average sales to assets and debt to assets ratios.

[f] From Table A7-2, using industry average betas.

[g] Suggested leveraged beta for a portfolio with leverage of .37, using Equation (2).

TABLE A7-2. A Portfolio Analysis of Gulf + Western Industries, 1975 ($ millions)

Group	S&P Industry Category	Industry Average Sales/Assets	Industry Average Debts/Assets	1974 G+W Sales[a]	Assets of a Company Comparable to G+W Group[b]	Debt of a Company Comparable to G+W Group[c]	Comparable Company's Assets as % of Portfolio's Assets[d]	Industry Beta[e]	Weighted Betas of Comparable Companies in Portfolio[f]
Food and agricultural products	Sugar	2.1	.45	$175	$ 85	$ 37	4.3%	.60	.026
Natural resources	Lead & zinc	1.2	.10	178	150	15	7.5	.72	.054
Paper & building products	Paper	2.1	.40	405	190	75	9.5	.90	.085
Financial services	Small loan finance	.6	.15	494	446[a]	70	22.4	1.35	.302
Leisure time	Movies	1.8	.30	298	165	50	8.3	1.65	.137
Automotive replacement parts	Automotive replacement parts	3.0	.10	225	75	7	3.8	1.70[g]	.063
Consumer products	Tobacco	2.1	.30	212	100	30	5.0	.85	.042
Manufacturing	Automotive OEM	2.3	.30	327	140	45	7.0	1.25	.104
	Capital goods machinery	1.8	.25	285	160	40	8.0	1.30	.068
	Electrical	2.0	.20	195	100	20	5.0	1.30	.088
Operating group's total				$2,794	$1,611	$389	80.8%		.969
Intangibles					100[a]		5.0	.969[h]	.048
Investments					284[a]	211	14.2	.95[i]	.105
Total					$1,995[j]	$600	100.0%		1.15

a G+W 1974 Annual Report.

b Probable assets of a company comparable to G+W's group. A comparison company is obtained by dividing G+W's group sales by industry average sales to assets.

c Probable debt of the comparison company. Determined by dividing company's probable assets by industry average debt to assets.

d Percentage of a portfolio similar to G+W invested in the company (industry).

e Beta of companies within that S&P grouping weighted by their equity market values.

f Amount of portfolio risk (beta) supplied by each group. Determined by multiplying the industry beta by the percentage of the portfolio invested in that industry.

g APS is publicly held, but its stock is thinly traded. Genuine Auto Parts was used for comparison.

h Intangibles arise from an excess investment over the equity acquired. Its risk matches that of the underlying assets (operating portfolio).

i Weighted average betas of Amfac, Kayser-Roth, and Flying Diamond.

j G+W's 1974 Annual Report listed this investment as 1,983 million, or within 1 percent of the comparable portfolio.

One can then compare different risk/return ratios to find the more efficient set by adjusting the beta (using Hamada's relationship) to reflect differing financial risks. Alternatively, one can adjust for the difference between a conglomerate's leverage and a comparable portfolio's leverage (based on industry norms) and thereby measure the inherent risk/return performance achieved by the conglomerate.

The results of an analysis of Gulf + Western Industries using this methodology are presented in Table A7-1. An analysis of a comparable portfolio is summarized in Table A7-2. Gulf + Western was a useful company to analyze, since its eight divisions have minimal overlap and are in distinctly different and identifiable businesses. When these divisions are grouped with Gulf + Western's investment portfolio, a nine-industry-security portfolio is achieved. This increases the accuracy of the comparison portfolio, since statistical measurement errors are reduced through the increased sample size and diversity.

As Table A7-1 indicates, there is no statistically significant difference between Gulf + Western's systematic risk, adjusted for leverage, and that of a comparable portfolio. The three systematic risk measures are within one standard deviation of each other. This would seem to indicate that the benefits Gulf + Western provide to its shareholders do not include reducing systematic risk.[5,6]

Notes and References

1. Harry O. Markowitz, "Portfolio Selection," *Journal of Finance* 7, March 1952; James Tobin, "Liquidity Preference as Behavior toward Risk," *The Review of Economic Studies* 25, February 1958; William F. Sharpe, "A Simplified Model for Portfolio Analysis," *Management Science,* January 1963; and John Lintner, "The Valuation of Risk Assets and the Selection of Risky Investments in Stock Portfolios and Capital Budgets," *Review of Economics and Statistics* 47, February 1965.

2. J. Fred Weston and S. K. Mansinghka, "Tests of Efficiency Performance of Conglomerate Firms," *Journal of Finance* 26, September 1971, and K. V. Smith and J. C. Schreiner, "A Portfolio Analysis of Conglomerate Diversification," *Journal of Finance* 24, June 1969.

3. Robert S. Hamada, "The Effect of the Firm's Capital Structure on the Systematic Risk of Common Stocks," *Journal of Finance* 22, May 1972.

4. The tax shield, or *TD*, accrues to the equity. Hence the market value of the equity will increase by the tax shield, *TD*, and decrease by the debt used instead of equity. Therefore, by replacing a certain amount of equity with an equivalent amount of debt, the total value of outstanding equity will only decrease by $D(1 - T)$.

5. This is not to say, of course, that conglomerate diversification cannot be justified by managers of diversified companies in terms of defensive strategy

(avoiding sales and profit instability, adverse growth developments, adverse competitive shifts, technological obsolescence, and increased uncertainties associated with the "core" business) or offensive strategy (applying advanced technology to businesses where technology has lagged or utilizing effectively special capabilities in financial planning and control). Neither does this point necessarily negate arguments that diversified companies can usefully (a) shield new business development from unrealistic shareholder demands, (b) subsidize high-potential businesses competing against established competitors with substantial resources, and (c) divorce earnings from reinvestment for specific businesses, thereby allowing both redeployment of cash from low- to high-profitability business and divestiture or liquidation of assets without threatening the survival of the company as a whole. Rather, the narrow question is whether or not managers of conglomerates have, in fact, been able to improve their companies' risk-return profiles over those of comparable portfolios of securities.

While portfolio theory has achieved significant credibility in academic and financial circles, it is not without its conceptual problems in its application to unrelated diversification. See Malcolm S. Salter and Wolf A. Weinhold, "Comparable Portfolios: Their Uses and Limits," mimeo, 1979.

6. Similar conclusions concerning the efficiency of conglomerate risk performance have been reached by several researchers. See, for instance, K. J. Smith and J. C. Scheiner, "A Portfolio Analysis of Conglomerate Diversification, *Journal of Finance* 24, June 1969; Randolph Westerfield, "A Note on the Measurement of Conglomerate Diversification," *Journal of Finance* 25, September 1970; J. Fred Weston, Keith V. Smith, and Ronald V. Shieves, "Conglomerate Performance Using the Capital Asset Pricing Model," *Review of Economics and Statistics* 54, November 1972; Baruch Lev and Gershon Mandelker, "The Micro-Economic Consequences of Corporate Mergers," *Journal of Business* 45, January 1972, and Ronald W. Melicher and David F. Rush, "The Performance of Conglomerate Firms: Recent Risk and Return Experience," *Journal of Finance* 28, May 1973.

Merger Guidelines of the Department of Justice

May 30, 1968

1. Purpose

The purpose of these guidelines is to acquaint the business community, the legal profession, and other interested groups and individuals with the standards currently being applied by the Department of Justice in determining whether to challenge corporate acquisitions and mergers under Section 7 of the Clayton Act. (Although mergers or acquisitions may also be challenged under the Sherman Act, commonly the challenge will be made under Section 7 of the Clayton Act and, accordingly, it is to this provision of law that the guidelines are directed.) The responsibilities of the Department of Justice under Section 7 are those of an enforcement agency, and these guidelines are announced solely as a statement of current Department policy, subject to change at any time without prior notice, for whatever assistance such statement may be in enabling interested persons to anticipate in a general way Department enforcement action under Section 7. Because the statements of enforcement policy contained in these guidelines must necessarily be framed in rather general terms, and because the critical factors in any particular guideline formulation may be evaluated differently by the Department than by the parties, the guidelines should not be treated as a substitute for the Department's business review procedures, which make available statements of the Department's present enforcement intentions with regard to particular proposed mergers of acquisitions.

2. General Enforcement Policy

Within the over-all scheme of the Department's antitrust enforcement activity, the primary role of Section 7 enforcement is to preserve and promote market structures conducive to competition. Market structure is the focus of the Department's merger policy chiefly because the conduct of the individual firms in a market tends to be controlled by the structure of that market, i.e., by those market conditions which are fairly permanent or subject only to slow change (such as, principally, the number of substantial firms selling in the market, the relative sizes of their respective market shares, and the substantiality of barriers to the entry of new firms into the market). Thus, for example, a concentrated market structure, where a few firms account for a large share of the sales, tends to discourage vigorous price competition by the firms in the market and to encourage other kinds of conduct, such as use of inefficient methods of production or excessive promotional expenditures, of an economically undesirable nature. Moreover, not only does emphasis on market structure generally produce economic predictions that are fully adequate for the purposes of a statute that requires only a showing that the effect of a merger "may be substantially to lessen competition, or to tend to create a monopoly," but an enforcement policy emphasizing a limited number of structural factors also facilitates both enforcement decision-making and business planning which involves anticipation of the Department's enforcement intent. Accordingly, the Department's enforcement activity under Section 7 is directed primarily toward the identification and prevention of those mergers which alter market structure in ways likely now or eventually to encourage or permit non-competitive conduct.

In certain exceptional circumstances, however, the structural factors used in these guidelines will not alone be conclusive, and the Department's enforcement activity will necessarily be based on a more complex and inclusive evaluation. This is sometimes the case, for example, where basic technological changes are creating new industries, or are significantly transforming older industries, in such fashion as to make current market boundaries and market structure of uncertain significance. In such unusual transitional situations application of the normal guideline standards may be inappropriate; and on assessing probable future developments, the Department may not sue despite nominal application of a particular guideline, or it may sue even though the guidelines, as normally applied, do not require the Department to challenge the merger. Similarly, in the area of conglomerate merger activity, the present incomplete state of knowledge concerning structure-conduct relationships may preclude sole reliance on the structural criteria used in these guidelines, as explained in paragraphs 17 and 20 below.

3. Market Definition

A rational appraisal of the probable competitive effects of a merger normally requires definition of one or more relevant markets. A market is any grouping of sales (or other commercial transactions) in which each of the firms whose sales are included enjoys some advantage in competing with those firms whose sales are not included. The advantage need not be great for so long as it is significant it defines an area of effective competition among the included sellers in which the competition of the excluded sellers is, *ex hypothesi,* less effective. The process of market definition may result in identification of several appropriate markets in which to test the probable competitive effects of a particular merger.

A market is defined both in terms of its product dimension ("line of commerce") and its geographic dimension ("section of the country").

(i) Line of commerce. The sales of any product or service which is distinguishable as a matter of commercial practice from other products or services will ordinarily constitute a relevant product market, even though, from the standpoint of most purchasers, other products may be reasonably, but not perfectly, interchangeable with it in terms of price, quality, and use. On the other hand, the sales of two distinct products to a particular group of purchasers can also appropriately be grouped into a single market where the two products are reasonably interchangeable for that group in terms of price, quality, and use. In this latter case, however, it may be necessary also to include in that market the sales of one or more other products which are equally interchangeable with the two products in terms of price, quality, and use from the standpoint of that group of purchasers for whom the two products are interchangeable.

The reasons for employing the foregoing definitions may be stated as follows. In enforcing Section 7 the Department seeks primarily to prevent mergers which change market structure in a direction likely to create a power to behave non-competively in the production and sale of any particular product, even though that powr will ultimately be limited, though not nullified, by the presence of other similar products that, while reasonably interchangeable, are less than perfect substitutes. It is in no way inconsistent with this effort also to pursue a policy designed to prohibit mergers between firms selling distinct products where the result of the merger may be to create or enhance the companies' market power due to the fact that the products, though not perfectly substitutable by purchasers, are significant enough alternatives to constitute substantial competitive influences on the production, development or sale of each.

(ii)   Section of the country. The total sales of a product or service in any commercially significant section of the country (even as small as a single community), or aggregate of such sections, will ordinarily constitute a geographic market if firms engaged in selling the product make significant sales of the product to purchasers in the section or sections. The market need not be enlarged beyond any section meeting the foregoing tests unless it clearly appears that there is no economic barrier (e.g., significant transportation costs, lack of distribution facilities, customer inconvenience, or established consumer preference for existing products) that hinders the sale from outside the section to purchasers within the section; nor need the market be contracted to exclude some portion of the product sales made inside any section meeting the foregoing test unless it clearly appears that the portion of sales in question is made to a group of purchasers separated by a substantial economic barrier from the purchasers to whom the rest of the sales are made.

Because data limitations or other intrinsic difficulties will often make precise delineation of geographic markets impossible, there may often be two or more groupings of sales which may reasonably be treated as constituting a relevant geographic market. In such circumstances, the Department believes it to be ordinarily most consistent with the purposes of Section 7 to challenge any merger which appears to be illegal in any reasonable geographic market, even though in another reasonable market it would not appear to be illegal.

[Market Measurement]

The market is ordinarily measured primarily by the dollar value of the sales or other transactions (e.g., shipments, leases) for the most recent twelve month period for which the necessary figures for the merging firms and their competitors are generally available. Where such figures are clearly unrepresentative, a different period will be used. In some markets, such as commercial banking, it is more appropriate to measure the market by other indicia, such as total deposits.

I.   Horizontal Mergers

4.   Enforcement Policy

With respect to mergers between direct competitors (i.e., horizontal mergers), the Department's enforcement activity under Section 7 of the

Clayton Act has the following interrelated purposes: (1) preventing elimination as an independent business entity of any company likely to have been a substantial competitive influence in a market; (ii) preventing any company or small group of companies from obtaining a position of dominance in a market; (iii) preventing significant increases in concentration in a market; and (iv) preserving significant possibilities for eventual deconcentration in a concentrated market.

In enforcing Section 7 against horizontal mergers, the Department accords primary significance to the size of the market share held by both the acquiring and the acquired firms. ("Acquiring firm" and "acquired firm" are used herein, in the case of horizontal mergers, simply as convenient designations of the firm with the larger market share and the firm with the smaller share, respectively, and do not refer to the legal form of the merger transaction.) The larger the market share held by the acquired firm, the more likely it is that the firm has been a substantial competitive influence in the market or that concentration in the market will be significantly increased. The larger the market share held by the acquiring firm, the more likely it is that an acquisition will move it toward, or further entrench it in, a position of dominance or of shared market power. Accordingly, the standards most often applied by the Department in determining whether to challenge horizontal mergers can be stated in terms of the sizes of the merging firms' market shares.

5. Market Highly Concentrated

In a market in which the shares of the four largest firms amount to approximately 75% or more, the Department will ordinarily challenge mergers between firms accounting for approximately the following percentages of the market:

Acquiring Firm	Acquired Firm
4%	4% or more
10%	2% or more
15% or more	1% or more

(Percentages not shown in the above table should be interpolated proportionately to the percentages that are shown.)

6. Market Less Highly Concentrated

In a market in which the shares of the four largest firms amount to less than approximately 75%, the Department will ordinarily challenge mergers between firms accounting for, approximately, the following percentages of the market:

Acquiring Firm	Acquired Firm
5%	5% or more
10%	4% or more
15%	3% or more
20%	2% or more
25% or more	1% or more

(Percentages not shown in the above table should be interpolated proportionately to the percentages that are shown.)

7.   Market with Trend toward Concentration

The Department applies an additional, stricter standard in determining whether to challenge mergers occurring in any market, not wholly unconcentrated, in which there is a significant trend toward increased concentration. Such a trend is considered to be present when the aggregate market share of any grouping of the largest firms in the market from the two largest to the eight largest has increased by approximately 7% or more of the market over a period of time extending from any base year 5–10 years prior to the merger (excluding any year in which some abnormal fluctuation in market shares occurred) up to the time of the merger. The Department will ordinarily challenge any acquisition, by any firm in a grouping of such largest firms showing the requisite increase in market share, of any firm whose market share amounts to approximately 2% or more.

8.   Non-Market Share Standards

Although in enforcing Section 7 against horizontal mergers the Department attaches primary importance to the market shares of the merging firms, achievement of the purposes of Section 7 occasionally requires the Department to challenge mergers which would not be challenged under the market share standards of Paragraphs 5, 6, and 7. The following are the two most common instances of this kind in which a challenge by the Department can ordinarily be anticipated:

(a) acquisition of a competitor which is a particularly "disturbing," "disruptive," or otherwise unusually competitive factor in the market; and

(b) a merger involving a substantial firm and a firm which, despite an insubstantial market share, possesses an unusual competitive potential or has an asset that confers an unusual competitive advantage (for example, the acquisition by a leading firm of a newcomer having a patent or a significantly improved product or production process).

There may also be certain horizontal mergers between makers of distinct products regarded as in the same line of commerce for reasons expressed in Paragraph 3(i) where some modication in the minimum market shares subject to challenge may be appropriate to reflect the imperfect substitutability of the two products.

9. Failing Company

A merger which the Department would otherwise challenge will ordinarily not be challenged if (i) the resources of one of the merging firms are so depleted and its prospects for rehabilitation so remote that the firm faces the clear probability of a business failure, and (ii) good faith efforts by the failing firm have failed to elicit a reasonable offer of acquisition more consistent with the purposes of Section 7 by a firm which intends to keep the failing firm in the market. The Department regards as failing only those firms with no reasonable prospect of remaining viable; it does not regard a firm as failing merely because the firm has been unprofitable for a period of time, has lost market position or failed to maintain its competitive position in some other respect, has poor management, or has not fully explored the possibility of overcoming its difficulties through self-help.

In determining the applicability of the above standard to the acquisition of a failing division of a multi-market company such factors as the difficulty in assessing the viability of a portion of a company, the possibility of arbitrary accounting practices, and the likelihood that an otherwise healthy company can rehabilitate one of its parts, will lead the Department to apply this standard only in the clearest of circumstances.

10. Economies

Unless there are exceptional circumstances, the Department will not accept as a justification for an acquisition normally subject to challenge under its horizontal merger standards the claim that the merger will produce economies (i.e., improvements in efficiency) because, among other reasons, (i) the Department's adherence to the standards will usually result in no challenge being made to mergers of the kind most likely to involve companies operating significantly below the size necessary to achieve significant economies of scale; (ii) where substantial economies are potentially available to a firm, they can normally be realized through internal expansion; and (iii) there usually are severe difficulties in accurately establishing the existence and magnitude of economies claimed for a merger.

II. Vertical Mergers

11. Enforcement Policy

With respect to vertical mergers (i.e., acquisitions "backward" into a supplying market or "forward" into a purchasing market), the Department's enforcement activity under Section 7 of the Clayton Act, as in the merger field generally, is intended to prevent changes in market structure that are likely to lead over the course of time to significant anticompetitive consequences. In general, the Department believes that such consequences can be expected to occur whenever a particular vertical acquisition, or series of acquisitions, by one or more of the firms in a supplying or purchasing market, tends significantly to raise barriers to entry in either market or to disadvantage existing non-integrated or partly integrated firms in either market in ways unrelated to economic efficiency. (Barriers to entry are relatively stable market conditions which tend to increase the difficulty of potential competitors' entering the market as new sellers and which thus tend to limit the effectiveness of the potential competitors both as a restraint upon the behavior of firms in the market and as a source of additional actual competition.)

Barriers to entry resting on such factors as economies of scale in production and distribution are not questionable as such. But vertical mergers tend to raise barriers to entry in undesirable ways, particularly the following: (i) by foreclosing equal access to potential customers, thus reducing the ability of non-integrated firms to capture competitively the market share needed to achieve an efficient level of production, or imposing the burden of entry on an integrated basis (i.e., at both the supplying and purchasing levels) even though entry at a single level would permit efficient operation; (ii) by foreclosing equal access to potential suppliers, thus either increasing the risk of a price or supply squeeze on the new entrant or imposing the additional burden of entry as an integrated firm; or (iii) by facilitating promotional product differentiation, when the merger involves a manufacturing firm's acquisition of firms at the retail level. Besides impeding the entry of new sellers, the foregoing consequences of vertical mergers, if present, also artificially inhibit the expansion of presently competing sellers by conferring on the merged firm competitive advantages, unrelated to real economies of production or distribution, over non-integrated or partly integrated firms. While it is true that in some instances vertical integration may raise barriers to entry or disadvantage existing competitors only as the result of the achievement of significant economies of production or distribution (as, for example, where the increase in barriers is due to achievement of economies of integrated production through an alteration of the structure of the plant as well as of the firm), integration accomplished by a large vertical merger will usually raise entry barriers or disadvantage competitors to an extent not accounted for by, and wholly disproportionate to, such economies as may result from the merger.

It is, of course, difficult to identify with precision all circumstances in which vertical mergers are likely to have adverse effects on market structure of the kinds indicated in the previous paragraph. The Department believes, however, that the most important aims of its enforcement policy on vertical mergers can be satisfactorily stated by guidelines framed primarily in terms of the market shares of the merging firms and the conditions of entry which already exist in the relevant markets. These factors will ordinarily serve to identify most of the situations in which any of the various possible adverse effects of vertical mergers may occur and be of substantial competitive significance. With all vertical mergers it is necessary to consider the probable competitive consequences of the merger in both the market in which the supplying firm sells and the market in which the purchasing firm sells, although a significant adverse effect in either market will ordinarily result in a challenge by the Department. ("Supplying firm" and "purchasing firm," as used herein, refer to the two parties to the vertical merger transaction, the former of which sells a product in a market in which the latter buys that product.)

12.   Supplying Firm's Market

In determining whether to challenge a vertical merger on the ground that it may significantly lessen existing or potential competition in the supplying firm's market, the Department attaches primary significance to (i) the market share of the supplying firm, (ii) the market share of the purchasing firm or firms, and (iii) the conditions of entry in the purchasing firm's market. Accordingly, the Department will ordinarily challenge a merger or series of mergers between a supplying firm, accounting for approximately 10% or more of the sales in its market, and one or more purchasing firms, accounting *in toto* for approximately 6% or more of the total purchases in that market, unless it clearly appears that there are no significant barriers to entry into the business of the purchasing firm or firms.

13.   Purchasing Firm's Market

Although the standard of paragraph 12 is designed to identify vertical mergers having likely anticompetitive effects in the supplying firm's market, adherence by the Department to that standard will also normally result in challenges being made to most of the vertical mergers which may have adverse effects in the purchasing firm's market (i.e., that market comprised of the purchasing firm and its competitors engaged in resale of the supplying firm's product or in the sale of a product whose manufacture requires the supplying firm's product) since adverse effects in the purchasing firm's market will normally occur only as the result of significant vertical mergers involving supplying firms with market shares in excess of 10%. There remain, however, some important situations in which vertical mergers which are not subject to challenge under paragraph 12 (ordinarily because the purchasing firm accounts for less than 6% of the purchases in the supplying firm's market) will nonetheless be challenged by the Department on the ground that they raise entry barriers in the purchasing firm's market, or disadvantage the purchasing firm's competitors, by conferring upon the purchasing firm a significant supply advantage over unintegrated or partly integrated existing competitors or over potential competitors. The following paragraph sets forth the enforcement standard governing the most common of these situations.

If the product sold by the supplying firm and its competitors is either a complex one in which innovating changes by the various suppliers have been taking place, or is a scarce raw material or other product whose supply cannot be readily expanded to meet increased demand, the merged firm may have the power to use any temporary superiority, or any shortage, in the product of the supplying firm to put competitors of the purchasing firm at a disadvantage by refusing to sell the product to them (supply squeeze) or by narrowing the margin between the price at which it sells the product to the purchasing firm's competitors and the price at which the end-product is sold by the purchasing firm (price squeeze). Even where the merged firm has sufficient market power to impose a squeeze, it may well not always be economically rational for it actually to do so; but the Department believes that the increase in barriers to entry in the purchasing firm's market arising simply from the increased risk of a possible squeeze is sufficient to warrant prohibition of any merger between a supplier possessing significant market power and a substantial purchaser of any product meeting the above description. Accordingly, where such a product is a significant feature or ingredient of the end-product manufactured by the purchasing firm and its competitors, the Department will ordinarily challenge a merger or series of mergers between a supplying firm, accounting for approximately 20% or more of the sales in its market, and a purchasing firm or firms, accounting in toto for approximately 10% or more of the sales in the market in which it sells the product whose manufacture requires the supplying firm's product.

14.   Non-Market Share Standards

(a) Although in enforcing Section 7 against vertical mergers the Department attaches primary importance to the market shares of the merging firms and the conditions of entry in the relevant markets, achievement of the purposes of Section 7 occasionally requires the Department to challenge mergers which would not be challenged under the market share standards of paragraphs 12 and 13. Clearly the most common instances in which challenge by the Department can ordinarily be anticipated are acquisitions of suppliers or customers by major firms in an industry in which (i) there has been, or is developing, a significant trend toward vertical integration by merger, such that the trend, if unchallenged, would probably raise barriers to entry or impose a competitive disadvantage on unintegrated or partly integrated firms, and (ii) it does not clearly appear that the particular acquisition will result in significant economies of production or distribution unrelated to advertising or other promotional economies.

(b) A less common special situation in which a challenge by the Department can ordinarily be anticipated is the acquisition by a firm of a customer or supplier for the purpose of increasing the difficulty of potential competitors in entering the market of either the acquiring or acquired firm, or for the purpose of putting competitors of either the acquiring or acquired firm at an unwarranted disadvantage.

15. Failing Company

The standards set forth in paragraph 9 are supplied by the Department in determining whether to challenge a vertical merger.

16. Economies

Unless there are exceptional circumstances, and except as noted in paragraph 14(a), the Department will not accept as a justification for an acquisition normally subject to challenge under its vertical merger standards the claim that the merger will produce economies, because, among other reasons, (i) where substantial economies of vertical integration are potentially available to a firm, they can normally be realized through internal expansion into the supplying or purchasing market, and (ii) where barriers prevent entry into the supplying or purchasing market by internal expansion, the Department's adherence to the vertical merger standards will in any event usually result in no challenge being made to the acquisition of a firm or firms of sufficient size to overcome or adequately minimize the barriers to entry.

II. Conglomerate Mergers

17. Enforcement Policy

Conglomerate mergers are mergers that are neither horizontal nor vertical as those terms are used in sections I and II, respectively, of these guidelines. (It should be noted that a market extension merger, i.e., one involving two firms selling the same product, but in different geographic markets, is classified as a conglomerate merger.) As with other kinds of mergers, the purpose of the Department's enforcement activity regarding conglomerate mergers is to prevent changes in market structure that appear likely over the course of time to cause a substantial lessening of the competition that would otherwise exist or to create a tendency toward monopoly.

At the present time, the Department regards two categories of conglomerate mergers as having sufficiently identifiable anticompetitive effects as to the subject of relatively specific structural guidelines: mergers involving potential entrants (Paragraph 18) and mergers creating a danger of reciprocal buying (Paragraph 19).

Another important category of conglomerate mergers that will frequently be the subject of enforcement action—mergers which for one or more of several reasons threaten to entrench or enhance the market power of the acquired firm—is described generally in Paragraph 20.

As Paragraph 20 makes clear, enforcement action will also be taken against still other types of conglomerate mergers that on specific analysis appear anticompetitive. The fact that, as yet, the Department does not believe it useful to describe such other types of mergers in terms of a few major elements of market structure should in no sense be regarded as indicating that enforcement action will not be taken. Nor is it to be assumed that mergers of the type described in Paragraphs 18 and 19, but not covered by the specific rules thereof, may not be the subject of enforcement action if specific analysis indicates that they appear anticompetitive.

18. Mergers Involving Potential Entrants

(a) Since potential competition (i.e., the threat of entry, either through internal expansion or through acquisition and expansion of a small firm, by firms not already or only marginally in the market) may often be the most significant competitive limitation on the exercise of market power by leading firms, as well as the most likely source of additional actual competition, the Department will ordinarily challenge any merger between one of the most likely entrants into the market and:

(i)   any firm with approximately 25% or more of the market;

(ii) one of the two largest firms in a market in which the shares of the two largest firms amount to approximately 50% or more;

(iii) one of the four largest firms in a market in which the shares of the eight largest firms amount to approximately 75% or more, provided the merging firm's share of the market amounts to approximately 10% or more; or

(iv)   one of the eight largest firms in a market in which the shares of these firms amount to approximately 75% or more, provided either (A) the merging firm's share of the market is not insubstantial and there are no more than one or two likely entrants into the market, or (B) the merging firm is a rapidly growing firm.

In determining whether a firm is one of the most likely potential entrants into a market, the Department accords primary significance to the firm's capability of entering on a competitively significant scale relative to the capability of other firms (i.e., the technological and financial resources available to it) and to the firm's economic incentive to enter (evidenced by, for example, the general attractiveness of the market in terms of risk and profit; or any special relationship of the firm to the market; or the firm's manifested interest in entry; or the natural expansion pattern of the firm; or the like).

(b) The Department will also ordinarily challenge a merger between an existing competitor in a market and a likely entrant, undertaken for the purpose of preventing the competitive "disturbance" or "disruption" that such entry might create.

(c) Unless there are exceptional circumstances, the Department will not accept as a justification for a merger inconsistent with the standards of this paragraph 18 the claim that the merger will produce economies, because, among other reasons, the Department believes that equivalent economies can be normally achieved either through internal expansion or through a small firm acquisition or other acquisition not inconsistent with the standards herein.

19.   Mergers Creating Danger of Reciprocal Buying

(a) Since reciprocal buying (i.e., favoring one's customer when making purchases of a product which is sold by the customer) is an economically unjustified business practice which confers a competitive advantage on the favored firm unrelated to the merits of its product, the Department will ordinarily challenge any merger which creates a significant danger of reciprocal buying. Unless it clearly appears that some special market factor makes remote the possibility that reciprocal buying behavior will actually occur, the Department considers that a significant danger of reciprocal buying is present whenever approximately 15% or more of the total purchases in a market in which one of the merging firms ("the selling firm") sells are accounted for by firms which also make substantial sales in markets where the other merging firm ("the buying firm") is both a substantial buyer and a more substantial buyer than all or most of the competitors of the selling firm.

(b) The Department will also ordinarily challenge (i) any merger undertaken for the purpose of facilitating the creation of reciprocal buying arrangements, and (ii) any merger creating the possibility of any substantial reciprocal buying where one (or both) of the merging firms has within the recent past, or the merged firm has after consummation of the merger, actually engaged in reciprocal buying, or attempted directly or indirectly to induce firms with which it deals to engage in reciprocal buying, in the product markets in which the possibility of reciprocal buying has been created.

(c) Unless there are exceptional circumstances, the Department will not accept as justification for a merger creating a significant danger of reciprocal buying the claim that the merger will produce economies because, among other reasons, the Department believes that in general equivalent economies can be achieved by the firms involved through other mergers not inconsistent with the standards of this paragraph 19.

20. Mergers Which Entrench Market Power; Other Conglomerate Mergers

The Department will ordinarily investigate the possibility of anticompetitive consequences, and may in particular circumstances bring suit, where an acquisition of a leading firm in a relatively concentrated or rapidly concentrating market may serve to entrench or increase the market power of that firm or raise barriers to entry in that market. Examples of this type of merger include:

    (i) a merger which produces a very large disparity in absolute size between the merged firm and the largest remaining firms in the relevant markets,

   (ii) a merger of firms producing related products which may induce purchasers, concerned about the merged firm's possible use of leverage, to buy products of the merged firm rather than those of competitors, and

  (iii) a merger which may enhance the ability of the merged firm to increase product differentiation in the relevant markets.

Generally speaking, the conglomerate merger area involves novel problems that have not yet been subjected to as extensive or sustained analysis as those presented by horizontal and vertical mergers. It is for this reason that the Department's enforcement policy regarding the foregoing category of conglomerate mergers cannot be set forth with greater specificity. Moreover, the conglomerate merger field as a whole is one in which the Department considers it necessary, to a greater extent than with horizontal and vertical mergers, to carry on a continuous analysis and study of the ways in which mergers may have significant anti-competitive consequences in circumstances beyond those covered by these guidelines. For example, the Department has used Section 7 to prevent mergers which may diminish long-run possibilities of enhanced competition resulting from technological developments that may increase interproduct competition between industries whose products are presently relatively imperfect substitutes. Other areas where enforcement action will be deemed appropriate may also be identified on a case-by-case basis; and as the result of continuous analysis and study the Department may identify other categories of mergers that can be the subject of specific guidelines.

21. Failing Company

The standards set forth in paragraph 9 are normally applied by the Department in determining whether to challenge a conglomerate merger, except that in marginal cases involving the application of Paragraph 18(a) (iii) and (v) the Department may deem it inappropriate to sue under Section 7 even though the acquired firm is not "failing" in the strict sense.

Suggested Readings on Corporate Diversification

General Background

Andrews, Kenneth R., *The Concept of Corporate Strategy*, Homewood, Ill.: Dow Jones-Irwin, Inc., 1971.

Ansoff, Igor, *Corporate Strategy*, New York: McGraw-Hill Book Company, 1965.

Bagley, Edward R., *Beyond the Conglomerates*, New York: AMACOM, 1975.

Barnard, Chester I., *The Functions of the Executive*, Cambridge, Mass.: Harvard University Press, 1938.

Brooks, John, *The Go-Go Years*, New York: Weybright & Talley, 1973.

Carroll, Daniel T., "What Future for the Conglomerate," *Harvard Business Review*, May–June 1969.

Chandler, Alfred D., *Strategy and Structure*, Cambridge, Mass.: The MIT Press, 1962.

Drucker, Peter, *Management: Tasks, Responsibilities, and Practice*, New York: Harper & Row, 1974.

Editors of *Fortune*, *The Conglomerate Commotion*, New York: The Viking Press, 1970.

Federal Trade Commission, *Economic Report on Conglomerate Merger Performance*, Washington, DC: U.S. Government Printing Office, 1973

Hackett, John T., "Drawbacks of Continuing Corporate Growth," *Harvard Business Review* 52, January–February 1974.

Levitt, Theodore, "Dinosaurs among the Bears and Bulls," *Harvard Business Review* 53, January–February 1975.

Markham, Jesse W., *Conglomerate Enterprise and Public Policy*, Boston, Mass.: Division of Research, Graduate School of Business Administration, Harvard University, 1973.

Mueller, Dennis C., "The Effects of Conglomerate Mergers: A Survey of the Empirical Evidence," *Journal of Banking and Finance 1*, November 1977, pp. 315–347.

Reid, Samuel R., *Mergers, Managers, and the Economy*, New York: McGraw-Hill Book Company, 1968.

————, *The New Industrial Order: Concentration, Regulation, and Public Policy*, New York: McGraw-Hill Book Company, 1976.

Rumelt, Richard P., *Strategy, Structure and Economic Performance*, Boston, Mass.: Division of Research, Graduate School of Business Administration, Harvard University, 1974.

Scherer, Frederick M., *Industrial Market Structure and Economic Performance*, Chicago: Rand McNally College Publishing Co., 1971.

Scott, Bruce R., "The Industrial State: Old Myths and New Realities," *Harvard Business Review* 51, March–April 1973.

Sloan, Alfred P., *My Years with General Motors*, New York: Doubleday, 1972.

Steiner, Peter O., *Mergers: Motives, Effects, Policies*, Ann Arbor, University of Michigan Press, 1975.

Formulating a Diversification Strategy

Aranow, Edward R., Herbert Einhorn, and George Berlstein, *Developments in Tender Offers for Corporate Control*, New York: Columbia University Press, 1978.

Biggadike, Ralph, "The Risky Business of Diversification," *Harvard Business Review 57*, May–June 1979, pp. 103–111.

Bing, Gordon, *Corporate Divestment*, Houston: Gulf Publishing, 1978.

Hayes, Robert, "New Emphasis on Divestment Opportunities," *Harvard Business Review* 50, July–August 1972, pp. 65–74.

Hilton, Peter, *Planning Corporate Growth and Diversification*, New York: McGraw-Hill Book Company, 1970.

Hovers, John, *Expansion through Acquisition*, New York: John Wiley & Sons, 1975.

Kitching, John, *Acquisition in Europe: Causes of Corporate Success and Failures*, Geneva: Business International, 1973.

Mace, Myles L. and George C. Montgomery, Jr., *Management Problems of Corporate Acquisitions*, Boston, Mass.: Division of Research, Graduate School of Business Administration, Harvard University, 1962.

Mergers and Acquisitions Series, Reprints from the *Harvard Business Review*.

Salter, Malcolm S. and Wolf A. Weinhold, "Diversification via Acquisition: Creating Value," *Harvard Business Review* 56, July–August 1978, pp. 166–178.

Vignola, Leonard, Jr., *Strategic Divestment*, New York: AMACOM, 1974.

Managing the Diversified Company

Berg, Norman A., "Strategic Planning in Conglomerate Companies," *Harvard Business Review* 43, May–June 1965, pp. 79–92.

———, "Corporate Role in Diversified Firms," Mimeo, Boston, Mass.: Division of Research, Graduate School of Business Administration, Harvard University, 1971.

Bower, Joseph L., *Managing the Resource Allocation Process,* Boston, Mass.: Division of Research, Graduate School of Business Administration, Harvard University, 1969.

———, "Management Decision-Making in the Large Diversified Firm," MSI Proceedings: Workshop on the Large Diversified Firm, Cambridge, Mass., November 1971.

Davis, Stanley M., and Paul R. Lawrence, *Matrix,* Reading, Mass.: Addison-Wesley Publishing Company, 1977.

Hall, William K., "SBUs: Hot, New Topic in the Management of Diversification," *Business Horizons,* February 1978, pp. 17–25.

Hamermesh, Richard G., "Responding to Divisional Profit Crises," *Harvard Business Review* 52, March–April 1977, pp. 124–130.

Lawrence, Paul R. and Jay Lorsch, *Organization and Environment,* Boston: Division of Research, Graduate School of Business Administration, Harvard University, 1967.

Leighton, Charles M. and G. Robert Tod, "After the Acquisition: Continuing Challenge," *Harvard Business Review* 47, March–April 1969, pp. 90–102.

Lorsch, Jay and Stephen A. Allen, *Managing Diversity and Interdependence,* Boston, Mass.: Division of Research, Graduate School of Business Administration, Harvard University, 1973.

Miller, Stanley, *Management Problems of Diversification,* New York: John Wiley & Sons, 1963.

Murthy, K., R. Srinivasa, and Malcolm S. Salter, "Should CEO Pay be Linked to Results?", *Harvard Business Review* 53, May–June 1975, pp. 65–73.

Pitts, R. A., "Strategies and Structures for Diversification," *Academy of Management Journal* 20, June 1977, pp. 197–208.

———, "Diversification Strategies and Organization Policies of Large Diversified Firms," *Journal of Economics and Business* 28, Spring–Summer 1976.

Salter, Malcolm S., "Tailor Incentive Compensation to Strategy," *Harvard Business Review* 51, March–April 1973, pp. 94–102.

———, "The Task and Tools of General Management," in Christensen, Berg, and Salter, *Policy Formulation and Administration,* Homewood, Ill.: Richard D. Irwin, 1976.

Stopford, John M. and Louis T. Wells, *Managing the Multinational Enterprise,* New York: Basic Books, Inc., 1972.

Williamson, Oliver E., *Corporate Control and Business Behavior,* Englewood Cliffs: Prentice-Hall, Inc., 1970.

Bibliography

Books and Published Manuscripts

Abell, Derek F. and John S. Hammond, *Defining the Business: Starting Point of Strategic Planning*, Englewood Cliffs, N.J.: Prentice-Hall, 1979.

Alberts, William W. and Joel E. Segall, eds., *The Corporate Merger*, Chicago: University of Chicago Press, 1967.

Andrews, Kenneth R., *The Concept of Corporate Strategy*, Homewood, Ill.: Dow Jones-Irwin, Inc., 1971.

Ansoff, H. Igor, *Corporate Strategy*, New York: McGraw-Hill Book Co., 1965.

Aranow, Edward R., Herbert Einhorn, and George Berlstein, *Developments in Tender Offers for Corporate Control*, New York: Columbia University Press, 1978.

Bagley, Edward R., *Beyond the Conglomerates*, New York:AMACOM, 1975.

Barnard, Chester I., *The Functions of the Executive*, Cambridge, Mass.: Harvard University Press, 1938.

Berle, Adolf A. Jr., *The Twentieth Century Capitalist Revolution*, New York: Harcourt, Brace, 1954.

————, *Power without Property*, New York: Harcourt, Brace, 1959.

———— and Gardiner C. Means, *The Modern Corporation and Private Property*, New York: Macmillan, 1932.

Cyert, Richard M. and James G. March, *A Behavioral Theory of the Firm*, Englewood Cliffs, NJ: Prentice-Hall, 1963.

Bierman, Harold Jr. and Seymour Smidt, *The Capital Budgeting Decision*, New York: Macmillan Publishing Co., 1971.

Bing, Gordon, *Corporate Divestment*, Houston: Gulf Publishing, 1978.

The Boston Consulting Group, *Perspectives on Experience*, Boston, Mass.: The Boston Consulting Group, 1968.

————, *Perspectives on Experience,* Boston, Mass.: The Boston Consulting Group, 1970.

————, *Perspectives on Experience,* Boston, Mass.: The Boston Consulting Group, 1972.

Bower, Joseph L., *Managing the Resource Allocation Process,* Boston, Mass.: Division of Research, Graduate School of Business Administration, Harvard University, 1970.

Braybrooke, David and Charles E. Lindblom, *A Strategy of Decision,* New York: Free Press, 1963.

Brooks, John, *The Go-Go Years,* New York: Weybright & Talley, 1973.

Chandler, Alfred D., *Strategy and Structure: Chapters in the History of Industrial Enterprise,* Cambridge, Mass.: The MIT Press, 1962.

Davis, Stanley M., and Paul R. Lawrence, *Matrix,* Reading, Mass.: Addison-Wesley Publishing Company, 1977.

Drucker, Peter F., *The Practice of Management,* New York: Harper & Row, 1954.

————, *Management Tasks, Responsibilities, Practices,* New York: Harper & Row, 1974.

Editors of *Fortune, The Conglomerate Commotion,* New York; The Viking Press, 1970

Federal Trade Commission, *The Merger Movement: A Summary Report,* Washington, D.C.: United States Government Printing Office, 1948.

————, Bureau of Economics, *Current Trends in Merger Activity, 1970,* Statistical Report No. 8, Washington, D.C.: United States Government Printing Office, March 1971.

————, *Current Trends in Merger Activity, 1971,* Statistical Report No. 10, Washington, D.C.: United States Government Printing Office, May 1972.

————, *Economic Report on Conglomerate Merger Performance, An Empirical Analysis of Nine Corporations,* Washington, D.C.: United States Government Printing Office, November 1972.

————, *Economic Report on Corporate Mergers,* Washington, D.C.: United States Government Printing Office, 1969.

————, *Large Mergers in Manufacturing and Mining 1948–1971,* Statistical Report No. 9, Washington, D.C.: United States Government Printing Office, May 1972.

————, *Statistical Report on Mergers and Acquisitions, 1973,* Washington, D.C.: United States Government Printing Office, July 1974.

————, *Statistical Report on Mergers and Acquisitions, 1974,* Washington, D.C.: United States Government Printing Office, October 1975.

————, *Statistical Report on Mergers and Acquisitions, 1975,* Washington, D.C.: United States Government Printing Office, November 1976.

————, *Statistical Report on Mergers and Acquisitions, 1976,* Washington, D.C.: United States Government Printing Office, November 1977.

————, *Statistical Report on Mergers and Acquisitions, 1977,* Washington, D.C.: United States Government Printing Office, December 1978.

Friedman, Milton S., *Capitalism and Freedom,* Chicago: University of Chicago Press, 1962.

Fruhan, William E., Jr., *Financial Strategy: Studies in the Creation, Transfer, and Destruction of Shareholder Value,* Homewood, Illinois: Richard D. Irwin, Inc., 1979.

Gort, Michael, *Diversification and Integration in American Industry,* Princeton: Princeton University Press, 1962.

Hilton, Peter, *Planning Corporate Growth and Diversification,* New York: McGraw-Hill Book Company, 1970.

Hovers, John, *Expansion through Acquisition,* New York: John Wiley & Sons, 1975.

Hunt, Pearson, Charles M. Williams, and Gordon Donaldson, *Basic Business Finance* (Fourth Edition), Homewood, Ill.: Richard D. Irwin, Inc., 1971.

Ibbotson, Roger B. and Rex A. Sinquefield, *Stocks, Bonds, Bills and Inflation: The Past (1926–1976) and the Future (1977–2000),* Charlottesville, Va.: Financial Analysts Research Foundation, 1977.

Jensen, Michael C., ed., *Studies in the Theory of Capital Markets,* New York: Praeger, 1972.

Kaysen, C. and D. Turner, *Antitrust Policy: A Legal and Economic Analysis,* Cambridge, Mass.: Harvard University Press, 1959.

Kitching, John, *Acquisition in Europe: Causes of Corporate Success and Failures,* Geneva: Business International, 1973.

Lawrence, Paul R., and Jay Lorsch, *Organization and Environment,* Boston, Mass.: Division of Research, Graduate School of Business Administration, Harvard University, 1967.

Lorie, James H. and Mary T. Hamilton, *The Stock Market,* Homewood, Ill.: Richard D. Irwin, Inc., 1973.

Lorsch, Jay W. and Stephen A. Allen III, *Managing Diversity and Interdependence,* Boston, Mass.: Division of Research, Graduate School of Business Administration, Harvard University, 1973.

Lynch, Harry H., *Financial Performance of Conglomerates,* Boston, Mass.: Division of Research, Graduate School of Business Administration, Harvard University, 1971.

Mace, Myles L. and George C. Montgomery, Jr., *Management Problems of Corporate Acquisitions,* Boston, Mass.: Division of Research, Graduate School of Business Administration, Harvard University, 1962.

Markham, Jesse W., *Conglomerate Enterprise and Public Policy,* Boston, Mass.: Division of Research, Graduate School of Business Administration, Harvard University, 1973.

————, "Survey of Evidence and Findings on Mergers," *Business Concentration and Price Policy,* National Bureau of Economic Research, Princeton: Princeton University Press, 1955.

Markowitz, Harry, *Portfolio Selection: Efficient Diversification of Investments*, New York: John Wiley & Sons, 1959.

Meeks, George, *Disappointing Marriage: A Study of the Gains from Merger*, Cambridge: Cambridge University Press, 1977.

Mergers and Acquisitions Series, Reprints from the *Harvard Business Review*.

Miller, Stanley, *The Management Problems of Diversification*, New York: John Wiley and Sons, Inc., 1963.

Myers, Stewart C., ed., *Modern Developments in Financial Management*, New York: Praeger, 1976.

Nelson, Ralph L., *Merger Movements in American Industry 1895–1956*, National Bureau of Economic Research General Studies #66, Princeton: Princeton University Press, 1959.

Newbould, Gerald D. and George A. Luffman, *Successful Business Policies*, London: Gower Press, 1978.

Reid, Samuel R., *Mergers, Managers and the Economy*, New York: McGraw-Hill Book Co., 1968.

————, *The New Industrial Order: Concentration, Regulation, and Public Policy*, New York: McGraw-Hill Book Co., 1975.

Requero, M. A., *An Economic Study of the Military Airframe Industry*, Department of the Air Force, October 1957.

Rumelt, Richard P., *Strategy, Structure and Economic Performance*, Boston, Mass.: Division of Research, Graduate School of Business Administration, Harvard University.

St. John's Law Review, *Conglomerate Mergers and Acquisitions: Opinion and Analysis*, Special Edition 44, Spring 1970.

Scherer, F. M., *Industrial Market Structure and Economic Performance*, Chicago: Rand McNally, 1971.

Selznick, Philip, *Leadership in Administration*, New York: Harper & Row, 1975.

Sharpe, William F., *Portfolio Theory and Capital Markets*, New York: McGraw-Hill Book Company, 1972.

————, *Investments*, Englewood Cliffs, NJ: Prentice-Hall, 1977.

Simon, Herbert A., *Administrative Behavior*, New York: Free Press, 1965.

Sloan, Alfred P., *My Years with General Motors*, New York: Doubleday, 1972.

Sperry, Robert, *Mergers and Acquisitions: A Comprehensive Bibliography*, Washington, DC: Mergers and Acquisitions, 1972.

Steiner, Peter O., *Mergers: Motives, Effects, Policies*, Ann Arbor: University of Michigan Press, 1975.

Stopford, John M. and Louis T. Wells, *Managing the Multinational Enterprise*, New York: Basic Books, Inc., 1972.

United States Congress, House of Representatives, *Hearings before the Antitrust Subcommittee of the Committee of the Judiciary*, 91st Congress, Part 3, 1969.

United States Department of Justice, *Merger Guidelines*, May 30, 1968.

Uyterhoeven, Hugo, Robert C. Ackerman, and John W. Rosenblum, *Strategy and Organization,* Homewood, Ill.: Richard D. Irwin, Inc., 1973.

Van Horne, James C., *Financial Management and Policy,* Englewood Cliffs, NJ: Prentice-Hall Inc., 1977.

Vignola, Leonard, Jr., *Strategic Divestment,* New York: AMACOM, 1974.

Weston, J. Fred and Eugene Brigham, *Managerial Finance,* New York: Holt, Rinehart & Winston, 1978.

White House, Task Force Report on Antitrust Policy (Neal Report), 115 *Congressional Record,* 1969, p. 13890.

Williams, J. B., *The Theory of Investment Value,* Cambridge, Mass.: Harvard University Press, 1938.

Williamson, Oliver E., *Corporate Control and Business Behavior,* Englewood Cliffs, N.J.: Prentice-Hall, Inc., 1970.

———, *Markets and Hierarchies: Analysis and Antitrust Implications*, New York: The Free Press, 1975.

Journal Articles

Abernathy, W. J. and K. Wayne, "The Limits of the Learning Curve," *Harvard Business Review* 52, September–October 1974, pp. 109–119.

Adams, William James, "Market Structure and Corporate Power: The Horizontal Dominance Hypothesis Reconsidered," *Columbia Law Review* 74, 1974, pp. 1276–1297.

Alberts, William W., "The Profitability of Growth by Merger," in William Alberts and Joel Segall, ed., *The Corporate Merger,* Chicago: University of Chicago Press, 1966.

Allan, Gerald B., *Note on the Use of Experience Curves in Competitive Decision Making,* Note #9-175-174, Division of Research, Graduate School of Business Administration, Harvard University, 1975.

———, *A Note on the Boston Consulting Group Concept of Competitive Analysis and Corporate Strategy,* Note #9-175-175, Division of Research, Graduate School of Business Administration, Harvard University, 1975.

Anderson, Theodore, H. Igor Ansoff, Frank Norton, and J. Fred Weston, "Planning for Diversification through Merger," *California Management Review* 1, Summer 1958, pp. 24–35.

Andress, F. J. "The Learning Curve as a Production Tool," *Harvard Business Review* 32, January–February 1954, pp. 87–97.

Ansoff, H. Igor and James C. Loentiades, "Strategic Portfolio Management," *Journal of General Management,* Autumn 1976, pp. 13–29.

Archibald, Ross T., "Stock Market Reaction to the Depreciation Switch-Back," *The Accounting Review* 47, January 1972, pp. 22–30.

Basu, S., "Investment Performance of Common Stocks in Relation to their Price-Earnings Ratios: A Test of the Efficient Market Hypothesis," *Journal of Finance* 32, June 1977, pp. 663–682.

Berg, Norman A., "Strategic Planning in Conglomerate Companies," *Harvard Business Review* 43, May–June 1965, pp. 79–92.

Berle, Adolf A., Jr., "Corporate Powers as Powers in Trust," *Harvard Law Review* 44, 1931, pp. 1049–1074.

———, "For Whom Corporate Managers are Trustees," *Harvard Law Review* 45, 1932.

Bicks, Robert A., "Corporate Mergers and the Antitrust Laws: Clayton Act, Section 7," in William W. Alberts and Joel Segall, eds., *The Corporate Merger,* Chicago: University of Chicago Press, 1968.

Biggadike, Ralph, "The Risky Business of Diversification," *Harvard Business Review 57,* May–June 1979, pp. 103–111.

Black, Fisher, Michael C. Jensen and Myron Scholes, "The Capital Asset Pricing Model: Some Empirical Tests," in M. C. Jensen, ed., *Studies in the Theory of Capital Markets,* New York: Praeger, 1972.

Blake, Harlan M., "Conglomerate Mergers and Antitrust Laws," *Columbia Law Review* 73, 1973, pp. 554–592.

Bok, Derek C., "Section 7 of the Clayton Act and the Merging of Law and Economics," *Harvard Law Review* 74, 1960, pp. 226–350.

Bower, Joseph L., "Management Decision Making in the Large Diversified Firm," MSI Proceedings: Workshop on the Large Diversified Firm, Cambridge, Mass., 1971.

Buckley, Adrian, "Growth by Acquisition," *Long-Range Planning* 8, August 1975, pp. 53–59.

Burck, Gilbert, "The Perils of the Multi-Market Corporation," *Fortune* 79, February 1967, pp. 130–138, 184–188.

Buzzell, R. D., B. T. Gale, and R. G. M. Sultan, "Market Share—A Key to Profitability," *Harvard Business Review* 53, January–February 1975, pp. 97–106.

Campbell, James S. and William G. Shephard, "Leading Firm Conglomerate Mergers," *Antitrust Bulletin* 13, 1968, pp. 1361–1379.

Carter, E. Eugene, "The Behavioral Theory of the Firm and Top-Level Corporate Decisions," *Administrative Science Quarterly* 16, December 1971, pp. 413–428.

Catry, Bernard and Michel Chevalier, "Market Share Strategy and the Product Life Cycle," *Journal of Marketing* 38, October 1974, pp. 29–34.

Conn, Robert G., "Performance of Conglomerate Firms: Comment," *Journal of Finance* 28, June 28, 1973, pp. 754–759.

Day, George S., "Diagnosing the Product Portfolio," *Journal of Marketing* 41, April 1977, pp. 29–38.

Didricksen, Jon, "The Development of Diversified and Conglomerate Firms in the United States, 1920–1970," *Business History Review* 46, Summer 1972, pp. 202–219.

Dodd, E. Merrick Jr., "Is Effective Enforcement of the Fiduciary Duties of Corporate Managers Practicable?" *University of Chicago Law Review* 2, 1935.

Dodd, Peter and Richard Ruback, "Tender Offers and Stockholder Returns: An Empirical Analysis," *Journal of Financial Economics* 5, December 1977, pp. 351–373.

Donaldson, Gordon C., "Financial Goals: Management vs. Stockholders," *Harvard Business Review* 41, May–June 1963, pp. 116–129.

Fama, Eugene F., "Multiperiod Consumption-Investment Decisions," *The American Economic Review* 60, March 1970, pp. 163–174.

———, "Efficient Capital Markets: A Review of Theory and Empirical Work," *Journal of Finance* 26, May 1970, pp. 383–417.

———, Lawrence Fisher, Michael C. Jensen, and Richard Roll, "The Adjustment of Stock Prices to New Information," *International Economic Review* 10, February 1969, pp. 1–21.

Fisher, L. and J. H. Lorie, "Rates of Return on Investments in Common Stock," *Journal of Business* 37, January 1964, pp. 1–21.

———, "Rates of Return on Investments in Common Stock: The Year-by-Year Record, 1926–1965," *Journal of Business* 41, July 1968, pp. 291–316.

Franks, J. R., J. E. Broyles and M. J. Hecht, "An Industry Study of the Profitability of Mergers in the United Kingdom," *Journal of Finance* 32, December 1977, pp. 1515–1525.

Goldberg, Lawrence G., "The Effect of Conglomerate Mergers on Competition, *Journal of Law and Economics* 16, April 1973, pp. 137–158.

———, "Conglomerate Mergers and Concentration Ratios," *Review of Economics and Statistics*, 1975, pp. 303–309.

Gonedes, Nicholas J., "Efficient Capital Markets and External Accounting," *The Accounting Review* 47, January 1972, pp. 11–21.

Gort, Michael, "Diversification, Mergers, and Profits," in William Alberts and Joel Segall, eds., *The Corporate Merger,* Chicago: University of Chicago Press, 1966.

Hackett, John T., "Drawbacks of Continuing Corporate Growth," *Harvard Business Review* 52, January–February 1974, pp. 6–8.

Hall, William K., "SBUs: Hot, New Topic in the Management of Diversification," *Business Horizons,* February 1978, pp. 17–25.

Hamada, Robert S., "The Effect of the Firm's Capital Structure on the Systematic Risk of Common Stocks," *Journal of Finance* 27, May 1972, pp. 435–452.

Hamermesh, Richard G., "Responding to Divisional Profit Crises," *Harvard Business Review* 52, March–April 1977, pp. 124–130.

Hayes, Robert, "New Emphasis on Divestment Opportunities," *Harvard Business Review* 50, July–August 1972, pp. 55–64.

Haugen, Robert A. and Terence C. Langetieg, "An Empirical Test for Synergism in Merger," *Journal of Finance* 30, September 1975, pp. 1003–1014.

Henderson, Bruce D., *The Experience Curve Reviewed IV: The Growth Share Matrix or the Product Portfolio*, Perspective 135, Boston: The Boston Consulting Group, 1972.

Hogarty, Thomas F., "The Profitability of Corporate Mergers," *Journal of Business* 43, 1970, pp. 317–327.

Holzman, Oscar J., Ronald M. Copeland, and Jack Hayya, "Income Measures of Conglomerate Performance," *Quarterly Review of Economics and Business* 15, Summer 1975, pp. 67–78.

Ibbotson, Robert B. and Rex A. Sinquefield, "Stocks, Bonds, Bills, and Inflation: Year-by-Year Historical Returns (1926–1974)," *Journal of Business* 49, January 1976, pp. 11–47.

Insilco Corporation (A) and (B), case #2-373-121 and 2-373-120, Graduate School of Business Administration, Harvard University, 1973.

Jensen, Michael, "Risk, the Pricing of Capital Assets, and the Evaluation of Investment Portfolios," *Journal of Business* 42, April 1969, pp. 167–247.

Jensen, Michael C. and William H. Meckling, "Can the Corporation Survive?" *Financial Analysts Journal*, January–February 1978, pp. 31–37.

Judelson, David N., "A Philosophy for a Conglomerate Company," *Business Horizons* 11, June 1968, pp. 5–13.

Kim, E. Han and John J. McConnel, "Conglomerate Mergers and the Co-insurance of Corporate Debt," *Journal of Finance* 32, May 1977, pp. 349–370.

Leighton, Charles M. and G. Robert Tod, "After the Acquisition: Continuing Challenge," *Harvard Business Review* 47, March–April 1969, pp. 90–102.

Lev, Baruch and Gershon Mandelker, "The Micro-Economic Consequences of Corporate Mergers," *Journal of Business* 45, January 1972, pp. 85–104.

Levitt, Theodore, "The Dangers of Social Responsibility," *Harvard Business Review* 36, September–October 1958, pp. 41–50.

Levitt, Theodore, "Dinosaurs among the Bears and Bulls," *Harvard Business Review* 53, January–February 1975, pp. 11–53.

Levy, Haim and Marshall Sarnat, "Diversification, Portfolio Analysis and the Uneasy Case for Conglomerate Mergers," *Journal of Finance* 25, September 1970, pp. 795–802.

Llewellyn, Wilbur, "A Pure Financial Rationale for Conglomerate Merger," *Journal of Finance* 26, May 1971, pp. 521–537.

Lintner, John, "Distribution of Incomes of Corporations Among Dividends, Retained Earnings and Taxes," *American Economic Review* 46, May 1956, pp. 97–113.

———, "Expectations, Mergers, and Equilibrium in Purely Competitive Securities Markets," *American Economic Review* 61, May 1971, pp. 101–111.

————, "Valuation of Risk Assets and the Selection of Risky Investments in Stock Portfolios and Capital Budgets," *Review of Economics and Statistics* 47, February 1965, pp. 13–37.

Malkiel, Burton G., "The Valuation of Closed-End Investment Company Shares," *Journal of Finance* 32, June 1977, pp. 847–860.

Malott, Robert H., "The Control of Divisionalized Acquisitions," in William Alberts and Joel Segall, eds., *The Corporate Merger*, Chicago: University of Chicago Press, 1966.

Mandelker, Gershon, "Risk and Return: The Case of Merging Firms," *Journal of Financial Economics* 1, December 1974, pp. 303–335.

Markowitz, Harry, "Portfolio Selection," *Journal of Finance* 7, March 1952, pp. 77–91.

Mason, Edward S., "The Apologetics of 'Managerialism'," *The Journal of Business* 31, January 1958, pp. 1–11.

Mason, R. Hal and Maurice B. Gondzwaard, "Performance of Conglomerate Firms: Portfolio Approach," *Journal of Finance* 31, March 1976, pp. 39–48.

Melicher, Ronald W. and David F. Rush, "The Performance of Conglomerate Firms: Recent Risk and Return Experience," *Journal of Finance* 28, May 1973, pp. 381–388

————, "Evidence on Acquisition-Related Performance of Conglomerate Firms," *Journal of Finance* 29, March 1974, pp. 141–150.

Mintzberg, Henry, "The Manager's Job: Folklore and Fact," *Harvard Business Review* 53, July–August 1975, pp. 49–61.

Mueller, Dennis C., "The Effects of Conglomerate Mergers: A Survey of the Empirical Evidence," *Journal of Banking and Finance* 1, November 1977, pp. 315–347.

Murthy, K., R. Srinivasa and Malcolm S. Salter, "Should CEO Pay Be Linked to Results?", *Harvard Business Review* 53, May–June 1975, pp. 66–73.

Myers, S. C. and S. M. Turnbull, "Capital Budgeting and the Capital Asset Pricing Model: Good News and Bad News," *Journal of Finance* 32, May 1977, pp. 321–333.

Pitts, R. A., "Diversification Strategies and Organization Policies of Large Diversified Firms." *Journal of Economics and Business* 28, Spring-Summer 1976.

————, "Strategies and Structures for Diversification," *Academy of Management Journal* 20, June 1977, pp. 197–208.

Porter, Michael E., "How Competitive Forces Shape Strategy," *Harvard Business Review* 57, March–April 1979, pp. 137–145.

Procter and Gamble, case #9-372-076, Graduate School of Business Administration, Harvard University, 1972.

Reed, Stanley Foster, "Corporate Growth by Strategic Planning Part II: Developing a Plan," *Mergers and Acquisitions,* Fall 1977, pp. 4–27.

Roll, R., "A Critique of the Asset Pricing Theory's Tests; Part 1: On Past and Potential Testability of the Theory," *Journal of Financial Economics* 4, March 1977, pp. 129–176.

Ross, S. A., "The Arbitrage Theory of Capital Asset Pricing," *Journal of Economic Theory* 13, December 1976, pp. 341–360.

Rostow, Eugene V., "To Whom and For What Ends is Corporate Management Responsible?" in Edward S. Mason, ed., *The Corporation in Modern Society*, Cambridge, Mass.: Harvard University Press, 1964.

Salter, Malcolm S., "Stages of Corporate Development," *Journal of Business Policy* 1, 1970, pp. 23–37.

————, "Tailor Incentive Compensation to Strategy," *Harvard Business Review* 51, March–April 1973, pp. 94–102.

————, "The Tasks and Tools of General Management—An Overview" in Christensen, Berg, and Salter, *Policy Formulation and Administration*, Homewood, Ill.: Richard D. Irwin, Inc., 1976.

———— and Wolf A. Weinhold, "Diversification via Acquisition: Creating Value," *Harvard Business Review* 56, July–August 1978, pp. 166–178.

Scott, Bruce R., "The Industrial State: Old Myths and New Realities," *Harvard Business Review* 51, March–April 1973, pp. 133–148.

Scott, James H., "On the Theory of Conglomerate Mergers," *Journal of Finance* 32, September 1977, pp. 1235–1250.

Schoeffler, Sidney, Robert D. Buzzell, and Donald A. Heany, "Impact of Strategic Planning on Profit Performance," *Harvard Business Review* 52, March–April 1974, pp. 137–145.

Schwartz, Samuel, "Merger Analysis as a Capital Budgeting Problem," in William Alberts and Joel Segall, eds., *The Corporate Merger*, Chicago: University of Chicago Press, 1966.

Sharpe, William F., "A Simplified Model for Portfolio Analysis," *Management Science*, January 1963, pp. 277–293.

Smith, K. J. and J. C. Schreiner, "A Portfolio Analysis of Conglomerate Diversification," *Journal of Finance* 24, June 1969, pp. 413–427.

Soldofsky, Robert M. and Dale F. Max, "Stocks and Bonds as Inflation Hedges," *MSU Business Topics*, Spring 1978, pp. 17–25.

Stevenson, Howard H., "Defining Corporate Strengths and Weaknesses," *Sloan Management Review* 17, Spring 1976, pp. 51–68.

Stigler, George, "Monopoly and Oligopoly by Merger," *American Economic Review, Papers and Proceedings* 40, May 1950, pp. 23–24.

Stonebaker, Robert J., "Corporate Profits and the Risks of Entry," *The Review of Economics and Statistics*, February 1976, pp. 33–40.

Stotland, Jack A., "Planning Acquisitions and Mergers," *Long-Range Planning* 9, February 1976, pp. 66–71.

Tilles, Seymour, "Strategies for Allocating Funds," *Harvard Business Review* 44, January–February 1966, pp. 72–80.

Tobin, James, "Liquidity Preference as Behavior toward Risk," *The Review of Economic Studies* 25, February 1958, pp. 65–85.

Treynor, Jack L. and Fisher Black, "Corporate Investment Decisions," in S. C.

Myers, ed., *Modern Developments in Financial Management,* New York: Praeger, 1976.

Turner, Donald, "Conglomerate Mergers and Section 7 of the Clayton Act," *Harvard Law Review* 78, May 1965, pp. 1313–1395.

Westerfield, Randolph, "A Note on the Measurement of Conglomerate Diversification," *Journal of Finance* 25, September 1970, pp. 909–914.

Weston, J. Fred and Surrenda Mansingkha, "Test of the Efficiency Performance of Conglomerate Firms," *Journal of Finance* 26, September 1971, pp. 919–936.

——, Keith V. Smith, and Ronald V. Shieves, "Conglomerate Performance Using the Capital Asset Pricing Model," *Review of Economics and Statistics* 54, November 1972, pp. 357–363.

Williams, Joseph T., "Capital Asset Prices with Heterogeneous Beliefs," *Journal of Financial Economics* 4, November 1977, pp. 219–240.

Wind, Yorma and Henry J. Claycamp, "Planning Product Line Strategy: A Matrix Approach," *Journal of Marketing* 40, January 1976, pp. 2–9.

Unpublished Manuscripts and Papers

Baughman, James P., "Problems and Performance of the Role of Chief Executive in the General Electric Company, 1892–1974," Mimeo, Boston, Mass.: Division of Research, Graduate School of Business Administration, Harvard University, 1974.

Berg, Norman A., "Corporate Role in Diversified Firms," Mimeo, Boston, Mass.: Division of Research, Graduate School of Business Administration, Harvard University, 1971.

——, "Allocation of Strategic Funds," Mimeo, Boston, Mass.: Division of Research, Graduate School of Business Administration, Harvard University, 1972.

Biggadike, Ralph, "Entry, Strategy, and Performance," unpublished doctoral dissertation, Graduate School of Business Administration, Harvard University, 1976.

Dougherty, Alfred F., Jr., "Statement before the Senate Committee on the Judiciary on the Merger Act of 1979," March 8, 1979.

Holland, Daniel M. and Stewart C. Myers, *Trends in Corporate Profitability and Capital Costs,* Sloan School Working Paper #999-78, Massachusetts Institute of Technology, May 1978.

Kusiatin, Ilan, "The Process and Capacity for Diversification through Internal Development," unpublished doctoral dissertation, Graduate School of Business Administration, Harvard University, 1976.

Rhee, Ghon S., "Post-Merger Systematic Risk: A New Look at the Diversification Effect," Working Paper 312, Graduate School of Business, University of Pittsburgh, 1978.

Rumelt, Richard, "Diversity and Profitability," Working Paper MBL-51, Graduate School of Management, University of California at Los Angeles, 1977.

Shenefield, John H., "Testimony before the Senate Committee on the Judiciary Concerning Conglomerate Mergers," March 8, 1979.

Case Law

Federal Trade Commission v. The Procter & Gamble Co., 58 FTC 1203 (1961), 63 FTC 1465 (1963), 358 F 2nd 74 (1976), 386 U.S. 568 (1967).

Fortner Enterprises, Inc. v. U.S. Steel Corporation, 394 U.S. 495 (1969).

Robothan v. Prudential Insurance Co., 64 N.J. Eq. 673, 53 Atl. 842 (1902).

U.S. v. Continental Can Co. et al., 378 U.S. 441, 449, 455, 457 (1964).

U.S. v. Griffith, 334 U.S. 100 (1948).

U.S. v. Grinnell Corp., 384 U.S. 563 (1966).

U.S. v. International Telephone & Telegraph (Canteen), 1971 Trade Cus. 73, 619 at 90, 545-59 (N.D., Ill., 1971).

U.S. v. International Telephone & Telegraph (Grinnel) 306 Fed. Supp. 766 (D. Conn., 1969), 324 Fed. Supp. 19, 24 (D. Conn., 1970).

U.S. v. International Telephone & Telegraph (Hartford) 306 Fed. Supp. 766 (D. Conn., 1969).

U.S. vs. Northern Securities Co., 120 Fed. 721 (April 1903), 193 U.S. 197 (March 1904).

U.S. v. Philadelphia National Bank, 374 U.S. 321 (1963).

INDEX

Index